Shaping a global women's agenda: women's NGOs and global governance, 1925–85

MANCHESTER
1824

Manchester University Press

Shaping a global women's agenda: women's NGOs and global governance, 1925–85

KAREN GARNER

Manchester
University Press
Manchester and New York

distributed in the United States exclusively
by PALGRAVE MACMILLAN

Published by Manchester University Press
Oxford Road, Manchester M13 9NR, UK
and Room 400, 175 Fifth Avenue, New York, NY 10010, USA
www.manchesteruniversitypress.co.uk

Distributed in the United States exclusively by
Palgrave Macmillan, 175 Fifth Avenue,
New York, NY 10010, USA

Distributed in Canada exclusively by
UBC Press, University of British Columbia, 2029 West Mall,
Vancouver, BC, Canada V6T 1Z2

British Library Cataloguing-in-Publication Data is available

Library of Congress Cataloging-in-Publication Data is available

ISBN 978 0 7190 8898 8 paperback

First published by Manchester University Press in hardback 2010

This paperback edition first published 2013

Printed by Lightning Source

Contents

Figures

Acknowledgements

I want to thank my friends and mentors who have encouraged me and supported this project in many ways and through the many years of its development. Most particularly I thank Debbie and Alan Cottrell, Seth Fein, Elaine Tyler May, Stephen G. Rabe and Leila J. Rupp. I also appreciate the generous assistance of many archivists who shared their expertise as I conducted research. Very special thanks go to Sheila Barnett at the World Young Women's Christian Association in Geneva, Switzerland, to Sarah Hutcheon at the Arthur and Elizabeth Schlesinger Library on the History of Women in America at the Radcliffe Institute, Harvard University in Cambridge, Massachusetts, to the director of the Sophia Smith Collection, Sherrill Redmon and to her always helpful staff at Smith College in Northampton, Massachusetts. Florida International University and SUNY Empire State College provided institutional support for which I am very grateful. My colleagues at these institutions also provided very generous moral support; their comments and suggestions along with those of very astute Manchester University Press readers have greatly improved this book. Most dear to my heart, I thank Chuck Vosganian for the love and laughter we share. Finally I dedicate this book to the next generation of my family with love: to Alyssa, Andy, Brad, Emily, Mateo and Megan.

Karen Garner

Abbreviations

AAUN	American Association for the UN
ANC	African National Congress
BMW	Barbara M. White Papers, Schlesinger Library, Radcliffe Institute, Harvard University, Cambridge, MA
CCCW	Committee on the Cause and Cure of War Papers, Schlesinger Library, Radcliffe Institute, Harvard University, Cambridge, MA
CEDAW	Convention on the Elimination of All Forms of Discrimination Against Women
CIDA	Canadian International Development Agency
CIMADE	Comité Inter-Mouvements Auprès des Evacués
CONGO	NGOs in Consultative Status with UN ECOSOC
CSW	Commission on the Status of Women
DAWN	Development Alternatives with Women for a New Era
DK	Dorothy Kenyon Papers, Sophia Smith Collection, Smith College, Northampton, MA
ECCO	Emergency Committee of Christian Organisations
ECOSOC	[UN] Economic and Social Council
FAO	Food and Agriculture Organization
FSM	Frieda S. Miller Papers 1909–73, Schlesinger Library, Radcliffe Institute, Harvard University, Cambridge, MA
HCOG	Papers of the High Commission of Occupied Germany, 1949–85, Sophia Smith Collection, Smith College, Northampton, MA
HRC	Human Rights Commission
IACW	Inter-American Commission of Women
ICG	International Consultative Group
ICW	International Council of Women
ICWPP	International Committee of Women for Permanent Peace

IFBPW	International Federation of Business and Professional Women
IFUW	International Federation of University Women
ILO	International Labour Organization
INSTRAW	International Research and Training Institute for the Advancement of Women
IPPF	International Planned Parenthood Federation
IRO	International Refugee Organization
IWSA	International Women's Suffrage Alliance
IWY	International Women's Year
JS	Josephine Schain Papers, Sofia Smith Collection, Smith College, Northampton, MA
KDC	Kathleen d'Olier Courtney Papers, 1878–1974, Women's Library, London, UK
LNU	League of Nations Union
LPM	Laura Puffer Morgan Papers, 1926–62, Peace Collection, Swarthmore College, Swarthmore, Pennsylvania
MEW	Mary Emma Woolley Papers, Mt. Holyoke College, Holyoke, MA
Morgan–Howes	Laura Puffer Morgan and Ethel Puffer Howes Papers, 1892–1962, Schlesinger Library, Radcliffe Institute, Harvard University, Cambridge, MA
NCCCW	National Committee on the Cause and Cure of War
NCOIWY	National Commission on the Observance of International Women's Year
NCPW	National Council for the Prevention of War
NCW	National Council of Women
NGO	non-governmental organisation
NIEO	New International Economic Order
NOW	National Organization for Women
OAS	Organization of American States
OMGUS	Office of the Military Government of the United States
P & D	Peace and Disarmament Committee of Women's International Organisations, 1931–40, Peace Collection, Swarthmore College, Swarthmore, Pennsylvania
PLO	Palestinian Liberation Organisation
RCN	Rachel Conrad Nason Papers, Schlesinger Library, Radcliffe Institute, Harvard University, Cambridge, MA
RW	Ruth Woodsmall Papers, Sophia Smith Collection, Smith College, Northampton, MA

SADC	Southern African Development Community
SCAP	Supreme Commander of the Allied Powers
SEWA	Self-Employed Women's Association
UDHR	Universal Declaration on Human Rights
UN[O]	United Nations [Organization]
UNCED	UN Conference on Environment and Development
UNESCO	UN Educational, Scientific and Cultural Organization
UNFPA	UN Fund for Population Activities
UNICEF	UN (International) Children's (Emergency) Fund
UNIFEM	UN Development Fund for Women
UNKRA	UN Korean Reconstruction Agency
UNRRA	UN Relief and Rehabilitation Administration
UNRWA	UN Relief and Works Agency
USAID	US Agency for International Development
USO	United Service Organization
WEC	World Ecumenical Council
WHO	World Health Organization
WIDF	Women's International Democratic Federation
WIL	Women's International League
WILPF	Women's International League for Peace and Freedom
WIN	Women's International Network
WREE	Women for Racial and Economic Equality
WUCWO	World Union of Catholic Women's Organizations
WYWCA	World Young Women's Christian Association
YWCA	Young Women's Christian Association

Introduction

Women's international organisations founded in the West shaped a global feminist political identity and defined women's issues within the context of the global governance system through most of the twentieth century. Formed at the turn of the century, these voluntary associations advocated for peace and women's suffrage, economic rights in the workplace, and social services for women, girls and families; they successfully interjected women's needs and feminist and humanitarian values into the operations of the male-dominated intergovernmental bodies that formed after the First World War within the League of Nations system and, after the Second World War, within the United Nations (UN) system. In the process, they transformed the norms of global governance, influenced public policy, especially in regard to human services, and raised women's status internationally. They established links between women's concerns and inclusive democracy, human rights, development and peacemaking, and illuminated connections between women's oppression and the exploitation of other oppressed groups in all regions of the world. In conjunction with other civil-society activists, they negotiated a strategic and indispensable role for non-governmental organisations (NGOs) in global politics.

Shaping a Global Women's Agenda documents international women's history through the lens of long-established liberal feminist organisations that dominated the global women's movement up through the UN Decade for Women; thereafter, new leaders and NGOs whose origins were in the global South and whose political orientations were often more socialist feminist or structuralist, challenged their supremacy.[1] The liberal feminist international organisations featured in this history emphasised human rationality, individual rights guaranteed by modern democratic states – such as property rights, voting rights, freedom of speech, freedom of religion, freedom of association – and state intervention in the form of labour laws, social services and regulation of vital industries to curb corporate greed and to guarantee equal access and equal protections for all.[2] Socialist feminists critique the inherent inequalities embedded in a capitalist class society and identify the interconnections to patriarchal power that pre-dates capitalism.[3] Structuralists emphasise that the state reflects dominant gender power relations and therefore it maintains a social structure of inequality through its laws and policies.[4]

As it traces the history of these dominant liberal feminist organisations, this study identifies 1925–85 as a distinct era in international women's history. It began with the founding of the Joint Standing Committee of Women's International Organisations in 1925 and culminated with the end of the UN Decade for Women in 1985, when the ascendancy of Western-led women's international organisations peaked. During this era men remained the primary holders of global power but women entered their ranks and began challenging the male-defined status quo and started to transform patriarchal consciousness.

Women's political leadership poses a significant problem for feminists. Women remain invisible in international politics, and many of their his-toric contributions to the League of Nations and UN global governance systems have been forgotten or disregarded.[5] This ongoing issue is both a cause and a consequence of women's limited political power within socie-ties worldwide. During the twentieth century, women secured the right to vote and to participate in politics in most, but not all, nations around the world. In spite of their talents and capabilities, however, only a few women have become leaders within existing male-defined national governments or intergovernmental bodies, and this situation continues to prevent the realisation of equitable gender power relations and the achievement of true political democracy.[6] As many feminist scholars have argued persuasively, the obstacles women face in efforts to enter government leadership, are structural, rather than personal.[7]

This book exposes patriarchal structures that have disadvantaged women in the gendered realm of international politics, where demonstra-tion of masculine gender traits, such as 'objectivity, rational interests, power as control, and the separation of instrumental political goals from morality' signals power.[8] Women can certainly demonstrate these mas-culine traits, despite the fact that, as Georgia Duerst-Lahti and Rita Mae Kelly argue, 'males who are much more aligned with masculinity than any female could be [sic] have gender power as a permeating resource to maintain their predominance'.[9] Yet historically some women have refused to employ masculine behaviours to acquire power and legitimacy. They sought equitable power for women on feminine-gendered and liberal femi-nist terms that emphasised peaceful conflict resolution and nurturance, and employed moral considerations and humanitarian values as the foun-dation for national and international policy making in order to transform big-power politics.

Shaping a Global Women's Agenda focuses on women who have occupied less visible leadership positions in world politics and who worked from within women's organisations to wield often indirect but critical feminine and feminist influence in international policy debates. If women have not occupied many formal or visible positions of power in global politics, they have nonetheless cultivated and used informal power to serve women's interests and to promote human welfare. The paradox explored here is that women have not achieved an equal measure of policy-making power within their societies or within the global governance system, yet the League of Nations and the UN both provided women with forums to challenge these inequalities and to lessen, if not eliminate, discriminations against women that limited their power and to force male-dominated governing bodies to acknowledge that women's rights are human rights. League of Nations and UN forums also provided opportunities for women to connect with one another in international associations and to define collectively 'global women's issues'.

Even as it illuminates an ongoing and only partially successful campaign to define an equal role for women policy makers vis-à-vis men in international politics, this history also reveals tensions among women whose nationalist and internationalist feminist identities came in conflict and who competed for access to power within the global women's movement. Without a doubt Western imperialist biases, including racism, moralism and classism, were embedded within women's international organisations founded at the apex of Western colonial expansion and were resented by non-Western women. Many of the Western feminist leaders of international associations were motivated by what the sociologist Nitza Berkovitch has described a 'colonial style internationalism' based on 'missionary zeal [that] stemmed from a notion that similar standards of behaviour should be set and similar state regulation should be imposed in all parts of the world'.[10] Yet these Western leaders were not uniformly blind to their biases. Moreover, they learned from their cross-cultural experiences and were affected by internationalising processes even as they shaped those processes.

At all points throughout the twentieth century women in international organisations represented a range of political standpoints and advocated competing political programmes across a spectrum from radical left to moderate right. After the Second World War, as East-West Cold War conflicts and North-South decolonisation struggles raged, women's international organisations were not exempt from the destabilising fallout. Socialist women's NGOs united to form the Women's International Democratic Federation (WIDF) in 1945 and this organisation promoted an alternative feminist internationalist political identity in UN forums and international

NGO coalitions throughout the post-war period. Additionally, after 1945, non-Western women were incorporated slowly into leadership positions within the historic women's organisations, as they were also included in UN chambers as government delegates and as representatives of 'new' NGOs. By the time the UN Decade for Women began, these developments undercut Western feminist hegemony and created a more truly global feminist movement. Yet as this book documents, whether or not the liberal feminist leadership of these Western-led women's international organisations is respected or denigrated, it is the foundation for what has followed; these historic women's organisations shaped the achievements that became possible for the more inclusive and representative global feminist movement that occurred after the UN Decade for Women.

Many histories of early twentieth-century Western feminism focus on the theoretical divide between social feminism – essentialising difference between male and female – and egalitarian feminism – denying difference. These accounts assign one or the other of these theoretical positions to specific women's organisations, usually in a strictly oppositional relationship to one another.[11] Yet the women's international organisations considered in this study more often went beyond the boundaries of these theoretical positions and, as circumstances demanded, employed various strategies to advance feminist empowerment. While not denying historic tensions, the episodes recounted here challenge the rigid dichotomy of Western feminist 'camps' in conflict, even as they provide an opportunity to evaluate the relative and situational effectiveness of social and egalitarian feminist strategies in overcoming anti-feminist objections to women's participation in international politics and diplomacy.

Finally this book historicises the relationships of women's international organisations to patriarchal power, a power that was neither static nor unitary within the system of global governance. While the women's international organisations remained separate women-only associations on principle, they worked effectively with gender-mixed coalitions, developing NGO networks with male-led organisations and working relationships with male diplomats and civil servants. As the historical record shows, women's international groups demonstrated a sophisticated understanding of the location and strategic exercise of power within the masculine realm of international politics.

The comprehensive records of the World Young Women's Christian Association, headquartered in Geneva, Switzerland since 1930, augmented by the records of other international organisations and activists, reveal how women's NGOs overturned the dominant gender discourse that relegated women to the private sphere and defined a public role for women within the systems of the League of Nations and the UN.[12] Since its inception as a national association of Protestant Christians in England in 1855 the Young Women's Christian Association (YWCA) has drawn together broad groups of women across class, race and cultural boundaries, created a discourse of women's empowerment, and helped to define the global feminist movement. Formed in Britain's industrial cities as voluntary associations of white, middle-class and usually married women from evangelical churches, YWCA chapters employed other white and generally single women as professional 'secretaries' to carry out a Social Gospel ministry that provided social services to needy populations of multi-ethnic working-class women and promoted humanitarian values among the middle and upper classes. Until the end of the nineteenth century, YWCA chapters expanded rapidly across Western Europe and North America. In 1894 a coalition of seven national associations in Great Britain, the United States, Norway, Sweden, Canada, Italy and British colonial India established the World YWCA, with headquarters and a small professional staff located in London.[13] The World YWCA's paid staff and officers elected from a pool of volunteers defined international policies and coordinated programmes to address women's needs and to establish the Christian Kingdom of God on Earth, where universal peace and social justice would prevail. Although Protestant Christian women founded the YWCA, it was not a fundamentalist organisation. It always emphasised humanitarian service, rather than proselytising. And the YWCA was an ecumenical association, never doctrinaire regarding Christian theology.

The World YWCA is featured because it is representative of the long-established women's international organisations and because this association's records provide specific examples that address questions regarding women's acquisition and use of power in the international arena. Moreover, the World YWCA played a leading role among those NGOs that were responsible for transforming the norms of global governance and formulating global gender policy during the 1925–85 period, when the YWCA grew from thirty to over eighty national chapters. Although two institutional histories commissioned by the World YWCA were published at the fifty- and hundred-year anniversaries of the association respectively, these accounts do not critically analyse the association itself or its relationships to other NGOs and intergovernmental bodies; this omission has left a serious gap in the histories of twentieth-century international politics and the global feminist movement.[14]

Like the Western women in their sister organisations of the first-wave international women's movement that Leila J. Rupp analysed so well – the International Council of Women (ICW, founded in 1888), the International Women's Suffrage Alliance (IWSA, founded in 1904), and the Women's International League for Peace and Freedom (WILPF, founded in 1919) – YWCA secretaries were secure in their white race and middle-class privilege, as they were buoyed by the moral force of Christianity.[15] These Western women called for humanitarian reforms to regulate imperial capitalism and for male recognition that 'natural rights' to life, liberty and property extended to all humankind, male and female, equally. Yet their reform campaigns exposed all women's inferior status within the global structure of gender power. Consequently they adopted more overtly feminist positions to challenge patriarchal power and achieve alternative and sometimes subversive power for women in national and international politics. Motivated by Christian internationalism and by feminism, by the early twentieth century the World YWCA embraced progressive social and political activism at the local, national, and international levels of organisation. YWCA women were extraordinary network builders. They were not academic theorists but were women of action who at several critical junctures led campaigns to define and mobilise the feminist politics that shaped League of Nations and UN gender policies and programmes and governance structures.

Western women's organisations promoted Christian internationalist and feminist values in order to achieve specific and practical results that would delegitimise militaristic global politics. Reaching their goals required political savvy, shrewd strategies and effective alliances among influential like-minded women and men who chose specific issues and fortuitous moments to enter into male-led international political debates. By the mid 1920s women's organisations were cultivating effective political skills and strategies within their individual associations, through national alliances, and through international coalitions. For example, beginning in 1920 YWCA publications called for regular 'contacts and cooperation' with other feminist women's organisations and with masculinist 'political bodies'.[16] In the United States, at the national level, in 1924 these goals inspired eleven American women's organisations to form the National Committee on the Cause and Cure of War (NCCCW). Led by the women's suffrage activist Carrie Chapman Catt, the NCCCW joined together in a cooperative peace-education project to mobilise women through annual conferences focusing on 'political and economic questions which were vitally tied up with questions of war and peace'.[17] At the international level twelve women's organisations together founded the Joint Standing Committee of Women's International Organisations in 1925 for the general purpose of increasing the number of women appointed to government delegations and to governing and advisory committees at the League of Nations. The founding of this global feminist alliance marked a new stage in the women's movement and created an expanded, more innovative and imaginative internationalism.

The Joint Standing Committee, which was renamed the Liaison Committee of Women's International Organisations as it grew in membership and purpose after 1931, met regularly in London and Geneva. Male diplomats and League of Nations officials recognised the Committee as 'the voice of the world's women' within the arena of international governance. This Committee as a body, and its member organisations individually, interceded regularly with states through League of Nations forums to promote world peace, women's economic and human rights, world health, child welfare, education, and the abolition of prostitution and trafficking in women and children, among many other international causes.[18]

Organised into three chronological periods, *Shaping a global women's agenda* documents the historical significance of women's entry into international politics during the First World War and their growing influence following the founding of the Joint Standing Committee of Women's International Organisations. Part I: 'Women's NGOs disarmament, 1925-40', explores the ways women's NGOs coordinated peace activism during the interwar era and focused women's interventions at the 1932 League of Nations Conference on the Reduction and Limitation of Armaments. During the League conference a YWCA woman led a coalition of activists drawn from the established women's organisations that became known as the Women's Disarmament Committee. As the conference progressed, the Women's Disarmament Committee monitored proceedings, invigorated the disarmament debate, mobilised public opinion, and developed productive relationships with the conference president, the League secretariat, government delegates, and fellow peace activists and internationalists.

Continuing to meet after the conference closed in 1934, the Women's Disarmament Committee expanded its original mandate; while it continued to lobby League members, it also generated additional public education campaigns focused on the Italian invasion of Ethiopia, the Spanish Civil War, the Sino-Japanese War, and more – all of which advanced its broader women's and human rights agendas. In connection with these broader goals women's international organisations also focused attention on women's economic and political status worldwide, and persuaded the League to include discussions of married women's nationality rights on the agendas of intergovernmental conferences and to establish a formal Inquiry on the Status of Women. All these activities challenged the masculinist norms that had historically determined the conduct of international politics and diplomacy. By legitimising NGO participation and positioning NGOs within international politics while delegitimising backroom political bargaining and big-power politics, women pressured the masculine political elite to reform the governance system espoused by the League of Nations. This reformation was certainly not completed during the 1930s, but the NGOs' authority in international politics increased exponentially, and NGOs influenced the organisation and operations of the United Nations Organization (UNO), especially the Economic and Social Council, after the Second World War.

Part II: 'Women's NGOs politics of war, 1940–70' exposes the vanguard role of Western women's organisations at the forefront of Allied NGO activities during the Second World War and at the UN after 1945. Here the wartime services of the Liaison Committee of Women's International Organisations are examined. Their humanitarian agenda became the foundation of the women's NGOs' unrealised internationalist vision of a collaborative post-war world community, which was subordinated as a consequence of the political pressures exerted by Cold War nationalism.

Part II explains how Western-led women's NGOs acquired more influence in the post-war UN system by building on wartime relationships to power. Drawing on these relationships, women's NGOs helped to draft provisions in the UN Charter that recognised women's and human rights, contributed to the Universal Declaration on Human Rights (UDHR), and persuaded governments to establish a Commission on the Status of Women within the UN system. As active participants in NGO coalitions, women's NGOs played a major role in elaborating the meaning of the NGO 'consultative status' to the UN Economic and Social Council (ECOSOC). In Part II, World YWCA activities, carried out in conjunction with the UN relief and refugee agencies, also provide concrete examples to illuminate how one women's organisation cultivated influential advisory and information-sharing relationships with the US State Department and UN secretariat through wartime and post-war service to refugees; furthermore the group helped to define Western women's role in Allied efforts to reconstruct democratic societies in post-war Germany and Japan.

Part II also examines the ways East-West politics of the Cold War era transformed feminist advocacy networks. Again drawing on the World YWCA as an example, Part II explains how and why the YWCA disengaged from pre-war relationships with the Liaison Committee of Women's International Organisations and established new and providential relationships with the UN Commission on the Status of Women and with a mixed-gender coalition of NGOs in the Conference of NGOs in Consultative Status with the Economic and Social Council of the United Nations (CONGO) during the 1950s and 1960s. During these decades women's international organisations were early advocates of women's involvement in 'technical assistance' development programmes at the UN. They provided arguments that linked national development to women's status in the Commission on the Status of Women and in forums sponsored by other UN agencies and positioned themselves to play key roles in the dramatic transformations in global-development and gender policies that occurred in the 1970s and 1980s.

Part III: 'Women's NGOs and the United Nations, 1970–85', examines women's organisations as they restructured and amplified relationships between NGOs and the evolving UN system. Since the 1970s the UN secretariat and government delegations recognised the essential contributions that NGOs made to the operations of UN agencies. This change was due, in large part, to the participation of NGOs in UN-designated 'Years' and 'Decades' focused on major global issues and in the corresponding UN World Conferences that developed global policy and programmes. The positive and vital impact of NGOs was apparent in determining the themes of UN programmes and conferences throughout the 1970s and 1980s, focusing attention on such critical global issues as the environment, disarmament, population, development and women. NGOs played key roles in mobilising popular and governmental support, setting conference agendas, influencing proceedings and implementing conference recommendations, as well as in planning concurrent forums specifically for NGO participants that were held parallel to the government-led UN conferences. In particular, during the World Population Year in 1974, women's NGOs collaborated with sympathetic UN officials and pressured governments to include women in global population policy planning and to recognise that women's control over their fertility was linked to national development and to the success of global population plans.

Part III also analyses the contributions of both 'old' and 'new' women's international NGOs in establishing the empowerment and advancement of women as a focal point within the system of the UN and in connecting broad intergovernmental initiatives promoting peace and conflict resolution, economic and social development, and democracy and human rights to women's roles and status in society during the UN Decade for Women. Perhaps most significantly, a more inclusive global feminist movement emerged through NGO struggles regarding access to power during the organisation of the UN Decade for Women conferences and corresponding NGO forums.

World YWCA records and the documents of the NGO forums deposited at the Sophia Smith Collection reveal the ways that NGOs which had formal consultative status worked inside the UN system, helped to define the themes of the UN Decade for Women, 'equality, development, and peace', and played important advisory roles during the Decade's three governmental conferences held in Mexico City (1975), Copenhagen (1980) and Nairobi (1985).[19] Women's NGOs also delineated the scope of the three parallel NGO forums, organised global feminist participation, and raised funds to carry out these forums. Three YWCA women provided organisational leadership as forum conveners. NGOs without formal consultative status that worked outside the system of the UN during the Decade raised many questions in regard to feminist modes of leadership and coercive uses of power. Nonetheless the NGO forums enabled thousands of women activists from all regions of the world to share their perspectives and priorities with one another and with government delegates, to monitor first-hand UN deliberations on global gender policy issues, and to focus world attention on the Decade's goals of gender equality, sustainable development and peace. The forums also inspired the organisation of ongoing international feminist networks that included leaders from the global South; these organisations emphasised global structural inequalities and the need for development within the Third World and transformed subsequent UN global gender policy.

The book concludes with an evaluation of the effectiveness of the leadership of Western-led women's international organisations in expanding women's power within the system of global governance. By documenting and analysing the history of women's international NGOs and their relationships to evolving global governance bodies, feminists can draw lessons for twenty-first-century activism. In a fundamental way this book was inspired by Karen Offen's conclusion to *European Feminisms 1700-1950: A Political History*. In its examination of the activist record of women's international organisations, *Shaping a global women's agenda* is also a 'construction – and transmission – of a feminist memory, a feminist past', as Offen described her history of modern European feminisms. Offen has laid down the challenge that this study takes on: 'The challenge then is to inform ourselves about what has been "already in place", the victories, the mistakes, the challenges, and to use this knowledge as a springboard to future feminist thought and action. We have far more important things to do than continually to reinvent the wheel.'[20]

Notes

1 This book focuses on the following women's international organisations that were included within the Joint Standing Committee of Women's International Organisations founded in 1925, and that continued with a few additions to membership through the Second World War. They are: the International Council of Women, the International Women's Suffrage Alliance, the World Young Women's Christian Association (YWCA), the Women's International League for Peace and Freedom, the International Federation of University Women, the World Union of Women for International Concord, the World's Young Women's Christian Temperance Union, St. Joan's Social and Political Alliance, the International Federation of Women Magistrates and Members of

the Legal Profession, the International Federation of Business and Professional Women, the International Cooperative Women's Guild and the American National Committee on the Cause and Cure of War. By the launch of the UN Decade for Women, the following women's international organisations were among the most active in establishing and promoting the UN Decade activities: the World YWCA, the International Alliance of Women (formerly the International Women's Suffrage Alliance), the International Council of Social Democratic Women, the International Council of Women, the International Federation of Business and Professional Women, the International Federation of University Women, the International Planned Parenthood Association, the Women's International League for Peace and Freedom, the World Council of Catholic Women's Organizations and the Women's International Democratic Federation.

2 Rosemary Tong, *Feminist Thought: A Comprehensive Introduction* (Boulder, CO: Westview Press, 1989), pp. 11–13.

3 Ibid., pp. 173–5.

4 Laurel Richardson, Verta Taylor and Nancy Whittier, *Feminist Frontiers*, 5th edition (Boston, MA: McGraw Hill Higher Education, 2001), p. 483.

5 Cynthia Enloe, *The Curious Feminist: Searching for Women in an Age of Empire* (Berkeley, CA: University of California Press, 2004), pp. 19–24.

6 Among many others, Canadian Member of Parliament the Honourable Audrey McLaughlin made this point in a speech delivered in 1997, as she asserted 'In my view, there is no genuine democracy unless our political institutions are comprised of at least fifty percent women. Gender equality is essential to true democracy.' The Honourable Audrey McLaughlin, 'The empowerment of women: searching for genuine democracy among the ashes of patriarchal rhetoric', speech delivered at the European Forum for Democracy and Solidarity Conference: 'Women in Central and Eastern Europe at the threshold of the XXI century', Prague, Czech Republic, 18–20 April 1997 (gos.sbc.edu/m/mclaughlin.html).

7 Charlotte Hooper has summarised the feminist scholarship documenting the masculinist structural biases in government bodies. Charlotte Hooper, *Manly States: Masculinities, International Relations and Gender Politics* (New York: Columbia University Press, 2001), p. 12: '[I]nternational relations is a world of traditional masculine pursuits – in which women have been, and by and large continue to be, invisible (Enloe 1990; Halliday 1991; Peterson and Runyan, 1993, 1988). The focus on war, diplomacy, states, statesmen, and high-level economic negotiations has overwhelmingly represented the lives and identities of men. This is because of the institutionalization of gender differences in society at large and the consequent paucity of women in high office. Between 1970 and 1990, for example, women worldwide represented under 5 percent of heads of state, cabinet ministers, senior national policymakers and senior persons in intergovernmental organizations (Peterson and Runyan, 1993, 6). States have historically been oppressive to women, who have often been denied full citizenship. Rights and duties of citizenship have depended upon the

bearing of arms, a duty by and large confined to men (Stiehm 1982). Men form
not only the decision makers, but also the law enforcers, backed by threats of
violence (Enloe 1987). In fact, masculine violence has become thoroughly
embedded, institutionalized, and legitimized in the modern state (Connell
1990).'

8 Ibid., p. 13. 'Realist' international relations theorists, like Hans Morgenthau
   defined these 'masculine gender traits'.
9 Georgia Duerst-Lahti and Rita Mae Kelly (eds), *Gender Power, Leadership and
   Governance* (Ann Arbor: University of Michigan Press, 1995), p. 19.
10 Nitza Berkovitch, *From Motherhood to Citizenship: Women's Rights and
   International Organizations* (Baltimore, MD: Johns Hopkins University Press,
   1999), p. 19.
11 Berkovitch, *From Motherhood to Citizenship*; Naomi Black, *Social Feminism*
   (Ithaca, NY: Cornell University Press, 1989); Karen Offen, *European Feminisms
   1700–1950, A Political History* (Stanford, CA: Stanford University Press, 2000).
12 World Young Women's Christian Association Papers, World Young Women's
   Christian Association, Geneva, Switzerland (hereafter WYWCA).
13 Germany joined the World YWCA in 1898 and France joined in 1900. Anna
   V. Rice, *A History of the World's Young Women's Christian Association* (New
   York: Woman's Press, 1947), p. 53.
14 Rice, *A History of the World's Young Women's Christian Association*; Carole
   Seymour-Jones, *Journey of Faith: The History of the World YWCA 1945–1994*
   (London: Allison and Busby, 1994). For a study of the international activism
   of the American YWCA, see also: Nancy Boyd, *Emissaries, The Overseas Work of
   the American YWCA, 1895–1970* (New York: Woman's Press, 1986).
15 Leila J. Rupp, *Worlds of Women: The Making of an International Women's
   Movement* (Princeton, NJ: Princeton University Press, 1997).
16 Papers of the YWCA of the USA, Sophia Smith Collection, Smith College,
   Northampton, MA (YWCA of the USA), Anna Owens, 'Women's international mind in industry', *Association Monthly* (December 1920), pp. 616–18;
   Katherine S. Gerwick, 'Along an international pathway, in our world program
   we are only following a trail blazed many years ago', *Woman's Press* (September
   1926), pp. 629–31; Charlotte Niven, 'Report of the General Secretary, May
   1924–June 1926', microfilm reel 78.
17 YWCA of the USA, Gerwick, 'Along an international pathway', p. 630.
   Member organisations of the National Committee on the Cause and Cure of
   War included: the American Association of University Women; Council of
   Women for Home Missions; Federation of Women's Boards of Foreign Missions
   of North America; General Federation of Women's Clubs; YWCA of the USA;
   National Council of Jewish Women; National Federation of Business and
   Professional Women's Clubs; National League of Women Voters; Women's
   Christian Temperance Union; National Women's Conference of American
   Ethical Union; and the National Women's Trade Union League.
18 Mary A. Dingman Papers, Schlesinger Library, Radcliffe Institute, Harvard
   University, Cambridge, MA (hereafter MAD), 'An experiment in cooperation,

1925–1945: the history of the liaison committee of women's international organisations', (Essex, England: W. Hart and Sons, Ltd., 1945), box 1.

19 International Women's Tribune Centre Records, 1970–2000, Sophia Smith Collection, Smith College, Northampton, MA (hereafter IWTC).

20 Offen, *European Feminisms*, p. 395.

Part I

Women's NGOs and disarmament, 1925–40

In the aftermath of the First World War, Western-led women's organisations engaged more actively and deliberately than ever before in international politics. Arguing that war-torn Europe had 'been decimated of its masculine creative potentialities' they demanded a role for women in the League of Nations and the International Labour Organization (ILO).[1] In 1925 women forged a new organisational network, the Joint Standing Committee of Women's International Organisations, to work together on collectively defined global 'women's issues'. Claiming a worldwide membership of over 45 million, the association members of the Joint Standing Committee and its offshoot, the Women's Disarmament Committee of the Women's International Organisations that formed in 1931, were led by women of extraordinary talents and deep convictions. They cultivated connections to male leaders in the interwar peace movement, Western governments and the League secretariat. While they drew upon the gender expectations of male leaders when they argued that women provided the necessary nurturing skills and humanitarian values to transform militaristic and hyper-masculine international relations, as world conflicts escalated they also learned to talk the tough talk of power politics in order to capture male leaders' attention and speak to their concerns in disarmament debates. Alternately they adopted strategies to work collaboratively on system reform from inside the male-defined intergovernmental bodies, and to protest male-defined operations from outside the global governance system.

The question then becomes why these women's voices are not recorded in the published histories of interwar international politics, particularly in accounts that focus on the League of Nations Conference on the Reduction and Limitation of Armaments that opened in 1932 when the Women's Disarmament Committee played critical activist roles. And why, by the mid-1930s, the Great Powers – the United States, Britain, France, Germany and Italy, whose national security concerns dominated the interwar decades – ultimately dismissed as impractical or even 'dangerous' women's peace advocacy, although it was realistic and nuanced and widely supported among global populations; nevertheless the Great Powers insisted on associating it with 'Communist' ideas.

The women whose contributions to interwar peacemaking are identified here were well known to one another and to government leaders. Yet in most cases these women, more concerned with promoting their causes than with achieving notoriety as individuals, never sought recognition for themselves. This self-effacing tendency in part explains women's historical invisibility.

At times, however, these leaders sought credit for their part in global peacemaking, as when the Women's Disarmament Committee campaigned openly for the Nobel Peace Prize in 1934. Yet at that time, and in the later published histories of the era, male leaders and scholars have often given pride of place to the words and actions of men.[2] Feminist scholars have recorded the women's role at the League Disarmament Conference and have highlighted the peace petition campaign that women's organisations conducted to publicise the opening plenary session of the conference in February 1932.[3] Nonetheless the published scholarship does not fully illuminate the legacy of the Women's Disarmament Committee. These omissions may be related to the preservation of historical records since the Committee's public reports and private letters are widely scattered in numerous archives. Although a concentration of these records that would reveal a more complete Committee history is not found in any single location, the research brought together here brings this history to light.

In the end, of course, the Women's Disarmament Committee did not achieve its self-defined goals. The Committee's activism did not prevent the arms race or the escalation of state-sponsored violence during the 1930s. The Committee's strategic appeals did not persuade Western European governments or the United States government to collaborate on arms reduction treaties or on internationalist economic and trade policies that might have weakened the appeal of fascist powers in Germany, Italy and Japan.

Moreover, the women who led the Disarmament Committee were not absolute pacifists, nor did they consistently promote egalitarian feminist campaigns for a universal declaration of women's equal rights. Their pragmatic political positions were determined by situations within specific contexts. To be sure, these women were not unprincipled. They defined visionary end goals that included the creation of a cooperative and peaceful world society where all human beings were valued and interacted as equals. Yet they accepted graduated and practical steps to achieve those ends and in some peace advocacy and feminist circles these compromises discredited their activism.

In addition their timidity in regard to opposing German persecution of Jewish populations in the early 1930s and their reluctance to work with leftists for fear of being identified as 'Communists' by anti-Communist

Western governments in the mid-1930s caused subsequent regrets and tarnished their historic feminist reputations.

While their global feminist perspectives were works in progress, the experiences of the women in these international organisations offered important lessons in establishing political relationships for succeeding generations of activists. Within the League of Nations system these women's persistence and creativity forged a role for non-governmental organisations (NGOs) that was carried over and expanded upon after the Second World War ended, the League dissolved, and the United Nations Organization (UNO) formed. Governments relearned the bitter lessons of war, but they also paid closer attention to the counsel of the NGOs, and this new understanding was due in large part to the reputations and relationships to power that the women's international organisations had established during the interwar years.

Notes

1 Florence Guertin Tuttle, *Women and World Federation* (New York: Robert M. McBride and Co., 1919), p. xii.
2 See coverage of women's contributions in published histories of the League of Nations Conference for the Reduction and Limitation of Armaments, including: League of Nations Archives, Geneva, Switzerland, IX Disarmament 1932.IX.19, 'Collaboration of women in the organization of peace', 12 February 1932, box R4218; Elmer Bendinger, *No Time for Angels: The Tragicomic History of the League of Nations* (New York: Alfred A. Knopf, 1975), pp. 271–2; Warren F. Kuehl and Lynne K. Dunne, *Keeping the Covenant: American Internationalists and the League of Nations, 1920–1939* (Kent, OH: Kent State University Press, 1997), pp. 52–3; Philip Noel-Baker, *The First World Disarmament Conference 1932–33, and Why it Failed* (Oxford, UK: Pergamon Press, 1979), pp. 73–4; F. P. Walters, *A History of the League of Nations* (New York: Oxford University Press, 1952), pp. 500–2.
3 Harriet Hyman Alonso, *Peace as a Women's Issue: A History of the U.S. Movement for World Peace and Women's Rights* (Syracuse, NY: Syracuse University Press, 1993), pp. 122–3; Gertrude Bussey and Margaret Tims, *Women's International League for Peace and Freedom, 1915–1965: A Record of Fifty Years' Work* (London: George Allen & Unwin, Ltd, 1965), p. 97; Cecelia Lynch, *Beyond Appeasement: Interpreting Interwar Peace Movements in World Politics* (Ithaca: Cornell University Press, 1999), pp. 97–9 and 184–6; Laura Puffer Morgan, 'Disarmament', in Harriet Eager Davis (ed.), *Pioneers in World Order: An American Appraisal of the League of Nations* (New York: Columbia University Press, 1944), pp. 42–57; Christy Jo Snyder, 'The influence of transnational peace groups on US foreign policy decision-makers during the 1930s: incorporating NGOs into the UN', *Diplomatic History* 27 (June 2003), 387–9. See also Arnold Whittick, *Woman into Citizen: The World Movement Towards the Emancipation of Women in the Twentieth Century with Accounts of the Contributions of the International Alliance of Women, the League of Nations and the Relevant Organizations of the United Nations* (London: Athenaeum, 1979), pp. 110–11.

1 Arrival of disarmament petitions from Britain in Geneva, January 1932. The World Young Women's Christian Association.

2 Parading the disarmament petitions in Geneva, 5 February 1932. The World Young Women's Christian Association.

3 Women march to the disarmament conference hall, 6 February 1932. The World Young Women's Christian Association.

4 The Bâtiment Electoral in Geneva, site of the 1932 League of Nations Conference on the Reduction and Limitation of Armaments.

5 Mary Dingman and Laura Puffer Morgan in Geneva 1932.

1

The First World War and its aftermath

Women's international organisations and the First World War

The First World War that pitted the British, French and Russian Allied Powers against the German, Austrian and Hungarian Triple Entente had sparked a surge of political activism among women's international organisations, but it also highlighted the dilemma that feminists have faced historically in their responses to war. Western male-led governments often denied women their full political rights as citizens because they did not fulfil the ultimate obligation of citizens – they did not put their lives on the line to fight in national armies in order to defend national policies. Yet women were also expected to have inherently peace-loving, nurturing and maternal natures, and to hate all wars in the abstract. If women opposed specific wars, however, and refused to support their governments' policies or their nations' troops as international conflicts raged, they were considered to be traitors. Based on these contradictory gendered expectations, Western feminist associations of the First World War era were caught in a bind.

Some Western feminists openly opposed the First World War and advocated for peace by making essentialist arguments, claiming that as women they must fulfil their roles as peacemakers. Succeeding generations of feminists, such as Jean Bethke Elshtain have since identified the counterproductive dangers of such essentialist arguments. By gendering peace feminine, Elshtain argues, war becomes masculine; fighting wars becomes a necessary rite of passage into manhood, thus perpetuating the war system.[1] Nonetheless appeals to women's 'natural' preferences for peace have been historically powerful because they coincide with deep and almost universal gender role conditioning. As Betty Reardon and other 'difference' feminists have explained, 'the social roles women have played throughout history . . . have led many to feel the burden of war, and value the opportunities of peace, more openly and more avidly than most men'.[2]

Carrie Chapman Catt, the pre-eminent leader in both the American and International Women Suffrage Associations during the early decades of the twentieth century, expressed commonly held essentialist feminist sentiments when she wrote to the *New York Times* in February 1915 to criticise the ongoing World War:

> The politics of men have embroiled the world in the most wholesale slaughter of the sons of mothers the world has ever known. That is a case where man's business of war and woman's business of conserving the race have clashed, and women are helpless to defend their own. Hundreds if not thousands of women have been forced to bear children by soldiers of their country's enemy all along the war zone. It becomes the terrible business of the mothers of the race to secure the right of political protest in every nation. When war murders the husbands and sons of women, destroys their homes, desolates their country and makes them refugees and paupers, it [the politics of men] becomes the undeniable business of women.[3]

Western feminist organisations that advocated for peace held a wartime Congress at The Hague in May 1915. Over 1,100 women delegates from twelve nations proposed plans for a mediated settlement to end the war and for a post-war international forum to settle future conflicts peacefully.[4] The American delegation, at that time representing the United States as a neutral power with Jane Addams as its spokeswoman, met with fourteen government leaders and presented peace proposals calling for 'neutral mediation, limitation of armaments, democratic control of foreign territories, removal of the economic causes of war, and "the further humanizing of governments by the extension of the franchise to women"'.[5] British activists Margaret Bondfield, Margaret Ashton and Kathleen Courtney together co-chaired a new organisation – the British Women's International League (WIL) – and forged a statement of feminine principles to guide post-war international relations: 'the principles of right rather than might, and of cooperation rather than conflict, in national and international affairs'.[6] Although they failed to persuade leaders of belligerent nations to sue for peace at that time, President Woodrow Wilson incorporated the women's ideas for a mediated settlement led by neutral nations and for a post-war League of Nations into his Fourteen Point Plan for peace in 1916.[7] The historian Deborah Stienstra has argued that 'these women broadened the scope of public discourse about the settlement of the war' even if their efforts did not overcome the predominant gender discourse that cast 'rational' men in leading roles determining wartime international affairs and relegated 'emotional' women to supporting roles as wives and mothers who kept the home fires burning.[8]

Other Western feminist organisations, such as the British and American national YWCAs, plunged into active war work to support their nations' economies and armed forces and in order to claim women's full political rights as citizens. Without a doubt these Western women who supported national war policies contributed to their nations' war-making capacities and made it possible for their leaders to wage war. As many scholars have documented, the First World War 'marked women's definitive entry into the war machine'.[9]

In the case of the First World War era YWCA, British and American secretaries went to France, Italy and Russia to provide support for Allied troops and to develop workers' associations and clubs for women and girls who laboured in munitions factories and wartime industries. As war raged in Europe, Western secretaries also led the expansion of YWCA national chapters in India, Japan and China and in several countries throughout Latin America. In these nations outside the war zones, YWCA secretaries continued pre-war collaborations with local women addressing the needs of women factory workers and a modernising middle class, monitoring factory safety inspections, lobbying for labour laws, establishing schools for women and girls, and allying with local women's rights and suffrage movements. In the immediate post-war period British and American YWCA secretaries also provided social services for war refugees in Czechoslovakia, Poland, Belgium, Romania, and the Baltic states.[10]

After the First World War ended, political energies once again surged through women's international organisations. With some notable exceptions during or immediately after the war, many Western governments and the Soviet Union granted women the right to vote in national elections, thus acknowledging women's contributions to national war efforts and signalling male approval for at least that minimal level of female political participation.[11]

Pushing for a much greater political role, women from the victorious Allied nations formed another joint delegation and appealed to Allied governments at the Versailles Peace Conference to include women in post-war intergovernmental bodies. The Inter-Allied Suffrage Conference – a coalition of the French Women's Suffrage Union, the International Women's Suffrage Alliance and the International Congress of Women – met with Allied government leaders and pressed for women's inclusion in the proposed League of Nations secretariat. They also urged the government leaders to address the global problems of trafficking in women and children, prostitution, the nationality of married women and women's suffrage, and they argued for the establishment of international education, health and arms control bureaus in the new League of Nations system.[12] Their efforts resulted in the addition of several provisions specifically addressing equal participation for women in the proposed League of Nations and attention to the needs of women and children in the proposed International Labour Organisation in the Versailles Peace Treaty.[13]

A separate coalition of American and European women's organisations led by Rose Schneiderman of the National Women's Trade Union League and Mary Anderson, chief of the Women in Industry Service, a US federal wartime agency, successfully lobbied for International Labour Organization (ILO) charter provisions to allow women to participate on an equal basis with men, representing the interests of member states, employers and workers. The ILO charter affirmed the principle of equal pay for equal work for men and women and established an inspection system to investigate workplace conditions, in which women were to be included as inspectors. [14]

When women from the defeated countries were denied visas and prevented from attending the Versailles Conference, rather than accepting the male-led Allied governments' decisions regarding the reconstruction of the post-war world, some feminist activists formed the International Committee of Women for Permanent Peace (ICWPP), which included women from the victorious Allied countries, the defeated Central Powers and the neutral nations. As an international statement of protest they organised an alternative peace conference in Zurich, Switzerland, that opened in May 1919, just as the Allies announced the harsh terms of the peace that were forced on defeated Germany in Versailles. Women at the Zurich conference condemned the 'morally indefensible' Versailles Treaty terms that heaped the blame for the war onto Germany and they predicted that disarmament of Germany alone would not promote permanent peace. [15] They also asserted that the League of Nations as it was created at Versailles, with its membership limited to Allied powers and neutrals, did not embody the inclusiveness or the democratic principles – self-determination for all nations, universal and equal reductions in arms, universal free trade and labour protections – that these women deemed critical foundations for the new intergovernmental body. [16]

The Zurich conference also drafted a Women's Charter, including reforms to secure women's social, political and economic equality and to abolish slavery and global trafficking in women. The Charter created a new international organisation based on the British WIL, the Women's International League for Peace and Freedom (WILPF). With membership opened to women of all nations, WILPF planned to marshal the 'moral' force of women behind the linked causes of world peace, women's rights, and human rights. WILPF soon established headquarters in Geneva, the new home of the League of Nations, and quickly formed national sections uniting liberal and socialist feminists who coordinated international campaigns for peace, women's equality and social justice. [17]

According to an American, Florence Guertin Tuttle, who combined practical guides for action with an urgent rallying cry in her 1919 book *Women in World Federation*, the First World War 'broke every shackle of tradition that had obstinately remained unbroken. It freed [women's] energies, liberated their minds and trained their activities as they had never been liberated and trained in the history of the world'. 'The only failure', Tuttle cautioned her fellow activists, 'that could really count would be a failure to convince women that world peace is equally woman's work; that if the world is ever again turned into a slaughterhouse, women will be equally responsible with men, and that the only way to secure a new world order is through supporting a new instrument that will make the guarding of our common humanity a common world task'.[18]

Women's international organisations agreed wholeheartedly with Tuttle. They were determined to involve women as participating members and to interject feminine and feminist perspectives into the newly formed League of Nations. They believed that women offered distinct and necessary perspectives on international issues that men did not traditionally bring to diplomatic negotiations.[19] 'Women', argued Rhoda McCullough of the American YWCA, 'approach facts from a different point of view and they seem to be moving toward new methods of solving international difficulties. Women want the facts underlying the causes of international friction, not as they have to do with "business," or "politics" or "economics" but in their direct relation to human life.'[20] Nonetheless, although they lobbied hard for women's inclusion in the intergovernmental body, only one British woman, Dame Rachel Crowdy, was appointed to a high-ranking position as head of the League Social Section that dealt with trafficking in women and children, among other issues, in 1921.

In order to increase the number of women appointed to government delegations and to the various governing and advisory committees at the League, in 1925 twelve women's organisations formed yet another coalition, the Joint Standing Committee of Women's International Organisations. This coalition included the International Council of Women, the International Women's Suffrage Alliance, the World Young Women's Christian Association, the Women's International League for Peace and Freedom, the International Federation of University Women, the World Union of Women for International Concord, the World's Young Women's Christian Temperance Union, St. Joan's Social and Political Alliance, the International Federation of Women Magistrates and Members of the Legal Profession, the International Federation of Business and Professional Women, the International Cooperative Women's Guild and the American National Committee on the Cause and Cure of War.[21] In 1931, with a name change to the Liaison Committee of Women's International Organisations, several groups joined the coalition including Equal Rights International, the League of Mothers and Educators for Peace, the World Organisation of Jewish Women, the European Federation of Soroptimist

Clubs, the League of Iberian and Latin American Women and the League of Jewish Women.[22]

The interwar histories of all these women's organisations are filled with accounts of linked campaigns to promote an astonishing array of progressive causes, including efforts to abolish slavery and trafficking in women and children, to halt international drug trafficking, to establish international agencies to aid migrants and refugees, to establish workplace regulations and labour laws to 'protect' the interests of women and children, and to gain women's 'equal rights'. Nearly all women's international organisations were active in many of these campaigns simultaneously. Women's goals and causes overlapped with one another, and organisations and individuals most commonly spread their attentions widely. By the mid-1920s, perhaps the broadest and most inclusive campaign was the one women waged for 'peace'.

The members of the broad-based and gender-mixed interwar peace movement represented a wide spectrum of positions, from liberal internationalists who supported the application of both political and economic sanctions to rein in aggressor states to absolute pacifists who rejected any use of coercive force. Yet all agreed that the entrenched norms of international politics that supported Western imperialism and secret diplomacy had to be transformed. Interwar peace activists shared the goal of establishing a new international order that supported democracy and racial and national equality. They opposed colonial hierarchies among nations and lobbied to integrate both Germany and the Soviet Union as full members in the new League of Nations. They promoted transparency and open diplomacy in League chambers to arrive at international treaties as the means for achieving the new world order.[23]

Interwar peace activists also inspired several government attempts to negotiate an international disarmament treaty and realise the provisions in the League of Nation Covenant Article 8 calling for 'the reduction of national armaments to the lowest point consistent with national safety and the enforcement by common action of international obligations'. Throughout the 1920s and into the 1930s, through various strategic campaigns, the interwar peace movement exerted constant pressure on reluctant League member nations to follow through with what the peace activists defined as the nations' 'disarmament pledges'.[24]

For the League member states – such as France – that sought guaranteed protection along their borders, resistance to arms reduction was linked to concerns for national security. Peace activists answered these concerns by arguing that national security could be safeguarded and national fears allayed through international cooperation and collective security pacts.[25] At the same time, during the 1920s, German diplomats demanded 'parity' from the League of Nations member states in regard to disarmament as well as to other international issues. According to the terms of the Versailles Treaty, defeated Germany had been stripped of its colonial territories and most of its industrial infrastructure and natural resources and was saddled with crippling war reparations payments; all of these terms had destroyed Germany's war-making capacity.[26] During the 1920s Germany sought reduction in reparations payments, the return of the port city of Danzig (Gdansk) from Poland, and restoration of Germany's pre-war stature as a major European power.

Peace activists were well aware of the economic hardships Germany experienced, and they focused attention on economic disparities as possible causes of another war. The Ruhr Valley crisis of 1922-23, when France occupied Germany's industrial region in retaliation for default on reparations payments, prompted British and American peace activists to support their governments' diplomatic efforts to reduce Germany's war debt. The resulting Dawes Plan negotiated by the US State Department in collaboration with American bankers in 1924, gave the interwar peace movement hope that more broad-based public peace campaigns could pressure governments to modify further the punishing economic terms of the Versailles Peace Treaty.[27]

In 1925 the peace movement also lobbied in support of the Locarno Treaties, which determined borders between France, Belgium and Germany and paved the way for Germany's entrance into the League as a full member nation. The Locarno Treaties gave peace activists confidence that other international agreements could be reached through the League of Nations or the World Court and that significant progress on negotiated disarmament could be achieved.[28]

Beginning in 1925, numerous Western women's organisations focused on cooperative strategies to resolve world conflicts; these included economic diplomacy, international arbitration and graduated disarmament achieved through new international agreements. In the United States the National Committee on the Cause and Cure of War launched internationalist public education campaigns and held the first of its annual conferences to expose the dangers of economic nationalism, and to promote disarmament and other peace-building strategies.[29]

In Britain in 1926 the WIL circulated a national Arbitration Petition: it received 500,000 signatures, documenting British popular support for the Protocol for the Pacific Settlement of International Disputes, proposed by two members of the Labour government, Lord Parmoor and Arthur Henderson, which called for compulsory arbitration of international disputes.[30] Public presentation of the petitions culminated with the Women's Pilgrimage for Peace, organised by WIL leaders Kathleen Courtney and

Emmeline Pethick-Lawrence. The nationwide demonstration coordinated the efforts of twenty-eight British women's organisations along with the League of Nations Union and the Quaker Friends Society. It united thousands of women from throughout England, 'countesses and charwomen' according to a *New York Times* reporter, who all journeyed on foot to rally in London's Hyde Park in June. The rally culminated in resolutions calling for international conflict resolution through arbitration, for an international disarmament conference, and for suffrage rights for British women under the age of thirty (women over the age of thirty were enfranchised on 10 January 1918).[31]

Clearly women in the peace movement had demonstrated their strong interest in international relations and their ability to mobilise pro-peace public opinion. Nonetheless by 1927 a 'business-as-usual' intransigence among the major world powers had resurfaced. After the League of Nations Assembly's first International Economic Conference in Geneva in May 1927 failed to reach agreements to reduce national tariff restrictions or to expand international trade, the Joint Standing Committee of Women's International Organisations could not persuade the gender-bound patriarchal League of Nations Council to include 'fresh' voices of women economic experts on the newly formed Economic Consultative Committee, made up of representatives of Geneva-based NGOs.[32] A League-sponsored Naval Disarmament Conference held in Geneva in the summer of 1927 also failed to produce new arms reduction agreements. Many observers faulted Britain's Conservative Party government, which refused to offer any concessions to reduce the size or strength of the British Navy.[33]

These setbacks were somewhat counteracted by the culmination of the peace movement's international campaign to 'outlaw war'. Salmon O. Levinson, a Chicago lawyer, had founded the American Committee for the Outlawry of War in 1921. He had enlisted influential supporters, including the US envoy James T. Shotwell, who knew that the French foreign minister, Aristide Briand, was pursuing an 'American Locarno' agreement with the US State Department after 1925 – that is, a bilateral treaty renouncing war and providing American guarantees to secure the French-German border. Shotwell and others pressured US Secretary of State Frank B. Kellogg to work with French Minister Briand to draft a universal declaration renouncing war as an instrument of national policy. In part influenced by the peace movement and in part mollified by the fact that the Paris Peace Pact 'required no real sacrifices and established no precise responsibilities' to obligate its signatories, in 1928, sixty-two nations signed the Kellogg-Briand Pact to outlaw war.[34]

While critics of the interwar peace movement judged the Kellogg-Briand Pact to be the height of 'interwar idealistic folly', Cecilia Lynch, a scholar of the peace movement, has argued that: 'In the longer term . . . the Pact would become the basis for a series of arguments put forth by both peace groups and governments . . . Peace activists used the Pact to justify disarmament and peaceful conflict resolution, whereas governments used the Pact as the basis for claims in favour of assistance in collective action against aggression.'[35] Although they, too, understood the Pact's practical limits,[36] women's international organisations frequently cited the Kellogg-Briand Pact and Article 8 of the League of Nations Covenant as 'legal' justifications to support their insistent calls for disarmament. At the same time, women activists also called attention to their gendered nurturing natures and their roles as mothers of boys who would grow up to be soldiers when making 'moral' demands for disarmament. This dual strategy was at once legalistic and visceral and it brought women's international organisations into the centre of action at the intergovernmental London Naval Disarmament Conference in 1930.

The London Naval Disarmament Conference and nationality rights

The London Conference that opened in January 1930 sought to improve on the naval construction ratios that had been negotiated by the United States, Great Britain, France, Italy and Japan in the Five Power Treaty at the Washington Conference of 1921-22. With support from United States President Herbert Hoover, the newly elected British Labour Party Prime Minister, Ramsay MacDonald, convened the international conference to halt a burgeoning naval arms race and to extend national fleet-building quotas to previously unlimited categories of warships, including submarines, naval destroyers and cruisers.[37]

British women's role in convening the London Conference, though indirect, was nevertheless influential. Ramsay MacDonald and the Labour Party had been voted into office with the critical support of British women's organisations. The Equal Suffrage Act in Britain had passed in 1928, gaining voting rights for all adult women. Exercising their new political power, British women launched a 1929 general election campaign to 'make the Kellogg Pact a reality'. They voted the Conservative Party government out of office and helped to elect a 'Parliament of Peacemakers'. As the only British party that promoted League of Nations diplomacy and an internationalist foreign policy for peace and disarmament, the Labour Party won many women's votes. Labour elected Ramsay MacDonald as Britain's prime minister. MacDonald in turn made several Cabinet appointments that women's and peace organisations applauded. He appointed Arthur Henderson, leader of the Union of Railwaymen and president of the Labour and Socialist International, to the post of foreign minister. MacDonald also selected Margaret Bondfield to head the Ministry of Labour, the first woman in British history to fill a Cabinet Secretary post.[38] With the sympathetic Labour government in office and a Naval Disarmament Conference on the near horizon, women's international organisations planned a joint action designed, once again, to mobilise public opinion and exert pressure on politicians to negotiate concrete arms reduction agreements.[39]

In the months leading up to the Conference, Japanese peace activists Uta Hayashi and Tsune Gauntlett collected 180,000 signatures supporting a petition for global disarmament and planned for its public presentation at the London meetings.[40] Leaders of women's organisations from the United States, Britain and France joined forces with the Japanese women activists at the Conference and formed the Women's Peace Crusade. As the London Conference opened the Peace Crusade delegation representing millions of women members of international organisations, met with Prime Minister MacDonald and with the Australian, New Zealand, Japanese and American foreign ministers.[41] Leading the Peace Crusade delegation, Margery Corbett Ashby, a British Liberal Party politician and president of the International Women's Suffrage Alliance, presented the peace petitions to the assembled Conference delegates and in her public address asserted that 'women [are] a new factor in international politics. They come here because they feel that women are not only idealists; they will represent in politics a very practical force'.[42]

Women in international organisations who actively campaigned for disarmament operated well within the political mainstream during the 1920s and 1930s as they forged alliances with powerful politicians, government bureaucrats and League officials. In many cases women leading these organisations had personal relationships with the power elite. Consequently these alliances were strong and effective. Margery Corbett Ashby, for example, was the daughter of Liberal Party MP Charles Corbett. She joined the British women's suffrage campaign through the National Union of Women Suffrage Societies as a young woman studying at Cambridge University. With her mother and sister, Margery Corbett pushed the Liberal Party to adopt a pro-suffrage position throughout the first decade of the twentieth century. After her marriage to Brian Ashby in 1910 Corbett Ashby continued to promote women's rights. She stood as a Liberal candidate for Parliament in Britain's first post-war elections. At the same time, she joined the International Women's Suffrage Alliance and represented the women's views at the Versailles Peace Conference. Although she was never elected to Parliament, during the interwar era Corbett Ashby waged seven active campaigns for office and represented the British government through several appointed diplomatic posts.[43] Lady Marian Parmoor, President of the World YWCA from 1924 to 1928, worked on international peace campaigns in conjunction with her husband, Charles Alfred Cripps, First Baron of Parmoor (1852–1941), a Labour Party leader in the House of Lords throughout the 1920s. Elsie Zimmern, who served as Honorary Secretary for the Joint Standing Committee and the Liaison Committee of Women's International Organisations through the 1920s and 1930s, was the daughter of Alfred Zimmern, a renowned British international relations scholar who served his nation in several diplomatic capacities at the League of Nations.

British women's organisations were particularly fortunate in their alliance with Labour Party leader Arthur Henderson during the interwar disarmament campaign. According to Henderson's parliamentary private secretary and leading member in the British League of Nations Union, Philip Noel Baker, 'From the day when he entered the Foreign Office as Secretary of State in the Second Labour Government in 1929, Arthur Henderson made it plain that the overriding purpose of his policy was to secure the execution of the pledges of Article 8 of the League of Nations Covenant and Part V of the Treaty of Versailles. His purpose was nothing less than the making of a World Treaty of Disarmament.' Indeed, these goals had inspired Henderson from the time he proposed the arbitration Protocol for the Pacific Settlement of International Disputes in 1924, and then as Britain's representative on the League of Nations Preparatory Commission for the Disarmament Conference in 1927.[44]

As Foreign Secretary and head of Britain's delegation to the League of Nations in 1929, Henderson included Helena Swanick in his diplomatic team. Swanick was a well-known peace advocate and one of the few women appointed to a national delegation at the League during the interwar years despite the best efforts of women's international organisations to put names of many qualified candidates before their government leaders.[45]

Only a very few women gained formal high-profile positions within the League of Nations secretariat, but they shared their inside information and access to power with the women's international organisations. British Dame Rachel Crowdy, for example, led the Social Section of the League secretariat that worked with Committee Five, the Committee that dealt with such social issues as trafficking in women and children, opium trafficking, intellectual cooperation and refugees. Beginning her work at the League in 1919, Crowdy was the only woman to head one of the secretariat sections, a position that followed in rank only to the Secretary General himself and to the three assistant secretary generals.[46] Crowdy established mutually beneficial relationships with the Joint Standing Committee of Women's International Organisations throughout the 1920s; she relied on the women's organisations' support for League of Nations initiatives and provided these organisations with advance notice

of League agenda items so that they could more effectively lobby government delegates.[47] When Crowdy retired from her post at the League in
1930, the Lithuanian Princess Gabriella Radziwell, who worked with
the secretariat's Information Section that performed the League's public
relations and education functions, became the chief source of inside information and adviser to the women's international organisations as they
sought greater influence within the League governance system.[48]

In addition to lobbying for disarmament at the 1930 London Naval
Conference, women's international organisations also engaged in a campaign to guarantee a woman's right to maintain her citizenship and the
passport of her own country of birth when she married a man from another
country. Numerous organisations supported a Joint Demonstration on the
Nationality of Married Women at The Hague Conference on the Codification
of International Law held in March 1930, asserting that women should
have equal rights as men to maintain their nationality after marriage.
Such organisations as Equal Rights International led by the Americans
Alice Paul and Doris Stevens of the International Women's Party and
Lady Margaret Rhondda, Chrystal MacMillan and Helen Archdale of the
British Six Point Group, claimed to represent the 'truly feminist' wing
of the women's movement that focused on achieving women's absolute
equal rights, without any distinctions from men, in all realms of society.
These women believed that an international treaty establishing married
women's nationality rights would open the door to an international treaty
guaranteeing women's universal equal rights.[49]

Many members of the Joint Standing Committee of Women's
International Organisations agreed that married women's right to main-
tain their own nationalities was a fundamental matter of fairness and
justice. At The Hague Conference, the International Council of Women,
International Alliance of Women, Women's International League for
Peace and Freedom, Inter-American Commission on Women, World Union
of Women for International Concord, All-Asian Conference of Women and
International Federation of University Women all joined Equal Rights
International in pressing for women's equal nationality rights. Although
male delegates to the conference rejected women's appeals, arguing that
women and their children were a vulnerable population that needed
the protective mantle of their husbands' citizenship, the League Legal
Committee agreed to hear the perspectives of the women's organisations
represented in a Consultative Committee that could make future proposals on women's nationality rights to the League General Assembly. The
women's organisations accepted this compromise, since they understood
that their Consultative Committee had been granted unprecedented privileges to hold meetings at the League of Nations secretariat offices and to

circulate memos and reports directly to the five permanent members of the League Council and to the General Assembly. The women's organisations fully intended to use the Consultative Committee structure as a platform to assert wider claims for women's equal rights.[50]

Organisations such as the World YWCA agreed with male delegates to The Hague Conference that at the time in world history, married women and their children needed special protections, and the YWCA decided not to participate with their sister organisations in the Joint Action for Married Women's Nationality Rights.[51] This issue, like that of women's equal rights in the workplace, exposed divisions within the Western liberal feminist movement during the 1930s.

All the Liaison Committee member organisations agreed that to achieve a just and peaceful world community, it was necessary to establish women's equal rights and status, guaranteed by national law in every country and by international law throughout the world. A number of women's organisations, however, believed that some campaigns to push for international treaties and universal declarations of women's equal rights, though desirable in principle, were less worth striving for in practice because they did not consider the negative effects those treaties could have on particular women in specific class and cultural locations. The YWCA, the Women's Trade Union League and several other organisations raised these arguments during the subsequent campaign for a women's equal rights treaty after 1935. They believed that an equal rights treaty would nullify protective labour laws regulating hours and types of work for women. These laws had been the result of hard-fought national campaigns in the first decades of the twentieth century, led by industrial reformers on behalf of workers in the West and in their colonies.

Women's international organisations faced a dilemma throughout the interwar era: how to define positions that promoted women's rights while still recognising that women's and men's productive and reproductive roles were different, though of equal value. Some egalitarian feminists who worked with Equal Rights International saw the solution to this difficulty in denying any difference with men, while other social feminists who worked with the YWCA demanded a broader definition of 'new feminism', one that argued for the necessity of women's gendered contributions to the widest array of progressive social reform and peace movements.[52]

The campaign for an international arms reduction treaty engaged social feminists in more active roles at the 1932 League Disarmament Conference, but egalitarian feminists also supported the 1930-31 peace petition drive that kicked off a new public relations offensive among women's international organisations. During the 1930s, women in organisations as different from one another as the YWCA and Equal Rights

International joined forces under the umbrella of the Liaison Committee of Women's International Organisations and worked together through the Committee's global network of activists to support progressive feminist projects.

Preparations for the disarmament conference

After Arthur Henderson became foreign minister in 1929, he appointed Lord Robert Cecil (Edgar Algernon Robert Gascoyne-Cecil, Viscount Cecil of Chelwood, 1864-1958) as Britain's representative to the ongoing preparatory commission for the League Disarmament Conference. Like Arthur Henderson, Lord Cecil also had strong ties to the women's international organisations. Cecil and Kathleen Courtney worked together in Britain's League of Nations Union throughout the interwar decades, and they shared the goal to reconcile the Union's 'pure pacifist' wing with the Union's majority members who supported negotiated disarmament treaties, backed by the collective security clauses in the League of Nations Covenant.[53] Born in 1864, the son of the British imperial diplomat and Prime Minister Lord Salisbury, Lord Cecil inherited power and privilege. Cecil claimed his seat in the House of Lords as a Conservative Party MP in 1904, before the First World War transformed his politics. Wartime service as minister of the blockade and assistant foreign minister fuelled Cecil's fervent desire for peace and his active support for the idealistic promise of the League of Nations. Over the decade of the 1920s practical experience in disarmament negotiations had tempered Cecil's idealism and he began the push to strengthen Article 16 of the League Covenant, which guaranteed collective economic sanctions and military responses by League member nations when an aggressive state attacked one of their members. By 1930 Cecil placed his hopes for peace in the League's collective security agreements.[54]

Many powerful League era diplomats sought support from women's organisations for their disarmament initiatives, and Henderson and Cecil both cultivated women's support both to convene an international disarmament conference and throughout the duration of the conference. These men understood women's power to influence public opinion. Male diplomats often appealed to women in language that affirmed traditional gender stereotypes and assumed women's pacific and nurturing maternal natures. Men identified a moral basis as defining women's political power. Women in international organisations often willingly acknowledged and embraced these traditional gender attributes, believing that these so-called 'feminine' traits were in fact the most admirable human qualities. However, they also asserted their claims to an equal measure of political power and their rights to participate actively in the public policy-making process.

The arms specialist Laura Puffer Morgan believed that women could use men's gender expectations to achieve greater roles in national and international politics. Born in Framingham, Massachusetts, in 1874 and educated at Smith and Radcliffe Colleges, Laura Puffer moved to Lincoln to teach mathematics at the University of Nebraska after graduation. There she met and married Raymond B. Morgan, a newspaperman who specialized in government affairs. They moved to Washington, DC in 1908. During the First World War Laura Puffer Morgan developed an avid interest in international politics. She focused on the international arms race as a key factor in the outbreak of war and on disarmament as the means to prevent war.[55] Beginning at the 1921-22 Washington Conference and continuing throughout the interwar years, Morgan developed expertise in modern weaponry and in tracking international military spending. As a leading member of the American Association of University Women, Laura Puffer Morgan also forged connections to the international peace movement.

In 1922 Morgan met the Quaker activist Frederick Libby who founded the National Council for the Prevention of War (NCPW) the previous year. Soon thereafter Morgan became an associate secretary for the NCPW – a coalition of women's, peace and internationalist organisations that cultivated public support for disarmament treaties, the World Court and the League of Nations as effective instruments to prevent the outbreak of international war.[56] Representing the NCPW during the interwar decades, Morgan attended international disarmament conferences and wrote analytical conference reports that were published and distributed by pacifists as well as by militarists. Colleagues described her as strong, rational, helpful, courageous, witty and constructive, but also as impatient with those who were uninformed, sentimental or superficial. Marshalling facts, presenting persuasive arguments and urging her friends and colleagues to act on their convictions were Morgan's forte. [57]

Confident and accomplished women like Morgan believed that gender stereotypes should not prevent women's entry into male-dominated politics; rather, women could use gender stereotypes to achieve outcomes that would serve the collective good of humanity. In November 1929 Morgan explained her views before the American National Council of Women in a speech entitled 'The Responsibility of Women in International Relations'.

> Because women are instinctively more interested than men in humanitarian projects and in matters of the common welfare, because they have more leisure for study and activity, because they have fewer financial entanglements, and as a result a more objective viewpoint and greater moral courage – in other words because they are free-er. For these reasons the activities of the women's organizations are needed in safeguarding and promoting

national legislation as well as that of the community in which they live. Every selfish interest is represented in Washington. To counteract these it is necessary to have some organized expression of humanity.

It is in this sense that I believe women are needed in international affairs. It is not enough that we should feel more keenly than men the sufferings of war and the blessings of peace, though that emotional reaction must necessarily spur us on to ever-increased efforts. We must dedicate to the settlement of actual current international problems our leisure, our freedom from entanglements, our objectivity, our idealism and our practical common sense.[58]

Laura Puffer Morgan argued that the key to men's acceptance of women in government policy-making positions was within women's power and control. Once women had developed expertise in political issues, men would be unable to ignore their views.[59] In order to participate in disarmament debates, women needed to acquire technical knowledge of weaponry and learn the specialised language of arms negotiations utilised by defence 'experts'. Without this knowledge at their disposal, women would be relegated to the political margins. Moral considerations were critical in mobilising public opinion but were less important to political and military strategists who occupied the formal seats of power at the negotiating tables. Morgan learned these lessons from her own personal experience and she was determined to enter the patriarchal realm of politics and to reform the system from within. She believed these lessons to be universally applicable to women everywhere. Certainly diplomats and military men in Geneva, London and Washington respected her advanced knowledge of weapons systems and defence budgets. When she became the technical adviser to the Women's Disarmament Committee after the League Disarmament Conference finally opened in February 1932, Morgan had already learned to speak the tough language of the military strategists.[60]

Although her subsequent efforts during the conference to counter the arguments of the male diplomats and generals who guarded their nations' military advantages were spirited and persistent, in the end they proved ineffective. Yet it was not the lack of 'realistic' expertise or political imagination on Morgan's part or on the part of the interwar peace movement that lay at the heart of the failed peace, as some historians have concluded. Rather, fears for national security, caused in part by worldwide economic depression, commanded the attention of national policy makers; the Great Powers would not agree on significant reductions in preparedness, whether in weapons, military budgets or size of armies.

Just after the London Naval Disarmament Conference concluded, however, hopes among women's international organisations for future success in negotiated disarmament were at a highpoint. Carrie Chapman Catt's National Committee on the Cause and Cure of War (NCCCW) hosted its annual conference in Washington in January 1930 and invited the peace activist Kathleen Courtney to be a featured speaker. Courtney was born in Chatham, Kent, in 1878 into an upper-middle-class British family. Her father, Major David Courtney of the Royal Engineers, and her mother, Alice Margaret d'Olier, raised her in Kensington. She studied at Lady Margaret Hall, the first women's college established at Oxford University. There she joined the National Union of Women Suffrage Societies and formed lifelong commitments to peace, social justice and women's rights. Courtney promoted these linked causes through her leadership at The Hague women's wartime conference in 1915, where she helped to found the British WIL, and at the Zurich women's post-war conference in 1919, where she helped to establish the Women's International League for Peace and Freedom.[61] Courtney's biographer, Beryl Haslam, has explained that Courtney's 'contribution to the causes of suffrage and internationalism was not in the realm of theory but as a first-rate organiser, lobbyist and speaker. As a leader, Courtney was held in great affection by her colleagues. She combined high principles with good sense, firmness and courtesy, as well as a sense of humour.'[62]

Never an absolute pacifist, Courtney expressed her faith in the diplomatic settlement of world conflict through the League of Nations. Unlike leaders in the American section of WILPF who were 'opposed to all war and all preparation for war, whether offensive or defensive, international or civil' Courtney and the British WIL adopted broader alliances within the international peace movement and advocated graduated disarmament through arbitrated agreement to fulfil the terms of Article 8 of the League of Nations Charter. Because of Courtney's leadership and dual membership in the British WIL and the British League of Nations Union, the two organisations collaborated often during the interwar decades. In 1930, at Carrie Chapman Catt's invitation, Courtney shared her views on peace and disarmament with American audiences at the NCCCW annual conference and during her subsequent cross-country speaking tour. After returning to London, she focused her energies on a new petition campaign to marshal popular support for international arms reduction agreements. German feminist and the WILPF leader Frieda Perlen had proposed an International Declaration on Disarmament, and British WIL and other women's NGOs seized on her idea and launched an ambitious drive to circulate disarmament petitions around the globe.[63]

Petitions for peace and disarmament

For the women's international organisations, petition campaigns were a well-used strategy to educate the public and pressure government officials to adopt progressive national legislation and international treaties. Women's organisations believed that petitions, signed by millions of concerned men and women, wielded moral and political power. Mobilising the strength and energy of relatively powerless individuals into a solid association based on shared goals and values defined the power of historic social movements in general and of women's movements in particular. Women's NGOs believed in the power of collective actions, and their activism at League forums in Geneva always called attention to the vast numbers they represented. Organisation leaders never spoke for themselves alone, but always in the name of millions of members worldwide. This condition explains in part why the names of so few leaders of the largest women's international organisations are recorded in history books. While few individual women sought the limelight, in the names of their organisations they applied political pressure with fierce moral conviction, as their collective appeal to government delegates attending the September 1930 eleventh session of the League of Nations General Assembly demonstrates:

> The undersigned organisations, representing more than forty millions of women working in various ways in fifty-six different countries of the world to forward international understanding and cooperation, feel impelled to call attention to an increasing and ominous tendency of the Press, general public and even Governmental circles to discuss, or admit in discussion, the possibility of another war; this is in utter disregard of the sacred pact formally renouncing war, which has just been signed by fifty-seven civilized nations . . .
>
> We demand of our statesmen, elected by the people, if they value their privilege of service, to increase their efforts and henceforward to make the whole-hearted observance of the Briand–Kellogg Pact the supreme charge of national honour and the safeguard of humanity.[64]

Copies of the women's statement were distributed to international journalists and to all 400 government delegates. Having been granted audiences with the president of the eleventh General Assembly and the German, British and the French foreign ministers, the women's organisations believed that their appeal made a powerful impression on the world's leading statesmen. Una Saunders, who represented the YWCA on the women's delegation, reported that in every meeting the diplomats praised women's efforts to promote the success of disarmament negotiations and promised to press their nations to fulfil Peace Pact obligations.[65]

In addition to women's joint action at the General Assembly session, throughout 1930 twenty-six national chapters of the Women's International League for Peace and Freedom had continued to circulate disarmament petitions inspired by Frieda Perlen, which demanded that the women's governments advocate for 'total and universal disarmament' at the planned-for League of Nations disarmament conference. National chapter petitions varied in minor points of wording, but in principle they aligned with the one circulated by the NCCCW in the United States:

> We, the undersigned women of the United States, URGE the International Disarmament Conference to satisfy the expectations of the world by putting Paragraph Eight of the Covenant into immediate and unhesitating effect by 'reduction of national armaments to the lowest point consistent with national safety.'
>
> The Allies and Associates pledged world disarmament to their adversaries; the Covenant promised it; great nations have solemnly agreed that international disputes arising shall be settled by peaceful methods without resort to war; and, lastly, the nations of the world, through the Briand-Kellogg Pact, and RENOUNCED war.
>
> The obvious next step is the bold reduction of every variety of armament. To do less would violate treaty obligations, awaken suspicion and start fresh war talk.
>
> The grant of our petition will make the assurances of peace invincible. War will cease when men will it.[66]

Supporting the WILPF petition campaign, Frederick Libby's National Council for the Prevention of War published an article in its September 1930 *News Bulletin* asserting, 'This work is good and ought to be prosecuted vigorously. The peoples and not the governments should rule in this heroic endeavour to banish war by destroying first its implements . . . The women of the world ought all to sign these petitions, for they are the first and the last losers.'[67] In Britain, over 600 local chapters of the League of Nations Union, urged on by Kathleen Courtney and Lord Robert Cecil, also reinforced the women's petition campaign, which was quickly becoming an international phenomenon.[68] Churches, trade unions, students and veterans groups joined women's organisations to mobilise widespread public support to pressure government leaders into negotiating a substantive international disarmament treaty. By early 1931 the petition campaign represented a global constituency. Conservative statesmen and military leaders dismissed the disarmament petitions as 'sentimental' and 'ignorant' of government interests, but sympathetic and influential statesmen – including French leaders Edouard Herriot and Henri de Jouvenel, Italy's Vittorio Scialoja, and the United States Senator William E. Borah – joined British Foreign Minister Arthur Henderson in welcoming the burgeoning public support for disarmament principles that they fervently believed in.[69]

At its annual conference in January 1931, the National Committee on the Cause and Cure of War voted to join with the Liaison Committee of Women's International Organisations to circulate WILPF peace petitions and to present them at the forthcoming League of Nations disarmament conference.[70] Carrie Chapman Catt's initial reservations about the project reflected her reluctance to work with what she defined as 'ultra feminist' organisations like Equal Rights International, which were also represented on the Liaison Committee. However, an exchange between NCCCW vice chair Henrietta Roelofs of the YWCA and Kathleen Courtney addressed Catt's concerns. Roelofs asked Courtney whether the Liaison Committee could function effectively with its disparate organisational membership, and whether a united approach would serve women's interests in the international arena.[71] Courtney answered with a carefully calculated affirmative response:

> First, as regards the Liaison Committee, it is just in this moment in the throes of coming to life. Whether it is going to function well or not, I do not know. But I think the best way to make it function will be to give it something to do . . .
>
> As regards your second question – is a united front more desirable or many approaches? My personal view it that what is all-important is that we should have a common purpose, that is to say, that within the limits of admitting certain divergences we should all be pressing for the same thing at the Disarmament Conference. If, at least in general principles, we have a common program I think the question of whether there is a united front or many approaches is less important.[72]

Courtney urged the NCCCW to support the petition campaign, and noted that British WIL had already collected 250,000 signatures in collaboration with the League of Nations Union and other national groups and was building a groundswell of British support for the disarmament conference.

Known for her leadership and organisational skills, Catt took up the challenge to meet and exceed the British numbers. In April 1931, Catt proposed that the eleven NCCCW member organisations collect the million American women's signatures that Catt believed would make the petition campaign influential and 'worthwhile'. The effort required tremendous 'energy and determination' and Catt pushed the women's groups to commit to the project: 'What I want to know is what each organization will do. Will you kindly send me your decision? Can you set your members to work and keep them at it until your quota has been secured?' Catt then revealed her vision, which turned out to be very close to the reality of what took place in Geneva when the disarmament conference finally opened in February 1932: 'I long to see a million American names being carried up the hill to the Disarmament Conference with a few splendid American women in charge. We want at least one eloquent and powerful woman to tell those men we are not going to accept "short change" this time.'[73]

Throughout 1931 NGOs reported on the progress of the international petition campaign in their publications. In April the National Council for the Prevention of War noted that England and Germany had each collected nearly 350,000 signatures, representing a 'solemn mandate' from the people favouring substantive disarmament agreements.[74]

The numbers were encouraging, but a few women, including Laura Puffer Morgan, were reminding the women's organisations that the petitions were only a first step. Millions of signatures might convince government delegates that they had popular support to negotiate significant arms reduction agreements, but women's associations had to take their efforts further, to involve themselves in the debates over specific treaty terms.

Prophetically, Morgan reminded women that if the negotiations were left to the 'experts' – that is, the military men 'whose professional interest is always enlisted on the side of expansion' – few, if any, reduction agreements would be reached. She also urged women to support realistic positions during the conference – to accept the principle of equal treatment for Germany, to advocate for limits on military budgets as well as reductions in weaponry, and to support the creation of a permanent international disarmament commission, with the active involvement of the United States in order to address the French demands for collective security.[75] Building popular support for these positions would require sustained public education campaigns on the part of women's organisations.

Peace advocates recognised these realities. The 1930-31 petition campaign was only one of the peace movement's many educational projects; women's organisations launched numerous initiatives aimed at developing a more profound understanding of those international issues that trigger violent world conflicts. The NCCCW, for example, sponsored a five-month-long European study tour from May to October 1931, to analyse the German position vis-à-vis the recovery of the 'Polish Corridor'. The Versailles Treaty had awarded this disputed strip of land, which divided Germany from East Prussia, to Poland; the corridor gave Poland access to the port city of Danzig, designated as a 'free port' – that is, a protectorate administered by the League of Nations. Rachel Conrad Nason, who would later go on to work for the US government, received an NCCCW scholarship to join the study tour and to write a report on Adolf Hitler's ambitions to restore Germany's eastern borders to their contours prior to the First World War. Nason was well connected to several women's international organisations and to the peace movement. Frederick Libby of the NCPW, Mary Woolley, president of Mt. Holyoke College and leader in the American Association of University Women, and Helen Thoburn of the American YWCA, all wrote letters of recommendation to the NCCCW supporting Nason. And all were interested to read her formal report to the NCCCW

'Hitler and the Corridor: A Study in the Cause and Cure of War', and to hear her informal impressions regarding the mood of the international community in Geneva, where she had observed the opening of the Twelfth League of Nations General Assembly session in September 1931. Nason was in Geneva when the Liaison Committee of Women's International Organisations formed the Women's Disarmament Committee and when the peace movement's plans to influence the outcome of the international disarmament conference seemed tantalisingly within reach.[76]

Notes

1 Jean Bethke Elshtain as quoted in Joshua S. Goldstein, *War and Gender: How Gender Shapes the War System and Vice Versa* (New York: Cambridge University Press, 2001), pp. 330–1.

2 Betty A. Reardon, *Women and Peace: Feminist Visions of Global Security* (Albany: State University of New York Press, 1993), pp. 15–16. See also Barbara J. Steinson, 'The mother half of humanity: American women in the peace and preparedness movements in World War I', in Carol R. Berkin and Clara M. Lovett (eds), *Women, War and Revolution* (New York: Holmes & Meier Publishing, 1980), pp. 259–84.

3 Quoted in Harriet Hyman Alonso, *Peace as a Women's Issue: A History of the U.S. Movement for World Peace and Women's Rights* (Syracuse, NY: Syracuse University Press, 1993), p. 61.

4 Leila J. Rupp, *Worlds of Women: The Making of an International Women's Movement* (Princeton, NJ: Princeton University Press, 1997), pp. 27–8.

5 Steinson, 'The mother half of humanity', p. 261.

6 Beryl Haslam, *From Suffrage to Internationalism: The Political Evolution of Three British Feminists, 1908–1939* (New York: Peter Lang, 1999), p.74.

7 Ibid., p. 70; Rupp, *Worlds of Women*, pp. 210–11. See also Lyman C. White, 'Peace by pieces: the role of nongovernmental organizations', *Annals of the American Academy of Political and Social Science* 264 (July 1949), p. 89.

8 Deborah Stienstra, *Women's Movements and International Organizations* (London: St. Martin's Press, 1994), p. 54.

9 Nicole Ann Dombrowski, 'Soldiers, saints or sacrificial lambs? Women's relationships to combat and the fortification of the home front in the twentieth century' in Nicole Ann Dombrowski (ed.), *Women and War in the Twentieth Century: Enlisted Without Consent* (New York: Garland Publishing Inc., 1999), p. 7.

10 Anna V. Rice, *A History of the World's Young Women's Christian Association* (New York: Woman's Press, 1947), pp. 153–69.

11 Many Western European nations, the United States and the Soviet Union granted women voting rights during or immediately after the First World War ended. Several exceptions include Spain, which granted women voting rights in 1930, and France and Italy, which granted women voting rights in 1945. Marilyn J. Boxer and Jean H. Quataert (eds), *Connecting Spheres: European*

Women in a Globalizing World, 1500 to the Present, 2nd edition (New York: Oxford University Press, 2000), p. 218.

12 Margaret Galey, 'Forerunners in women's quest for partnership', in Anne Winslow (ed.), *Women, Politics and the United Nations* (Westport, CT: Greenwood Press, 1995), p. 4; Rupp, *Worlds of Women*, p. 211.

13 Stienstra, *Women's Movements*, p. 56.

14 Carol Riegelman Lubin and Anne Winslow, *Social Justice for Women: The International Labor Organization and Women* (Durham, NC: Duke University Press, 1990), pp. 1 and 25.

15 Haslam, *From Suffrage to Internationalism*, p. 140.

16 Cecilia Lynch, *Beyond Appeasement: Interpreting Interwar Peace Movements in World Politic.* (Ithaca: Cornell University Press, 1999), p. 56.

17 Haslam, *From Suffrage to Internationalism*, p. 142; Rupp, *Worlds of Women*, pp. 29–31 and 40; Alonso, *Peace as a Women's Issue*, pp. 81–3.

18 Florence Guertin Tuttle, *Women and World Federation* (New York: Robert M. McBride and Co.), 1919, pp. xii–xiv.

19 Galey, 'Forerunners in women's quest for partnership', p. 4; Rupp, *Worlds of Women*, p. 211; Stienstra, *Women's Movements*, p. 56; Preface by Margery Corbett Ashby, President of the International Woman Suffrage Alliance, in D. M. Northcroft, *Women at Work in the League of Nations* (London: Page and Pratt, Ltd, 1923), pp. 1 and 25–8.

20 YWCA of the USA, Rhoda E. McCullough (ed.), *Association Monthly* (March 1922); Arnold Whittick, *Woman into Citizen: The World Movement Towards the Emancipation of Women in the Twentieth Century with Accounts of the Contributions of the International Alliance of Women, the League of Nations and the Relevant Organizations of the United Nations* (London: Athenaeum, 1979), p. 93.

21 MAD, 'An experiment in cooperation, 1925–1945: history of the liaison committee of women's international organisations', box 1.

22 WYWCA, 'Résumé of the work of the disarmament committee of the women's international organisations, up to April 1, 1932', box 283.

23 Lynch, *Beyond Appeasement*, pp. 28–30 and 35.

24 Ibid., p. 63.

25 YWCA of the USA, Gerwick, 'Along an international pathway', *Woman's Press* (September 1926), pp. 629–31.

26 Elmer Bendinger, *No Time for Angels: The Tragicomic History of the League of Nations* (New York: Alfred A. Knopf, 1975), p. 126.

27 Lynch, *Beyond Appeasement*, p. 68.

28 Ibid., pp. 75–6.

29 Gerwick, 'Along an international pathway,' pp. 629–31.

30 Lynch, *Beyond Appeasement*, pp. 70–5.

31 'Women foes of war marching on London', *New York Times* (12 June 1926): 4.

32 WYWCA, Joint Standing Committee of Women's International Organisations, Meeting Minutes, 28 November and 16 December 1927, and 7 February 1928, 'Reports, Minutes, International Organizations', 1928–1929', box 261.

33 Lynch, *Beyond Appeasement*, p. 79.

34 Thomas G. Paterson, J. Garry Clifford, Kenneth J. Hagan, *American Foreign Relations: A History Since 1895, Vol. II*, 4th edition (Lexington, MA: D. C. Heath and Company, 1995), pp. 145–6.
35 Lynch, *Beyond Appeasement*, p. 90; Alonso, *Peace as a Women's Issue*, p. 88.
36 Charles DeBenedetti, *The Peace Reform in American History* (Bloomington, IN: Indiana University Press, 1980), p. 121.
37 Paterson, Clifford and Hagan, *American Foreign Relations*, p. 174.
38 Haslam, *From Suffrage to Internationalism*, p. 184.
39 Philip Noel-Baker, *The First World Disarmament Conference 1932–33, and Why it Failed* (Oxford, UK: Pergamon Press, 1979), p. 42.
40 Alonso, *Peace as a Women's Issue*, p. 118; Jacqueline Van Vorhis, *Carrie Chapman Catt: A Public Life* (New York: Feminist Press, 1987), p. 211.
41 Gertrude Bussey and Margaret Tims, *Women's International League for Peace and Freedom 1915–1965: A Record of Fifty Years' Work* (London: George Allen & Unwin, Ltd., 1965), p. 91.
42 Lynch, *Beyond Appeasement*, p. 98.
43 Papers of Margery Irene Corbett Ashby, 1869–1879, Brief Biography, The Women's Library, London, UK (aim25.ac.uk/cgi-bin/search2?coll_id=6696&inst_id=65; accessed 1 January 2008).
44 Noel-Baker, *The First World Disarmament Conference*, pp. 54–8; F. P. Walters, *A History of the League of Nations* (New York: Oxford University Press, 1952), p. 441.
45 Haslam, *From Suffrage to Internationalism*, p.185.
46 D. M. Northcroft, *Women at Work in the League of Nations* (London: Page and Pratt, Ltd. 1923), p. 11.
47 WYWCA, Elsie Zimmern to Mary Dingman, 22 December 1927, box 261.
48 Winslow, *Women, Politics and the United Nations*, p. 5.
49 Karen Offen, 'Women's rights or human rights? International feminism between the wars', in Patricia Grimshaw, Katie Holms and Marilyn Lake (eds), *Women's Rights and Human Rights* (New York: Palgrave, 2001), pp. 246–7; Carol Miller, 'Geneva – the key to equality: inter-war feminists and the League of Nations', *Women's History Review*, 3:2 (1994), pp. 224–6.
50 Miller, 'Geneva – the key to equality', pp. 227–8.
51 WYWCA, Charlotte Niven to Margaret Hiller, 19 March 1930, box 256.
52 Offen, 'Women's rights or human rights?', pp. 247–8.
53 J. A. Thompson, 'Lord Cecil and the pacifists in the League of Nations Union', *Historical Journal* 20 (1977), p. 949; Haslam, *From Suffrage to Internationalism*, p. 180.
54 Thompson, 'Lord Cecil', pp. 953–4.
55 Papers of Laura Puffer Morgan and Ethel Puffer Howes, 1892–1962, Schlesinger Library, Radcliffe Institute, Harvard University, Cambridge, MA (hereafter Morgan–Howes Papers), 'Opening remarks of Mrs. James Austen Stone, former chairman of the Women's Joint Congressional Committee [at Laura Puffer Morgan Memorial Service, 1962]', box 1.
56 DeBenedetti, *The Peace Reform in American History*, p. 113.

57 Laura Puffer Morgan Papers, 1926–1962, Peace Collection, Swarthmore College, Swarthmore, PA (hereafter LPM), Remarks by H. Duncan Hall, Member of the Board of Directors, Institute for World Organization, at AAUW Memorial Service, 4 October 1962 and Remarks by Mrs. Ruth W. Tryon, Former Editor for the AAUW and Staff Associate for the Fellowship Fund, at AAUW Memorial Service, 4 October 1962.

58 Morgan–Howes Papers, 'The responsibility of women in international relations', 4 November 1929, box 2.

59 Ibid. See also Morgan–Howes Papers, 'Shall we leave it to the experts?', for the *Christian Advocate* c. October 1931, box 1.

60 LPM, Roland Hall Sharpe, 'Active for disarmament', *Christian Science Monitor* (28 December 1932); Morgan–Howes Papers, Benjamin Gerig to Frederick J. Libby, 3 May 1934, box 7.

61 The Papers of Kathleen d'Olier Courtney, 1878–1974, The Women's Library, London, UK (hereafter KDC).

62 Haslam, *From Suffrage to Internationalism*, pp. xxv and 156–8.

63 Ibid., pp. 186–7.

64 Committee on the Cause and Cure of War Papers, Schlesinger Library, Radcliffe Institute, Harvard University, Cambridge, MA (hereafter CCCW), 'Appeal of the women to the world's statesmen', September 1930, box 18.

65 YWCA of the USA, Una M. Saunders, 'Women and the world's statesmen, representatives of six organizations in Geneva launch an appeal for peace', *Woman's Press* (December 1930), pp. 831–2.

66 CCCW, National Committee on the Cause and Cure of War petition to the disarmament conference at Geneva, c. 1931, box 21.

67 Morgan–Howes Papers, 'Conservative financial journal supports program of Women's International League for total and universal disarmament', National Council for the Prevention of War *News Bulletin* IX: 9 (September 1930), box 2.

68 Noel Baker, *The First World Disarmament Conference*, pp. 65–8.

69 Walters, *A History of the League of Nations*, p. 445.

70 Ruth Woodsmall Papers, Sophia Smith Collection, Smith College, Northampton, MA (hereafter RW), 'National Committee on the Cause and Cure of War, list of resolutions', January 1931, box 46.

71 CCCW, Henrietta Roelofs to Kathleen Courtney, 3 February 1931, box 18.

72 CCCW, Kathleen Courtney to Henrietta Roelofs, 13 February 1931, box 19.

73 CCCW, Carrie Chapman Catt to the National Committee on the Cause and Cure of War', 1 April 1931, box 21.

74 Morgan–Howes Papers, 'Remarkable progress abroad with universal disarmament petition', National Council for the Prevention of War *News Bulletin* 10:4 (April 1931), box 2.

75 LPM, 'The issues of the general disarmament conference: what should be the position of the United States?', 1931, box 7.

76 Rachel Conrad Nason Papers, Schlesinger Library, Radcliffe Institute, Harvard University, Cambridge, MA (hereafter RCN), 'Biographic notes', 6 June 1973, box 1.

2

Working for disarmament and peace

The twelfth general assembly of the League of Nations

For years women's international organisations had been meeting in Geneva when the League of Nations held its annual general assembly sessions that convened in September. Several Liaison Committee member organisations, including the World Young Women's Christian Association (WYWCA) and Women's International League for Peace and Freedom (WILPF), had relocated their world headquarters to the centre of international governance and maintained a year-round presence in Geneva, but the September general assembly brought the full forces of the women's organisation leadership to the city, as the government delegates also gathered from around the world. In the 1920s the Joint Standing Committee of Women's International Organisations established a tradition of inviting all female government delegates and women serving in the League secretariat to an annual dinner in their honour, and the Liaison Committee continued the tradition throughout the 1930s. These dinners provided women's international organisations with special access to the elite women who offered their insider perspectives on League business and used their influence to support the women's organisations' agenda. In September 1931, as the Liaison Committee established the Women's Disarmament Committee to coordinate activism at the upcoming League disarmament conference, dinner conversation focused on the long-desired disarmament treaty.[1] Kathleen Courtney, the featured speaker at the dinner, introduced the leaders of the newly formed Women's Disarmament Committee.[2]

Selection of the Women's Disarmament Committee leadership had caused little real controversy among the women's organisations, but some momentarily tense manoeuvring took place. Carrie Chapman Catt, described by friends and foes alike as conservative, diplomatic, domineering and brilliant, had reigned supreme over the early-twentieth-century women's suffrage movement and her impact on the interwar women's peace movement, if not dominant, was great.[3] As the Women's

Disarmament Committee formed, Catt campaigned behind the scenes for selection of 'moderate' feminist leaders.[4] Henrietta Roelofs, Catt's deputy in Geneva, reported on the meeting of 5 September, when the Disarmament Committee formed. Kathleen Courtney presided and displayed 'unusual gifts for administration and for integrating a group', gifts that were needed to satisfy the various women's organisations in attendance when they supported different candidates for the various Committee officer posts. Courtney was selected as the Women's Disarmament Committee vice chair. Rosa Manus of the International Women's Suffrage Alliance, Catt's admirer and ally since they met at the Amsterdam International Women's Suffrage Alliance (IWSA) conference in 1908, was selected as the Committee secretary.

Rosa Manus had formed an intimate friendship with Carrie Chapman Catt through their shared association with the IWSA (International Women's Suffrage Alliance), and she looked upon Catt as a second mother.[5] Born into a wealthy Jewish family in Amsterdam in 1881, Rosa Manus led a sheltered life in her youth, prevented by her father's sense of propriety from attending public schools and from pursuing any occupation beyond philanthropy. When the IWSA hosted an international Congress in Amsterdam in 1908, two leading Dutch feminists, Aletta Jacobs and Johanna Naber, invited Manus to represent the new generation of energetic activists that was needed to carry on the quest for women's rights. Following the Amsterdam Congress, Manus joined the Dutch women's suffrage movement and in 1910 became a 'special organiser' for the IWSA. Manus played a leading role arranging international conferences for the next thirty years. Together with Aletta Jacobs, Manus coordinated local arrangements for the Women's Peace Congress held at The Hague in 1915, and, after the First World War ended, she continued to work for peace through the IWSA and through WILPF.[6]

When Manus was named secretary of the Women's Disarmament Committee, a minor power struggle between the IWSA and the International Council of Women (ICW) ensued. The formidable Lady Aberdeen (Ishbel Maria Marjoribanks Gordon, Lady Aberdeen), a Scottish Marchioness led the ICW and sat at the head of the table, 'with her long pearl ear drops, her elaborate ostrich-plumed hat and her spectacles on the end of her nose'. Lady Aberdeen pushed for the selection of Laura Dreyfus-Barney as Committee chair, with the expectation that the Women's Disarmament Committee headquarters would be located in Paris.[7]

Laura Clifford Barney was born into a wealthy and artistic family in Cincinnati, Ohio, in 1879; she had also dedicated her energies to mobilising women in the quest for peace during the interwar years. Raised in privilege in Washington, DC and enjoying frequent European holidays,

Laura Barney and her sister Natalie followed their mother, the 'bohemian' painter Alice Pike Barney, and moved to Paris in 1900. There Barney met the Canadian May Ellis Bolles, who introduced her to the Baha'i religion. Barney converted to Baha'i, a faith that emphasises the unity of all peoples and religious traditions into a peaceful and integrated global community. A wealthy woman in her own right after she inherited a fortune on her father's death in 1902, Laura Barney married into more wealth when she wed the French scholar Hippolyte Dreyfus in 1911. Dreyfus, from a prominent Parisian Jewish family, had also converted to the Baha'i faith and became a leading scholar, teacher and translator of Baha'i scriptures from the original Persian texts. From 1904 onward Laura Barney collaborated with Dreyfus on several scriptural translations, and, after they married, both adopted the surname Dreyfus-Barney. During the First World War Hippolyte served as a postal censor in Marseilles. Laura worked with the American Ambulance Corps (1914–15) and with the American Red Cross (1916–18). When the war ended, she founded a children's hospital in Avignon. In 1925 the French government honoured her wartime service.[8]

Dreyfus-Barney also joined the ICW after the First World War.[9] Beginning in 1926 she served as ICW point of contact to the League of Nations Institute of Intellectual Cooperation located in Paris and became a strong advocate for League efforts to promote peace and disarmament. Lady Aberdeen hoped that Laura Dreyfus-Barney would head the Women's Disarmament Committee, but she was disappointed. Dreyfus-Barney was selected as the second vice chair, and Mary Agnes Dingman of the World YWCA, who seemed both 'neutral and able' to the IWSA and the ICW, was named Committee chair.[10]

Born in 1875, Mary Dingman was the eldest daughter of a devout Methodist doctor, James Alva Dingman. Humanitarian service and the evangelical spirit of the Social Gospel Movement guided his country medical practice. Later in life Dingman recalled the long horse-drawn buggy rides she made with her father to visit patients and his urging her onto a life of service to others. After graduating from New Paltz Normal School in 1899 Dingman taught school in Brooklyn until her parents' deaths. Continuing her education at Columbia Teachers College, Dingman earned a bachelor's degree in 1910, joined the faculty at Wellesley College, and taught history and economics. In 1914, Florence Simms, a progressive-era reformer, hired Dingman to join the Industrial Department at the American YWCA, and there she found her Christian service calling.[11]

In 1917 the American YWCA sent Dingman to France to establish clubs and educational programmes for women working in the munitions factories. The French government welcomed American YWCA's assistance, but food and government funds were scarce. Dingman pushed and prodded French authorities to devote precious resources to the women workers. Her persistent appeals to French Minister Edouard Herriot were legend among Dingman's friends:

> 'Like Jacob', they joked, 'she would not let him go unless he blest her – that is, gave her what she requested! She had learned, somewhat haltingly, a few French phrases. She uttered these with conviction, and with gestures. "The girls' morale is at stake. They *must* have centers. They *must* have hot lunches. They *must* have release from the tension. They *must* learn what the war is about. *Il est faut!* (It is necessary.)"'

She received the permissions she needed and the amused but respectful sobriquet, 'Mademoiselle Il est faut'. After the war ended, the French government honoured Dingman with two national service medals.[12]

After joining the World YWCA staff in London as chief industrial secretary in 1921, Dingman travelled throughout Europe, East Asia, Australia and New Zealand, developing model education programmes for female factory workers and training YWCA secretaries to implement these programmes with sensitivity to local conditions. In carrying out these duties, Dingman became an expert in industrial labour conditions and in industrial reform movements initiated in modern Western nations and in their colonies.[13] She spent over a year in China, from January 1924 to June 1925, working with the Chinese YWCA and the Industrial Commission of the Chinese National Christian Council, lobbying the Shanghai Municipal Council to establish progressive factory labour laws and safety regulations in foreign-owned enterprises within the concession zones.[14]

Through her extensive travels to organise industrial training schools and camps during the 1920s Dingman developed an international cohort of socially conscious YWCA secretaries and a global network of progressive industrial reformers. In London she worked with the well-known labour leaders and reformers Margaret Bondfield, Constance Smith and Agatha Harrison. Describing her impressions of Mary Dingman's warmth and energy in 1924, an Australian YWCA board member wrote:

> As World's Y.W.C.A. Industrial Secretary, Miss Dingman seems to live out exactly what it means, as she has all the qualities necessary to fill every part of that office. First, she belongs to every part of the world; then she is intensely interested in all questions relating to women and girls everywhere; she is also a sincere Christian, 'seeking first those things that are above', She enjoys the cooperation and fellowship of the big Association fondly wherever she meets with members . . . and she endeavours with all her powers to bring the women and girls in Industry to the abundant life that can only come in the service of Jesus Christ.[15]

In addition to the benefits of Dingman's international experience and global feminist networks, her home organisation, the World YWCA, offered the Women's Disarmament Committee office space at its Geneva headquarters as well as clerical assistance provided by Evelyn Beresford Fox. The British organisation secretary Evelyn Fox had also joined the World YWCA staff in London in the early 1920s, and had moved with the organisation to its new world headquarters in Geneva in 1930. YWCA records contain very few biographical details but they document Fox's integral role in social and industrial programme planning at the World YWCA throughout the 1920s, 1930s and 1940s. Evelyn Fox also shared Mary Dingman's humanitarian values and became Dingman's great friend, life-long companion and working partner.

To complete the Women's Disarmament Committee leadership, Clara Guthrie d'Arcis was named Committee treasurer. Born in 1878 into a well-connected family in New Orleans, Louisiana, Clara Guthrie was the daughter of James B. Guthrie, a distinguished member of the Louisiana Bar; her grandfather Judge E. T. Merrick had served as Chief Justice of the Supreme Court of Louisiana, and her grandmother Caroline E. Merrick was active in Southern women's organisations during the late nineteenth century. In 1911 Guthrie met and married a Swiss businessman, Ludovic d'Arcis. She then moved to Geneva and joined d'Arcis in running a successful import business for American automobiles and other American-made consumer goods. During and after the First World War, d'Arcis promoted United States–Swiss trade relations. In neutral Switzerland, Clara also led fundraising efforts to provide food for child victims of the war. In 1915 she founded the World Union of Women for International Concord, believing that a new and peaceful world order could be realised through education initiatives, led by women. Her experiences as a peace activist and international businesswoman convinced d'Arcis that economic causes of war were paramount. Bankers and industrialists, she argued, who funded wars and produced arms and war materials had to be re-educated to support peace. She believed that moral considerations must factor into business decisions and businessmen must be enlisted for practical plans to promote peace.[16]

As an essentialist feminist Clara Guthrie d'Arcis asserted that women had a special role to play in the peace movement, one that had nothing to do with selfish power politics or partisanship and everything to do with women's maternal concern for the preservation of human life. As she frequently explained, 'We have no axe to grind, we are concentrating on it, and as mothers and potential mothers we are naturally concerned with conserving human life . . . But until economic forces are behind us we can do comparatively little.'[17]

Together Mary Dingman, Laura Puffer Morgan, Clara Guthrie d'Arcis, Laura Dreyfus-Barney, Kathleen Courtney and Rosa Manus – four Americans, one British and one Dutch, and all known to each other through shared feminist and peace activist circles – became the working core of the Women's Disarmament Committee. Representing the 14 member organisations of the Liaison Committee of Women's International Organisations, these six Western women often claimed to speak for over 45 million women worldwide.[18]

Josephine Schain, an American leader active in several interwar women's organisations, joined Henrietta Roelofs in witnessing the formation of the Women's Disarmament Committee, and she asserted that the Committee leadership was well chosen. Roelofs reported Schain's observation to Carrie Chapman Catt: '[T]he fact that Mary Dingman is an American and knows our [National Committee on the Cause and Cure of War] movement will help us a lot, and she will keep us in touch with everything and will welcome most eagerly any suggestions from us.'[19]

Indeed, when Catt subsequently wrote to Dingman to propose a presentation plan for the petitions at the League of Nations disarmament conference, she awarded her seal of approval: 'I am very glad Miss Dingman, that you are the Chairman. You are a very safe girl.'[20] Yet Dingman, aged fifty-six at the time she took up the leadership of the Women's Disarmament Committee, would display an intense commitment to the cause of arms reduction and peace building and was not as deferential as Catt imagined.

As the twelfth League of Nations general assembly session opened in 1931 and 'the world' came to Geneva, the women's international organisations plunged into the annual festivities. Rachel Nason reported on the scene; she noted that despite the fact that the United States was not a League member, Americans with internationalist sympathies had flooded into the city and joined the diplomatic community in its mixture of political and social events. In fact, the United States government sent numerous official representatives to Geneva to safeguard the United States' national interests and to monitor League actions. At the highest ranks Consul General Prentiss Gilbert was based in Geneva, and Minister to Switzerland Hugh R. Wilson also sat on the League Third Committee on Arms Reduction. Nason noted contrasts between the formally orchestrated diplomatic receptions hosted by the various national delegations and nightly sessions in the smoke-filled cafés, where diplomats and lobbyists engaged in insider gossip that exposed a more candid view of national ambitions than statesmen would dare to reveal in the League Assembly Halls. She was drawn into the steady stream of Liaison Committee meetings because of her association with the NCCCW and she joined Henrietta Roelofs, Josephine Schain, Rhoda McCullough and Elsie Parsons who represented the coalition of American women's organisations at the international gatherings. In addition to the dinner for the eighteen women who served on national delegations to the League in 1931, the Liaison Committee member organisations also sponsored a series of luncheons and lectures by diplomats, including Salvador de Madariaga of Spain, and international relations experts, such as Alfred Zimmern and William Rappard, an American who taught at the Graduate Institute for International Studies in Geneva. At teas and dances hosted by various organisations and embassies, Nason heard speeches, proposals, and pleas pushing for the opening of the disarmament conference without further delays or evasions.[21]

Spanish Minister Salvador de Madariaga sympathised with the women's organisations' causes. In addition to supporting the disarmament conference, de Madariaga proposed a resolution to the League Committee Three in early September that gave women's organisations their opportunity to associate formally the Women's Disarmament Committee with the League's disarmament conference plans.[22] Spain's resolution that was adopted by Committee Three and then by the general assembly put the League on official record as calling on the women's international organisations, known to represent 'the great value of women to the work of peace and the good understanding between nations', 'to cooperate more fully in the work of the League'.[23] The resolution gave the Liaison Committee members another opportunity to remind League members that Article 7 of the League Covenant opened all positions at the League 'equally to men and women', and while the women's organisations intended to mobilise public support for League disarmament initiatives, they also sought formal power.[24]

Then, on 18 September 1931, Japan unexpectedly attacked Chinese troops in Manchuria. Spain's resolution and general planning for the disarmament conference were abruptly sidelined. The international crisis demanded a League response, not least because China formally requested League intervention. Japan had violated the League Covenant as well as the Kellogg–Briand Pact of Paris, both international agreements that it had pledged to support. In the ensuing League Assembly debates, de Madariaga argued that the Pact of Paris required its sixty national signatories to intervene to stop the fighting so as to allow a diplomatic resolution to proceed; League members could not, however, agree on collective intervention.[25]

Lord Robert Cecil, leading Britain's delegation to the League at the time, advocated a Western 'show of force' and economic sanctions to pressure Japan to retreat. Instead Cecil's own British government proposed an investigative Commission led by Lord Lytton (Victor Bulwer-Lytton, 2nd Earl of Lytton) to sort through the competing claims of the Chinese and Japanese governments. China claimed that it had been the victim of an unprovoked attack; Japan brought forth a long list of provocations that jeopardised its economic interests and the physical safety of its citizens in Manchuria. Even after further Japanese attacks on the civilian Chinese population in Shanghai on 28 January 1932, the British government refused to take Cecil's advice to force Japan to retreat, a decision that prompted his resignation from the British delegation to the League in February, just as the disarmament conference opened.[26] When the Conference on the Reduction and Limitation of Armaments convened on 2 February 1932, Cecil, one of its greatest proponents, held no official position in the British government from which to influence proceedings. Like the women's organisations, Lord Cecil had to rely on informal power, moral claims and connections to those on the inside to promote his views.

The Women's Disarmament Committee and conference preparations

Throughout the autumn of 1931 League diplomats focused on the conflict in China and the Women's Disarmament Committee pushed forward with its petition campaign. Mary Dingman and others on the Women's Disarmament Committee understood the far-reaching consequences of Japanese aggression, and they were aware that the dangerous conflict necessarily consumed the League's attention, but they urged the League Council to open the disarmament conference in February as planned. Dingman wrote to the League Council:

> We [the Women's Disarmament Committee of the Women's International Organisations] are committed heart and soul to the cause of peace and are working together in the greatest collective effort women have ever undertaken for the success of the Disarmament Conference called for February 2, 1932. But we are deeply troubled over the situation in Manchuria. The fact that one country has been invaded by the armed forces of another, and that this military occupation continues seems to us a flagrant violation of the Covenant of the League of Nations and the Kellogg Peace Pact, and gives defenceless nations a sense of insecurity so great that any effort towards disarmament is doomed to failure. As long as this occupation continues, the balance of power is on the side of the use of force and puts the success of the Disarmament Conference in the greatest danger . . . We welcome the appointment of a Committee of Enquiry but we are convinced that until evacuation takes place, this Committee will not be able to do its work freely and effectively.[27]

Dingman also launched a vigorous letter-writing campaign, advising Liaison Committee organisations to use their newsletters, journals and local peace networks to focus public support for the disarmament conference.[28]

Dingman and Rosa Manus continued with their plans to present petitions at the conference's opening plenary session. This presentation was originally intended to be the conclusion of the women's activism and the Committee wanted to make the event as memorable as possible, to capture the attention of the world's media and the world's statesmen.[29] Dingman and Manus, guided by Carrie Chapman Catt's suggestions, sought an international spokeswoman to present their petitions to the assembled delegations, someone with the stature and prestige of Jane Addams or the British preacher and peace activist Maude Royden. Yet Dingman also suggested the Disarmament Committee's activism should not end with the presentation of petitions but should continue as long as the conference proceeded.[30]

With plans percolating for continuing their work beyond the conference opening, Clara Guthrie d'Arcis launched the first in a series of fundraising campaigns. Appealing to the women's organisations represented on the Committee, d'Arcis proposed the Disarmament Dollar Drive urging the organisations to collect a dollar from each of their members. Such a successful drive would put millions of dollars, and the corresponding political influence that money commanded, towards waging the international disarmament campaign.[31] Subsequent appeals for funds laid out conservative budgets for creating a permanent display of the petitions along with educational materials focusing on issues of war and peace, to be put on view at the League of Nations Assembly Hall in Geneva; this plan was estimated to cost between $30,000 and $50,000. The continuing peace work of the Committee for the run of the conference, a period estimated to be of ten months' duration, was estimated to require an additional $75,000. At the time the request was made, in December 1931, the Committee had a total operating budget of only $1,000 to wrap up the petition campaign and to make a formal presentation of the petitions at the conference. D'Arcis emphasised women's ability to launch progressive social projects and to wage political campaigns, which had achieved impressive results in the past on shoestring budgets; she was convinced that women's proven record of efficiency would persuade donors to fund the important disarmament campaign at the amounts she was requesting.[32]

The struggle for funding was an ongoing battle for the Women's Disarmament Committee, and what d'Arcis and her fellow Committee members considered praiseworthy in regards to women's ability to work effectively with limited budgets the male power elite often found laughable. According to a satirical article written by a reporter, Guy Hickok, that was published in the *New York Eagle*, when a member of the Women's Disarmament Committee had approached a prominent statesman in Geneva to seek his advice about how the women's organisations could wield greater influence at the disarmament conference, the man suggested that they collect a dollar from each of the forty million women the women's organisations claimed to represent. Hickok reported that the man explained:

> 'If you come down here with $40,000,000 I can guarantee you will have the conference in your pocket.' After the Committee member replied that collecting that amount of money was practically impossible, the man suggested that each member contribute ten cents, or even one cent, and the coffers of the Women's Disarmament Committee would be full. When he learned that the Women's Committee had an operating budget of $1,000, he replied, 'You represent 40,000,000 women determined to end war? Determined to end war? And all they will do to end war is to give an average of one-four-hundredth of a cent a piece?' The interview ended.[33]

In contrast to the diplomat's view, the Women's Disarmament Committee found that even the strongest supporters among the women's organisations were initially shocked at the amount of money that d'Arcis proposed to raise. Carrie Chapman Catt reminded Mary Dingman of the devastating impact that worldwide depression had had on the American national economy in 1932 – an economic crisis the Europeans had been struggling to overcome for years. She scolded Dingman and the Committee for requesting over $125,000, which seemed an exorbitant sum at the time: 'We have talked the matter over and we conclude that the presentation of the petitions should not cost more than a few hundred dollars and, perhaps, not that. It would be thoroughly inappropriate to spend all that money, even if you had it. It must be remembered that this is not the year for making a splurge.'[34]

Yet even without the vote of confidence that funding for their work would have provided, League officials appreciated the public support that the Women's Disarmament Committee had mobilised, and the secretariat cultivated mutually beneficial relationships with Dingman and her colleagues. Directed by Secretary General Sir Eric Drummond, the League secretariat joined the women's organisations in urging nations to appoint women to their conference delegations. With the power to advise rather than mandate, the secretariat, like the women's organisations, relied on the informal power of persuasion to influence government action. When it came to the disarmament conference secretariat, however, Sir Drummond could exert more pressure. Dingman asked Drummond to intervene to persuade the League-appointed president of the conference, the British Labour Party leader Arthur Henderson, to allocate time during the opening sessions, when the national delegates delivered their preliminary remarks to the General Assembly, for the presentation of the millions of disarmament petitions collected by women's, labour, student and peace organisations around the world. The Women's Disarmament Committee also sought, and received, reserved seating at public sessions of the conference and copies of conference documents as they were released to the press.[35]

At the time he was appointed conference president in May 1931, Arthur Henderson was Britain's foreign secretary and head of Britain's delegation to the League of Nations. His long political record demonstrated enthusiastic support for the League's founding principles of international cooperation to ensure peace. However, the Labour Party had lost an election to the rival Conservative Party in October 1931 and Henderson was no longer directing Britain's Foreign Office by the time the Conference finally opened in February 1932. Henderson, too, had to rely on personal diplomacy to convince his own government and Foreign Secretary Sir John Simon, and the governments of the world, that disarmament was both desirable and achievable in practice.[36]

In the past Henderson had supported peace education campaigns waged by British women's organisations and he had admired the women's efforts to rouse public sympathies for support of progressive government policies. His reluctance to allow time for the presentation of peace petitions at the opening session of the conference may have been due to his fears that in light of Japan's attack on China, which exposed the League's impotence, the conference would become a public charade, or so Carrie Chapman Catt interpreted the situation.[37]

Philip Noel Baker later wrote that Henderson supported the unprecedented role that non-governmental organisations (NGOs) played in presenting their petitions and views before a government conference, but that 'traditionalists' within the League opposed the NGOs' intrusion into the opening ceremony.[38] Nonetheless, without Henderson's firm commitment to including a public presentation of the petitions on the plenary agenda, neither Jane Addams nor Maude Royden were willing to travel to Geneva. Undaunted, the Women's Disarmament Committee continued to collect petitions, and in Britain Kathleen Courtney and Margery Corbett Ashby lobbied the women's cause with Henderson. In mid-January, the Women's Disarmament Committee estimated that petitions recording between four and five million signatures would be sent to Geneva by women's organisations worldwide.[39]

The disarmament conference

At the same time as the Liaison Committee claimed to represent the voice of women of the world in Geneva, other women's organisations representing alternate perspectives also planned interventions at the disarmament conference. The American Women's Peace Union was one of these small but vocal organisations, driven by a few leading members who expressed absolute pacifist views through news releases and grass-roots letter-writing campaigns.[40]

In 1931 a leader of the Women's Peace Union, Frieda Langer Lazarus, single-handedly raised $2,000 to sponsor her attendance at the conference. Arriving in Geneva in January 1932, Lazarus launched a public relations campaign to bring attention to the Women's Peace Union demands. Welcoming 'all . . . interested in working for immediate, universal and complete disarmament', Lazarus set up organisational headquarters with a British ally, Isabel Ashby of War Resisters International, marked by a neon sign that flashed 'Total Disarmament Now!'.[41]

Opposed to collaboration with any group that fell short of the absolute pacifist position, Lazarus and Ashby operated in isolation. They refused to join with the Women's Disarmament Committee in their petition drive or in the public presentation ceremony that ultimately took place at a special conference plenary session on 6 February. In March 1932 Lazarus returned to the United States; her experiences in Geneva had so embittered her that she wrote an article for her hometown Brooklyn newspaper entitled 'Why Women Failed at Geneva'. Highly critical of the Women's Disarmament Committee because it supported a conference that promised at best to negotiate gradual arms reductions and dismissing its leaders who seemed to have no real plans for continuing activism beyond the presentation of petitions, Lazarus blamed the Women's Committee 'failure' on 'the lack of the right leadership to uphold an ideal'. If women from the American chapter of WILPF had been at the helm of the Women's Disarmament Committee, Lazarus believed the pacifist position would have been represented more vigorously and effectively.[42]

In Britain the League of Nations Union (LNU) had also developed a prescription for the success of the disarmament conference that recognised Germany's claims for parity and called for a 25 per cent reduction in national arms budgets to be carried out over the course of five years, and bans on building and stockpiling 'aggressive' weapons of war. These realistic proposals, the LNU argued, addressed the major points of difference within the international community: Germany's legitimate demands that the World War victor nations must meet the terms of the Versailles Peace Treaty in order to gain equality for Germany, and reliance on the collective defence of the League members to provide security for all. Like the women's organisations, the LNU focused on building public opinion that would pressure government leaders to follow through and negotiate substantial arms reductions agreements on these terms. The LNU utilised the press to publicise its proposals and held grass-roots town meetings at the local level, as well as grand-scale national and international congresses and demonstrations to muster public support throughout the 1930s. Yet according to the historian Donald Birn, the LNU's fundamental assumptions, shared by the Women's Disarmament Committee, were flawed:

> From the start the Union had placed emphasis on the role of world opinion and on pacific means for settling disputes. It had been loath to suggest to the British public that such tactics – a League-sponsored economic boycott in particular – might fail or lead to war. Collective security was thus not understood to involve risks, or even to be the basis for the defence of Britain. It was talked about instead as an alternative to war, a policy, which by mobilizing the strength of the law-abiding nations would eliminate the need for large national armies. This helps to explain why League supporters saw no contradiction between advocating it at the same time they pressed for disarmament.[43]

As national delegations converged on Geneva at the end of January 1932, the Japanese ruthlessly bombed the Chinese civilian population in Shanghai, once again violating commitments to the League of Nations Covenant and the Kellogg–Briand Pact and outraging the international community. In the long term Japan's aggression marked the beginning of violent international conflicts that led to the Second World War. In the short term Japan's actions challenged the aims and purposes of the disarmament conference in ways that the delegates never overcame, according to contemporary observers as well as later historians.[44] Sent to report on the disarmament conference for the National Council for the Prevention of War, Laura Puffer Morgan wrote to Frederick Libby that she had been travelling on the same train to Geneva with the president of the conference, Arthur Henderson, who was thin and ill, when he heard the demoralising news coming out of China. The Women's Disarmament Committee had organised a welcoming party on the train platform to celebrate Henderson's return to Geneva and to demonstrate its enthusiastic support for the conference. Yet, Morgan reported:

> it sounds like a very joyful occasion, but it wasn't. I never met such concentrated gloom . . . There were rumours that Sir Eric Drummond was completely discouraged and that no one could foresee what attitude the League was likely to take . . . The refusal of Lord Cecil to serve on the British delegation everyone interpreted – and this is literally every English person with whom I have talked – as due to his realization that there was nothing hopeful in their policy toward Disarmament . . . No one feels like predicting what will happen and no one can see how the Disarmament Conference can proceed until the situation in the Far East is somewhat clarified.[45]

Morgan had travelled to Geneva in exalted company. On her ocean crossing she joined two members of the American delegation to the disarmament conference, Senator Claude Swanson of Virginia and Dr Mary

Woolley, President of Mount Holyoke College. The American delegation was to be led by Charles Dawes, the United States ambassador to Britain. It also included Hugh Gibson, the United States ambassador to Belgium, and Norman H. Davis, an American businessman who had served as an adviser to President Woodrow Wilson. Davis resided in Geneva and had served on several League of Nations Commissions.

By the time the conference opened, Gibson had replaced Dawes as head of the American delegation, and Hugh R. Wilson, the United States minister to Switzerland, joined the delegation as well. Republican President Herbert Hoover appointed Swanson, a Democrat and leader on the Senate Foreign Relations Committee, because Swanson had the reputation of being an 'expert' on naval affairs. Morgan believed that President Hoover generally supported reduction of land armaments, but wanted to preserve the size and strength of the American Navy and so appointed Swanson to represent the United States' interests.[46]

Mary Woolley had been appointed as a concession to American women's organisations. These organisations had lobbied hard for the appointment of Judge Florence Allen, a Democrat, but they rallied to Woolley's side when it became clear that Hoover intended to appoint a woman who was a member of the Republican Party.[47] Although she was considered timid and the women's NGOs wanted a forceful voice on the delegation, they backed Woolley with all the power their collective support could provide.[48]

Woolley was one of only five women appointed to national delegations at the disarmament conference. Margery Corbett Ashby was also appointed as an alternate delegate for Great Britain, along with Winifred Kydd from Canada; Anna Poradowska-Szelagowska, who had served on Poland's delegation to the League Twelfth Assembly and was active in the International Women's Suffrage Alliance; and Dr Pauline Luisi, a medical doctor who presided over the Alliance of Women in Uruguay. In the small minority, and conscious that they had been appointed to their conference delegations because they were women, the female delegates often felt pressured to articulate the gendered ways that they would contribute to conference negotiations, in contrast to their male counterparts. Woolley stressed that she would represent the 'human element', as opposed to the feminist perspective, at the conference:

> Women have been criticized for thinking in terms of persons. To them a country is not an abstraction, it is a place inhabited by people . . . This is all to the good. In this attitude there is hope. They keep close to the human. I hesitate to say this – because I may sound sentimental and I do not wish to be regarded as a sentimentalist – but I do think we should go to this Disarmament Conference with a consciousness of our kinship, as members of the same human family.[49]

At a pre-conference gathering hosted by the Women's Disarmament Committee Margery Corbett Ashby summed up her views about women's gendered contribution to the upcoming arms negotiations:

> Women are solid about this question of peace . . . It has been said that 'progress in mechanical invention has far outrun progress in moral and social control'. Therefore the great chance of the Disarmament Conference lies in proving that moral and social control can outrun even mechanical invention and lift humanity to the place where it will be master and not mastered. Such things are particularly woman's concern. Humanity has got to see that the question of armaments is understood as an international rather than a national responsibility. If this conference can bring forth a convention which accepts this principle, it will have accomplished much.

Anna Paradowska-Szelagowska asserted that: 'There can be no effective disarmament without moral disarmament.'[50] Thus the women's delegates took on the roles of representing the 'human element' during conference negotiations and of advocating for what became known as 'moral disarmament', that is, educational initiatives and cultural exchanges to develop common pacific values to guide national policies and to resolve world conflicts. Meeting regularly during the first several months of conference sessions, the women defined themselves as a distinctive group, somewhat apart from the male-led delegations. The women delegates' efforts were mirrored and augmented at every point by the Women's Disarmament Committee and its member organisations worldwide. Indeed, emphasis on the preservation of human life and moral persuasion were the dominant themes when the Women's Disarmament Committee presented petitions with a record of over nine million signatures to a special conference plenary session on 6 February.

On 6 February 1932, early in the morning of the opening plenary session, a truck filled with paper petitions waited by the service entrance to the Bâtiment Electoral, the great hall where the conference met in general assembly. Several American women from the NCCCW, dispatched to Geneva by Carrie Chapman Catt, met with the organiser of the day's events, Rosa Manus, to unload the trucks. Manus and her deputies unloaded the truckload of boxes of paper petitions into the lobby of the assembly hall, where they would be visible to all the national delegates as they arrived and took their seats. Then they rushed to the nearby Palais Eynard where women volunteers representing the petitioning nations were gathered to march in procession through the Promenade des Bastions, across the Place Neuve, to the Bâtiment Electoral for the formal presentation. When they reached the Palais, there was mass confusion. Manus and Dingman had planned a procession of the fifty six petitioning nations, represented by four women each, marching in formation to the assembly hall – a total of 224 women in procession. But many more women had arrived and were ready to march. Through sheer force of will, Manus and her fellow Disarmament Committee officers managed to line up an orderly procession, making sure that all the designated marchers wore white sashes across their shoulders that showed in gold letters the names of their nations and white armbands emblazoned with the word *Pax*. [51]

The women marched across the Place Neuve led by the five officers of the Women's Disarmament Committee: Mary Dingman, Laura Dreyfus-Barney, Kathleen Courtney, Clara Guthrie d'Arcis and Rosa Manus. When they reached the assembly hall the women filed in, two by two, their arms loaded with stacks of petitions. [52] Arthur Henderson called Mary Dingman to the lectern. Addressing the conference on behalf of 'the greatest collective effort that women have ever undertaken'[53] she asserted:

> Behind each of these names stands a living personality, a human being oppressed by a great fear, the fear of the destruction of our civilization, but also moved by a great will for peace that cannot be ignored and must not be denied . . . A great vision has become clear to the eyes of this generation – the vision of the forces of humanity working together toward one single aim, towards a new world order based on mutual understanding and international goodwill. We look to you to bring us one step nearer to that vision of peace in our time. It is not for ourselves alone that we plead, but for the generations to come. To us women, as mothers, the thought of what another great war would mean for our children is the strongest incentive impelling us to spend ourselves in the endeavour to make their lives secure from such a disastrous fate. [54]

Next Kathleen Courtney and Rosa Manus called out the names of the petitioning countries and the women filed in procession up to a table below President Henderson, seated on a dais at the head of the assembly room, and deposited the scrolls and sheaves of paper. [55]

At that point in the ceremony representatives of several other organisations addressed the government delegations. The International Union of Catholic Women's Organizations, International Christian Organizations, International Students' Organizations, Veterans of the World War, the Second International of Communist Workers of the World, the International Federation of Trade Unions, and Lord Robert Cecil representing the International League of Nations' Societies, all appealed to the conference delegates to make some real and substantial arms reduction agreements to increase the chances for peace. [56] Following the plenary session, the petitions were put on permanent display in the entrance hall for the duration of the conference, which continued to meet in public sessions through 1934. [57]

The international press described the presentation ceremony as a profoundly moving 'spectacle'. The journalists also noted that the delegates seemed genuinely affected by the speakers' emotional pleas. Nonetheless, as arms negotiations got under way, government representatives quickly returned to their predominant focus on safeguarding national interests.[58] One of Carrie Chapman Catt's NCCCW correspondents wrote from Geneva in May:

> A well known journalist said here Friday night, speaking before the Women's Disarmament group, 'Your presentation of Petitions was an unforgettable and a completely forgotten event. Not one of these delegates who march back and forth in the corridor where, through the courtesy of Mr. Henderson, the Petitions are bravely displayed, ever glances at them or thinks of them or of Public Opinion which is hoping for peace.' Yesterday the Assembly met in extraordinary session, no representative except Sir John Simon of the big men of the big powers being present.'[59]

Sceptical journalists and diplomats quickly dismissed hopes for the success of the disarmament conference.[60] Yet their cynicism emboldened Mary Dingman to prod the member organisations of the Women's Disarmament Committee to redouble their efforts to promote arms reductions agreements. In 1932 the worldwide economic crisis, Japan's attack on China, and the rise of the ultra-nationalist and militaristic National Socialist Party in Germany, all commanded attention from world leaders and their military advisers. Dingman believed that these world problems were all intimately connected to the outcome of the disarmament conference. Conference success was the key to solving world problems; it was not an idealistic pipe dream distracting from the real issues of the day.

Arthur Henderson shared Dingman's urgent sense that the international crises demanded progressive steps towards disarmament and international cooperation rather than a retreat to self-serving nationalist positions. As he officially opened the conference, Henderson entreated government delegates to press on:

> I refuse to contemplate even the possibility of failure, for if we fail no one can foretell the evil consequences that might ensue . . . I feel bound to refer to the fact that at the moment when this conference begins its work we are confronted with a situation of extreme gravity . . . It is imperative that all the signatories of the League of Nations Covenant and other international treaties should make it their business to ensure the strict observance of those great safeguards against acts of violence and war . . . The world wants disarmament; the world needs disarmament. We have it in our power to help fashion future history.[61]

Encouraged by demonstrations of public support, Henderson called on the women's organisations to keep up their public education campaigns.

When the first phase of the conference sessions ended on 24 February, after the heads of diplomatic delegations laid out in broad strokes their nations' chief concerns regarding disarmament proposals, Henderson wrote to French WILPF leader Camille Drevet 'I have been deeply impressed by the manifestations of public support for the work of the Conference, and I venture to express the hope that you and your friends who are in favour of success will not relax your efforts until it has brought its work to a successful conclusion.'[62] As Henderson turned over the specific work of disarmament negotiation to the government delegations and their expert advisers, Dingman formulated plans for the Disarmament Committee's next steps.

The Women's Disarmament Committee defines its work

At a meeting held on 23 February, the Women's Disarmament Committee outlined the basic positions it intended to advocate at continuing conference sessions. According to the women present, they represented not just one national perspective, but a universal woman's view, the 'greatest measure of women's agreement upon defined and essential propositions'. These included the establishment of national and international structures to supervise private industry and state manufacture of arms and ammunition, total bans on naval and military aircraft, total bans on chemical and bacteriological warfare, abolition of aggressive weapons of war, limits on military spending on all other categories of weapons, the establishment of a permanent International Disarmament Commission to support disarmament provisions in the League Covenant and the Pact of Paris and the implied collective actions to prevent war. Finally the Committee supported proactive peace education efforts carried out in the name of moral disarmament.[63] The Committee member organisations were asked to confirm their agreement with the proposed peace platform.

While the member organisations generally agreed that the Committee should continue to press for disarmament and monitor conference proceedings, Carrie Chapman Catt, speaking for the NCCCW, was less enthusiastic. Catt reminded Dingman that the Committee had formed solely to support the general aims of the disarmament conference. 'All of us are favourable to the abolishing of war and many of the elements which keep war going. But', she wrote further, 'I should like to know on behalf of the [NCCCW] whether it is your intention to work for those more specific and aggressive things, for if it is we do not feel that we can join in that procedure. We sent four women to Geneva to safeguard the travel of our petitions and to aid you in their presentation in any way they could. The last thing we expected was that they would share in making a program without consultation of their constituents as to what women should collectively ask for in Geneva.'[64] Mary Dingman and Kathleen Courtney sent Catt their spirited reply:

> Our Disarmament Committee was formed to help the Disarmament Conference achieve the greatest possible degree of success. We do not feel that we were confined to the one task of the presentation of petitions. That was a wonderfully successful effort in focusing attention of the Conference to the worldwide desire for disarmament. Now that the Conference is sitting we are bound to be concerned not with the support of disarmament in general, but with definite and specific proposals for achieving disarmament in practice.
>
> If we are to make any contribution to the work of the Conference it must be by giving support to those specific measures which we believe can achieve results, and by calling on organizations to prepare public opinion in each country to accept these proposals, and to make the reciprocal concessions necessary to arrive at genuine reduction and limitation. The Conference may arrive at a point where one country may block the way. The women in that country may help break the impasse. We must face, fearlessly and intelligently, the issues and help to lead in the tremendous effort before us to free the world from the menace of war.[65]

As she left Geneva to return to Holland to care for her sick mother, Rosa Manus wrote to Josephine Schain and added her personal endorsement of the Women's Disarmament Committee work for her good friend and mentor Catt to consider:

> The women of the world have done a great piece of work for public opinion in collecting signatures and holding meetings in favour of Disarmament all over the world, but we may not stop. Something real must be done from the women, we may not and cannot have another war and the women must stand strongly together and tell the statesmen that we do not care to which party and country they belong, but that no human lives may be offered again, this crime may not recommence.[66]

Catt's discouraging words did not dissuade Committee members in Geneva from following through with their plans. Arthur Henderson had met with Dingman and Committee representatives in mid March, reviewed their peace proposals, and assured them that their work applied critical pressures to government delegations that should not be abandoned.[67] Pressing women's organisations for their continued support, Clara d'Arcis submitted her Treasurer's Report to the presidents of member organisations with pleas to persevere:

> The women's organisations have made a real place for themselves and established a sphere of influence in the Conference, the extent of which even the most conservative of people in high places tell us we have never fully

realized. We are considered a power and a force and great things are expected of us, great courage and loyalty in being true to our declarations. The good name of women as energetic defenders of Peace of the world is at stake and depends on the next months upon the activity of the Women's Disarmament Committee.[68]

The public sessions of the disarmament conference were disheartening; they were, for the most part, filled with diplomats' public posturing as they presented their national views in the most positive lights. In the opening week the Soviet delegate Maxim Litvinoff injected momentary excitement into the conference hall when he presented a sweeping plan for abolishing a wide range of land, air and naval armaments and outlawing chemical and bacteriological weapons as well as incendiary bombs.[69] Litvinoff's disarmament proposal was defeated by a vote of 52 to 2, emphasising how far out of sync the Soviet plan was from the general view of government delegates.[70]

The French delegation insisted that firm guarantees for collective security be established before any disarmament agreements were negotiated, while the United States, Great Britain and the Scandinavian countries proposed that specific arms reduction agreements should be negotiated before any sort of international security force was contemplated.[71] After the general assembly established a Political Commission and technical Land, Naval, Air and Budgetary Commissions to hammer out specific agreements, substantive disarmament negotiations moved to private sessions. Thereafter the Great Powers represented at the conference – the United States, Britain, France, Italy and Japan – conducted negotiations in secret consultations with one another, following traditional practices that ambitious participants like Spain's Salvador de Madariaga and Czechoslovakia's Eduard Beneš thoroughly resented.[72] The German diplomat who was initially willing to consider 'compromises' with the Great Powers, Chancellor Heinrich Brüning, was forced to resign the chancellorship and left the conference in May 1932. From the end of April through May and the first three weeks in June the technical commissions took over, and the conference moved into its 'Dark Ages' as a contemporary observer termed it. 'So far as the records are concerned, aside from technical quibblings [sic], this period was a complete, unquestioned, unequivocal blank.'[73]

In the meanwhile, drafting volunteers whenever they could, the Women's Disarmament Committee attended all public sessions of the conference and reported on the proceedings in a steady stream of communiqués, journal articles and circular letters to the member organisations; these reports were subsequently distributed among women's groups all over the world, and were sent to other organisations upon request.

According to Committee records, thirty NGOs apart from Committee members, forty journalists and sixty-four magazines had requested news from the Women's Disarmament Committee, as of 1 April 1932.[74]

D'Arcis and Dingman devised a plan to produce and sell 'Disarmament Postcards' that bore a picture of Arthur Henderson and quoted his opening remarks to the government delegates to raise funds to continue their work. During the first two years of the conference 50,000 postcards were distributed in twenty seven countries, and brought in a small profit and much-needed operating funds.[75]

In May 1932 the Women's Disarmament Committee hosted a study conference in Geneva to educate influential NGO leaders about the underlying conference issues; this event featured several prominent speakers including Senator Louis de Brouckère of Belgium who spoke on 'Qualitative and Quantitative Disarmament and Budgetary Limitation'; Baron von Rheinbaden of Germany who addressed the topic of 'Trade in and Manufacture of Armaments'; and Margery Corbett Ashby who discussed 'Moral Disarmament'.[76] In the summer of 1932 Mary Dingman and Kathleen Courtney also organised a two-week course for Speakers on Disarmament held at the International School in Geneva. Thirty students from six countries enrolled.

In June 1932, immediately after the announcement of his nomination as the Republican Party candidate in the upcoming presidential election, President Herbert Hoover pumped new life into the governmental negotiations at the disarmament conference. Hugh Gibson addressed an emergency session of the general assembly to deliver Hoover's proposals suggesting abolition of all tanks, chemical warfare, large mobile guns, and all military aircraft; the number and tonnage of battleships to be reduced by one-third; aircraft carriers, cruisers, destroyers, reduced by one-quarter and treaty tonnage of submarines reduced by one-third. The size of national militaries were to be reduced as Germany's army had been according to the terms of the Versailles Treaty; nations could retain armies only for 'the maintenance of internal order in connection with the regular peace forces of the country' with some adjustments for nations that governed colonial territories.[77]

Hoover's proposals won some significant support including the enthusiastic endorsement of the Women's Disarmament Committee.[78] The Soviet Union also accepted Hoover's proposals immediately. Germany and Italy accepted, but with reservations on points where Germany believed inequalities still existed. France pressed for the addition of collective security guarantees. Japan rejected the proposals outright because they kept Japan's naval strength proportionately weaker than those of the United States and Great Britain.[79] Britain also practically rejected Hoover's proposals by offering complicated counter-proposals aimed at preserving British naval strength.[80] Foreign Secretary Sir John Simon warned the British Parliament that if the nations did not disarm, Hitler's power within Germany would rise and Germany would surely rearm, yet he could not persuade the hawks within Britain's Conservative government to support Hoover's formulations.[81]

Representatives of various NGOs in Geneva, including the Women's Disarmament Committee, signed a joint statement urging conference delegates not to adjourn unless they could agree on at least one major arms reduction plank to rally public support and declare that all nations accepted the principle of equality as the basis for any arms reduction agreements.[82] Ultimately, however, although Hoover's plan was debated seriously, the most national delegates would agree to before adjourning was a weak compromise proposed by the Czech delegate, Eduard Beneš. The governments resolved to be 'guided by the general principles underlying President Hoover's declaration' – that is, the nations agreed in principle to the reduction of armaments, with no mention of 'equality' or 'collective security' in the resolution wording.[83] At this point Germany withdrew from the conference.

As the disarmament conference adjourned on 23 July 1932, a group of NGOs met at the YWCA headquarters of the Women's Disarmament Committee to strategise for the future. Far from conceding defeat, they decided to support the anaemic conference resolution as a 'step toward progress' and to press on. As Mary Dingman argued, 'the organizational machinery must not be allowed to disappear and all are studying ways and means of continuing our efforts til the very end of this Conference . . . We cannot give up the struggle at this point.'[84]

Together leaders of the Geneva-based NGOs formed the International Consultative Group (ICG) to continue disarmament advocacy. Along with Mary Dingman, Kathleen Courtney and Evelyn Fox, who represented the Women's Disarmament Committee, leaders of several international Christian organisations, as well as student and veterans groups, joined with representatives from League of Nations societies and internationalist organisations. They met regularly in Geneva to share information and plan joint actions until the League of Nations suspended its meetings in Geneva in 1940, following the outbreak of the European war. Laura Puffer Morgan, who represented the coordinated activism of sympathetic American NGOs in Geneva, was a founding member of the ICG. At this time Morgan also joined the Women's Disarmament Committee as its technical adviser.[85]

The Women's Disarmament Committee received a much-needed vote of confidence in October 1932, when the Nobel Institute in Norway recognised the association's valuable peace work performed in relation to the disarmament conference and sent a grant of 2000 kroner to support its ongoing efforts.[86] The League-sponsored governmental conference also revived when the Five Power Agreement negotiated by Great Britain, the United States, France, Germany and Italy in December 1932 secured Germany's promise to rejoin the conference, with guaranteed equality of status, when sessions resumed in January 1933. Norman Davis, US president-elect Franklin Roosevelt's adviser in Geneva, facilitated Germany's return to the conference,[87] and disarmament activists speculated that a new cooperative energy might inspire the United States and European governments in the new year ahead.[88]

Notes

1 Founding member organisations of the Women's Disarmament Committee included: the International Alliance of Women for Suffrage and Equal Citizenship, the International Council of Women, the World Young Women's Christian Association, the Women's International League for Peace and Freedom, the World Union of Women for International Concord, the International Federation of Business and Professional Women, the International Soroptimist Club, the International Federation of University Women and the National Committee on the Cause and Cure of War.
2 Peace and Disarmament Committee of Women's International Organisations, 1931–1940, Peace Collection, Swarthmore College, Swarthmore, PA (hereafter P & D Committee), Minutes of the Disarmament Committee of the Women's International Organisations, 5 September 1931.
3 Jacqueline Van Voris, *Carrie Chapman Catt: A Public Life* (New York: Feminist Press, 1987).
4 RCN, Rachel Conrad Nason to unidentified recipient from Geneva, 2 September 1931, box 1.
5 Leila J. Rupp, *Worlds of Women: The Making of an International Women's Movement* (Princeton, NJ: Princeton University Press, 1997), pp. 197 and 199.
6 Ibid., p. 61; Francesca de Haan, 'A "truly international" archive for the women's movement (IAV, now IIAV): from its foundation in Amsterdam in 1935 to the return of its looted archives in 2003', *Journal of Women's History*, 16:4 (2004), pp. 149–50.
7 CCCW, Henrietta Roelofs to Carrie Chapman Catt, 6 September 1931, box 18.
8 Shapour Rassekh, Biographical Materials Hippolyte Dreyfus-Barney and Laura Dreyfus-Barney, *Encyclopedia Iranica* (online at: iranica.com/articles/v7/v7f5/v7f571.html), Mary Kinnear, *Woman of the World: Mary McGeachy and International Cooperation* (Toronto: University of Toronto Press, 2004), p. 182.

9 Rupp, *Worlds of Women*, pp. 15–19. The ICW was founded in 1888 to coordinate broad-based women's volunteer organisations into a global sisterhood of support for a range of issues during the interwar years, including peace, women's suffrage, the abolition of trafficking in women, public health, child welfare, narcotic drug controls and more.

10 CCCW, Henrietta Roelofs to Carrie Chapman Catt, 6 September 1931, box 18.

11 Morgan–Howes Papers, 'Mary A. Dingman, 1875–1961' [brief bio] by Julia Capen, box 5.

12 P & D Committee, 'The international board: Mary A. Dingman, president', c. 1937; MAD, 'A service of thanksgiving for Mary A Dingman, 9 April 1875–21 March 1961', 21 April 1961, box 1.

13 YWCA of the USA, Recruitment letter for Industrial Summer School 1922, January 1922, microfilm reel 78.

14 Karen Garner, *Precious Fire: Maud Russell and the Chinese Revolution* (Amherst, MA: University of Massachusetts Press, 2003), pp. 56–7 and 70.

15 YWCA of the USA, 'Accounts from Australian YWCA of Mary Dingman's visit to their country and review of industrial relations in 1924', microfilm reel 78.

16 P & D Committee, 'Madame Clara Guthrie d'Arcis', c. 1937.

17 CCCW, Biographical information Madame Clara d'Arcis, box 18.

18 WYWCA, 'Résumé of the Work of the Disarmament Committee of the Women's International Organisations, up to April 1, 1932', box 283.

19 CCCW, Henrietta Roelofs to Carrie Chapman Catt, 6 September 1931, box 18.

20 CCCW, Carrie Chapman Catt to Mary Dingman, 16 October 1931, box 18.

21 RCN, Rachel Conrad Nason to unidentified recipient, 11 September 1931, box 1.

22 P & D Committee, Disarmament Committee of the Women's International Organisations to Delegates to League of Nations General Assembly, 18 September 1931.

23 MAD, Mary Dingman to the Member Organisations of the Disarmament Committee, 24 September 1931, box 2.

24 MAD, Mary A. Dingman to Salvador de Madariaga, 16 September 1931, box 2.

25 The Earl of Lytton, 'The twelfth assembly of the League of Nations', *International Affairs*, 10 (November 1931), pp. 751–2.

26 Christopher Thorne, 'Viscount Cecil, the government, and the Far Eastern crisis of 1931', *Historical Journal* 14 (1971), pp. 805–9.

27 MAD, Mary Dingman to Council Members of the League of Nations, 23 November 1931, box 2.

28 P & D Committee, Mary Dingman to Member Organisations from the Disarmament Committee of the Women's International Organisations, 29 October 1931.

29 MAD, Rosa Manus to Member Organisations of the Women's Disarmament Committee, 25 November 1931, box 2.

30 CCCW, Mary Dingman to Carrie Chapman Catt, 5 November 1931, box 18.

31 P & D Committee, 'Disarmament dollar drive', Clara d'Arcis to Emily Green Balch, WILPF, 5 December 1931.

32 CCCW, Appeal from the Disarmament Committee of the Women's International Organisations, December 1931, box 11.

33 Mary Emma Woolley Papers, Mt. Holyoke College, Holyoke, MA (hereafter MEW), Guy Hickok, '40 million women try to end war on $1000', *New York Eagle* (30 January 1932), Scrapbooks, Geneva 1932.

34 CCCW, Carrie Chapman Catt to Mary Dingman, 7 January 1932, box 18.

35 MAD, Mary Dingman to Sir Eric Drummond, 1 January 1932, box 2.

36 Philip Noel-Baker, *The First World Disarmament Conference 1932–33, and Why it Failed* (Oxford, UK: Pergamon Press, 1979), p. 61; F. P. Walters, *A History of the League of Nations* (New York: Oxford University Press, 1952), p. 442.

37 CCCW, Carrie Chapman Catt to Rosa Manus, 7 January 1932, box 18.

38 Noel-Baker, *The First World Disarmament Conference*, p. 73.

39 P & D Committee, Minutes of the Disarmament Committee Meeting, 15 January 1932.

40 Harriet Hyman Alonso, *The Women's Peace Union and the Outlawry of War, 1921–1942* (Knoxville, TN: University of Tennessee Press, 1989), pp. 24–8.

41 Ibid., pp. 98–131.

42 Ibid., p. 140.

43 Donald S. Birn, *The League of Nations Union, 1918–1945* (Oxford, UK: Clarendon Press, 1981), pp. 90–4.

44 H. Arthur Steiner, 'The Geneva disarmament conference of 1932', *Annals of the Academy of Political and Social Science*, 168 (July 1933), p. 213; F. S. Northedge, *The League of Nations, Its Life and Times, 1920–1946* (Leicester, UK: Leicester University Press, 1986), pp. 161–4.

45 Morgan–Howes Papers, Laura Puffer Morgan to Frederick Libby, 31 January 1932, box 3.

46 LPM, Laura Puffer Morgan, 'The challenge of the disarmament conference', *American Teacher*, January 1932.

47 CCCW, Carrie Chapman Catt to President Herbert Hoover, 4 December 1931, box 21.

48 CCCW, Carrie Chapman Catt to Judge Florence Allen, 21 December 1931, box 18; Carrie Chapman Catt to Presidents of the Member Organisations in the Committee on the Cause and Cure of War, 29 December 1931, box 21.

49 MEW, 'This woman's war . . . for peace', *Daily Herald*, (11 January 1932), Scrapbooks, Geneva 1932.

50 MEW, 'Women express goal of peace at arms parley', *Christian Science Monitor* (5 February 1932), Scrapbooks, Geneva 1932.

51 CCCW, Elvira Fradkin to Carrie Chapman Catt, 8 February 1932, box 18.

52 Adele Schreiber's report on the presentation of the petitions to the Disarmament Conference on 6 February in *International Women's News*, March 1932, in Arnold Whittick, *Woman into Citizen: The World Movement Towards the Emancipation of Women in the Twentieth Century with Accounts of the Contributions of the International Alliance of Women, the League of Nations and the Relevant*

Organizations of the United Nations (London: Athenaeum, 1979), p. 110; MAD, *Vox Populi* (Vox Populi Committee, Geneva, Switzerland, 1933 ed.), box 2.

53 CCCW, 'Appeal and programme of the women's disarmament committee', c. January 1932, box 11.

54 MAD, 'Address presented to the disarmament conference', 6 February 1932, box 6.

55 WYWCA, 'Résumé of the work of the disarmament committee of the women's international organisations, up to April 1, 1932', box 283.

56 MAD, *Vox Populi*, box 2.

57 WYWCA, 'Statement of the disarmament committee of the women's international organisations in relation to the Conference for the Reduction and Limitation of Armaments', box 283.

58 MAD. One of these reports from an unnamed newspaper is found in R. E. Haestier, 'Guilt-edged insecurity', c. February 1932, box 1.

59 CCCW, Mrs Nathaniel H. Bilder to Carrie Chapman Catt, 1 May 1932, box 18.

60 Elmer Bendinger, *No Time for Angels: The Tragicomic History of the League of Nations* (New York: Alfred A. Knopf, 1975), pp. 275–8; 'Foreign news', *Time Magazine* (8 February 1932): 14.

61 MEW, 'Arms conference opens; delayed while League debates China crisis', *Daily Hampshire Gazette* (2 February 1932), Scrapbooks, Geneva 1932.

62 Margaret Bussey and Gertrude Tims, *Women's International League for Peace and Freedom, 1915–1965: A Record of Fifty Years' Work* (London: George Allen & Unwin, Ltd, 1965), p. 102.

63 WYWCA, 'Statement of the disarmament committee of the women's international organisations in relation to the Conference for the Reduction and Limitation of Armaments' 23 February 1932, box 283.

64 CCCW, Carrie Chapman Catt to Mary Dingman, 7 March 1932, box 11.

65 CCCW, Mary Dingman and Kathleen Courtney to Carrie Chapman Catt, 11 April 1932, box 18.

66 Josephine Schain Papers, Sofia Smith Collection, Smith College, Northampton, MA (hereafter JS), Rosa Manus to Josephine Schain, 19 April 1932, box 7.

67 YWCA of the USA, Evelyn Fox, excerpts from letters to Miss Hiller [YWCA of USA], 16 and 17 March 1932, microfilm reel 78.

68 P & D Committee, Clara Guthrie d'Arcis, 'Treasurer's report', c. April, 1932.

69 MEW, 'Soviets urge full abolition of armaments', *New York Herald and Herald Tribune*, 12 February 1932, Scrapbooks, Geneva 1932.

70 'Eagle, lion, bear', *Time Magazine* 19: 10 (7 March 1932).

71 Steiner, 'The Geneva disarmament conference of 1932', p. 214.

72 Noel-Baker, *The First World Disarmament Conference*, pp. 83–4.

73 Steiner, 'The Geneva disarmament conference of 1932', p. 216.

74 WYWCA, 'Résumé of the work of the disarmament committee of the women's international organisations, up to April 1, 1932', box 283.

75 MAD, Disarmament committee of the women's international organisations,

report from September 1931 to June 1933, box 2; Morgan–Howes Papers, 'Disarmament committee of the women's international organisations, what it is, what it has done, what it proposes to do, why its work should be continued', c. 1933, box 2.

76 P & D Committee, 'The women's disarmament policy', c. May 1932.

77 League of Nations Archives, League of Nations Registry File 7B/21261/596/, 'Conference for the Reduction and Limitation of Armaments, Preliminary Report of the Conference, November 1935', p. 5, box R4221.

78 CCCW, 'World's women welcome Hoover proposals', Mary Dingman to Ruth Morgan, National Committee on the Cause and Cure of War, 28 June 1932, box 18.

79 Steiner, 'The Geneva disarmament conference of 1932', p. 217.

80 Hanson W. Baldwin, 'The naval tangle, the need of a new approach is now indicated', *New York Times* (18 December 1932).

81 Noel-Baker, *The First World Disarmament Conference*, pp. 104–5.

82 MAD, 'Memorial' drafted and signed by members of Disarmament Committees in Geneva, 16 July 1932, box 2.

83 YWCA of the USA, Text of the Resolution Adopted by the Disarmament Conference, 23 July 1932, microfilm, reel 78.

84 CCCW, Mary Dingman to 'Friends in America', 28 July 1932, box 18.

85 Morgan–Howes Papers, 'Draft report of meetings of representatives of disarmament committees in Geneva', 23 and 26 July 1932, box 3.

86 P & D Committee, 'Nobel committee recognizes women's work', Disarmament Committee Press Release no. 137, October, 1932.

87 Clarence A Berdahl, 'American foreign policy', *American Journal of Sociology* 38 (May 1933), p. 852.

88 P & D Committee, Kathleen Courtney, 'Has the tide turned at Geneva?', 12 December 1932.

3

The peace is threatened

Resurgent nationalism in 1933

As the disarmament conference resumed in 1933 government diplomats in Geneva vehemently expressed nationalist views, reflecting the prevailing moods in their national capitals.[1] After advancing its army farther into north Chinese territory, Japan withdrew from the League of Nations in March 1933, while it abstrusely retained its delegation at the disarmament conference.[2] British Prime Minister Ramsay MacDonald presented a new draft Disarmament Convention to the conference general assembly on 16 March, but his arms reduction proposals fizzled as conflict continued in China, and as aggressive governments led by Mussolini's Fascist Party in Italy and Hitler's National Socialist Party in Germany threatened international peace. In early April 1933 the British ambassador in Berlin began informing his government about the Nazi Party's violent persecution of Germany's Jewish populations. As anti-Semitic aggression mounted in Germany, President Franklin Roosevelt weighed in on international disarmament debates with his administration's support for Ramsay MacDonald's disarmament proposals, and Roosevelt called for bans on offensive weapons accompanied by a non-aggression treaty.[3]

Mary Dingman and the Women's Disarmament Committee also began discussing their response to Nazi Party attacks on the Jewish population in April. After seeking advice from several women leaders in Geneva, including Dame Rachel Crowdy, Dingman asked Women's Disarmament Committee member organisations to sign a joint appeal to Chancellor Adolf Hitler, the Nazi Party leader. Dingman circulated a letter for Committee member approval, with plans to send it first to the German government and then to release it to the international press:

> Herr Hitler: The organisation of which we, the undersigned are members, representing more than forty-five millions of women in fifty-six countries, has since its creation stood for Disarmament both moral and material. It has

upheld the principle of equal status and striven consistently to create a public opinion in favour of international cooperation and understanding.

It is therefore with sorrow and dismay that we have read the recent proclamations by your Excellency regarding the Jews in Germany.

The Jewish people are scattered throughout the world, and action such as this must carry with it worldwide consequences, for social injustice in any one country is a fruitful source of discord in all. Discriminative action against race or religion must inevitably breed mistrust and enmity and destroy the spirit of confidence and friendly understanding which is the basis of moral disarmament and peace between nations. Recognizing that your Government 'considers the Christian religion as the solid foundation of the morality of the nation' we earnestly appeal to your Excellency to inaugurate measures in accordance with the Christian principles of justice and mercy, thus many thousands will be delivered from suffering and that 'ideal of liberty,' which your National Government feels 'must once again become sacred to the German people', will be asserted.[4]

The Women's Disarmament Committee did not send Dingman's letter to Adolf Hitler. Mary Dingman personally believed that silence in the face of Nazi injustice undermined the 'spiritual power' of Christian womanhood, however, like the Christian Churches in Germany that 'submit[ted] to the authority of the State', she submitted to the majority will of the Committee member organisations to let Hitler's policies toward the Jews go unchallenged. She wrote apologetically to her colleague Vera Cushman at the American YWCA headquarters in New York:

> We had an emergency meeting of the Disacom [Women's Disarmament Committee] and decided not to send the letter to Hitler. There will probably be a mixed [gender] committee created in Geneva to take action on this question. We, Disacom, cannot go on with it as it is so far reaching and outside our competence. The stories of suffering are so sad. So many pacifist social democrats are losing their jobs and being put in concentration camps.[5]

Yet as world conflict steadily escalated throughout the decade, under Mary Dingman's leadership the Women's Disarmament Committee drafted many resolutions of protest and sent letters and made public appeals to the League and to national governments denouncing attacks on civilian populations during the Italian invasion of Ethiopia in 1935, the Spanish Civil War in 1936, and as Germany and Japan launched imperialist attacks on weaker nations after 1937. The women's international organisations also tracked the fortunes of their Jewish friends and organisational leaders in Germany, Austria, Holland and other states that fell under Nazi control. The women intervened, sometimes effectively and sometimes without results, to secure their friends' release from prisons or to facilitate their emigration to Britain or the United States.

Carrie Chapman Catt, usually the voice of moderation when it came to joint women's actions, was one of the first and most outspoken feminist critics of Hitler's persecution of the Jews in Europe from 1933 onwards.[6] Catt's close friend, Rosa Manus, who aided Jewish refugees in Holland, sent Catt first-hand reports that prompted Catt to form the Protest Committee of Non-Jewish Women Against Persecution of Jews in Germany. Catt pressured American women's organisations to condemn Germany's anti-Jewish pogroms and she lobbied the Roosevelt administration to ease United States immigration laws to allow entry to European Jewish refugees seeking asylum.[7]

By June 1933 world leaders turned their attention to the League-sponsored World Economic Conference in London. The disarmament conference adjourned soon after the economic conference opened but planned to reconvene in Geneva in October. Throughout the rest of the summer disarmament conference president Arthur Henderson continued his rounds of personal diplomacy and travelled to the European capitals to meet foreign ministers in Britain, Germany, Italy and France on their home grounds. By the end of summer France, alarmed at Germany's open preparations for war, insisted on greater security measures and would only agree to slow, phased disarmament over an eight-year period to reach equality with Germany. In September Germany officially rejected the French proposals and demanded immediate disarmament by the Great Powers.[8]

Faced with the growing climate of fear and distrust in Geneva, the Women's Disarmament Committee initially continued its focus on peace education. Hosting a second study conference in Geneva for non-governmental organisation (NGO) leaders at the end of May, Dingman called on her international networks to lead study sessions. Salvador de Madariaga headed the discussion on the use of military aircraft to wage wars; Maurice Bourquin, Belgium's delegate to the League of Nations, spoke on collective security. Laura Morgan and Kathleen Courtney also led sessions on disarmament conference proceedings and Lord Robert Cecil addressed the conference luncheon. NGO representatives who attended the study conference expressed their firm commitments to lobbying for the goals of the disarmament conference.[9] Yet after the Women's Committee study conference ended, Laura Morgan met with Norman Davis, who expressed little hope for further progress at the League-sponsored conference.[10]

As the disarmament conference adjourned in June, the Women's Disarmament Committee officers believed the time had come to dissolve their committee as well and to continue peace work in other forums. The Committee's allies, led by Arthur Henderson, raised an immediate outcry. If the Women's Disarmament Committee dissolved, Henderson wrote to

Clara d'Arcis, it would be a 'tragedy' both for the conference and for the world community that longed for peace.

> I cannot find words enough to express my appreciation of what your Committee has done during the last seventeen strenuous months since the disarmament Conference began. Since your first magnificent demonstration on February 6 when you and others voiced to the Conference the longings and aspirations of the people of the world, it has become increasingly clear that public opinion would play a great part in determining the outcome of our labours. It has become increasingly plain that in so difficult a matter Governments will not commit themselves to the grave decisions that are required unless they are required, unless they are certain that the opinion of their peoples is solidly behind them . . .

Henderson ended his letter with the plea, 'the women of the world have never taken up a cause so pregnant with good or evil for future generations. I hope they will not abandon it before we have won the final victory which will establish enduring peace.'[11]

The Committee received similar heartfelt appeals from the outgoing secretary general of the League, Sir Eric Drummond, as he prepared to turn over leadership of the secretariat to Joseph Avenol; from Lord Robert Cecil; and even from the head of the German delegation to the conference, Ambassador Rudolf Nadolny.[12] These appeals convinced the women to persevere and to join with the International Consultative Group in another rousing demonstration of public support for the goals of the League conference at its reopening ceremony in October.[13]

Collaborations between the Women's Disarmament Committee and its fellow NGOs in the International Consultative Group had continued throughout the spring 1933 session of the disarmament conference. The NGOs had among themselves hashed out a succinct 'Six Point Plan' and they had collectively lobbied for it at the spring conference session.

The Plan became the basis for the autumn campaign as well. The Plan boiled down difficult disarmament issues to their essential components that addressed the main points of contention among the Great Powers. The first and second points were linked: an international disarmament treaty should not allow any measure of German rearmament to reach parity with the world powers but should disarm the League member nations, according to the principle expressed in Article 8 of the League of Nations Covenant. The third point called for abolition of 'aggressive' categories of weapons of war, of all military aircraft, and of all chemical and bacteriological weapons. The fourth point called for the limitation of national arms budgets. The fifth and sixth points were also linked, calling for international monitoring of the size and strength of national armies and of arms manufacturing and trade, to be conducted by a permanent International Armaments Regulatory Commission.[14]

According to Laura Morgan's analysis of the Six Point Plan, French demands for security would be met by bans on German rearmament and strict international supervision over the size of national armed forces, military budgets and over weapons manufacture and sales. German demands for parity would be met if the world powers carried out their disarmament pledges to maintain only defensive armies. Hitler's threats of impending German rearmament provided the Great Powers with strong incentives to act together to prevent such a resolve from happening. Norman Davis had announced to the League that the United States was willing 'to go as far as the other States in the way of reduction. We feel that the ultimate objective should be to reduce armaments approximately to the level established by the peace treaties; that is, to bring armaments as soon as possible through successive stages down to the basis of a domestic police force.'[15] The groundwork was laid for an international disarmament treaty, or so the Women's Disarmament Committee believed, because the stakes were so high. As the Committee explained in its publications, '"Success" will mean a treaty that both France and Germany will sign and a period of stability which will allow time to build a firmer foundation for peace. "Failure" will mean the re-arming of Germany and unlimited competition among nations in preparation for war.'[16]

Germany's abrupt withdrawal from the disarmament conference on 14 October came on the heels of an equally shocking announcement by Sir John Simon that Britain and France had agreed to allow Germany some limited rearmament, under strict international supervision, thus moving toward international armaments parity.[17] In spite of British and French concessions Hitler had already decided to rally the German people's nationalist fervour behind claims that Germany had been fundamentally abused by the terms of the Versailles Treaty and by the continuing duplicity of the World War victor nations. In a telegram sent to Conference President Henderson, Germany announced:

> In light of the course of recent discussions of the Powers concerned have taken in the matters of disarmament, it is now clear that the Disarmament Conference will not fulfil what is its sole object, namely, general disarmament. It is also clear that this failure of the Conference is due solely to the unwillingness of the highly armed states to carry out their contractual obligation to disarm. This renders impossible the satisfaction of Germany's recognized claim to equality of rights, and the condition of which the German Government agreed at the beginning of this year to take part in the work of the Conference thus no longer exists. The German Government is accordingly compelled to leave the Disarmament Conference.[18]

At this point the United States for all practical purposes withdrew from the conference as well. Norman Davis returned to Washington, and Roosevelt temporarily gave way to the dominant national mood of isolationism expressed by the United States Congress.[19]

Yet while governments pulled back from the conference, the NGOs did not retreat. Joining with the Women's Disarmament Committee, the National Committee on the Cause and Cure of War (NCCCW) had organised town meetings and demonstrations across the United States throughout September and early October to rally American support for the reopening of the disarmament conference on 15 October, just as national branches of women's organisations continued activism in other countries.[20]

In Geneva conference supporters carried on with their planned demonstration. A crowd of 2,000 pledged support for the International Consultative Group (ICG) Six Point Plan and urged Arthur Henderson to work for its adoption in spite of Germany's withdrawal. Lord Cecil, Rosa Manus, Laura Morgan and H. L. Henriod, representing the International Christian Organisations, met with Henderson to express collective popular support for disarmament goals on behalf of their organisations and millions of members worldwide.[21]

Henderson matched the activists with equal resolve to press forward, and he issued his reply:

> My message to you is that the struggle for disarmament will not be treated as a scrap of paper. It cost ten million dead and twenty million wounded to bring the League of Nations into being. We will not break faith with the dead, who fell that there should be no more war . . . To you, who represent public opinion I would say, nail your flag to the mast of the League. Make the will to peace stronger and more steadfast than the will to war.[22]

Henderson and the NGOs continued to tout the efficacy of public opinion to influence government policy because the power of persuasion was the only power at their disposal. Peace advocates faced entrenched militarist traditions and government leaders who believed that strength in arms guaranteed national security. Peace and disarmament activists believed with equally strong convictions that steady peace education work would ultimately transform militaristic attitudes and lead to changes in government policy. During the autumn of 1933 disarmament conference sessions Henderson rallied to inspire his NGO allies, as they inspired him:

> To secure disarmament, we must break with ancient and powerful traditions. We must induce governments to give up the belief in their own armed force as the basis of their national safety, and to put their faith in international agreements to cooperate and to settle disputes peacefully. Armaments

and national safety become matters of world concern and both must be subordinated to the rule of Law as embodied in the treaties. It is public opinion and public opinion alone, which can make governments realize these facts sufficiently and vividly to give them the courage to act.

It is impossible to exaggerate the importance of the educational and propaganda work done by the organizations, and notably by the Women's Organizations, which have sent in petitions to the League, held meetings, and explained to public opinion precisely what must be done to get disarmament. It is through this work that disarmament has become a burning political issue which no government can refuse to face. It is this work that in the long run will make disarmament inevitable and peace secure.[23]

Yet when the conference adjourned in November, once again the delegates had failed to reach any agreements on arms reduction. By early 1934 Germany, France and Britain all sharply increased their arms budgets, briefly stimulating the European economy and escalating an international arms race.[24] The United States kept its distance from the disarmament conference and from most of the League's political debates even as it collaborated on international economic and social policy initiatives.[25] Throughout 1934 the disarmament conference met in general assembly only twice, in January and May. At the same time, conference commissions continued to debate various treaty issues, including abolition of the so-named 'aggressive' weapons of war, regulations on the use of aircraft in war and arms budget limitations, as well as the formation of a permanent international Disarmament Commission. While commission work registered few agreements, government delegates continued to meet and disarmament advocates gained some solace from that fact.[26]

The women's disarmament committee campaigns for the 1934 Nobel Peace Prize

As the new year began, the bleak international situation did not deter the Women's Disarmament Committee. Committee officers instead launched a new campaign to rally their supporters. With votes of confidence from prominent statesmen and their fellow international organisation leaders in Geneva spurring them on, Dingman and d'Arcis initiated a campaign for the 1934 Nobel Peace Prize. The Women's Committee and their NGO cohorts in Geneva placed the Committee at the centre of organisational efforts to build public opinion in support of the disarmament conference since 1931, and they considered themselves at the moral centre of the peace and disarmament movement as well.[27] Lord Robert Cecil penned the formal nomination letter to the Nobel Prize Committee and praised the Women's Disarmament Committee as a truly representative organisation that had conducted widespread peace education and mobilised world-wide public opinion in favour of the aims of the disarmament conference. Moreover, Lord Cecil asserted, 'if the Peace Prize were awarded to this Committee it would not only be a recognition of work already done, but a guarantee of the continuance of the work in the future. The Prize would be devoted to extending and developing the activities of the Committee, and would thus be a contribution toward women's work for peace for years to come.'[28] This, too, was the Committee's hope: to be recognised for past contributions to peace work but also to build up resources for continuing peace education in the future.[29]

An array of international leaders endorsed the Women's Committee's Peace Prize nomination. The French minister Edouard Herriot; Spain's ambassador to France, Salvador de Madariaga; Dr Mary Woolley; US Secretary of the Navy, Claude Swanson; Norman Davis; and the Chinese foreign secretary Wellington Koo, along with many other leading members of the League secretariat, international scholars, activists and government delegates to the League, all penned letters of support for the Committee to the Nobel Prize Committee.[30] The Nobel Committee recognised a world leader in disarmament activism when it awarded the Peace Prize in 1934, but it was not the Women's Disarmament Committee. Rather, it was the president of the disarmament conference, Arthur Henderson.

In his presentation speech a member of the Nobel Prize Committee, Johan Ludwig Mowinckel, recognised Henderson's singular efforts to secure a disarmament treaty, 'There he stands, in the struggle and the work itself, a lonely man. The words of Bjørnson to Emile Zola during his fight for justice in the Dreyfus case come to mind: "A single man against millions – the proudest sight to be seen".'[31] Yet Henderson was far from alone in his pursuit of world disarmament, as the records of the vigorous interwar peace movement attest. Even though Mowinckel's words erased the important contributions of the Women's Disarmament Committee and the international NGOs, they were vital components of the disarmament movement, which continued to campaign for arms reduction by attacking the arms industry in 1934.

As the British League of Nations Union launched its 'Peace Ballot' campaign in the spring of 1934 to register, once again, the support of British voters for the aims of the Disarmament Conference, the Women's Disarmament Committee formulated plans to target corporate business-men, whose political clout with government policy makers was more influential than the average citizen's.[32]

The 1934 bestselling book *Merchants of Death* by H. C. Engelbracht had exposed the economic manipulations and war profiteering that arms man-ufacturers and bankers had engaged in during the First World War. United

States congressional investigations led by Senator Gerald Nye confirmed Engelbracht's findings. In response to these revelations the treasurer of the Women's Committee, Clara d'Arcis, appealed to American businessmen who made automobiles and other consumer goods that sold well in peace time, to analyse their financial records and to reach the conclusion that supporting peace was the more enlightened and most profitable business decision to make. She urged businessmen to add their company names to the 'peace roll of industry' and to 'put peace in their budgets' and to make donations to support the Women's Disarmament Committee's peace education work.[33] Clara d'Arcis explained the campaign in her letter of appeal to American businessmen:

> We believe that businessmen accustomed to practical planning and forecasting and to obtaining results, could, through pressure on their national governments in different parts of the world, hasten a gradual, reciprocal and balanced reduction and limitation of these restrictions, quotas, tariffs, etc., which are today strangling the world. These are essentially business problems rather than political, and as business problems they still have to be dealt with . . .
> We will merely add that women, representing the overwhelming majority of consumers by handling their home budgets, can easily be brought to see that economic disarmament touches them quite as nearly as military disarmament . . . Undoubtedly two of the greatest forces for constructing peace are women and business – we want to bring that into closer cooperation.[34]

The Women's Disarmament Committee had distributed hundreds of copies of Gerald Nye's February Senate Resolution that opened the US government investigation of the arms industry, as well as hundreds of copies of an influential article that appeared in *Fortune* magazine in March 1934.[35] *Fortune* magazine had published 'Arms and the Men' by Eric Hodgins that further exposed the venality of the European arms traders and presented a powerful argument for arms control.[36] American isolationists pointed to these exposés and hoped to build congressional support for legislation that supported American neutrality in the event that another war broke out in Europe or in Asia. The internationalist Women's Disarmament Committee reported the same evidence in order to gain support for international disarmament agreements, regulation of the arms industry, and strict limitations on national military budgets.

In September 1934, when Margery Corbett Ashby spoke before women delegates to the fifteenth general assembly of the League of Nations, she, too, focused on the United States investigations of the arms industry, as they revealed self-serving collaborations among arms manufacturers, government military establishments and the scientific research community that developed new weapons and methods of warfare. 'Against these forces of evil', Corbett Ashby explained, 'we have the ministers for the peace departments of governments distracted and disunited, research starved, social services diminished or suspended, the industries that depend on peace and prosperity quarrelling for dwindling markets instead of combining against that evil octopus, the armaments . . . [industry], which is sucking the prosperity of the world.' Corbett Ashby urged the women's international organisations 'to keep our heads cool and our hearts warm, expose each new hypocrisy, fight each new corruption, devote ourselves to education and use our political powers, where we possess them, on the side of organised peace'.[37]

Although government delegates to the disarmament conference were no longer meeting in general assembly, a treaty for the Regulation and Control of the Manufacture and Trade in Arms seemed to be nearing the point of agreement in Commission work in early 1935, and this imminent success encouraged the Women's Disarmament Committee and its fellow peace activists. Gerald Nye wrote to Mary Dingman to praise the Committee for publicising the findings of United States congressional investigations and to register his support for any treaty to regulate the arms industry that might come out of Geneva.[38]

The seeming near-agreement on arms control offered one of the few positive signs for peace advocates in 1935. A clash between Somali soldiers patrolling the disputed border between Italian Somaliland and Ethiopian forces in December 1934 had prompted Italian dictator Benito Mussolini to send Italian troops into Ethiopia in February 1935 and to launch his bid for colonial expansion in Africa. The Ethiopian emperor, Haile Selassie, turned to the League to pressure Italy to back down, but the French and British, who could have exerted effective pressure on Mussolini, instead focused on narrowly defined national interests and failed to act. Emperor Selassie made a similar appeal to United States Secretary of State Cordell Hull, but the Americans, too, seemed reluctant to interfere with Italy's Ethiopian power play.[39]

In March, the League faced a further challenge from Paraguay, which had been warring with Bolivia for control of the Chaco region on its northern border since 1932. In January 1935 the League sent Paraguay demands to cease fire by 24 February, or sanctions would be applied. The deadline came and went without change in Paraguay's war policy. Rather, Paraguay left the League, and the Great Powers once again failed to act.[40]

Britain, France, Italy and Germany, all continued rearming with no end in sight. In mid March, Margery Corbett Ashby resigned her post as Britain's delegate to the disarmament conference, stating that 'it was impossible to pretend she was any longer in sympathy with [her] Government's policy with regard to disarmament'.[41]

By the summer of 1935 the Women's Disarmament Committee was at a crossroads. Although some conference Commissions continued to meet, in truth the League disarmament conference was dead. Arthur Henderson, now very ill, had no more energy to pump internationalist will into the nationalistic Great Powers. Mary Dingman's service contract with the World YWCA was about to undergo a change; she would no longer be based in Geneva, but was to begin a series of prolonged industrial training tours in the United States and Asia. Dingman had already spent much of the spring of 1935 abroad, representing the World YWCA and conducting training courses for national chapters in South America. While Laura Puffer Morgan had been on a speaking tour in the United States and Laura Dreyfus-Barney travelled with her husband in the Middle East, Kathleen Courtney had worked with Clara d'Arcis to maintain the Women's Disarmament Committee presence in Geneva, but Courtney was ready to return to London, and d'Arcis could not carry on alone. The Committee again considered dissolving, but, after a week-long reunion in Geneva in June, the Committee devised an alternative plan.

The Committee renamed itself the Women's International Organisations for Peace and Disarmament. Mary Dingman signed a three-year employment contract to continue as the Committee's full-time, Geneva-based president and took leave from her duties at the World YWCA. With a vote of confidence from the Committee member organisations and a broad mandate to carry out peace and disarmament campaigns on a worldwide basis, the Committee was reborn.[42] Among the Committee's first actions at the sixteenth session of the League of Nations general assembly, which opened in September 1935, was participation in a joint delegation of the women's international organisations that met with Secretary-General Avenol and General Assembly President Eduard Beneš. Kathleen Courtney spoke on behalf of the women's organisations to appeal for League action to honour Covenant disarmament pledges. The Committee also sent a public letter of appeal to Benito Mussolini to withdraw Italian troops from Ethiopian soil and to show the world the way to peace.[43]

As the women's international organisations continued peace work in Geneva they also launched a collective effort at the sixteenth general assembly to persuade League delegates to revisit the question of women's equal right to maintain their nationality after marriage, and to initiate consideration of a universal women's equal rights treaty in League deliberations. After much lobbying by those Latin American nations that had already pledged support for women's equal rights at the Conference of American States meeting in Montevideo in 1933, and by the Women's Consultative Committee on Nationality that had formed in 1930, the 1935 League general assembly agenda included a discussion on the nationality and status of women. The League Council invited the Liaison Committee of Women's International Organisations to present their views and organisational statements were circulated among the League member nations.

The International Alliance of Women, led by Margery Corbett Ashby, expressed the most commonly held women's organisation view:

> We believe that for the League of Nations to draw up an International Convention which, without in any way infringing upon national sovereignty, should ask the contracting States to agree that the participation of their citizens in the affairs of the State shall not depend on sex, would be truly in the interests of international life. It is surely an essential basis for all international cooperation between States that Governments should speak in the name of their entire peoples, and no Government which refuses to all its adult inhabitants [equal rights] as citizens can so speak with any degree of reality [as representing the nation].

The World YWCA expressed a contrary view, and asserted that an 'Equal Rights treaty . . . is not an adequate method of dealing with so complicated a problem as the equality of status between men and women in all departments of life. Such a method cannot take into account the claims of motherhood and of family nor can it allow for the great variety of social and economic conditions in different countries.' The YWCA, along with the Women's Trade Union League and the International Women's Cooperative Guild, feared that a universal Equal Rights Treaty would nullify the protective labour legislation that women factory workers relied on; at the same time they were concerned about restrictions on women's right to work of the kind that governments in economically depressed nations had been imposing throughout the 1930s. The women proposed instead that the League conduct an inquiry into the status of women worldwide, one that would investigate women's legal and actual status. The findings could guide further international actions to promote women's equality. [44]

The League secretariat consequently asked governments and the women's international organisations to submit national data on women's suffrage rights, parental rights, and rights to choose their domicile, to work, to own property and to control their earnings. The report based on the preliminary data that women's organisations collected was far from complete in its international coverage, but it revealed women's unequal status in the world in general, with wide variations from country to country. In 1937 the League General Assembly voted to conduct a formal Inquiry into the Status of Women utilising the most modern social science research methods. A Committee of international experts, composed of four women and three men, was formed to direct the inquiry, and the women's international organisations remained actively involved in its progress over the next several years, until the outbreak of war in Europe caused its demise.[45]

Italy goes to war and fascist aggression mounts

In spite of serious peacemaking efforts led by NGOs, government leaders failed to deter the war makers among their ranks. When Italy launched an armed invasion of Ethiopia on 2 October 1935 neither the British nor the French governments intervened; both nations preferred cultivating friendly relations with Mussolini's government so as to win Italy as a future ally to check Hitler's aggression in Europe.[46]

In response to the Italian aggression on 5 October the women's organisations in Geneva issued another urgent appeal to the League of Nations Council to work immediately for peace.[47] On 10 October the Council concluded that Mussolini had violated the League Covenant by invading Ethiopia, but the decision of whether to impose economic sanctions or an arms embargo on Italy or to do nothing at all was left to the individual League member nations. Women's and peace organisations in Geneva cheered when fifty nations elected to halt arms sales and cease loans to Italy.[48]

However, the United States and the Soviet Union, neither League members, continued to sell arms and other key commodities, such as oil, steel and cotton, to Italy without restrictions. The United States government allowed American businesses to continue arms sales even though the majority public opinion, educated by American women's organisations, supported the League's call for sanctions. A temporary 'peace' was proposed in December when British and French diplomats negotiated a settlement that ceded 60,000 square miles of Ethiopian territory to Italy and designated 160,000 additional square miles in southern Ethiopia as 'a zone of economic expansion and settlement reserved for Italy', while it granted to Ethiopia a corridor of land through Italian Somaliland territory to link the landlocked nation to the Indian Ocean.[49] Ethiopia immediately rejected these terms and called for renewed League intervention. Fighting resumed in January 1936. Throughout the spring of 1936 Italian warplanes dropped poison gas bombs on both military and civilian targets and forced Ethiopia to surrender its territory to Italy in May.[50]

In the middle of the Ethiopian crisis, on 21 October 1935 Arthur Henderson died after a long illness. The Women's Peace and Disarmament Committee grieved for the loss of a strong leader in its cause. In November Laura Morgan spoke at a memorial service held for Henderson in Geneva; she asserted that one of Henderson's great strengths had been to represent the will of the 'common people' who desired peace through disarmament.

In every public speech and, Morgan believed, in every private negotiation, Henderson had emphasised the people's demands for peace, 'which he believed in the end would prevail'.[51]

In the fall of 1935 disarmament advocates began to fight among themselves regarding the best way to express the 'people's will' to world leaders. The British League of Nations Union, with significant aid from the British WIL and other women's organisations, had led a door-to-door People's Ballot canvassing campaign in 1934 that had achieved a fair measure of success by mid-1935.[52] The Peace Ballot had polled nearly twelve million British voters on their views on several questions to determine support for continued disarmament negotiations to restrict or abolish weapons of war, international regulation of the weapons industry and international sanctions to deter aggressor states. The results of the poll were announced at a mass rally in London's Albert Hall in late June, and a League of Nations Union delegation, led by Lord Robert Cecil, presented the results as a record of popular support for peace to British Conservative Prime Minister Stanley Baldwin.[53]

The Women's International League for Peace and Freedom criticised the LNU Peace Ballot because the LNU did not use the outcome of the polls to demand a response from elected leaders.[54] The American chapter of the Women's International League for Peace and Freedom (WILPF), led by Mabel Vernon, and at the international WILPF organisation in Geneva, led by American Emily Greene Balch, initiated a more proactive global Peace Mandate campaign in September 1935 to renew demands on world governments:

> Stop immediately all increase of armaments and armed forces.
> Use existing machinery for peaceful settlement of present conflicts.
> Secure a World Treaty for immediate reduction of arms as a step toward Complete World Disarmament.
> Secure international agreements founded on recognition of world interdependence to end the economic anarchy which breeds war.
> As we sign this mandate, people in all countries of the world are signing it with us, united in the determination to secure Permanent Peace.[55]

WILPF sent a delegation to present the signatures to world leaders at the Seventeenth General Assembly of the League of Nations as the campaign concluded in September 1936, having collected over 14 million signatures. The People's Mandate campaign topped the achievement of the nine million signatures on petitions presented at the 1932 disarmament conference by the Women's Disarmament Committee.[56]

This campaign aroused the jealousy of Mary Dingman and her fellow Committee officers, who believed they had been sidelined in the women's peace movement, where they claimed leadership. On 16 October 1935 WILPF further bypassed Dingman's Committee when it organised a Consultative Conference of the Women's International Organisations at its Geneva headquarters to plan a joint women's action to condemn Italy's attack on Ethiopia. Although all organisational members of the Women's Disarmament Committee were invited to the Consultative Conference, along with representatives of two left-wing women's organisations, the Comité Mondial des Femmes Contre le Guerre et le Fascisme and the Internationale Syndicate Rouge, Mary Dingman's Committee was not consulted in advance, and Committee officers felt disrespected.[57]

YWCA leaders who felt a special loyalty to Mary Dingman also resented WILPF's actions in organising the People's Mandate campaign, only asking for the support of other women's organisations well after the fact. Cornelia van Asch van Wijck, the president of the World YWCA, wrote to Evelyn Fox and criticised WILPF's leadership style: 'In their [WILPF] way of arranging for this mandate the first conditions for cooperative work – consultation beforehand and willingness to give in on details – are ignored completely. This is exactly like that effort in October . . . They say our cooperation is urgently needed. Well, then it ought to have been asked and really used for common constructive work at a much earlier period.'[58] Kathleen Courtney felt loyalty to her home organisation, the British chapter of the Women's International League (WIL), but she, too, wrote to Evelyn Fox to express her concerns: 'Actually I regret this "Mandate" scheme. I do not see how it can be successful, for it has been ill prepared and hastily put into practice, and I fear it may queer the pitch for something similar that is really well worked out.'[59] Nonetheless, in spite of their reservations, the YWCA and British WIL both joined the campaign to collect signatures of support for the People's Mandate that demanded government action.[60]

Internal squabbling among women's international organisations, however, was the least of their worries, as Italy resumed its Ethiopian campaign in January 1936. In March, Adolf Hitler, emboldened by Italy's military successes in Africa and the League's ineffective response, invaded the Rhineland border region separating Germany from France, Luxembourg, Belgium and the Netherlands. The Rhineland, German territory before the First World War, had been demilitarised according to the terms of the 1925 Locarno Treaty. Following the rationale that Germany was reoccupying German territory and had done so without using force, the British government offered no protest. The French, fearing that any resistance on their part would lead to war, did not demand a German retreat.[61]

As soon as Hitler invaded the Rhineland, Italy renewed gas bombing of Ethiopia's armies and its civilian population. Haile Selassie's daughter, the Princess Tschai, appealed to women's international organisations to bring their moral force to bear on world leaders in Geneva: 'This suffering and torture is beyond description, hundreds of our countrymen are screaming and moaning with pain. Many, many of them are unrecognisable since the skin has been burned off their faces. These are facts.' Princess Tschai appealed to women to protest this violation of the 1925 protocols signed by all League members – including Italy – banning the use of poison gas as a weapon of war.[62]

Unable to ignore Ethiopia's heart-rending pleas for help, the Women's Disarmament Committee immediately expressed outrage at Italy's treaty violations and breach of human rights and appealed to the League Committee of Thirteen that sought a negotiated settlement of the war to renew its efforts to bring about a just peace.[63]

Drawing on women's moral power and invoking the sanctity of international treaties, however, did not move German or Italian leaders. Moreover it frustrated women who struggled to define an effective course of action. In June 1936 the Women's Disarmament Committee once again organised a summer course on current international problems for leaders of NGOs; the focus was to be on the economic causes of war, disarmament and collective security. There was little enthusiasm for these efforts among the women's organisations, however.[64] YWCA president Cornelia van Asch van Wijck wrote to Mary Dingman: 'Something must be done! But what? Personally I must say I am most sceptical as to the possible influence of a conference as proposed. These sorts of conferences have been held so much now, these demonstrations have been so frequent, that I cannot become enthusiastic about this one and I fear it will mean a great deal of effort with practically no results. To a meeting like this only the convinced ones come.'[65] In the United States, Henrietta Roelofs expressed the women peace activists' frustration in a speech she delivered to Presbyterian Church women in 1936:

> No question seems to be so near the heart of a woman as that of peace or war. And yet she seems to have almost no influence on the policies of her government when fateful decisions are made. When in modern times do we find an example of the women of a country refusing to support a war? Do they really believe that God can bless the murdering of the children whom they bear? Do they believe that there are more important things than life itself? Granted that we were all ignorant and deluded during the World War, are not all our eyes open now to the causes of war? . . .
>
> We, the Christian nations, go on making preparations to kill each other, and the women who might be expected to rise in a mighty army against war, for the most part content themselves with educating themselves on the so-called 'international situation'. Education without action – of what use is it?[66]

At the League of Nations, Swedish delegate Kerstin Hesselgren voiced similar frustrations with women's lack of power in international politics. As Sweden's representative Hesselgren could address the general assembly and express what she defined as the 'women's perspective' even if it was ignored by male leaders:

> I have been listening with the greatest interest to these fine and eloquent speeches but I have found no ray of hope in them.
> 50 nations give in to one aggressor.
> 50 nations let a small power, one of its own members, to fall to the ground . . .
> A few years ago the League of Nations asked for the collaboration of women – we answered by pleading by millions all over the world for disarmament, what was the result? Not disarmament but rearmament all over the world.[67]

Notes

1 F. P. Walters, *A History of the League of Nations* (New York: Oxford University Press, 1952), pp. 541–4.

2 League of Nations Archives, Registry File 7B/ 2717/596, 'Communication from the Japanese Delegation', box R4218.

3 George Scott, *The Rise and Fall of the League of Nations* (London: Hutchinson & Co. Publishers, Ltd, 1973), p. 278.

4 MAD, Mary Dingman to Women's Disarmament Committee Members, 12 April 1933, box 2.

5 YWCA of the USA, Mary A. Dingman to Vera Cushman, YWCA of the USA headquarters [in handwritten postscript], 24 April 1933, microfilm reel 78.

6 Harriet Hyman Alonso, *Peace as a Women's Issue: A History of the U.S. Movement for World Peace and Women's Rights* (Syracuse, NY: Syracuse University Press, 1993), p. 142.

7 Jacqueline Van Vohis, *Carrie Chapman Catt: A Public Life* (New York: Feminist Press, 1987), p. 214.

8 Scott, *The Rise and Fall of the League of Nations*, p. 280; Walters, *A History of the League of Nations*, pp. 548–9.

9 P & D Committee, 'Report of the study conference', 30 May 1933.

10 YWCA of the USA, Evelyn Fox to Sarah Lyon, 31 May 1933, microfilm reel 78.

11 CCCW, Arthur Henderson to Clara Guthrie d'Arcis, 8 June 1933, box 18.

12 CCCW, Secretary General Sir Eric Drummond to Clara Guthrie d'Arcis, 15 June 1933 and Lord Robert Cecil, Viscount of Chelwood to Clara Guthrie d'Arcis, 5 July 1933, box 18; P & D Committee, Rudolf Nadolny, German Ambassador, Head of the German Delegation to the Disarmament Conference, 13 June 1933.

13 MAD, 'Project for a mass meeting to be held in Geneva, Sunday, October 15, 1933', c. July 1933, box 2.

14 Morgan–Howes Papers, Memo, International Consultative Group, 19 July 1933, box 3.

15 CCCW, 'The disarmament conference: how it can succeed, a six point program', c. September 1933, box 21.
16 CCCW, 'World disarmament campaign, October 1–15, 1933', c. September 1933, box 21.
17 Elmer Bendinger, *No Time for Angels: The Tragicomic History of the League of Nations* (New York: Alfred A. Knopf, 1975), p. 291.
18 League of Nations Archives, Registry File 7B/7341/596, Telegram from the German Secretary of State for Foreign Affairs, Baron von Neurath, 14 October 1933, box R4218.
19 Walters, *A History of the League of Nations*, p. 550.
20 CCCW, National Committee on the Cause and Cure of War to Laura Puffer Morgan, 6 October 1933, box 21.
21 MAD, 'Deputation to the president of the disarmament conference from the organisations responsible for the great public meeting held under the auspices of the International Consultative Group for Disarmament in Geneva', 15 October 1933, box 2.
22 Scott, *The Rise and Fall of the League of Nations*, p. 287.
23 MAD, 'A message from Mr. Henderson, president of the disarmament conference', 27 October 1933, box 2.
24 Walters, *A History of the League of Nations*, p. 551.
25 Warren F. Kuehl and Lynne K. Dunne, *Keeping the Covenant: American Internationalists and the League of Nations, 1920–1939* (Kent, OH: Kent State University Press, 1997), pp. 142–7.
26 Walters, *A History of the League of Nations*, pp. 552–4.
27 P & D Committee, Clara d'Arcis to Kathleen Courtney, 4 January 1934.
28 CCCW, 'Viscount Cecil to the Nobel committee presenting the candidature of the Peace and Disarmament Committee of the Women's International Organisations for the Nobel Peace Prize', c. January 1934, box 18.
29 MAD, 'Disarmament committee of the women's international organisations, Summary or Supplementary Report of Activities, June 1933–March 1934', box 2.
30 P & D Committee, List of supporters of the Women's Disarmament Committee Nobel Prize nomination, May 1934.
31 Johan Ludwig Mowinckel, Nobel Peace Prize 1934, presentation speech, 10 December 1934 (nobelprize.org/nobel_prizes/peace/laureates/1934/press.html).
32 Donald S. Birn, *The League of Nations Union, 1918–1945* (Oxford, UK: Clarendon Press, 1981), pp. 142–54.
33 CCCW, 'The women's international peace roll, the peace roll of industry, a plebiscite of the business world', c. 1934, box 18.
34 JS, Clara Guthrie d'Arcis to Mr C. M. Woolley, President of the American Radiator Company, 5 December 1935, box 10.
35 MAD, Kathleen D. Courtney and Laura Puffer Morgan to the Presidents of the Women's International Organisations, 28 September 1934, box 2.

36 Stuart D. Brandes, *Warhogs: A History of War Profits in America* (Lexington, KY: University of Kentucky Press, 1997), p. 208.

37 MAD, 'Mrs. Corbett Ashby's speech at the luncheon', 13 September 1934, box 2.

38 P & D Committee, Senator Gerald P. Nye to Mary Dingman, 13 February 1935.

39 Bendinger, *No Time for Angels*, pp. 348–51.

40 Clarence K. Streit, 'League's position unheroic on Chaco', *New York Times* (3 March 1935).

41 P & D Committee, Disarmament committee meeting minutes, 12 March 1935.

42 P & D Committee, Dorothy Heneker, honorary secretary and K. D. Courtney, vice president, to Disarmament Committee of Women's International Organisations members, August 1935; Peace and Disarmament Committee meeting minutes, 11 September 1935.

43 P & D Committee, Peace and Disarmament Committee meeting minutes, 14 September 1935; Yale Divinity School Library, 'Geneva at assembly time', *World's YWCA Monthly* (October 1935).

44 League of Nations Archives, Registry File 3A/19352/13900, Report to League of Nations on the Nationality and Status of Women: Statements Presented by International Women's Organisations, 30 August 1935.

45 'The United Nations and the status of women', *United Nations Review* 8 (March 1961), p. 22.

46 Birn, *The League of Nations Union*, p. 156.

47 P & D Committee, 'A new appeal from women to the governments of the Council of the League of Nations', 5 October 1935.

48 P & D Committee, K. D. Courtney and L. P. Morgan to Members of the Peace and Disarmament Committee, 24 October 1935.

49 Bendinger, *No Time for Angels*, pp. 356–60.

50 John H. Spencer, 'The Italian–Ethiopian dispute and the League of Nations', *American Journal of International Law* 31 (October 1937), pp. 614–30.

51 Morgan–Howes Papers, Laura Puffer Morgan, memorial remarks for Arthur Henderson c. November 1935, box 4.

52 Beryl Haslam, *From Suffrage to Internationalism: The Political Evolution of Three British Feminists, 1908-1939* (New York: Peter Laug, 1999), p. 197.

53 YWCA of the USA, 'Public affairs: international relations', *Woman's Press* (September 1935), p. 402.

54 Gertrude Bussey and Margaret Tims, *Women's International League for Peace and Freedom 1915–1965: A Record of Fifty Years' Work* (London: George Allen & Unwin, Ltd, 1965), p. 145.

55 WYWCA, Mabel Vernon, WILPF, to Cornelia van Asch van Wijck, 19 November 1935, box 267.

56 Bussey and Tims, *Women's International League for Peace and Freedom*, p. 147.

57 WYWCA, Report prepared for the World YWCA executive committee meeting, re: the Disarmament Committee of International Women's Organisations, 11–13 November 1935, box 283.

58 WYWCA, Cornelia van Asch van Wijck to Evelyn Fox, 9 December 1935, box 267.

59 WYWCA, Kathleen Courtney to Evelyn Fox, 10 December 1935, box 267.

60 WYWCA, Mary Gertrude Fendall, on Behalf of Mabel Vernon, Campaign Director for People's Mandate, 4 February 1936, box 267.

61 Bendinger, *No Time for Angels*, pp. 367–8.

62 P & D Committee, 'These are facts', Princess Tschai, president of Ethiopia's Women's Work Association to Lady Gladstone, chairman of the Women's Advisory Council of the League of Nations Union, as printed in the *News Chronicle*, London, 25 March 1936.

63 P & D Committee, 'Protest to the Committee of Thirteen from the Peace and Disarmament Committee of the Women's International Organisations', 31 March 1936.

64 WYWCA, Outline for Study Conference on 'Present international problems', 10–11 June 1936, box 267.

65 WYWCA, Cornelia van Asch van Wijck to Mary Dingman, 2 May 1936, box 267.

66 Henrietta Roelofs, from a speech delivered at a Women's Fellowship Dinner at the General Assembly of the Presbyterian Church USA in 1936, in Mary S. Sims and Rhoda E. McCullough (eds), *Women and Leadership* (New York: Woman's Press, 1938), pp. 64–5.

67 MAD, 'Address of Miss Kerstin Hesselgren, delegate of the Swedish government at the Assembly of the League of Nations', 3 July 1936, box 2.

4

Fascism, Communism and war

The 1936 World Congress for Peace

In Europe, with war imminent, women's peace and popular-front organi-
sations decided to host jointly a World Congress for Peace (Rassemblement
Universel pour la Paix). Initially planned for Geneva, the Congress location
was changed to Brussels, Belgium, where it opened in early September
1936, just preceding the opening of the seventeenth League of Nations
General Assembly session. Well-known internationalists launched the
International Peace Campaign and convened the World Congress. Lord
Robert Cecil, Philip Noel Baker, and the 1933 Nobel Peace Prize winner,
Norman Angell, all leaders in the British League of Nations Union; Margery
Corbett Ashby of the International Alliance of Women, French Minister of
State Edouard Herriot, trade union leader Leon Jouhaux; and socialist
politician, Pierre Cot, all jointly served on the World Congress executive
committee. Rosa Manus served as the organising secretary.

The International Peace Campaign sought to renew national commitments to international treaties, to halt the arms race among the Great
Powers, and to register popular support for the League of Nations as the
instrument to settle international disputes without resort to war. With
the involvement of representatives from a wide range of labour, religious,
women's, youth, veterans' and religious NGOs that operated in forty-three
countries worldwide and spanned the political spectrum from moderate
liberal to radical Communist, the International Peace Campaign claimed
to speak for 400 million organisational members. While the International
Peace Campaign enjoyed popular support, conservative politicians and
militarists in fascist and non-fascist states, along with the Roman Catholic
Church, all condemned the World Congress for Peace as a Communist-
front stunt designed to compromise national security.[1]

Representing the Women's Disarmament Committee, Mary Dingman
also feared the consequences of the right-wing's accusations that
Communists were manipulating the International Peace Campaign and, to

a certain extent, she agreed with the charges. By the mid-1930s red-scare tactics had pressured women's organisations to back away from radical demands for peace, and Dingman had seen the French socialist Camille Drevet of WILPF forced to leave Switzerland because of her politics when her residency permit was not renewed in June 1935.[2] In December 1935 Henrietta Roelofs wrote to Kathleen Courtney and described the growing anti-Communist climate in the United States:

> One of the greatest problems which the active workers for peace are now facing is the revived movement to weed out the 'Reds' in this country. State after state has been passing sedition legislation tending to curb freedom of speech and freedom of assembly. The YWCA is being attacked in various sections of the country, and the attacks are becoming more virulent. It seems no longer possible to simply ignore them ... A book has been written called 'The Red Network' which purports to give facts showing communist leanings of leaders in colleges, church groups, women's organizations and so forth, which are working on peace. I think that we are in for a very difficult time during the next few years.[3]

However, with the trusted allies Lord Cecil, Philip Noel Baker and Rosa Manus spearheading the International Peace Campaign, Dingman endorsed the World Congress and signed the Call to Women that circulated among women's international organisations on behalf of the Women's Disarmament Committee.[4] Yet even as the Call to Women went forth, Dingman began to express serious misgivings about Communist influence within World Congress planning sessions. She suggested at one point that the Women's Disarmament Committee withdraw its endorsement and pull out of the Congress.

Dingman raised the anti-Communist alert after meeting with the Congress organising committee in Brussels in July 1936. As the Congress date neared, the working members of the organising committee, among them several vocal Communists, decided to switch the location of the event from Geneva to Brussels. The decision was made against Dingman's wishes because of the prevailing conservative climate in Geneva. Dingman believed that this change in location signalled that the Communists were 'taking over' the Congress. With Lord Cecil and Philip Noel Baker not actively involved in Congress details, and with Rosa Manus seeming to acquiesce to the leftist leadership, Dingman feared that the Communists would seize the opportunity to attack fascist leaders in Germany and Italy and to praise the Communist leaders in the Soviet Union. As Dingman explained her objections to these developments, 'It is one thing to attack dictatorships, suppression of liberty, etc., wherever found and another to vent all this passion against specific countries.' But Dingman also revealed that with the change in venue, and the centre of activities removed from Geneva, the Women's Disarmament Committee's home ground, the Committee would lose some measure of leadership at the Congress. Instead, Dingman feared that Gabrielle Duchene, President of the Comité Mondial des Femmes Contre la Guerre at le Fascisme and leader in the French chapter of the Women's International League for Peace and Free (WILPF), would become the leading light among women at the Congress, and she jealously objected to that eventuality. [5]

While Philip Noel Baker offered assurances that he and Lord Cecil were actively involved with the Congress planning and had a large stake in the Congress's success, Dingman's fellow Committee members overruled her.[6] Kathleen Courtney argued that the range of organisations involved would preserve 'balance' in the Congress programme.[7] Rosa Manus asserted that the movement's allies and strength were found among the political left, and not among the anti-Communist right wing. When the decision was made to hold the Congress in Brussels, Manus wrote to Carrie Chapman Catt:

> There are political difficulties in Geneva . . . [The] Council of Geneva . . . are all afraid, afraid about having the Communist trade unions etc., coming into this country and they think our Congress is too 'left'. But we think the 'left' are much more in favour of peace than the 'right' and if some countries may have more people of the left who are cooperating with us, for instance France and Spain, we quite well know that some others, England for instance, are mostly of the right. We can only be thankful that for the first time we have all the forces combined for one effort.'[8]

Laura Puffer Morgan reassured her cautious friends and constituents that the Communists were not dominating the International Peace Campaign. Yet she also warned moderates that if they withdrew their support from the peace movement, they only strengthened the extremists they feared. Moderates needed to commit to activism, and not retreat, in order to bolster international peace efforts: 'It would be unfortunate if the American organizations working for peace, by withholding their help from a great world movement at a critical moment should prevent its development just as the American government by refusing to join the League of Nations dealt it a blow from which it has never recovered.'[9]

From thirty-five countries, 40, 000 delegates turned out for the World Congress in Brussels, and speakers strictly adhered to the four agreed-upon goals of the International Peace Campaign: they expressed support for existing international treaties, disarmament, collective security and international cooperation through the system of the League of Nations. The huge crowd of nearly 30,000 delegates and onlookers crowded into the Brussels public stadium for the opening ceremony applauded wildly for Lord Cecil and Pierre Cot, co-presidents of the World Congress. A special session on women's role in the peace movement was attended by 600 women, chaired by Josephine Schain of the American National Committee on the Cause and Cure of War (NCCCW). Mary Dingman and Gabrielle Duchene shared the duties of recording secretary at the women's session, where the discussion focused on effective methods of peace education and on ways to include more women in governing bodies at both the national and international levels. All in attendance pledged continued cooperation among women's groups in the future. Popular-front sentiments prevailed among the women delegates, and first-hand accounts of the wars in Ethiopia and Spain heightened everyone's sense of urgency to restore world peace before armed conflicts spread further.[10]

Although she feared that the leadership of the Women's Disarmament Committee had been diminished in Brussels, back in Geneva, Mary Dingman was again recognised as the 'voice of women' in the global peace movement. On 1 October Dingman joined Lord Cecil and ten other non-governmental organisations (NGO) leaders who spoke to government delegates at the seventeenth League of Nations General Assembly and reported on the World Congress for Peace. Dingman announced that women worldwide were united for peace; her remarks revealed no hint of the reservations she felt about Communist women's political motives at the Congress. Dingman claimed that:

> we [women] are linked together in our efforts to establish the supremacy of international law over armed violence and to have free and open discussion of all grievances which might be provocative of war . . . We women are deeply in earnest about this question of war and peace. We realize that it is a matter of life or death to millions and our mission is to conserve life. We believe that moral laws govern the universe; that if we work in harmony with them there will be political security and economic plenty for all.

In that spirit of unity Dingman quoted from Gabrielle Duchene's address to the women in Brussels: 'Women believe that peace is indivisible. They want peace for all . . . They consider that it is the lack of solidarity between the nations that want peace at the present time which constitutes the strength of the war-makers.'[11]

Civil war in Spain

The 'lack of solidarity between the nations that want peace' that Gabrielle Duchene decried was evident in the international reaction to the Civil War in Spain. General Francisco Franco and his anti-Communist 'Nationalist' forces, armed by Hitler and Mussolini's fascist regimes, attacked Spain's Republican Government in Madrid in July 1936. With no material aid from the French or British governments who led twenty-seven nations in forming an International Non-Intervention Committee, the Republicans foundered under Franco's assaults. Justifying the non-intervention policy, British Foreign Secretary Anthony Eden addressed the League assembly in September and explained that Spain was in the middle of an internal 'ideological conflict' and that the League of Nations Covenant did not permit interference in such a case.[12] Germany and Italy's membership on the Non-Intervention Committee showed the meaninglessness of the international action as the fascist nations continued to aid Franco. To counter fascist intervention, the Soviet Union and Mexico led popular-front efforts and sent soldiers to fight along with other material support for the Republican armies, but Franco's well-supplied forces prevailed and defeated the Republicans by early 1939.

Beginning with the first Nationalist assaults in July 1936, the women's international organisations expressed sympathy for the Republican government forces under attack and for the suffering Spanish people. They were also concerned, however, with preserving 'neutrality' in regard to 'civil' conflicts. At first the Women's Disarmament Committee and other Geneva NGOs supported the non-intervention policy of the Western powers.[13] Like the League, the NGOs adhered to a narrow definition of the Spanish conflict as a civil war, one that was, therefore, outside the scope of concerns of the intergovernmental body.[14] In November, however, the British Women's Peace Crusade tried to enlist the Peace and Disarmament Committee to call on the League Council to take action according to Article 11 of the League Covenant, which declared, 'Any war or threat of war, whether immediately affecting any of the Members of the League or not, is hereby declared a matter of concern to the whole League, and the League shall take any action that may be deemed wise and effectual to safeguard the peace of nations.' The Women's Disarmament Committee still refused to appeal to the League Council asserting that any League efforts to mediate the conflict would be rebuffed by the Republicans because mediation would confer legitimacy on Franco's Nationalist insurgents. Moreover, as the Committee and approximately thirty allied NGOs within the International Consultative Group in Geneva understood the situation, in order for League members to intervene with other measures, the members would have to be unanimous in their decision, and there was no such agreement among nations in regard to the Spanish Civil War.[15]

In autumn 1936, as the Spanish War raged, the NGOs like the Western governments defined the war as a contest between competing totalitarian ideologies that threatened liberal democracies yet offered no clear path for intervention. Representatives of the Geneva-based NGOs laid out the puzzling problem for their organisational constituents:

> Europe today is dominated by political types which have perhaps never before been encountered by students of politics, and one does not get beneath the surface of the problem if one classifies them merely as dictatorships. They are something much more than that. They represent the expressions of whole peoples rather than the voices of isolated individuals. The political life of Europe is today dominated by States motivated by concepts which give political ideals the qualities of religions. Whole nations are impelled by ideas of 'racial superiority' of 'imperial destiny' or 'proletarian rights' to the point where they become absolutely plastic material in the hands of leaders who have concrete plans and challenging programs to offer.[16]

The Spanish War came to be defined as a 'dress rehearsal' for armed conflicts that brewed in Austria and Czechoslovakia, as Germany formulated plans to build its European empire.[17] When German bombers supporting Franco's ground forces attacked a civilian population and destroyed the Spanish city of Guernica in April 1937, the world witnessed the brutal terror tactics that fascist forces would employ without hesitation in the global war to come. At that point all the Women's Disarmament Committee could do was to register their horror, condemn the slaughter of 'innocent civilians', and call on the League to reconsider the non-intervention policy that it, too, had advocated.[18] By 1938 the Committee officers recognised the folly of the non-intervention policy. It had only prevented Spain's Republican government from purchasing arms openly from the Western powers that could have been used to defend it against fascist attacks.[19]

Although the Women's Disarmament Committee continued to meet for the next several years, organising occasional study conferences and publishing scores of informational news analyses that chronicled the mounting aggression in Europe and Asia, the Committee had lost the energy to imagine new peace actions. After several months of serious illness Clara d'Arcis died on 12 May 1937, and Mary Dingman especially felt the loss of her beloved friend and Geneva colleague.[20] The Committee remained active as ever, hosting events for distinguished women visitors to Geneva and introducing them to contacts in the League secretariat, but it was no longer innovative.[21]

When Japan attacked China on 7 July 1937, there was no immediate reaction from the Women's Disarmament Committee. Mary Dingman's close contacts in the World YWCA headquarters kept her well informed about Japanese and Chinese women's involvement in their national crises, but there were no immediate responses from the Committee, or its Euro-centred organisational members, to the outbreak of war in Asia. All waited for the League of Nations to meet in General Assembly in September to formulate a plan. On 28 September the League assembly passed a resolution denouncing the bombing of civilian towns in China, but made no broader statement to condemn Japan's war of conquest in Asia. The Women's Disarmament Committee appealed to League members to recognise the Japanese aggression as a threat to international peace and to impose international sanctions.[22] After the Chinese delegate, Wellington Koo, also made an urgent appeal to the League to take action, the League voted to express its moral support for China but it urged member nations to determine their own national policies in regard to providing material support to the Chinese government. Thus the League took another weak and unsatisfying stand that provided no leadership for the Women's Disarmament Committee to follow.[23] Subsequently the Committee issued plaintive appeals to its member organisations to work towards building public opinion to support government intervention to stop Japanese aggression.[24]

Germany's annexation of Austria in March 1938 brought renewed calls among Committee officers for cooperation among League member nations. Travelling in Australia, far from the European centre of action at the time, Kathleen Courtney criticised British and French acquiescence to Hitler's actions and called for collective sanctions against the fascist state.[25] In Geneva, the Committee published its account of the international community's reaction. The majority of international journalists, NGOs and the League secretariat, discouraged and pessimistic, believed that the League had reached a new low point in its role as a collective deterrent to aggressors. The most that pessimists hoped for was that Mussolini would be threatened by Hitler's coup in Austria, and that, as a result, the fascist alliance would dissolve. All anticipated that the German occupation of Czechoslovakia would be Hitler's next step, unless some dramatic change in the international situation transpired.[26]

Laura Morgan argued that the League still provided a forum for 'weak and oppressed' states to appeal to the conscience of the world, but that Britain and France had abandoned all the democratic principles that the League claimed to embody and had forfeited their leadership among democratic nations.[27] Morgan's assessments were confirmed when British and French leaders met with Hitler and Mussolini in Munich in September 1938 and agreed among themselves that Hitler's annexation of the Czechoslovakian Sudetenland would go forward without challenge; Germany occupied the rest of Czechoslovakian territory in March 1939. Although, according to Kathleen Courtney, they were 'overwhelmed with shame', the women's organisations, like the weak beleaguered states of the world, had little influence over big-power politics.[28] All they could do was issue moralistic appeals for international cooperation.[29] The 'task of women's organisations', the Women's Disarmament Committee counselled, was to strengthen 'moral values and the maintenance of the moral basis of international cooperation and of collective action . . . and to work for their realisation'.[30]

The individual Committee officers did what they could to aid and protect their Jewish friends. In January 1939 Dingman recounted the story of the Braun family in letters she sent to her family and friends in America:

> I am having an interesting experience these days. Feeling that it wasn't right to have two empty beds when so many refugees are homeless I decided to invite one to come and stay with me. The one recommended by the Committee for Intellectual Refugees turns out to be Frau Gerda Braun a mezzo soprano from the Munich State Opera House. She left Germany four or more years ago and went with her daughter to Italy. Recently the Italian authorities refused to extend her permission to stay there so she was obliged to leave. The daughter is with a family and she was allowed to stay. The Refugee Committee said that Frau Braun was willing to do the house work that is the only gainful occupation that the refugees are allowed to do in Geneva . . .
>
> It is unbelievable the persecution Jews are suffering. Made to leave their country, all their money and property taken away from them, without a proper passport they are turned out across the border. They can never go back and no country really wants them . . . I don't know how the people working with these refugees day after day can stand it. And millions in the world who have status in a country, a home and some degree of economic security are so absorbed in their own affairs that they give barely a thought to all these people in need. If only I can find some work for Frau Braun. She is very likeable, is naturally light-hearted and keeps up good courage.[31]

In October she continued the Braun's saga, which ultimately ended with their emigration to America:

> I've been busy with the Brauns, trying to get the mother off from Bordeaux on the *Washington* and the daughter from Milan on the *Rex*. I've had to advance the passage money for both personally as the Jewish agencies have been so slow and their visas for America are expiring the 5th of November. If only they arrive safely, and after a chance to get rested (they've had a terrible time), find something to do, I shall be so thankful. I've been working on this case for a year and a quarter. It is incredible what they have been through. [handwritten note included: '1939 – They arrived safely'.][32]

The League of Nations Inquiry on the Status of Women

As international relations deteriorated the Liaison Committee of Women's International Organisations turned its energies from supporting peace actions to focusing on the League of Nations Inquiry into the Status of Women that the League Eighteenth General Assembly had formally initiated in September 1937. Margery Corbett Ashby offered to monitor the Inquiry proceedings and to lobby for an equal rights treaty in Geneva.[33] To be sure, most League member nations and the League Legal Committee that studied the problem of women's status never supported an equal rights treaty. They believed that women's rights were a matter for individual states to determine and that an international treaty would have no practical value because it could not be enforced. Yet the League had agreed to conduct a comparative study of national laws regarding women's political and civil rights, just as the International Labour Organization(ILO) had agreed to conduct an independent inquiry into women's economic and labour rights.[34]

According to the historian Carol Miller, the interwar peace work performed by women's international NGOs laid important groundwork for the Inquiry into the Status of Women. Women's organisations had created networks of influence among the international governance community. These networks were used to bring 'women's issues', such as the status of women inquiry, onto the League of Nations agenda. Certainly the most adamant equal rights activists, like Alice Paul and Dorothy Evans, and organisations like Equal Rights International, had played critical roles since the 1930 League Conference on the Codification of International Law. They too had raised the male diplomats' consciousness regarding concerns for women's status and rights. But such organisations as the Women's Disarmament Committee, which had established strong relationships with diplomats and League civil servants in Geneva, had defined a legitimate place for women in the system of international governance.[35]

On 30 September 1937 the League General Assembly adopted a resolution that established a Committee of Experts to conduct an Inquiry into the Status of Women, with the cooperation of the International Institute for the Unification of Private Law, the International Institute of Public Law and the International Bureau for Unification of Penal Law.[36] Four women and three men were selected to serve on the Inquiry Committee. Kerstin Hesselgren from Sweden had served as a national delegate to the ILO and to the League and knew the League system well. Madame Suzanne Bastid-Basdevant from France, Dr. Anka Godjevac from Yugoslavia, Judge Dorothy Kenyon from the United States, Professor H. C. Gutteridge from Great Britain, Monsieur de Ruelle from Belgium and Paul Sebestyen from Hungary all had university law degrees. The Committee was charged with determining the scope and methods of the Inquiry, and these were the first time-consuming tasks the appointed Committee confronted when it convened for the first time in April 1938.[37] Several years' worth of data collected by the women's international NGOs regarding the application of laws to protect women's rights was turned over to scientific institutes in Rome and Paris, to determine whether any of the information could be used and to direct the women's organisations in future collaborations.[38]

Women's organisations used the full range of their informal power to influence the course of the Inquiry, beginning with the selection of women to serve on the Committee of Experts. Dorothy Kenyon, a New York lawyer and judge, was well known to YWCA women, who recommended that she be included on the Committee of Experts as soon as it was rumoured that an American woman would be selected.[39] Born in 1888 into a wealthy New York family, Kenyon was educated at Smith College and then went on to study law at New York University. Active in the American Civil Liberties Union, the American Association of University Women, and the League of Women Voters, Kenyon had long-established connections and was well respected among American women's organisations.[40] When the Liaison Committee sought suggestions to forward to the League secretariat, Henrietta Roelofs immediately forwarded Kenyon's name to the World YWCA with a strong endorsement. After her appointment, when Kenyon made her initial visit to Geneva, Mary Dingman and Evelyn Fox arranged their usual round of introductions, luncheons and dinners under the auspices of the Women's Disarmament Committee to welcome Kenyon into their League of Nations world.[41] From that point onward they kept Kenyon well supplied with Liaison Committee and Disarmament Committee publications and provided their informed interpretation of international events for Kenyon's consideration.

Along with other women's NGOs in Geneva,[42] Dingman and Fox also fêted the other women delegates serving on the Committee of Experts and shared their views on widening the scope of the Inquiry, which the Committee of Experts initially proposed to limit to Western nations, where 'reliable' data could be gathered.[43] Moreover, they cultivated friendly relations with Hugh Mackinnon Wood of the League secretariat, the designated assistant to the Committee of Experts in the Inquiry. The Liaison Committee pushed Mackinnon Wood to use his influence with the Committee of Experts, persuading it to expand the scope of the Inquiry to include countries in the Middle East and South Asia, where women's rights and status were governed by Islamic and Hindu religious laws as well as by civil codes. Mackinnon Wood also supplied the Liaison Committee with reports and data that the League provided to the Committee of Experts, so that the women were well informed about the progress of the Inquiry during long months when the Inquiry proceeded through the work of the scientific institutes rather than in public sessions in Geneva.[44] Liaison Committee representatives in Geneva passed all this information on to their organisations' national chapters and the chapters were instructed to share information about the League Inquiry widely with other national and local women's groups around the globe.[45]

When the Committee of Experts met with the women's organisations at a last public meeting called in January 1939 to report on the status of the Inquiry, their conclusions were limited, a state of affairs that frustrated the women's organisations, which had been collecting data since 1935 and hoped for some substantial results to use in the campaign for women's equal rights. The Committee of Experts, however, emphasised the rigorous methods of scientific research; the Committee explained that much of the data that the women had submitted to the scientific institutes, such as statistics regarding women's participation in the political life of nations, was not useful or reliable from a scientific standpoint. Moreover, when the women's organisations had reported individual cases of discrimination, they had not provided sufficient scientific documentation. The scope of the Inquiry had been extended to include Middle Eastern and Asian nations as the women's organisations had desired, but this increased the work of the scientific institutes and the Committee of Experts estimated that it could not produce even a preliminary report for at least a year.[46]

In spite of its seeming lack of progress, the Inquiry continued quietly for the next several years. Even after Germany invaded Poland in September 1939 and Britain and France went to war with the fascist powers, the League continued international cooperation on some social questions, such as the Inquiry into the Status of Women. Finally, in 1941, the Inquiry was forced to cease work, and its findings were shelved. Dorothy Kenyon preserved some of the compiled reports, and these resurfaced when the women's international organisations lobbied to revive the Inquiry after the war ended and as the United Nations Organization (UNO) was formed.[47]

The denouement of the women's disarmament committee

By January 1939 the inevitability of war in Europe gripped the Geneva community. Women's NGOs, like the World YWCA, had already begun transforming their operations. YWCAs in Czechoslovakia and Austria began service to refugee populations that continued throughout the war. British YWCAs had opened job-training centres for Jewish émigrés who managed to escape from German territories.[48] Women's Disarmament Committee members also began planning their next stages of wartime activism. Evelyn Fox's duties at the World YWCA refocused on coordinating and expanding the YWCA's wartime refugee service. Laura Puffer Morgan left Geneva in early January. She returned to the United States to join the ranks of American internationalists who lobbied for greater

American involvement with the world conflicts in Europe and Asia and who envisioned a wartime world leadership role for Franklin Roosevelt.[49] From her home in London, Kathleen Courtney expressed her deep sadness at Morgan's departure, understanding that it portended the 'end of an era' of internationalist idealism:

> I simply hate the thought of your leaving Geneva without an immediate and definite prospect of return. I don't know when I felt anything of this sort so acutely. I shall miss you terribly in Geneva, both when I am there and when I am not there, for I have counted on you in innumerable ways perhaps even more than I realise myself. Your departure also gives me a pang because it seems to me to be as it were the end of an era. Do you remember that evening in February 1932 when you and your secretary came into the Hotel des Familles to meet Hilda Clark and me and how excited and hopeful we all felt then? How horribly times have changed, have they not?[50]

On behalf of the British Women's Peace Crusade, Courtney continued to correspond with Morgan and other American friends in the NCCCW who advocated the internationalist perspective in American foreign-policy circles.[51]

From Geneva, Dingman maintained contacts with Courtney and Morgan, seeking their advice on the Women's Disarmament Committee's next steps in light of the world crisis.[52] As she issued reports and news releases to Committee member organisations, Dingman also planned to return to the United States in autumn 1939. She hoped to work with American women's organisations to coordinate an international women's peace congress in conjunction with the NCCCW annual conference in January 1940, then to end her term as president of the Disarmament Committee and remain in America.[53] At a September meeting of the International Consultative Group – held soon after war was declared – Dingman and her fellow NGO leaders issued a statement of principles as many made plans to leave Geneva. With the future of the League of Nations unclear, the organisations continued to promote international cooperation or, as they defined it 'sane internationalism'. 'Directly and indirectly', the leaders asserted,

> organisations have done what they could to influence governments both in Geneva and, still more importantly, in the capitals of the Great Powers. Admittedly our success has been very limited, and today we are more than ever convinced of the necessity for patient educational propaganda, in season and out of season, for those principles and practices without which there is no hope of durable peace between nations.[54]

In October Geneva began to experience the effects of the war; Polish refugees began arriving in the city and shared their first-hand accounts of the horrors of war. Dingman planned her departure with a heavy heart.[55] Laura Dreyfus-Barney returned to Geneva in December to host Dingman's farewell dinner and to lead the long list of Dingman's friends and colleagues in praise of her devotion to the causes of peace and disarmament.[56]

From her home in Amsterdam, Rosa Manus had maintained an important connection with the Women's Disarmament Committee over the years, even though her direct involvement with Committee activities had been occasional. Family obligations had kept her in Holland, where she had worked to establish an archive for women's international organisations, based on the collected records that Aletta Jacobs bequeathed to her when Jacobs died in 1929. Together with the Dutch economics professor Posthumus van der Goot, Manus collected materials from women's groups and feminist libraries around the world after the archive opened in 1935. When the Germans overran Holland in 1940, the archive was confiscated and moved to Berlin; no doubt the Germans believed that documents collected by Rosa Manus, a Jewish feminist whose association with the 1936 World Congress for Peace tied her to the Communist world as well, contained dangerously subversive information that the Nazis wanted to suppress. When the Germans were defeated, the Soviets looted the archive and transported it to Moscow, where it remained until 2003. Then, after long negotiations, the papers that Rosa Manus collected and preserved were returned to the International Archive for the Women's Movement in Amsterdam, where they are currently housed.[57]

From Holland in 1939 Manus's letters to her close friends in America gave the European war a fearful immediacy, but they also revealed that Manus's focus was on the future:

> I am convinced that in Europe there are far more peace-loving people than war-loving people but the magnetism of that one man seems to paralyse everyone. Until last year the real gentlemen still believed they could make him act as a gentleman too!
>
> What are we to do? We are helpless and in a small neutral country like ours one can only see that everything is properly prepared at the frontiers, that is all; our army is pretty strong and everything is well organised. My sister's sons are of course doing their duty; I was on the field just amongst the soldiers when my nephew read out to his 150 men the war declaration on that dreadful Sunday afternoon; I thought I felt like sinking through the ground!
>
> I am glad your Cause and Cure of War Committee is trying to educate the women to create public opinion for joining the world organisation when the time comes.
>
> I certainly am thinking ahead too, and I think women should prepare now and demand already now that when peace negotiations start, at least some of the women should be in the committee with the men; 2) at that time they

must have ready a well prepared plan and 3) they must then see that in each and every country women are prepared to make public opinion support their plan.[58]

Rosa Manus did not survive the war. When war broke out in 1939, Manus organised the Amsterdam Women's Volunteer Corps, which was active in the Dutch anti-Nazi movement and opposed German influence in Holland. The Germans dissolved the Corps in 1940 and the Gestapo arrested Rosa Manus in April 1941. In a letter that Carrie Chapman Catt sent out to the women's organisations in July 1942, after rumours of Manus's death began circulating among her friends, Catt shared the reminiscence of another mutual friend: 'Memories of Rosa have been crowding in my mind. I can see her bustling around in Paris, Amsterdam, Berlin, and Istanbul. I'm sure that when the crisis came, she met it with courage. The same persistence which made her an organizer would stiffen her against the blows of fate.'[59] Later it was learned that Manus had been imprisoned in a succession of concentration camps until she died in Ravensbrück in 1943.[60]

After her return to the United States, Dingman began an active career on the lecture circuit, sharing her knowledge of international relations and preaching the gospel of international cooperation. When the Japanese attacked Pearl Harbor in December 1941 and the United States at last entered the world war, Dingman joined the Women's Action Committee for Victory and Lasting Peace to promote her vision of a cooperative world, in which women played an active role in politics and government. Dingman's often repeated message was the creed she lived by: 'If world peace is ever to be achieved, women all over this broad land of ours *must* be made to understand and shoulder their responsibilities. One woman alone can do little, but our united strength can accomplish miracles.'[61]

Notes

1 Donald S. Birn, *The League of Nations Union, 1918–1945* (Oxford: Clarendon Press, 1981), pp. 173–5; Gertrude Bussey and Margaret Tims, *Women's International League for Peace and Freedom, 1915–1965: A Record of Fifty Years' Work* (London: George Allen & Unwin, Ltd, 1965), p. 148.
2 WYWCA, Mary Dingman to Gertrude Baer, WILPF Chairman, 20 June 1935, box 258.
3 CCCW, Henrietta Roelofs to Kathleen Courtney, 3 December 1935, box 11.
4 JS, 'A call to women', c. June 1936, box 7.
5 JS, Mary Dingman to members of the executive board of the Disarmament Committee, 25 July 1936, box 10.

6 WYWCA, Mary Dingman to 'Dear colleague' [on Disarmament Committee], 12 August 1936, box 267.

7 WYWCA, Kathleen Courtney to Mary Dingman, 28 July 1936, box 267.

8 JS, Rosa Manus to Carrie Chapman Catt, 24 June 1936, box 7.

9 Morgan–Howes Papers, Laura Puffer Morgan, 'The Brussels Congress and the International Peace Campaign', 1936, box 2.

10 JS, Henrietta Roelofs, 'Report Rassemblement Universel Pour la Paix; International Peace Conference, Brussels Belgium', 3–8 September 1936, box 7.

11 MAD, 'Message to the assembly of the League of Nations, the voice of women', 1 October 1936, box 1.

12 Konni Zilliacus, League of Nations Secretariat Information Section in unpublished autobiography, *Challenge to Fear* (Spartacus Educational website: spartacus.schoolnet.co.uk/FWWleague.htm).

13 Bussey and Tims, *Women's International League for Peace and Freedom*, pp. 141–2; WYWCA, Message from World YWCA and Peace and Disarmament Committee to National YWCA Secretaries, 15 September 1936, box 267.

14 P & D Committee, Laura Puffer Morgan, 'The seventeenth assembly of the League of Nations' Peace & Disarmament Committee, press release no. 168, 28 October 1936.

15 P & D Committee, Laura Puffer Morgan, 'Conclusions reached concerning the possibility of mediation either by the League of Nations or by individual states in the Spanish Civil War', Peace and Disarmament Committee, press release no. 170, 12 November 1936.

16 P & D Committee, 'Certain ideological conflicts and their repercussions upon international relations', International Consultative Group, survey no. 11, 22 February 1937.

17 Morgan–Howes Papers, Laura Puffer Morgan, for *World Affairs Chronicle*, 2 March 1937, box 1.

18 MAD, 'Action taken re [Guernica] Spain' distributed by the Peace and Disarmament Committee, 29 April 1937, box 2.

19 P & D Committee, 'One hundred and first session of the League Council', Peace and Disarmament Committee, press release no. 217, 30 May 1938.

20 WYWCA, Dorothy Heneker to Mary Dingman, 14 May 1937; Kathleen Courtney to Mary Dingman, 14 May 1937, box 267.

21 MAD, Peace and Disarmament Committee annual report 1936–1937, September 1937, box 2.

22 WYWCA, Mary Dingman to member organisations of the Peace and Disarmament Committee, 30 September 1937, box 267; MAD, Mary Dingman to M. Vilhelms Munters, chairman of the advisory committee of twenty-three of the League of Nations, 5 October 1937, box 2.

23 MAD, Mary Dingman to member organisations of the Peace and Disarmament Committee, 6 October 1937, box 2.

24 WYWCA, Ruth Woodsmall, World YWCA to Tsai Kwei, China YWCA, 7 July 1938, box 218.

25 Beryl Haslam, *From Suffrage to Internationalism: The Political Evolution of Three British Feminists, 1908–1939* (New York: Peter Lang, 1999), p. 201.

26 Dorothy Kenyon Papers, Sophia Smith Collection, Smith College, Northampton, MA (hereafter DK), 'Geneva watches Austria', Peace and Disarmament Committee, press release no. 212, 30 March 1938, box 41.

27 P & D Committee, 'One hundred and first session of the League Council'.

28 Haslam, *From Suffrage to Internationalism*, p. 202.

29 WYWCA, Response to International Consultative Group survey 'Regarding the present activities of international organisations in Geneva', 9 March 1939, box 283.

30 KDC, 'The Peace and Disarmament Committee of the Women's International Organizations', c. September 1938, box 454.

31 MAD, Mary A. Dingman to family and friends, 31 January 1939, box 1.

32 MAD, Mary A. Dingman to family and friends, 22 October 1939, box 1.

33 DK, Elsie Zimmern to Dorothy Kenyon, 25 March 1938, box 39.

34 League of Nations Archives, Registry File 3A/36390/33769, Committee for the Legal Status of Women, First Session, Provisional Minutes, Second Meeting, 4 April 1938, 'Collaboration with the Women's International Organizations'.

35 Carol Miller, '"Geneva – the key to equality": inter-war feminists and the League of Nations', *Women's History Review* 3:2 (1994), pp. 237–9.

36 DK, League of Nations, status of women, report submitted by the first committee to the assembly, Kirsten Hesselgren (Sweden) Rapporteur, 25 September 1937. League of Nations Official A. 54. 1937. V, box 40.

37 Arnold Whittick, *Woman into Citizen: The World Movement Towards the Emancipation of Women in the Twentieth Century with Accounts of the Contributions of the International Alliance of Women, the League of Nations and the Relevant Organizations of the United Nations* (London: Athenaeum, 1979), pp. 130–2.

38 DK, 'League of Nations, committee for the study of the legal status of women, note by the secretariat on certain questions which require consideration', 3 January 1938, box 39.

39 DK, Henrietta Roelofs to Dorothy Kenyon, 3 December 1937, box 39.

40 Kate Weigand and Daniel Horowitz, 'Dorothy Kenyon, feminist organizing 1919–1963', *Journal of Women's History* 14 (2002), p. 126.

41 DK, Evelyn Fox to Dorothy Kenyon, 11 March 1938, box 39.

42 Liaison Committee representatives in Geneva included Margery Corbett Ashby, Emilie Gourd, representing the International Alliance of Women; Anne Weigle, representing the International Federation of University Women; Marguerite Nobs, representing the Union of Women for International Concord; Renee Girod, representing the International Council of Women; Evelyn Fox, representing the World YWCA; J. C. H. H. de Vinck, representing the International Union of Catholic Women; Alice Paul, representing the Women's Party International and the Consultative Committee on Women's Nationality, Dorothy Evans, representing Equal Rights International; Gertrude Baer, representing the Women's International League for Peace and Freedom; and Winifred Le Sueur, representing Open Door International.

43 WYWCA, Evelyn Fox to Cornelia van Asch van Wijck, 9 April 1938; Evelyn Fox to Elsie Zimmern, 9 April 1938, box 287.

44 WYWCA, Evelyn Fox to Hugh Mackinnon Wood, League of Nations, Committee on the Status of Women, 25 April 1938, box 287; League of Nations Archives, Registry File 3A/19189/13900, Evelyn Fox to Hugh Mackinnon Wood, 3 May 1938.

45 DK, Emilie Gourd, Corresponding Secretary, International Alliance of Women for Suffrage and Equal Citizenship, to President of the Alliance Auxiliaries, 24 May 1938, box 39.

46 DK, League of Nations Committee for the Study of the Legal Status of Women, Second Session, eighth meeting, 7 January 1939, box 40.

47 DK, Dorothy Kenyon to Malcolm Davis, Associate Director, Carnegie Endowment for International Peace, 1 July 1943, box 39; WYWCA, 'History of the Committee on the Legal Status of Women Appointed by the League of Nations in 1938', 12 September 1945, Liaison Committee of International Women's Organisations, Minutes, Correspondence, 1941–47.

48 RW, Marianne Mills to World's YWCA council members, 24 December 1938, box 43.

49 Morgan–Howes Papers, Peace and Disarmament Committee meeting minutes, 9 January 1939, box 7.

50 Morgan–Howes Papers, Kathleen Courtney to Laura Morgan, 11 January 1939, box 7.

51 JS, Kathleen Courtney to Josephine Schain, letters 1939–1940, box 11.

52 Morgan–Howes Papers, Mary Dingman to Laura P. Morgan, 3 May 1939, box 2.

53 WYWCA, Annual Report 1938–1939 Peace and Disarmament Committee of the Women's International Organisations, September 1939, box 283.

54 WYWCA, From International Consultative Group [on Disarmament and Peace Questions] 'Deputation to Mr. C. [Carl] J. Hambro, Chairman of the League's Supervisory Commission', 26 September 1939, box 284.

55 MAD, Mary A. Dingman to family and friends, 22 October 1939, box 1.

56 CCCW, Laura Dreyfus-Barney to Peace and Disarmament Committee Member Organizations, 14 December 1939, box 18.

57 Francesca de Haan, 'A "truly international" archive for the women's movement (IAV, now IIAV): from its foundation in Amsterdam in 1935 to the return of its looted archives in 2003', *Journal of Women's History* 16: 4 (2004), pp. 148–58.

58 JS, Rosa Manus to Josephine Schain, 9 October 1939, box 7.

59 MAD, Mary Dingman, Laura Puffer Morgan, and Laura Dreyfus-Barney to Members of the Women's Disarmament Committee, 20 July 1942, box 1.

60 de Haan, 'A "truly international" archive for the women's movement', p. 159.

61 MAD, 'From the Women's Action Committee for Victory and Lasting Peace', c. 1942, box 1.

Part II

Women's NGOs and politics of war, 1940–70

Activist leaders in Western-led women's organisations confronted faith-shaking events during the Second World War and yet they continued to adhere to the liberal feminist values that had inspired their interwar work. After war broke out in Europe in 1939 most women leaders in Allied nations shunned pacifism; they performed wartime service work inspired by patriotism and a sense of duty to preserve their national homelands in response to the fascist threat.[1] They spoke of their long-term goals – to promote transcendent human values and equal treatment for women – as 'universal' feminist goals. In performing war service work they continued to cultivate relationships to Allied government leaders and, in turn, the women's organisations earned their own measure of power and prestige. Yet during this era of war and dislocation for many Eastern European and Asian peoples the Western women's organisations faced many challenges to their claims to speak for 'humanity', or, more specifically, for the 'women of the world'. Consequently, they vigorously debated and steadily amended their vision of the post-war world order in response to these challenges.

The United States government and its Western European allies were also challenged by the post-war re-emergence of the Soviet Union as a rival axis of power. The Soviets opposed Western plans to reconstruct the post-war world following an ambitious world capitalist economic and geopolitical agenda and they objected to the West's nuclear weapons monopoly. The post-war rise of the socialist Soviet Union and its satellite-state sphere in Eastern Europe transformed global superpower relations into a state of Cold War and redefined the global governance system that the West had designed to mediate international relations.

Women's international organisations were also compelled to redefine their global women's agenda based on the new Cold War world order. Cold War East-West politics overruled visions of a collaborative 'one-world' community that many Western internationalists touted during the Second World War. In the immediate aftermath of the war socialist women proposed an alternative 'liberation' model in the international forums provided by the newly formed system of global governance, the United Nations Organization (UNO). Western women's campaigns for equal rights, for human rights and for the spread of liberal democratic governing systems patterned after those of the Western governments, all had to respond to the alternatives proposed by the theory of socialist democracy and the political rhetoric of non-Western women. The contest between Eastern and Western worldviews was particularly evident in the annual sessions of the Commission on the Status of Women (CSW) that soon supplanted the Liaison Committee of Women's International Organisations as the main forum for debate and collective activism of the women's international non-governmental organization (NGOs).

Nonetheless, within the CSW and in other government and intergovernmental bodies that addressed 'women's issues' in the post-war era Western-led organisations were remarkably successful in continuing to build relationships to government power, in shaping institutional discourses and in promoting their liberal feminist agendas among intergovernmental forums – even as socialist and other non-Western women contested their plans. A steady flow of information circulated among the Western-led NGOs, government representatives and the United Nations secretariat that benefited all parties and the women's NGOs provided the CSW delegates with their greatest support.

Among the women's organisations the World YWCA's wartime and post-war activities provide clear illustrations of the ways that Western-led organisations operated in the global governance sphere, how they influenced the agendas of intergovernmental bodies and were influenced by those bodies, and why governments and the United Nations secretariat recognised some of their so-called 'women's issues' as important and why others were not so acknowledged. While broader institutional considerations provided political opportunities for the success of women's organisations like the World YWCA, the influence of a few individuals – the 'organisational entrepreneurs' who provided vision, charisma, experience and expertise, and insider connections – cannot be overlooked.[2] The examples discussed here illuminate how one of these individuals, the World YWCA general secretary Ruth Woodsmall, built influential information-sharing and advisory relationships with the US State Department and with the various United Nations (UN) agencies that were organised to meet the needs of refugee populations displaced by wars, where American interests prevailed. In the post-war era, Woodsmall, an American woman, made key organisational decisions to withdraw from the Liaison Committee of the Women's International Organisations and to join the newly formed NGO networks that engaged directly with UN agencies in order to maximise the privileges associated with NGO consultative status to the United Nations Economic and Social Council agencies. Thereafter, YWCA programmes became more dependent on UN agency and government funding, and funding considerations increasingly influenced programming decisions. Finally Ruth Woodsmall also contributed in key ways to United States cultural diplomacy programmes to teach 'American democratic values' to Japanese and German women during the post-war military occupations of the defeated fascist powers in the late 1940s and early 1950s.

These specific examples based on YWCA experiences show how women's organisations operating within a male-led global governance system dominated by East-West superpower politics shaped global gender policy. The system placed limits on women's power and assumed a patriarchal world order where national security interests and militarism still trumped social and humanistic considerations and diplomacy in most cases of world conflict. Women's participation in the global governance system did not completely transform the system, as will be shown here. Women, too, acted according to their nationalistic political and cultural biases. Yet through the steady pressure of NGO activism women's power and status also became a concern of global governance bodies as did human rights more generally. Moreover, women's NGOs continued to collaborate with male-led NGOs to expand the influence of 'civil society' in shaping the agendas, norms and programmes of the intergovernmental agencies within the UN system.

Notes

1 Nicole Ann Dombrowski, 'Soldiers, saints or sacrificial lambs? Women's relationships to combat and the fortification of the home front in the twentieth century', in Nicole Ann Dombrowski (ed.), *Women and War in the Twentieth Century: Enlisted Without Consent* (New York: Garland Publishing Inc., 1999), p. 11.

2 Jutta M. Joachim, *Agenda Setting, the UN, and NGOs: Gender Violence and Reproductive Rights* (Washington, DC: Georgetown University Press, 2007), p. 33.

6 Ruth Woodsmall in Japan at girls' middle school during the World Young Women's Christian Association visitation, November 1947.

7 Ruth Woodsmall, director of the Women's Affairs Division of the Office of the Military Government of the United States in Germany, c. 1950.

5

Second World War activism and service

Women's international organisations plan for the post-war world

As war zones expanded across Europe women's organisations were forced to respond to racist hatred and violence directed against European-Jewish communities and other 'undesirable' populations, so named by the fascist states. The fascists' aid to General Franco during the Spanish Civil War, German annexation of Austria and Czechoslovakia, Italy's occupation of Albania, and Germany and the Soviet Union's alliance and subsequent invasion and division of Poland, all finally brought forth a declaration of war from British and French Allied powers in September 1939. All of these conflicts created waves of refugees seeking safety and asylum from brutal and merciless armies. Above and beyond the horrific genocide of over six million European-Jews that began with Adolf Hitler's attacks on 'non-Aryans' in 1933 and that escalated steadily into mass detentions followed by mass exterminations of the Jewish peoples within the reach of the German Third Reich during the 1940s, the Second World War surpassed the First World War in the use of violence and terror directed at civilian populations.[1] Without the power, moral or otherwise, to persuade governments to disarm and negotiate their way through political and economic conflicts during the 1930s women's international organisations were compelled to deal with the realities of the war that they could not prevent. Given the high value that women placed on preservation of human life, their war work focused on alleviating human misery and on planning for the post-war world.

Although women activists in the Liaison Committee member organisations were certainly discouraged that their peace work had failed so miserably they continued to plan for a post-war global community based on peaceful cooperation and democratic values. They envisioned a post-war world where women played equal roles with men in political as well as social institutions at the local, national and international levels. The political education they acquired at the League of Nations and as activists in their home counties during the interwar decades served as the foundation for women's wartime discussions of post-war reconstruction. Women's international organisations continued in every public and private forum open to them to express the themes that women's equal participation in all levels of government was necessary to ensure peace and to realise true democracy, and that women's rights were human rights that must be guaranteed in post-war societies. Western women and men in non-governmental organisations (NGOs) who shared an internationalist ethos believed that if the fascists triumphed in the world war then all hope for a peaceful, democratic world where human rights were respected would be destroyed.[2]

At the International Women's Suffrage Alliance (IWSA) Conference held in Copenhagen in July 1939 that took place as the Western powers contemplated a declaration of war against the fascist aggressors IWSA President Margery Corbett Ashby chastised the Western democracies for failing to incorporate women into the political sphere. The fascists had a theory – however objectionable and imperfectly implemented – that women should serve the state through their reproductive roles, providing the state with new citizens and soldiers and mothering the nation. In the Western democracies Corbett Ashby asserted:

> [M]en have no theory about women's place but accept them as an intrusion into 'man's sphere' with philosophic or annoyed patience. They make room for us by their side and yet do not elaborate a counter theory to that of fascism and say to the young women 'What kind of world do you women want, what form of society suits you, what handicaps do you want to be free from? I have my ideas and you can help or hinder me, but if we can pool our ideas and work for our common ideal no force can withstand us.'

She concluded that 'Democracies only survive if their theories of equality are logically carried out and women's needs and women's gifts are felt by men to be an intrinsic part of the community.'[3] Drafting a statement of principles the IWSA conference delegates declared:

> The woman's battle is that of all mankind. There can be no freedom for women when freedom is no longer a recognised right for every individual. There can be no justice or economic freedom for women, when all justice is dependent on the will of an oligarchy.
> Now we live through difficult times in which life based on our principles is at stake. Therefore women, with men, true to their fundamental principles, must defend a system which will lead to greater justice, freedom, real peace, general prosperity and more happiness for all.[4]

Thus women's international organisations set their wartime goal: to articulate their vision of a post-war democratic world society.

Mary Dingman and her fellow members of the Women's Disarmament Committee also began a discussion of the new world they desired in the summer of 1939 as they planned for an 'Intercontinental Conference of Women Leaders' to be held in conjunction with the annual January Conference on the Cause and Cure of War in Washington, DC. After she returned to the United States at the end of 1939 Dingman continued conference arrangements even though wartime travel restrictions prevented many European women from attending. Nonetheless an impressive group of women's organisation leaders from Europe, Latin America, Canada and India[5] together debated several crucial global governance issues: whether to reform the League or to create a new 'permanent world society' and whether collective security could effectively oppose aggressor nations in the future.[6] Fifty women gathered in Washington in January 1940 and their discussions produced various proposals for a post-war peace conference that would involve ordinary citizens as well as governments in order to place human welfare at the heart of any intergovernmental body that might be created.[7]

As the Washington women's conference discussed post-war issues the Women's International League for Peace and Freedom (WILPF) leader Gertrud Baer also began to float proposals for an International Declaration of Human Rights 'as a basis for whatever form the World State or Organisation may take in the coming new order'.[8] Baer, a German-Jewish woman, was forced to leave her European home during the war but she remained an active leader in the international women's movement and published a newsletter that circulated from her new home base in New York City.[9] Women's international organisation representatives on the Liaison Committee began to discuss Baer's ideas at their ongoing meetings in Geneva and London. They made lists of civil rights that must apply to every individual citizen regardless of sex, race or creed, and debated the rights of nations within international governance structures.[10] In 1941, after incorporating suggestions drawn from these discussions, Baer formulated a draft human rights convention that she entitled the 'International Declaration of the Rights of Man'; she forwarded the document to the London Liaison Committee for its consideration and support. Beginning with Article 1, 'The undersigned States pledge themselves to confer on all their inhabitants equal rights as to life, freedom, work and earnings, and to grant complete protection to all in their territories, without distinction of nationality, sex, race, language, religion, or conviction', and continuing through twelve additional articles specifying inviolable human rights, Baer's declaration concluded '[This Declaration] is the fundamental law for mankind throughout the whole world'.[11]

Yet even though the Liaison Committee generally supported the concept of an international declaration of human rights, several organisational members did not want the outspoken Gertrud Baer to speak for them. Since Baer had been living in the United States, the American chapter of WILPF had disassociated itself from Baer because the American WILPF leaders held firm to their absolute pacifist convictions. They supported the US government's continuing policy of neutrality in summer 1941 and Baer vigorously advocated armed opposition to the fascist powers.[12] The dilemma of whether to adhere strictly to pacifism and oppose war or to support the fight against fascist powers challenged Euro-American feminists once again, as it had in 1914. At this moment in history, however, the choice to support the war against the fascist powers seemed clear to many activist women. Henrietta Roelofs, for example, wrote to Kathleen Courtney in 1940 that American internationalists were 'doing all we can in our speaking to set forth clearly the alternatives which we are facing – the struggle between the two types of civilization and that it is Britain who stands between us and the loss of all we hold dear. . . . If Hitler's new world order controls the world then there will be no chance for us to move toward democracy and freedom.'[13]

While pacifists and isolationists still opposed American entry into the war throughout 1941, American internationalists including Henrietta Roelofs and Laura Puffer Morgan actively promoted American leadership in world affairs. As soon as the war broke out in Europe, American internationalists promoted American leadership in all realms of the battle against totalitarian fascism – as a combatant in the military struggle, as a model and champion of democracy and human rights, and as a leader in reconstructing peaceful and cooperative global relations in the post-war world. Yet even though the majority of American citizens opposed the spread of global fascism and felt an emotional kinship to nations under fascist attack, many still opposed direct military involvement in the wars in Europe or Asia and retained their anti-war convictions until Japan attacked United States territory.

Nonetheless, from 1939 onwards President Franklin Roosevelt's administration recognised the serious global threat to American national security and aided anti-fascist British, French and Chinese governments through economic measures and with logistical support. After June 1941, when Germany attacked the Soviet Union, the United States began to aid the USSR as well. By the summer of 1941 the United States had transformed its industries to become the 'arsenal of democracy' and supplied war materials including ships, planes, tanks, guns, as well as food and other materials to the anti-fascist Allies.[14]

In August 1941 President Roosevelt and British Prime Minister Winston Churchill met in conference off the coast of Newfoundland and devised a statement of principles that they agreed to uphold in the post-war world. The Atlantic Charter articulated the Anglo-American commitment to resolve conflicts peacefully, to oppose all wars of conquest, and to support national self-determination for all peoples, free trade, access to raw materials, international cooperation, just labour standards, social welfare and freedom of the seas. After the Atlantic Charter was concluded Winston Churchill predicted privately to his War Cabinet that American actions 'would become more and more provocative . . . [and Roosevelt] would look for an "incident" which would justify him in opening hostilities' against the fascist powers. Japan's attack on Pearl Harbor in December 1941 provided the incident that brought the United States into the war.[15]

In the 1939–41 period leading up to the US entry into the war, American internationalists actively shaped a new role for the United States in global governance. In autumn 1940 the League of Nations records and most of the secretariat staff were relocated to the campus of Princeton University in New Jersey for the duration of the war, while a few League offices were transported to London. Thereafter, American internationalists continued their campaign to transform the League into an intergovernmental organisation that could preserve the post-war peace and protect human rights, as well as expand America's political and economic power in the post-war world.

Since the end of the First World War Canadian-born internationalist James T. Shotwell had been involved through mostly informal advisory roles in advancing 'scientific progressive' policies to guide the United States government conduct of international relations. In various initiatives, such as those to establish the International Labour Organization (ILO) and to formulate the Kellogg-Briand Pact, Shotwell had worked on behalf of the Carnegie Endowment for Peace and in collaboration with US government officials to replace traditional methods of conducting diplomacy in secrecy with rational and empirically derived collective agreements determined by groups of professional 'experts.' In 1939 when he was a professor at Columbia University, Shotwell established the Commission to Study the Organization of Peace.[16] The Commission conducted nationwide study groups and sponsored public debates. The outcomes of these meetings were shared in a series of radio broadcasts that focused on 'the changing nature of war, the aftermath of the World War, disarmament, existing international institutions, the problems of America and the Far East, an inter-democracy federal union, the possible bases of organizing peace in Europe, peaceful change, peace enforcement, markets, and raw materials'.[17]

The American Association of University Women, along with several other NGOs, sponsored the Commission. Nonetheless its 'expert' members – the scholars, government officials, lawyers and businessmen who were charged with determining 'the fundamental bases of lasting peace' – included few women. As the Commission itself admitted, women's contributions to the Commission were 'inconspicuous' until the American National Council of Women (NCW) surveyed the 'feminine viewpoint' and presented its findings to the Commission in 1940.[18] The NCW polled a wide range of American women's organisations regarding provisions that must be included in a post-war settlement in regard to war debts and other costs of war, settlement of post-war national boundaries and dissolution of colonies, disarmament, protection of women's and human rights, migration, tariffs and world trade and economic resources, and protection of children in regard to their health, nutrition, housing and education, sending the results of their polls to the Commission experts.[19]

Like the NCW, the Young Women's Christian Association (YWCA) called on its members to think hard about the post-war world and to make their ideas and interests known to political leaders. Internationalist YWCA women deplored 'selfish nationalism' and 'sinful aggression' that 'opposed God's will' and destroyed world peace, yet their strong Christian religious faith prevented them from retreating from the new demands of wartime humanitarian service work. Indeed, their wartime experiences convinced YWCA leaders more than ever that a global network of women partnered in cross-cultural service associations was necessary to preserve humanity, so argued the World YWCA general secretary, Ruth Woodsmall, as war broke out in Europe in 1939.[20] Ruth Woodsmall delivered several speeches addressing the topic 'Building a new world' in the United States during 1941 and 1942; she urged her female audiences to adopt a Christian internationalist perspective to support post-war reconstruction initiatives:

> We must ask ourselves unflinchingly: what kind of world are we ourselves building? Are we deluding ourselves that we can live in a compartment kind of world in which we hope to keep our *own* security, our *own* freedom, oblivious to the security or freedom of others? What kind of a world do we really want? For we only build the type of world that we believe in. Are we prepared in order to achieve it? These are the questions which only we ourselves can answer . . .[21]

Ruth Woodsmall, born in Atlanta, Georgia in 1883, was the daughter of Harrison S. Woodsmall, a lawyer and teacher, and Mary Elizabeth Howes, an art teacher, and the sister of Helen Woodsmall Eldridge, a missionary who served in India. She grew up in Indiana where her Christian home became a centre for visiting missionaries. She studied liberal arts at the University of Nebraska and then completed her master's degree in English at Wellesley College in 1906. Between 1906 and 1917 she taught classes and served as principal at high schools in Colorado and Nebraska. During the First World War she joined the YWCA of the USA's wartime service operations directing Hostess Houses for soldiers in training at Camp Pike in Arkansas and for American troops fighting in France.

After the war, Woodsmall became a YWCA foreign secretary; she was sent to the Middle East where she served as the regional executive secretary until 1928. During these years and in the two years following on from a fellowship from the Laura Spellman Rockefeller Foundation she conducted research on modernising changes that impacted on women's lives in Islamic and Asian societies. From 1930 to 1932 Woodsmall travelled throughout South and East Asia as a member of the John D. Rockefeller-sponsored Layman's Foreign Mission Inquiry for China, Japan, India and Burma. She interviewed native Christian women in these countries about the impact that Christian values had on gender and other traditional social relationships. Her research resulted in several books published in the 1930s: *Eastern Women Today and Tomorrow* and *Moslem Women Enter a New World.* Because of her extensive international experience and sharp intellect in 1935 the World YWCA Executive Board hired Woodsmall for the post of general secretary at its Geneva headquarters.[22]

Following her appointment as general secretary Woodsmall expanded further the World YWCA's relationships with other international organisations that also focused on women and youth. As Woodsmall took on the most visible public leadership position at the YWCA, collaborations with the League of Nations disarmament initiatives and with the League-sponsored Inquiry into the global status of women continued, as did the YWCA's cooperation with League efforts to develop international conventions to prohibit trafficking of women and children and in numerous studies and programmes launched by the ILO regarding women's work. In addition to ongoing projects with intergovernmental agencies and with sister members of the Liaison Committee, under Woodsmall's direction the YWCA also worked closely with several Geneva-based international Christian organisations including the World Council of Churches, the World Student Christian Federation and the World Young Men's Christian Association.[23] As soon as the European war broke out in 1939 the YWCA joined with these organisations to form the Emergency Committee of Christian Organizations (ECCO). ECCO coordinated relief measures for refugees, prisoners of war and other internees with the Red Cross and with various emergency relief committees formed by other NGO associates.[24]

Due to the relationships that Ruth Woodsmall embraced and expanded after 1935, the World YWCA established a long record of collaborative associations with a wide range of world organisations and advocated Christian internationalist and liberal feminist values through these networks throughout the 1930s and 1940s. During wartime the YWCA extended its influence within joint initiatives launched by women's and other NGOs and built its reputation as a powerful and central voice for women's concerns among Allied intergovernmental bodies. Nevertheless, the YWCA's moral compass did not always point clearly towards the most humane actions as the following episodes reveal.

The Liaison Committee faces wartime challenges

As the war raged, women's international organisations continued to debate whether the Liaison Committee was a body that could speak collectively for its member organisations. The women's associations believed in the power of women's collective voice but, at times, individual organisations would not support specific actions that a few members of the London Liaison Committee tried to initiate during the war. Una Saunders represented the World YWCA at the London Liaison Committee meetings and corresponded regularly with Ruth Woodsmall at YWCA headquarters in Geneva and Washington, DC and sought out Woodsmall's guidance regarding YWCA positions and Liaison Committee actions. After 1939 several women tried to persuade the Liaison Committee member organisations to take bolder stands on human rights issues. Katherine Bompas of the International Women's Suffrage Alliance and Madame Grabinska, a Polish women's organisation leader who was living in exile in London, pushed Liaison Committee members to issue explicit statements of principle regarding their demands for women's equal rights, and to condemn the German atrocities against Jewish and other persecuted peoples in Europe. In 1941 they proposed that the Liaison Committee issue the following statement on post-war reconstruction:

> Believing in the Fatherhood of God and the Brotherhood of Man and therefore in the dignity and worth of human personality, we maintain that all schemes of reconstruction and post-war settlement should recognize the inviolable right of the individual to life and bodily integrity, the right to worship and earn, to contract, to possess and use property, to marry and participate in family, civic, and national life, to speak and to write according to the conscience and ability of the individual, irrespective of *sex*, race, creed, or class . . .
>
> Lastly expressing unqualified condemnation of the fact that the aggressors in the present war are, in territories occupied by them, applying measures directed against civilian populations in defiance of the most sacred laws of humanity as well as of the law of nations, through a policy of extermination and spoliation against:
> a. individuals . . .
> b. spiritual values . . .
> c. material values . . .

and that a regime which maintains a reign of terror over nations and individuals in the name of a so-called new order, represents a terrible decline in the standard of civilisation.

We declare that it is necessary to prepare without delay suitable plans to ensure that the world of tomorrow shall be made secure by a lasting peace and freed forever from the menace of political hegemony.[25]

Most of the representatives on the London Liaison Committee agreed with Margery Corbett Ashby that work for women's equal rights should proceed as a separate initiative by the individual member organisations but that the condemnation of the fascist powers should be released by the whole Liaison Committee as a joint statement of Protest Against Disregard of International Law and of Dictates of Humanity, clearly conveying the women's organisations' unity. Yet the joint statement of protest caused further debate and was amended several times before the Liaison Committee organisations publicly released it to the international press in November 1942.[26]

Una Saunders believed that international organisations with national chapters still operating in fascist states – such as the World YWCA – could not support a statement that might cause their chapters to suffer political reprisals. She believed that each organisation should decide independently whether to issue anti-fascist statements or not; this was not a matter for Liaison Committee collective action. Moreover she did not believe that she had the authority to sign a Liaison Committee statement on behalf of the YWCA without the express approval of the YWCA Executive Board.[27] Ruth Woodsmall agreed with Saunders' reasoning and further clarified the YWCA's position: 'We cannot indulge in condemnation protest statements. It is not the function, as you say, for an international women's group – and particularly of a world Christian group.'[28]

Madame Grabinska vehemently disagreed and she continued to prod the women's organisations to denounce fascist terrorism and policies of genocide. She appealed to the women's organisations to exercise their moral power regardless of politics: 'The least that women's organisations can do, though unable to give practical help, is to give open expression to their moral indignation, and political changes which happen to occur cannot affect the moral issue, which remains the same and it is only with the moral, not the political aspect, with which the resolution is concerned. After the war the women of persecuted countries will ask "what attitude did women in the free countries take up and how did they show their horror at our sufferings?"'[29]

As the London Liaison Committee member organisations continued to debate and edit the Protest Against Disregard of International Law and of Dictates of Humanity they also took steps to provide some practical help for women and girls in occupied countries who would be liberated when – they hoped – the Allies won the war. Anticipating great needs for trained social workers to provide health, nutrition and other social services in European nations after the war ended, the Liaison Committee formed an Allied Advisory Committee that received aid from the British War Council and established emergency training programmes for social workers. Kathleen Courtney organised the training programme and recruited British women as well as European refugees from Poland, Czechoslovakia and Yugoslavia who were living in London. As Courtney described the Liaison Committee's training programmes in June 1942: 'experts in social science gave their advice; the National Council of Girls Clubs made the services of their organisers available; lecturers and teachers – experts in their subjects – were found willing to help; rooms for both the lectures and for a common room were put at our disposal, and the course is now successfully running in London.'[30]

Also by mid-1942 both the British War Office and US State Department had documented evidence regarding the Jewish extermination programme that German forces systematically followed as they occupied Soviet and Polish territories. Already the Jewish ghetto in Warsaw had been decimated, its population reduced by over 300,000. Exterminations at the Auschwitz internment camp in Poland had begun and the German Nazi death camps would claim the lives of over six million Jewish victims by the end of the war. Yet the British and United States governments failed to rescue or find safe havens for Jewish refugees who fled from the genocide that Adolf Hitler's forces unleashed until after 1944.[31] By the end of 1942 Madame Grabinska also provided testimonies documenting the Nazi atrocities to the Liaison Committee as she shared copies of the Polish *Fortnightly Review* with Committee members. In its December issue the *Review* reported:

> Since July 22nd last anything from several dozen to several hundred Jews have been murdered everyday in Warsaw, by shooting in the streets and houses. These murders are committed every day during round-ups of people who are carried off to be killed, Among six to ten thousand people are rounded up every day, for deportation; between fifty and a hundred old people, cripples, and infirm are taken to the cemetery to be shot and buried. If anyone has any doubt whether it would be possible to kill off five, six, or ten thousand people in one day, they can be convinced by the thousands of witnesses at Otwock, Rembertow, Siedice, Minsk Mazowieki, Lomza, and many more localities, People at each of these places have seen anything from two to ten thousand people murdered in the course of a few hours.[32]

At last moved to take some action, Liaison Committee members appealed to their governments to aid Jewish refugees who fled from German-occupied territories. In November 1942 the organisational members on the Liaison Committee – including the YWCA – finally signed and published the Protest Against Disregard of International Law and of Dictates of Humanity. For this somewhat delayed action they earned the gratitude of the Women's International Zionist Organisation and recognition from the American first lady, Eleanor Roosevelt.[33]

In 1943 debates over feminist strategies continued when the Liaison Committee organised a Conference on the Status of Women in the Postwar World. The purpose of the conference attended by over 100 international women leaders who resided in London was to discuss strategies to promote women's equality in the future but also to record the history of the League of Nations Inquiry on the Status of Women and the Liaison Committee's role initiating and supporting the Inquiry.[34] In a further effort to document its accomplishments the Liaison Committee also published a booklet entitled 'Women and the Post-war World' that summarised the Committee's wartime service work and listed its wartime resolutions pledging support for the equal status of men and women and women's equal right to work in the post-war era and its protest against war crimes and promotion of human rights.[35] This publication was part of a concerted campaign that Liaison Committee members directed at the Allied governments urging them to include women in United Nations Organization (UNO) intergovernmental agencies as they were being established to reconstruct the post-war world.[36] The United Nations Relief and Rehabilitation Administration (UNRRA) was one such agency where the Liaison Committee women's organisations believed they could and should play important roles.[37]

YWCA wartime service: a case study in women's internationalism

The World YWCA with national and local chapters spread far and wide throughout Europe and East Asia focused much of its war work on service to persecuted populations who became prisoners of war and refugees in efforts to address human needs that the governments neglected. Throughout the 1930s anti-Semitism and economic nationalism weakened and restricted the Western European governments' aid to Jewish peoples who were desperate to emigrate from their German and Eastern European homelands. Consequently the League of Nations' response to the persecuted Jewish populations was very limited even after the fascist powers withdrew from the League.[38] According to Evelyn Fox who joined a Liaison Committee delegation that delivered a resolution urging the League to 'organise relief and assistance by every possible means' for the millions of refugees displaced by the Nazi blitzkrieg campaigns of spring

1940, the League secretariat wanted to provide aid but had no funds or authorisation from the League member states to do so. Evelyn Fox wrote to Elsie Harper of the YWCA of the USA:

> The League is handicapped by a total lack of financial resources. Hence in regard to the financial aspect of the problem the support of the United States is most important. If the American Government could come in on this scheme and could in any way guarantee support it might make all the difference between the life and death of millions of people.[39]

Yet the US government's response to the refugee problem was limited too. The US immigration policy dating from the 1924 National Origins Act had defined specific quotas regarding numbers of immigrants admitted from each country and it discriminated against immigrants from Southern and Eastern Europe, the regions of Europe where Jewish populations were under attack. Moreover American immigration officials strictly enforced entry rules for immigrants, turning away those who had health problems, or could not guarantee that they had financial resources to support themselves, or had a criminal past. Yet German state-sponsored terrorism had often ruined the health of immigrants who sought refuge, the National Socialist government laws prohibited Jewish peoples from taking any savings or property out of the country, and many of those who fled had also broken other German laws and so were labelled criminals. Adding further barriers to Jewish immigration to the United States, American labour groups and anti-Communist conservatives opposed lifting immigration quotas for various so-called 'nationalistic' reasons believing the European immigrants would fill jobs that employed American workers or that European-Jewish refugees would introduce radical and subversive ideas to undermine 'American values'.[40]

Beginning in the autumn of 1938 YWCA women in Czechoslovakia ministered to the thousands of refugees who fled to Prague, Brno and other cities in efforts to escape the fascist onslaught. Unlike some other local relief organisations, the YWCA did not turn away Jewish refugees but converted its club rooms and camps into dormitories and coordinated services, resources and funds from various municipal sources. Local YWCAs provided baths and meals as well as shelter and care for displaced women and children. The World YWCA also helped young Eastern European women immigrate to England where they were given shelter and job training by local British YWCA chapters.[41] Other national and local European YWCAs initiated similar refugee services as needs arose and the World headquarters assisted with moral and material support. From 1938 onwards the majority of Evelyn Fox's work assignments involved travel to various Eastern European cities and, after 1940, she frequently travelled to southern France, in order to assess refugee needs and to bring World YWCA news to the refugee centres.

In mid-1939 the World YWCA published an appeal to Christians worldwide to respond to the needs of the Jewish refugees with Christian compassion and material aid rather than giving in to anti-Semitic and nationalist fears and continuing to ignore the refugee problem:

> Surely Christian teaching demands neighborliness, friendship, love and forgiveness, even of one's enemies. This is the stern reality of our faith. There are others – and they represent a fairly large group of Christians – who would do something for the refugees, for their Jewish neighbors, and for stemming the tide of anti-Semitism. It is for these that the Church and its auxiliary agencies, such as the YWCA, must provide leadership, guidance, and a programme and plan of action.[42]

By 1940 YWCA women provided refugee, internee and prisoner-of-war services in Poland, Romania, Hungary, France and Germany in collaboration with the Red Cross, the International Save the Children Fund, the Young Men's Christian Association (YMCA), European governments and other American mission societies.[43] Acting with these agencies the YWCA provided emergency relief, but soon YWCA work evolved into ministering to spiritual needs, and developing language classes, job skills training, recreation and other programmes for the longer-term rehabilitation of those who fled from the war zones.[44] YWCA publications printed first-hand accounts of refugee experiences to emphasise the human dimension of the war and to cultivate compassion and empathy within its organisational ranks and beyond.[45]

Ruth Woodsmall more than any other single individual within the Association defined the YWCA wartime service that laid the foundations for post-war reconciliation. Woodsmall outlined the wartime tasks of the YWCA, balancing spiritual directives with practical service in a list that she sent to national chapters in January 1940, beginning with the 'primary task of every National Association is to help their members in their mental and spiritual struggle to find and obey God's will in their own situation . . . A Christian movement like the YWCA can render no greater service . . . than to give clear and convincing expression to the essential verity of our Christian faith.' Her list followed with injunctions to prepare for the post-war peace by supporting wartime labour laws that safeguarded labour standards for women factory workers, to study economics and political affairs in order to participate in post-war public life, and to provide critical wartime service to refugees. As Woodsmall concluded her appeal for wartime study and service she reminded Association women: 'These claims for service offer an unusual opportunity to demonstrate the central Christian purpose of the organisation . . . The YWCA should use this unusual opportunity . . . to widen the field of its contact with women workers, extend its area of influence and increase its leadership.'[46] World YWCA President Cornelia van Asch van Wijck worked closely with Woodsmall throughout Woodsmall's tenure as general secretary and it was her opinion that 'the World's YWCA [became] known, and favourably known, to Kings and Queens, Presidents of Republics, Ambassadors and Statesmen, diplomatists, educationalists . . . largely due to Ruth Woodsmall's skill in seeing where links should be formed, and in forming them.'[47]

Woodsmall's vision was put into practice by Evelyn Fox who coordinated YWCA services and by new staff members who joined the World organisation during the war. Beginning in 1940, Danish secretary Benedicte Wilhjelm coordinated service work with the YMCA War Prisoners Aid organisation in Berlin and after November 1942 Alice Arnold took over this increasingly dangerous work.[48] Dr Alice Arnold, a Swiss woman born in 1904 who earned her doctorate in law at the University of Leipzig in Germany, had begun full-time service to 'stateless' refugees who had fled to Geneva where she worked for the International Red Cross in 1940. In 1942 the World YWCA hired Alice Arnold and sent her to work in Berlin where the World organisation maintained contact with the struggling German YWCA led by Hulda Zarnack.[49] As soon as war was officially declared in 1939 German authorities pressured Zarnack to sever ties with the World office but she refused to do so.[50] Nonetheless she was forced to restrict YWCA activities to Bible study classes for adult women only.[51] When government restrictions made it impossible for the German YWCA to provide educational, recreational or spiritual services to women prisoners of war and internees as other European associations had established, the World YWCA was allowed to send members of its World staff into Germany to coordinate those services with other volunteer international agencies. Ruth Woodsmall was admitted into Germany to meet with Zarnack through 1940 with special permissions secured through the German Church Ministry.[52]

Likewise, the French national YWCA was not allowed to operate within the German-occupied zones of France. In southern France the YWCA worked through the Comité Inter-Mouvements Auprès des Evacués (CIMADE). CIMADE was a joint committee organised to provide service to French refugees that was formed by the YMCA, YWCA, the World Student Christian Movement, the Boy Scouts and Girl Guides. German armies had invaded France after they overran Belgium in May 1940 and a mass exodus of over eight million French civilians fled the blitzkrieg into the south of France. In June the French government led by Marshal Philippe Pétain signed an armistice with Germany and his 'collaborationist' government then negotiated the terms of repatriation for the refugees in the south. Those who refused German citizenship were not allowed to return to their homes. Nor were 'Jews, communists, socialists, foreigners' who fell outside the bounds of German citizenship allowed to repatriate. After the Germans closed off repatriation in November one million refugees remained in unoccupied southern France. Among them French civilians from the regions of Alsace and Lorraine refused as a group to return to their homes under German terms and remained in the south until the war ended.[53]

Madeline Barot who joined the YWCA in 1939 and CIMADE in 1940, not only worked with refugee populations setting up camps and finding homes for the refugees with southern families, but also supported French resistance efforts and led groups of Jews who fled from the Nazis across the borders into neutral Switzerland. CIMADE workers provided the Jewish émigrés with false identification papers and passports and conducted the escort work themselves because, as Barot explained, 'It didn't seem wise to trust our "travellers" to professional agents, who seemed too conspicuous or dishonest. We had to accompany them ourselves.'[54] After the war ended Barot described CIMADE activities during the first years of war:

> CIMADE took charge of work and made the relief of those in concentration camps its main objective. The camps were multiplying because the Nazis were interning political refugees from Spain and from Central Europe. Jewish deportees began to arrive in these camps and, by autumn 1940, about 70,000 were interned . . .
>
> In August 1942 came the beginning of the great tragedy – the mass deportations of the Jews. The 'deportables' were crowded into wagons which bore them across the border to an unknown fate; to death. The CIMADE staff of Rivesaltes were on hand, arguing step by step, the case of each of those under their care. If CIMADE staff did not succeed in saving their charges in this way, they often helped them to escape.
>
> The director hid the residents in the woods and on farms. The alarm increased and a system of watchers was set up in a certain house, which, although isolated by woods, commanded a view of the neighbouring roads. At the slightest sign of danger, those who were threatened would disappear. A tunnel, dating no doubt from the time of Huguenot persecutions, provided refuge.[55]

Although Britain suffered greatly under German bombing raids from 1940 onward, the nation remained free of German occupation. German bombs that flattened large sections of British cities destroyed many British YWCA buildings but YWCA operations nonetheless expanded during the wartime – even more so than they had during the First World War. British YWCA women along with their sisters in the Liaison Committee organisations continued to meet in London and together coordinated home front war production and relief work and found homes and provided job training for European refugees. According to a British YWCA report, by early 1940 the YWCA was also 'officially recognized as *the* women's organisation to serve women's units of the Navy, Army Air Force, and the Military Nurses. A great part of its emergency war work consists in providing leisure time facilities for these mobilised girls and women.'[56] In cooperation with the British YMCA, the YWCA also served British armed forces overseas, opening clubs, hostels and canteens, and supporting British troops in many capacities.[57]

Operating outside the war zones the American and Canadian YWCAs also provided some direct services to war refugees who immigrated to North America. More importantly, these national chapters raised emergency funds for YWCAs that provided refugee services in Europe and China. Most of the United States and Canadian YWCA war work was devoted to working with women in home front industries and serving men and women in their nations' militaries. In January 1941 the YWCA of the USA joined the United Service Organization (USO) formed by the US government to coordinate services for American armed forces.[58]

American and Canadian women also played a larger role than previously on the World YWCA Executive Committee as the world organisation opened up an office in Washington, DC in September 1940 to serve as a temporary wartime headquarters. Although the Geneva office also remained open during the war and was staffed by Evelyn Fox and Benedicte Wilhjelm and other volunteers, travel in and out of neutral Switzerland, surrounded by war zones, was difficult and dangerous. In spite of wartime challenges Ruth Woodsmall continued to travel throughout Europe, the Middle East, and Asia, but she travelled from the organisation's new Washington, DC base. Located in the United States national capital the World YWCA collaborated closely with the US State Department during the war and in its immediate aftermath. Woodsmall cultivated relationships with the US government officials, meeting, for example, with Ruth Shipley at the Passport Division who facilitated YWCA wartime travel arrangements into and out of war zones.[59] These relationships also led to further expansion of YWCA war service work after the United States entered the war in December 1941 and allied with the British, Free French, Chinese and Soviet governments against the combined fascist forces.

After the United States joined the anti-fascist Allied Powers who christened themselves the United Nations in January 1942, neither government aid for war refugees nor rescue of Jewish peoples increased significantly until 1944. Until that time volunteer agencies including the YWCA continued to provide the majority of refugee services. Private donations funded their efforts. At the end of 1943, however, the forty-four governments of the Allied Powers established UNRRA to meet the tremendous demands for emergency services for refugees in Europe and Asia that the voluntary agencies could not fulfil, including food, fuel, clothing, emergency shelter, public health and medical care. Headed by American director generals – first Herbert Lehman and later Fiorello LaGuardia – UNNRA developed relief policies and administered a $4 billion budget that was donated by member governments. Most of the budget funding, $2.7 billion, flowed from the United States government. Consequently, the United States exerted strong political influence over the agency whenever it could. Over the life of the agency, until it was dissolved in 1947, UNRRA provided relief for over one million displaced persons during the war and helped to repatriate refugees when the war ended.[60]

As soon as Allied government representatives began to organise UNRRA in December 1943 Ruth Woodsmall wrote to the United States representative, Francis Sayre, and proposed a meeting to discuss the refugee services that volunteer agencies had provided and to promote affiliation with UNRRA.[61] In February 1944 Woodsmall met with Mary Craig McGeachy who had been appointed as director of welfare for UNRRA and who was charged with establishing relationships between UNRRA and the NGOs.

McGeachy was well known to Woodsmall and the women's international organisations. Born into an Ontario-Scottish family in 1901, McGeachy joined the Student Christian Movement at the University of Toronto during the First World War and developed an interest in international affairs and in the newly formed League of Nations. After graduation and several years' experience teaching history and English, McGeachy set off for a year of travel in Europe. Not wanting to return to Canada after she arrived in Europe, McGeachy found work with the League of Nations secretariat in Geneva. From 1928 onwards she was employed in various League offices, with advancing responsibilities, until the war broke out. After helping to transport League records to London she went to work for the British government and its newly established Ministry of Economic Warfare. She maintained close contacts with women's international organisations through the London Liaison Committee. After 1943, McGeachy concentrated on post-war planning in her Ministry work and with women's organisations. In 1944 McGeachy went to work with UNRRA and moved to her new office in Washington, DC.[62]

At their February 1944 meeting Woodsmall and McGeachy discussed the relationship that UNRRA hoped to form with non-governmental agencies. McGeachy noted that after the Allied powers defeated fascist forces and reoccupied territories in Greece and the Balkans, refugee services would be expanded and relief workers employed by NGOs could play key roles. While UNRRA could not pay the relief workers' salaries, McGeachy offered travel and expense funds if the workers operated under UNRRA supervision. In regard to the relief workers that UNRRA planned to hire directly McGeachy assured Woodsmall that men and women would be considered equally on the basis of their qualifications and no job categories would be restricted to men only.[63]

Following this meeting Woodsmall recommended numerous qualified women social workers to fill UNRRA posts in the occupation zones. She also invited McGeachy to speak to YWCA women regarding 'Recent Developments in UNRRA – Trends and Underlying Policies'.[64] As UNRRA programmes developed, the United States and British governments assumed responsibilities for administering relief in separate zones of the liberated countries; within those zones American and British YWCA secretaries worked under their home nations' UNRRA supervision. The World YWCA also sent international staff to establish relief work in the liberated territories, working through local YWCA chapters when they could be found.

In addition, the YWCA maintained joint operations with international Christian organisations on the Emergency Committee that had formed in Geneva in 1939 and these organisations shared information and developed a common approach to their cooperative work with UNRRA.[65] Although it was not problem free, Woodsmall's close relationship with Mary McGeachy facilitated fruitful working relationships with UNRRA and with its successor agency, the International Refugee Organization (IRO) that the UN established in 1948 to deal with refugee populations who could not or would not return to their countries of origin.[66]

The small World YWCA professional staff that had remained in Geneva had built up an admirable record of refugee and internee service throughout the war. Benedicte Wilhjelm and Evelyn Fox travelled from Geneva into France and back on a regular basis, monitoring and facilitating YWCA collaborations with Madeline Barot and CIMADE. As the Allies liberated France in 1944, CIMADE aided the small numbers of Jews who had survived the concentration camp at Drancy and also began internee service to French collaborators who were imprisoned by the Allied liberation forces.[67] Dr Alice Arnold had continued her work with refugees and prisoners of war in Berlin and Austria in conjunction with the YMCA and planned to assist with the repatriation process. In the spring of 1945 through her connections with the International Red Cross Arnold travelled into Poland to meet with women who had been imprisoned in Warsaw.[68]

World YWCA Executive Board member Elsa Bernadotte Cedergren, the Swedish comtesse de Wisborg, had also travelled with her husband, Hugo Cedergren who directed YMCA wartime service to prisoners of war, to refugee and internment camps across Europe throughout the war. Elsa Cedergren wrote frequent reports about camp conditions for women and children and sent them to Ruth Woodsmall. The YWCA published these accounts in association journals and they formed the basis of the YWCA's decision to continue rehabilitative services to refugee populations when the war ended.[69] Defining the value of YWCA services to internees in Germany Elsa Cedergren wrote in 1944:

> The German government allows a secretary of the World's YWCA [Alice Arnold] to visit the British and American women in the internment camps, and I have been permitted to go with her. The Red Cross is doing all it can for the internees, but the YWCA is the only women's organisation allowed to visit the camps, and its representatives bring something which no one else can. We are the only women from outside the country in which they are interned whom these women ever meet, and to see the faces of women who do not belong to the enemy country, to know that we have come to try to make life a little easier and better for them means a great deal to them.[70]

As the war concluded, the YWCA continued its work with European refugees through associations with UNRRA, ECCO and CIMADE. After 1948 it collaborated with the newly formed IRO and expanded its mission to serve refugee populations beyond Europe.[71] After 1950, the YWCA collaborated with the UN High Commission on Refugees (UNHCR) that replaced the IRO. Throughout these years Alice Arnold continued to direct YWCA refugee service as her leadership role in forming World YWCA policy on social and international questions also increased. In 1947, commenting on YWCA service to war refugees in Asia, Arnold reminded YWCA women that 'our personal and collective Christian responsibility is at stake in this matter'.[72] Under Alice Arnold's guidance YWCA refugee programmes expanded over the post-war decades and corresponding relations with governments and UN agencies expanded and became closer as well.

Notes

1 Nicole Ann Dombrowski, 'Soldiers, saints or sacrificial lambs? Women's relationships to combat and the fortification of the home front in the twentieth century', in Nicole Ann Dombrowski (ed.), *Women and War in the Twentieth Century: Enlisted Without Consent* (New York: Garland Publishing Inc., 1999), pp. 9–10.
2 KDC, Henrietta Roelofs to Kathleen Courtney, 20 October 1940, box 456.
3 Arnold Whittick, *Woman into Citizen: The World Movement Towards the Emancipation of Women in the Twentieth Century with Accounts of the Contributions of the International Alliance of Women, the League of Nations and the Relevant Organizations of the United Nations* (London: Athenaeum, 1979), pp. 137–8.

4 P & D Committee, 'News bulletin', press release no. 263, September 1939.

5 CCCW, List of women invited to Washington, DC conference by Mary Dingman, 27 December 1939, box 21.

6 CCCW, Letter of invitation from Mary Dingman, 4 January 1940, box 21.

7 MAD, 'Some essential elements of a permanent world society', 26 January 1940, box 2.

8 CCCW, Laura Dreyfus-Barney to Peace and Disarmament Committee Member Organisations, 14 December 1939, box 18.

9 Leila J. Rupp, *Worlds of Women: The Making of an International Women's Movement* (Princeton, NJ: Princeton University Press, 1997), p. 46.

10 WYWCA, 'Suggestions for a programme of post war reconstruction to be considered by the International Women's Organisations', 1941.

11 WYWCA, Liaison Committee meeting minutes, London, 26 June 1941.

12 KDC, Henrietta Roelofs to Kathleen Courtney, 7 July 1941, box 456.

13 KDC, Henrietta Roelofs to Kathleen Courtney, 20 October 1940, box 456.

14 Robert L. Messer, 'World War II and the Coming of the Cold War', in John Carroll and George C. Herring (eds), *Modern American Diplomacy* (Wilmington, DE: Scholarly Resources, Inc., 1996), p. 121.

15 Robert D. Schulzinger, *U.S. Diplomacy Since 1900*, 4th edition (New York: Oxford University Press, 1998), pp. 176–8.

16 Charles DeBenedetti, 'James T. Shotwell and the science of international politics', *Political Science Quarterly* 89:2 (June 1974), pp. 379–95.

17 Smith Simpson, 'The commission to study the organization of peace', *The American Political Science Review*, 35:2 (April 1941), pp. 317–20.

18 Ibid., p. 319.

19 'Women undertake wide peace study', *New York Times* (26 May 1940): D6.

20 RW, 'Annual report of the general secretary, 1938–1939', box 36.

21 RW, 'Building a new world', c. 1941–42, box 9.

22 Ruth Frances Woodsmall Papers, Sophia Smith Collection, Smith College.

23 Anna V. Rice, *A History of the World's Young Women's Christian Association* (New York: Woman's Press, 1947), pp. 224–7; YWCA of the USA, Charlotte T. Niven, 'The YWCA in the world', *Woman's Press* (December 1936), pp. 530–1.

24 YWCA of the USA, 'Emergency committee reports', *Woman's Press* (February 1940), pp. 81 and 87.

25 WYWCA, Preliminary Draft on Reconstruction drawn up by the sub-committee [of the Liaison Committee of Women's International Organisations] for further consideration c. April 1941, box 277.

26 WYWCA, Liaison Committee meeting minutes, 30 October 1942, box 277.

27 WYWCA, Una Saunders to Anne Mills, 23 May 1941, box 277.

28 WYWCA, Ruth Woodsmall to Agatha Harrison, 19 July 1941, box 277.

29 WYWCA, Liaison Committee meeting minutes, 22 July 1941, box 277.

30 WYWCA, Letter to the *Times* (London) from Kathleen Courtney, Chairman, Women's Inter-Allied Training Committee, 25 June 1942, box 277; YWCA of the USA, Kathleen Courtney, 'Women and the Allies plan to rebuild', *Woman's Press* (November 1942), pp. 471–2.

31 Thomas G. Paterson, J. Garry Clifford and Kenneth J. Hagan, *American Foreign Relations A History Since 1895*, vol. II, 4th edition (Lexington, MA: D. C. Heath and Company, 1995) p. 238.

32 WYWCA, *Polish Fortnightly Review* London, 1 December 1942 attached to Liaison Committee meeting minutes, 15 January 1943, box 278.

33 WYWCA, Liaison Committee meeting minutes, 24 February 1943, box 278.

34 WYWCA, 'Liaison Committee of Women's International Organisations: [conference on] the status of Women in the post war world', London, 6 March 1943, box 278.

35 WYWCA, 'Women and the post war world' published by the Liaison Committee, London, c. 1943.

36 WYWCA, Liaison Committee meeting minutes, 10 September 1943, box 278.

37 WYWCA, Liaison Committee meeting minutes, 26 October 1943, box 278.

38 Leon Gordenker, *Refugees in International Politics* (New York: Columbia University Press, 1987), p. 21.

39 WYWCA, Evelyn Fox to Elsie Harper, 1 June 1940.

40 Paterson, Clifford and Hagan, *American Foreign Relations*, pp. 235–7.

41 RW, Marianne Mills to World's Council Members, 24 December 1938, box 43.

42 Yale University Divinity School Library, 'The crisis in world Jewry and Christian responsibility', *World's YWCA Monthly* (July 1939).

43 'Emergency committee reports', pp. 81 and 87.

44 YWCA of the USA, 'Lighting the world's darkness', *Woman's Press* (April 1940), pp. 161–2.

45 YWCA of the USA, 'Europe has a question', *Woman's Press* (September 1940), pp. 366–7.

46 RW, Ruth Woodsmall to national general secretaries, 15 January 1940, box 42.

47 WYWCA, Cornelia van Asch van Wijck, 1963, Who's Who File: 'Ruth Frances Woodsmall'.

48 Rice, *A History of the World's Young Women's Christian Association*, pp. 247–8; Carole Seymour-Jones, *Journey of Faith: The History of the World YWCA 1945–1994* (London: Allison and Busby, 1994), pp. 47–8.

49 WYWCA, Who's Who File: 'Alice Arnold'.

50 RW, Ruth Woodsmall to Mrs. John D, Rockefeller, 28 February 1940, box 17.

51 Rice, *A History of the World's Young Women's Christian Association*, p. 250.

52 RW, Ruth Woodsmall to World YWCA executive committee members, 9 March 1940, box 18.

53 Nicole Ann Dombrowski, 'Surviving the German invasion of France: women's stories of the exodus of 1940', in Dombrowski (ed.), *Women and War in the Twentieth Century*, pp. 128–33.

54 Seymour-Jones, *Journey of Faith*, pp. 20–1.

55 YWCA of the USA, 'The story of CIMADE', *Woman's Press* (September 1945), pp. 7–8.

56 WYWCA, 'Report of some aspects of the work of the World's Young Women's Christian Association prepared for the League of Nations Advisory Committee on Social Questions', 30 April 1940, box 284; YWCA of the USA, 'One clear design', *Woman's Press* (February 1941), p. 75.

57 Rice, *A History of the World's Young Women's Christian Association*, p. 252.

58 YWCA of the USA, 'Why We're in the USO', *Woman's Press* (June 1941), p. 270.

59 RW, Ruth Woodsmall to Marianne Mills, 22 April 1940, box 42.

60 Gordenker, *Refugees in International Politics*, pp. 22–3; Paterson, Clifford and Hagan, *American Foreign Relations*, p. 240.

61 WYWCA, Ruth Woodsmall to Francis B. Sayre, US State Department, 2 December 1943, box 278.

62 Mary Kinnear, *Woman of the World: Mary McGeachy and International Cooperation* (Toronto: University of Toronto Press, 2004).

63 WYWCA, Interview with Mary McGeachy, UNRRA Chief of Division of Welfare [conducted by Ruth Woodsmall], 21 February 1944, box 225.

64 WYWCA, Ruth Woodsmall to Mary McGeachy, UNRRA, 11 and 13 April 1944, box 278.

65 RW, 'Relationship of the national YWCA and the World's YWCA to the United Nations Relief and Rehabilitation Administration [UNRRA]', June 1944, box 49.

66 WYWCA, Ruth Woodsmall to Mary McGeachy, 21 June 1944, box 278; Interview with Miss Mary McGeachy [conducted by Ruth Woodsmall], 9 October 1944, box 225.

67 Yale University Divinity School Library, 'The CIMADE carries on', *World's YWCA Monthly* (April 1945).

68 RW, Ruth Woodsmall to World YWCA executive committee members, 9 May 1945, box 18.

69 WYWCA, Consultative meeting of British members with Miss Ruth Woodsmall, 2 November 1944.

70 YWCA of the USA, 'What internment means', *Woman's Press* (September 1944), pp. 381–2.

71 WYWCA, Alice Arnold to Ruth Woodsmall, 23 September 1947, World YWCA Service to Displaced Persons.

72 YWCA of the USA, 'Spring comes to displaced persons', *Woman's Press* (March 1947), pp. 9–10.

6

Forging a role at the United Nations

The founding of the United Nations

Throughout the Second World War, women's international organisations had actively supported women's equal participation in war service as well as in government planning for the post-war world. As the war concluded with the defeat of the fascist powers, women's organisations continued to push for equal participation in the new global governance system that replaced the League of Nations: the United Nations Organization (UNO). In spite of the progressive vision for the post-war world that Allied leaders Winston Churchill and Franklin Roosevelt had articulated in the 1941 Atlantic Charter, practical planning for the new UNO had proceeded behind closed doors during the fall of 1944 at the Dumbarton Oaks mansion in the Georgetown neighbourhood of Washington, DC. Leaders of the major Allied Powers formulated the preliminary draft of the United Nations Charter. According to the historian Robert Hildebrand 'the Big Three [the United States, Britain and the Soviet Union] saw the defence of their own security, the protection of their own interests, and the enjoyment of the fruits of their victory in the world war as more important than the creation of an international organisation to maintain world peace'. The draft Charter defined the (UN) that was to be led by a powerful Security Council with five permanent members; France and China joined the three major Second World War Allies on the proposed Council. Each Security Council member held veto power over substantive decisions. A general assembly to include all other UN member states was envisioned as a weak advisory body.[1] The draft Charter also did not include any provisions designating collaborative or advisory roles for non-governmental organisations (NGOs).[2] But as the Charter was released for study in preparation for the UN organisational conference that was held in San Francisco, from 25 April to 26 June 1945, the Allied nations that planned to become UN member states and NGOs challenged the major powers' global governance plans.

At the San Francisco conference NGOs rallied to interject their collaborative vision of the new system of global governance into the UN Charter. NGOs succeeded in 'strengthening and formalising' their own roles in the UN system and 'greatly enhanced the UN's role in economic and social issues and upgraded the status of the Economic and Social Council (ECOSOC) to a "principal organ" of the UN'.[3] The sociologists John Boli and George M. Thomas have analysed the long-term development of a world polity across the twentieth century through the systems of the League of Nations and the UN and the roles that NGOs have forged for themselves in those systems. Boli and Thomas have explained that the twentieth-century systems of global governance cannot be reduced to economic or political interactions between nation-states. These systems have included cultural components and NGOs have contributed significantly to creating and defining the principles on which a 'world culture' has been based. Twentieth-century world culture has been defined by: 'universalism', that is, recognition that humans everywhere have similar needs and desires; 'individualism', or acknowledging that members of world bodies are individuals with human rights; 'rational voluntaristic authority', meaning that responsible governing bodies act collectively through rational procedures and determine cultural rules that are just, equitable and efficient; 'human purposes of rationalising progress', referring to the understanding that global development includes not only economic considerations but also individual self-actualisation, collective security and justice; and 'world citizenship', or recognising that every individual is endowed with certain citizenship rights and obligations.[4]

Boli and Thomas have challenged neo-realist international relations theories that assert that only states matter as international actors. They argue that states sometimes defer to pressures from international NGOs, too. 'In mobilizing around and elaborating world-cultural principles, INGOs lobby, criticize, and convince states to act on those principles, at least in some sectors and with respect to some issues.' From the League of Nations era and into the UN era the global status and rights of women has been such an issue in which women's NGOs have taken the lead and have persuaded governments to adopt their point of view. [5]

Women's international organisations were intensely interested in the founding of the UN and hoped to expand women's roles within the new intergovernmental body. They knew that women's voices must be heard during the San Francisco conference debates regarding the language and substantive content of the UN Charter in order to promote human rights and fundamental freedoms for the entire world's people and women's equal rights and equal participation in governing the post-war world. [6] The Liaison Committee sent letters to the governments that would be attending the San Francisco Conference stating these goals; it also urged the governments to include women on their national delegations and in the newly formed UN secretariat.[7] Several London Liaison Committee members including Kathleen Courtney went to San Francisco to advocate for women at the UN organising conference.[8]

The conference was attended by 521 national representatives from forty-nine nations in San Francisco, presided over by the conference chairman, the US Secretary of State Edward R. Stettinius, Jr. As in the past, few women – only fourteen – were included as official national delegates.[9]

Nonetheless, many women attended the conference and made their presence felt through their advisory coalitions. For example, the US State Department named only one woman, Virginia Gildersleeve, the dean of Barnard College, to the US delegation. Several women who worked at the State Department and in the Women's Bureau at the Department of Labor, however, advised the US delegation. They invited representatives of several American women's organisations including the American Association of University Women, the General Federation of Women's Clubs, the National Federation of Business and Professional Women's Clubs, the National League of Women Voters and the Women's Action Committee for Victory and Lasting Peace, to offer advice to the US delegation on 'women's issues', too.[10]

As the American example demonstrates, the few female national delegates were backed by networks of women's organisations. These women used their formal and informal power to its fullest extent and lobbied vigorously for male recognition that, as Dorothy Kenyon phrased it, 'women are people and women's rights are human rights'.[11] As a result of their efforts several clauses were added to the UN Charter drafted at Dumbarton Oaks that made this point explicit. The Charter Preamble included an affirmation of human rights for all persons and of men and women's equal rights. And, in Article I Section 3 regarding the purposes of the UN, the members pledged to promote and encourage 'respect for human rights and for fundamental freedoms for all without distinction as to race, *sex*, language or religion'. Article VIII opened all positions in the secretariat equally to men and women.[12]

The sociologist Nitza Berkovitch has interpreted the inclusion of these clauses into the Charter as representing a new international emphasis on human rights that was a reaction to the wartime atrocities committed by the Germans and by their Axis Power allies. As the Allied Powers created a new world order through new or reconstituted intergovernmental bodies these 'supranational institutions were expected to set standardised guidelines to be followed and implemented by all nation-states as far as the well-being and rights of their respective citizens were concerned. What used to fall under the sole jurisdiction of nation-states – the rights of their inhabitants – now became a concern for the international community. This context enabled women's rights to be placed on the world agenda.'[13]

Although an internationalist climate of opinion that was ready to accept women's rights into the new world governance organisation had been created, these clauses might not have been added to the UN Charter without the effective pressure exerted on the male conference delegates by NGO activists in coalition with individual feminists serving on the Australian, Brazilian, Dominican Republican and Mexican delegations: Jessie Street, Bertha Lutz, Minerva Bernardino and Amalia Gonzales Caballero de Castillo Ledón.

Ruth Woodsmall's assessment of women's activism at the San Francisco conference recognised the important roles played by these feminists who were willing to push male delegates to acknowledge women's rights. According to Woodsmall, Jessie Street was 'a rather typical feminist – very nice woman, not very clear in her thinking, somewhat of a single-track mind. She represented the extreme left section of the women at San Francisco who pressed hard at all times the question of the inclusion of women'. Woodsmall contrasted Street's efforts with the attitude of US delegate Virginia Gildersleeve who, Woodsmall explained, was 'rather indifferent' to feminist issues, and 'represents perhaps the extreme right, women who have achieved and are not particularly concerned about promoting the forward advance of women, although essentially their own example is an influence for progress'. Gildersleeve had stated outright that she was not at the conference to 'represent women' but was there '*sui generis*', selected on the basis of her own merits and not because she was a woman.

Woodsmall also commented on Bertha Lutz who proposed that the newly organised ECOSOC should establish in addition to a Human Rights Commission a separate Commission on the Status of Women to recognise and protect women's gender-specific interests in all UN agencies and commissions – whatever their focus might be. According to Woodsmall, '[Bertha Lutz] and Mrs. Street were on the alert for the protection of women's interests. One can be critical of their methods, but perhaps not of their ultimate achievement, as they succeeded in getting the participation of women adequately included in the Charter even though they antagonised people in the process.'[14]

A US State Department newsletter published in 1980 also recalled the events at the 1945 San Francisco United Nations conference and the key roles played by these few outspoken feminist women who swayed the course of the conference outcome:

> The struggle to get women recognized in the Charter of the United Nations was led by Jessie Street (Australia), Bertha Lutz (Brazil), and Minerva

Bernardino (Dominican Republic) aided by Amalia Ledon (Mexico) and Isabel Urdaneta (Venezuela). These women spearheaded the movement to get a special clause included in the Charter specifying the eligibility of women to hold any position within the United Nations system (Article 8) . . .

In arguing for the inclusion of Article 8 . . . Jessie Street pointed out that in practically every country in the world at the time women were excluded from occupying various positions just because the law did not specifically state that women were eligible. Bertha Lutz added that it had always been held that women were included in the general term 'men', and that this also resulted in women being precluded from taking part in public affairs. That such a statement on the status of women was necessary, she went on, was proved by looking at the number of women participating in the [San Francisco] Conference. Only 1% of the delegates were women, and there were no women in the policy making body of the United Nations.[15]

Women's organisations waged a lively debate at the San Francisco conference about whether ECOSOC should include a separate Commission on the Status of Women to articulate specific women's rights and to monitor international progress in achieving those rights. There were two competing views expressed by different groups of women at San Francisco. Generally, American leaders who defined themselves as pragmatists, no 'extreme "Equal Righters" among them' agreed that a separate, probably women-only, international Commission on Women would be marginalised in the UN System. Virginia Gildersleeve and her advisers – the judge Dorothy Kenyon, the director of the National Consumers League Mary Anderson, the director of the Women's Bureau at the Department of Labour Frieda Miller, and the State Department representatives Ruth Shipley and Emily Hickman – all argued that a separate women's commission 'would be less effective than a technical committee under the proposed Human Rights Commission'. They believed that other UN agencies and offices could better address specific problems of women in their areas of concern.[16] Gildersleeve explained their point of view: 'Women should be regarded as human beings . . . If they should be segregated in this special feminine Commission, then it might well happen that men would keep them out of other commissions or groups, saying that they had plenty of scope in their own organisation. This would be contrary to what we were working for – no discrimination because of sex.'[17]

On the opposite side of the question, European women generally and Latin American delegates Bertha Lutz, Minerva Bernardino and Amalia Castillo Ledón and Australian delegate Jessie Street believed that a women's commission was necessary to promote women's rights. They reasoned that patriarchal attitudes that had long discriminated against women were still the international norm. As Dorothy Kenyon explained their views, 'the habits of centuries did not change so quickly and . . . what was still needed was a spark plug to watch out for women's interests'.[18] The Europeans and Latin American women argued that women needed a dedicated office at the UN because women's societal roles were different from men's and some of their interests were gender specific. This 'separatist' view ultimately prevailed and was upheld within the UN system until recent years. After the UN Decade for Women concluded in 1985 the emphasis shifted to 'mainstreaming' or integrating women and a gender perspective into all UN programmes and activities.[19]

As the UN defined the Economic and Social Council and its Commissions and Sub-Commissions in February 1946, however, the two viewpoints reached a temporary compromise and a Sub-Commission on the Status of Women, reporting to the Commission on Human Rights that was to be led by Eleanor Roosevelt, was formed 'to study the conditions and prepare reports on the political, civil, and economic status and opportunity of women with special reference to discrimination and limitations placed on them on account of their sex'.[20]

Women's organisations define joint projects in UN forums

Following the San Francisco conference, women's international organisations struggled to define common goals and projects for joint activism. The long-established organisations that had worked persistently to establish relationships with male power holders at the League of Nations wanted to ensure that their histories were recorded and that new organisations entering the international arena would learn from their experiences. The Liaison Committee published its own history with this purpose in mind and long-serving leaders among these established women's groups continued to fill leadership positions in many post-war associations.[21] Dorothy Kenyon produced the preliminary reports of the League of Nations Inquiry on the Status of Women that she had safeguarded during the war with the hope that the women's organisations would revive the project in the postwar era.[22] Yet as these older leaders pushed for future activism that would build on past accomplishments they often found that younger activists who were new to international politics did not appreciate what seemed like meagre advances in women's power and status.

The historian Deborah Stienstra has asserted that women's rights activists have made few gains at the international level because patriarchal states and intergovernmental bodies were historically 'unwilling to undertake the radical restructuring of their economies and societies that would be necessary to bring about the changes that many women's movements are requesting'. Stienstra argued further that 'mainstream' women's organisations have not pushed for these radical changes because they have been appeased by the inclusion of broad statements supporting the principal of equality in international agreements, like the statements included in the UN Charter. These statements have not been fully implemented, yet they have seemingly mollified liberal women's rights activists.[23] Stienstra's assessment must be revised. It is true that the historic leaders of Western-dominated international organisations were proud of their accomplishments adding inclusive language and asserting women's rights in UN documents, actions which were considered radical in the context of the times. However, they were not satisfied with those accomplishments alone but continued to define new goals that they could pursue collectively to abolish all forms of discrimination against women and to advance women's status globally in the post-war period.

As part of the search to determine the next steps to raise women's global status in September 1945 the League of Women Voters invited a group of American women leaders to an all-day Conference on the United Nations and the Special Interests of Women that was held in Washington, DC. Ruth Woodsmall, Laura Puffer Morgan, Laura Dreyfus-Barney and Mary Dingman were among those invited to share their international expertise, as were Eleanor Roosevelt, Dorothy Kenyon, Carrie Chapman Catt, and numerous women who worked in the State Department and the Women's Bureau at the Department of Labour, along with leading journalists, educators and a congresswoman. Anna Lord Strauss, president of the League of Women Voters, chaired the conference.[24]

The Washington conference assessed what had taken place at San Francisco, as well as the League-era history of women's international activism as it had been carried out through the Liaison Committee of Women's International Organisations, the International Labour Organization (ILO), and the Inter-American Commission on Women, an intergovernmental agency within the Organization of American States (OAS) that formed in 1928 in conjunction with the Sixth International Conference of American States held in Havana, Cuba. Based on what they culled from the record of their past accomplishments conference participants discussed how to maximise women's influence at the new UN.[25]

Dorothy Kenyon urged American women to call for the renewal and expansion of the League of Nations Inquiry on the Status of Women and argued that up-to-date data regarding global discrimination against women could serve as the basis for future women's activism. The Liaison Committee planned to build on its past influence within the system of the League of Nations at the new UN and to expand its organisational membership to incorporate new women's international NGOs forming in the post-war era. Frieda Miller, director of the Women's Bureau at the US

Department of Labour, reported that the ILO was expected to continue as an intergovernmental agency within the UN system and she urged women to support US government ratification of ILO conventions regarding equal pay for equal work performed by men and women. The Inter-American Commission on Women had established a valuable network for exchange of information among women in the Western hemisphere and also hoped to increase women's influence in the UN system.[26] Although it had not collaborated much with the European-based Liaison Committee during the interwar years, the Inter-American Commission, too, had built an impressive record of feminist activism during the League of Nations era. In 1933, following the OAS Conference held at Montevideo, women from Latin American countries had appealed to the League to draft an equal rights treaty. Latin American women had been among the strongest advocates pushing for the League of Nations Inquiry into the Status of Women that was undertaken in 1937. The Inter-American Commission on Women had also collected data on women's civil and political equality on a country-by-country basis even before the League began its official Inquiry.[27]

  The long-running problem of persuading the United States government to appoint qualified women to international posts was also discussed and the conference agreed that 'unless specific nominations are made [naming qualified women], the tendency is to appoint men'. The experienced women attending the conference understood that government delegates and UN officials needed to possess political skills and technical qualifications as well as 'international experience' but they knew of many American women who met these requirements. They concluded that the best strategy to increase the number of women appointed to UN posts was to identify specific women nominees for State Department consideration and then provide 'unanimous support' from the women's organisations for their appointments. Once again women's collective pressure was needed to gain entry into the male-dominated intergovernmental body.

  The conference also debated the proposed UN Commission on the Status of Women. As they had argued at the San Francisco conference, numerous women asserted that a separate commission could isolate 'women's issues' when it was agreed that all issues proposed for consideration at the UN concerned women. Virginia Gildersleeve sent a letter that articulated this perspective: 'Women of all nations are agreed on the desirability of doing everything possible to improve the position of women. We differ only as to machinery. I am anxious that nothing should be done to isolate women, but I hope we shall rather insist on their being regarded as "people" as we have long tried to do in this country.'[28] Other women, however, challenged Gildersleeve and argued that women's specific interests would be ignored in male-led UN agencies even if women were employed in those agencies without a Commission on the Status of Women monitoring their work and focusing attention on women's needs. In the end, this counter-argument prevailed.

In December Anna Lord Strauss sent the conference recommendations to American women's organisations for their review and endorsement. Strauss outlined an American women's agenda for post-war activism at the UN that supported the establishment of a UN Commission on the Status of Women to be composed of both men and women national delegates; the Commission should advise ECOSOC on questions regarding women's rights and status and equal participation in international governance. The conference also recommended that the Inquiry on the Status of Women be revived and that a UN International Conference on Women be convened as early as 1946.[29] The international women's conference would serve several purposes:

> to a) review the status of women in the various countries of the world; b) determine the responsibility of member governments for improving their status; c) explore opportunities and suitable procedures for UN assistance in this effort and d) establish more effective liaison between private organisations of women whose collaboration will be essential to achieve the desired goal of fundamental freedom for all without distinction as to race, sex, language or religion.[30]

When the Liaison Committee met in London in January, members also considered calling for an international women's conference – convened by NGOs themselves and not under UN management – to determine a global women's agenda. According to Margery Corbett Ashby 'a joint conference would carry far more weight in putting forward women's point of view than a number of separate conferences held by each international organisation'. Such a conference could also educate younger women activists about the historical record of women's global activism. Yet several women's organisations including the International Women's Cooperative Guild, the International Council of Women, and the World Young Women's Christian Association (YWCA) were already planning post-war conventions to discuss their own organisational priorities and they were not enthusiastic about Corbett Ashby's joint conference proposal.[31] The Liaison Committee was never able to organise the large-scale joint conference that Corbett Ashby envisioned and the UN did not host an international woman's conference bringing together representatives of national governments and women's NGOs until 1975 during International Women's Year.

Just as they had forged a role for themselves at the San Francisco UN Charter conference, women's organisations also established an informal advisory role at the inaugural session of the UN General Assembly that convened in London in January and February 1946; they arranged meetings with the few women appointed to national delegations and exercised their well-developed networking skills. Among the government appointees Eleanor Roosevelt served on the US delegation and Frieda Miller of the Women's Bureau at the Department of Labour and Dorothy Fodsick from the State Department advised her. The French delegate Marie Hélène Lefaucheux had been an active member in the French resistance and had been elected to the Paris Committee of Liberation, the Provisional Municipal Assembly of Paris and the first post-war French National Assembly. The New Zealand delegate Jean R. MacKenzie was first secretary to the High Commissioner of New Zealand and had a long record of government service in national and international posts.[32] Minerva Bernardino who led feminist activism at the San Francisco conference represented her nation, the Dominican Republic, at the General Assembly meetings. Bernardino also met with the London Liaison Committee and introduced the work of the Inter-American Commission on Women. The Danish delegate Bodil Begtrup was a member of the National Council of Women and had served her government in several capacities at the League of Nations.[33]

With the women's organisations behind them, these delegates and twelve other women delegates to the inaugural UN session were conscious that they represented 'women' as well as their nations at the UN meetings. The women delegates came from different cultural backgrounds yet they shared common commitments to women's and human rights.[34] They displayed their gender consciousness when they issued a joint statement in the form of an Open Letter to the Women of the World from the Women Delegates and Advisers at the First Assembly of the United Nations that Marie Hélène Lefaucheux drafted and Eleanor Roosevelt presented to the General Assembly:

> In view of the variety of tasks which women performed so notably and valiantly during the war, we are gratified that seventeen women representatives and advisers, representing eleven Member states, are taking part at the beginning of this new phase of international effort. We hope their participation in the work of the United Nations Organisation may grow and may increase in skill and insight. To this end we call on the Governments of the world to encourage women everywhere to take a more active part in national and international affairs, and to women who are conscious of their opportunities to come forward and share in the work of the peace and reconstruction as they did in war and resistance.[35]

Government delegates expressed their general support for the women's statement but, since it was not presented in the form of a resolution, no formal government endorsement was made. In her study, *Women, Development and the UN* the development specialist Devaki Jain has argued that the Open Letter deliberately 'stressed the roles, responsibilities, and contributions of women' and encouraged women to enter the public sphere, yet the statement 'did not speak of rights or lack of rights'. Jain has attributed this moderate and strategic stance to the influence of Eleanor Roosevelt who had been schooled in the conservative political culture of the United States where women had to 'prove their capacity to be good citizens'.[36]

The Sub-Commission on the Status of Women was more forthright in its assertion of women's rights. This assertiveness was linked to its charge and to its composition. The Sub-Commission was charged to submit proposals, recommendations, and reports to the Human Rights Commission (HRC) 'about how to raise the status of women to equality with men in all fields of human enterprise' and the HRC then determined whether to act or to forward these proposals to ECOSOC or the UN General Assembly.[37] The Economic and Social Council appointed the first nine national delegates to the Sub-Commission on the Status of Women; like all UN bodies membership represented a carefully calibrated geographical and political distribution. Delegates included women from the East and West, Communist and non-Communist countries, and North and South, the industrialised and non-industrialised developing worlds. Bodil Begtrup was elected as chair of the Sub-Commission. Her sister delegates included Minerva Bernardino who was elected as vice-chair, Angela Jurdak from Lebanon, Bani Amrit Kaur from India, Gabriela Mistral from Chile, Madame Vienot from France and Wu Yi-fang from China. The Soviet Union and Soviet-dominated Poland also sent delegates to serve on the Sub-Commission. These Eastern bloc delegates were not named by ECOSOC, but were selected by their Communist Party governments and they joined the Sub-Commission when it met for the first time in April and May 1946 in New York.[38]

Even though the Sub-Commission – and the Commission on the Status of Women (CSW) that replaced it – were part of an intergovernmental body and the delegates who served on the CSW represented their governments, those appointed were almost always women who also supported the advancement of women's global status.[39] Moreover, from the very beginning women's organisations played an influential role in setting the CSW's agenda and defining its subsequent work. Women's NGOs established themselves as a channel for information about women's needs and interests representing the fifty-one original UN member states and speaking for women in many non-member states where the women's organisations had national chapters and contacts.[40] Women's organisations also pushed to enlarge the Sub-Commission and supported its transition to full Commission status.

After the inaugural UN meetings had concluded in March, back in the United States American organisations met with US government representatives to discuss the scope and programme of the Sub-Commission. They argued that the Sub-Commission membership should include an American woman and the United States government agreed.[41] Soon thereafter, during ECOSOC's first summer session held in New York in May 1946, Sub-Commission chair Bodil Begtrup argued persuasively to raise the Sub-Commission to full Commission status when she asserted 'in view of the importance of this world-wide scheme which covers, in fact, the condition of half the population of the world, the work ought to have the best possible working conditions and not be dependent upon another Commission, and that it would give this work more weight in the social field if it was done by a full Commission'.[42] Following Begtrup's appeal to ECOSOC and with the US government's full support, in June a fifteen-member Commission on the Status of Women was created with new reporting lines directly to ECOSOC.

The US government appointed Judge Dorothy Kenyon as its delegate on the enlarged CSW that met for the first time in February 1947.[43] Kenyon had continued her campaign to revive the League of Nation's unfinished Inquiry on the Status of Women and this became one of the US-backed projects on the Commission's agenda at the 1947 opening session.[44] Some CSW delegates such as Minerva Bernardino and numerous women's organisations opposed this project. Recalling the history of the 1937-39 League Inquiry, women's organisations believed that long periods spent collecting data would prevent the Commission from acting on women's behalf but Kenyon answered their objections:

> I do not agree with your idea that collection of material on the subject of the status of women will halt or deflect the work of the Commission itself in any way. Certainly we want action and all the action we can get. The collecting of material is not the job of the Commission but of the Secretariat, subject to whatever supervision the Commission chooses to give it. Our Commission is not like the old Committee of the League of Nations which was given only one job, namely to make the legal study. The UN Commission has the whole broad field, with no holds barred, to whatever it can get away with.[45]

When the CSW met at Lake Success, New York for its first formal session the Commission defined its broad guiding principles to raise the status of women and eliminate gender-based discriminations against women in law and practice and outlined future plans to establish legal foundations for women's equality.[46] The CSW's agenda, as the international human rights scholar Laura Reanda has argued, represented 'Western thought and political priorities . . . promoting equal rights and opportunities for women as individuals'. According to Reanda's brief history of the Commission on the Status of Women, during the early Cold War era, CSW delegates usually discussed women's rights apart from the context of other global developments, such as decolonisation, the anti-nuclear peace movement and social and economic development initiatives in the Third World. This represented the influence of Western delegates who overruled, at times, the wishes of the Commission's socialist and non-Western members.[47]

Despite its Western orientation during its first decade and a half of operation, the CSW nonetheless helped to redefine international norms regarding women's roles and status and promoted significant acknowledgement of women's rights among governments. In part this was because from its beginnings the Commission was determined to work with other UN specialised agencies whose mandates encompassed women's rights issues, and these included initially the HRC and the HR Sub-Commission on Prevention of Discrimination and Protection of Minorities, the United Nations Educational Scientific and Cultural Organization (UNESCO), the ILO, and various other agencies that formed as the UN system expanded over the years. These inter-agency connections cultivated influential allies among government delegates and the UN secretariat and worked to the CSW's great advantage. As Devaki Jain has explained:

> Representatives of these bodies could sit in on CSW meetings and vice versa. There was also provision for collaborative ventures – sharing of and commenting on reports, requests for preparation of studies and so forth. This kind of interagency collaboration on the subject of women's rights broadened the perspective as well as the network of accountability. It sent a clear message that women's issues did not just relate to the CSW; in fact, it challenged the likelihood of ghettoization and predicted what feminists would say much later, 'All issues are women's issues.'[48]

In fact, Dorothy Kenyon articulated that very message in 1947 as she shared her belief in the potential of the Commission in a statement she released to the press:

> Women's place is in the world, and that means in the home and everywhere else where she is needed – which nowadays is just about everywhere. Women are no minority group, either, but actually are in the majority in the world today. This fact alone gives women increasing responsibilities. Women certainly belong in the UN organization and there is a great field of work for them to do there. I consider that the establishment of this Commission on the Status of Women of the UN is a great historical event and I am happy to have a share in it.[49]

NGOs and consultative status with the UN Economic and Social Council

With the establishment of the new system of global governance at the UN in 1945–46, NGOs sought to expand the limited role they played within the League of Nations and to formalise NGO participation on a wide range of issues. In the revised UN Charter adopted by government delegates at the San Francisco conference Article 71 directed ECOSOC to 'make suitable arrangements for consultation with non-governmental organizations which are concerned with matters within its competence'.[50] At the UN General Assembly inaugural meetings held in 1946 NGOs, with women's organisations at the forefront, lobbied energetically to define their new 'consultative status' with ECOSOC and its Commissions and agencies in the broadest of terms. Even as they negotiated the parameters of consultative status the Liaison Committee was among the first group of NGOs to apply for the new designation.[51] Soon afterwards, several organisational members of the Liaison Committee including the World YWCA also requested independent consultative status.

In spite of their collective goals, women's organisations continued to guard their individual organisational prerogatives to take independent action when their views did not coincide with Liaison Committee majority opinion. In the immediate post-war period some organisational members including the YWCA believed, according to Ruth Woodsmall, that:

> the Liaison Committee central group in London tends to freely make general pronouncements in the name of the total committee without recognizing the need for full previous consultation. The representatives of the World's YWCA have always acted as a constant check on this free-lance method of voicing world organisation opinion. We need to find a way for effective action when action is needed, but to avoid the free-lance over-all easy pronouncement plan.[52]

The decision to request consultative status as independently was viewed as the solution to this problem and ECOSOC eventually agreed with the women's arguments.

An ECOSOC Committee on Arrangements for Consultation reviewed NGO applications and awarded consultative status to well-credentialled NGOs with international scope, established headquarters, democratic constitutions, no past associations with fascist governments and expertise in formulating policy or implementing programmes that addressed the social and economic questions considered by ECOSOC or its agencies or commissions. ECOSOC awarded consultative status to NGOs in ranked categories with distinct privileges according to rank. What was initially termed Category A Consultative Status was reserved for broad-based NGOs that had demonstrated expertise in a wide range of economic and social issues. NGOs with Category A status could attend meetings and consult with ECOSOC member states or agencies on policies or issues under debate, add items to ECOSOC or agency agendas, submit written or oral statements at

ECOSOC or agency meetings, and receive all ECOSOC or agency reports, publications and communications from the secretariat. These NGOs had unprecedented access to government delegates and to the UN secretariat in the UN system. NGOs with Category B status held the privileges of Category A NGOs but within their more limited and proscribed areas of expertise. They could attend ECOSOC or agency meetings, and so on, when topics were discussed that concerned their designated areas of expertise. Category C status was reserved for NGOs with more limited or technical focus to their activities and they could make occasional contributions to the work of ECOSOC or agencies. [53] The Liaison Committee and several of its member organisations including the YWCA were awarded Category B Status in 1947.[54] Within the first decade of the founding of the UN, twenty women's organisations were granted consultative status, 18 per cent of all NGOs so designated by ECOSOC.[55]

Within the UN system NGOs historically influenced agenda setting, policy formation, and programme implementation among a range of UN agencies. The women's international organisations enjoyed their greatest substantive influence with the UN Commission on the Status of Women. Nonetheless, the women's NGOs also influenced agendas and global governance processes in many other UN agencies, such as UNESCO, the HRC, the Food and Agriculture Organization (FAO), the United Nations (International) Children's (Emergency) Fund (UNICEF), the United Nations High Commission for Refugees (UNHCR), the World Health Organization (WHO), the ILO, and more. According to the international relations scholar Peter Willetts, NGOs with consultative status:

> [firstly] have access to all UN documents once these have been officially circulated [and through these documents NGOs can gain high levels of information about the political process] . . . Secondly, NGOs have security passes giving them access to all the buildings, including the lounges, bars and restaurants used by the diplomats. They . . . have access to the delegates . . . Thirdly, being awarded consultative status gives an NGO a legitimate place within the political system. This means the NGO activist is seen as having a right to be involved in the process.[56]

Representing global civil society NGOs have democratised the system of global governance at the UN and have steadily expanded the system to encompass much more than state-to-state relations.

With UN headquarters established in New York in 1946 and with many global governance operations that continued in Geneva, Paris and Vienna, international NGOs had to determine how they could consult effectively and exert influence within the dispersed UN system. In order to gain more leverage and influence in global governance deliberations women's organisations including the YWCA joined an umbrella coalition in 1948: the Conference of Non-governmental Organisations in Consultative Status with ECOSOC (CONGO). Soon after CONGO was established its members also formed sub-committees that focused on human rights, development, disarmament, the status of women, and racism and decolonisation. CONGO and its subcommittees facilitated NGO networking as well as information sharing with the UN secretariat and UN member states.[57]

In addition to joining CONGO the YWCA appointed a full-time staff member as the Association's consultant at UN headquarters in New York. The first consultant, Marion Royce, a Canadian, studied the workings of the UN system, advised the YWCA Executive Committee about issues where it could present statements and propose resolutions before ECOSOC commissions, lobbied government delegates and the UN secretariat on behalf of women's interests and engaged in public relations work for the YWCA in UN forums. In 1949 Alice Arnold became the YWCA's second UN consultant. Arnold attended annual sessions of the Commission on the Status of Women, UNESCO and FAO held in New York, Geneva, and elsewhere. Numerous YWCA volunteers served as consultants at dispersed UN agency meetings in New York, Paris, Rome, Vienna and Geneva.[58] These volunteers were long-time YWCA members; some had served on the Executive Committee or in other unpaid leadership positions and were knowledgeable about YWCA and global gender policy.

As Ruth Woodsmall planned to retire in 1947 she worked hard to define her legacy by amending the World YWCA's relationship with the Liaison Committee of Women's International Organisations and by establishing relationships with newly formed NGO networks and with UN intergovernmental bodies. Woodsmall believed, and the YWCA Executive Committee concurred, that the relationship with the Liaison Committee had changed for the worse in the post-war period. A new, young honorary secretary presided over Liaison Committee meetings at the London headquarters; Gwendolyn Home Peel had replaced the ageing Elsie Zimmern, and under Home Peel's leadership the Liaison Committee seemed to act as an 'executive committee' formulating positions on its own behalf rather than continuing to function as a liaison facilitating communication among individual women's organisations so that they could act together in specific instances when their goals coincided.[59]

Woodsmall also wanted to guard the World YWCA's growing influence and privileges within the UN system. Woodsmall believed this status would erode over time if the ECOSOC and its agencies assumed that the Liaison Committee spoke for the collective 'voice of women'. Finally after several years of weighing the costs and benefits of formal association with other women's organisations, in 1950 the YWCA officially resigned its membership in the Liaison Committee.[60] The Executive Committee ago-nised over this decision because it wanted to retain close contacts with the women's organisations that historically had defined the global women's agenda. However, the World YWCA believed it could continue to define universal women's needs based on input from its own national asso-ciations that operated worldwide and could better influence global gender policy through consultative relationships built with UN agencies.

Ruth Woodsmall believed these UN relationships were critical for expanding YWCA influence in regard to global actions affecting women and girls, promoting YWCA values of democratic inclusiveness within the UN system, and convincing the sometimes hesitant YWCA members that women must play an active role in post-war politics at the local, national and international levels. In the post-war years and often in conjunction with UN agencies the World YWCA formulated programmes aimed at 'stimulating political interest among women and girls' in politics at all levels. The YWCA developed 'citizenship training' programmes in the established Western democratic states, in the reconstructed fascist states, and in the newly independent post-colonial states. At a post-war leader-ship conference sponsored by the YWCA in Switzerland in June 1946, Ruth Woodsmall, Cornelia van Asch van Wijck and Elsa Cedergren defined Christian women's leadership and promoted political involvement for young YWCA leaders in training. Elsa Cedergren articulated the World YWCA's post-war message when she told the students:

> Women's contribution is essential to the political life of the community . . .
> The community needs the motherliness of the woman in the very best sense
> of the word; it needs the personal touch, the practical common sense and
> the clear, direct thinking characteristic of women – because they are close
> to the springs of life . . . In the community or state there are not special
> women's interests, neither are there special men's interests. There are only
> Human interests.[61]

Notes

1 Thomas J. Paterson, J. Garry Clifford and Kenneth J. Hagan, *American Foreign Relations: A History Since 1895*, vol. II, 4th edition (Lexington, MA: D. C. Heath and Company, 1995), p. 241.
2 Peter Willetts, 'What is an NGO?' *UNESCO Encyclopedia*, Article 1.44.3.7 Nongovernmental Organizations (staff.city.ac.uk/p.willetts/CS-NTWKS/NGO-ART.HTM#Start).
3 Ibid.
4 John Boli and George M. Thomas, 'World culture in the world polity: a century of international nongovernmental organization', *American Sociological Review* 62 (April 1997), pp. 180–2.

5 Ibid., pp. 186–7.

6 WYWCA, Liaison Committee meeting minutes, 19 February 1945, box 278.

7 WYWCA, Amended draft of letter to governments invited to the San Francisco Conference, 3 April 1945, Liaison Committee Meeting Minutes.

8 Beryl Haslam. *From Suffrage to Internationalism: The Political Evolution of Three British Feminists, 1908–1939* (New York: Peter Lang, 1999), p. 205.

9 Karen Offen, 'Women's rights or human rights? International feminism between the wars', in Patricia Grimshaw, Katie Holms and Marilyn Lake (eds), *Women's Rights and Human Rights* (New York: Palgrave, 2001), p. 249.

10 WYWCA, Liaison Committee meeting minutes, 21 April 1945, box 278.

11 Dorothy Kenyon, 'Victories on the international front', *Annals of the American Academy of Political and Social Science* 251 (May 1947), p. 19.

12 Deborah Stienstra, *Women's Movements and International Organizations* (London: St. Martin's Press, 1994), pp. 77–8.

13 Nitza Berkovitch, *From Motherhood to Citizenship: Women's Rights and International Organizations* (Baltimore, MD: Johns Hopkins University Press, 1999), pp. 102–3.

14 WYWCA, Ruth Woodsmall to Marianne Mills, 11 August 1945, box 291.

15 Schlesinger Library. Radcliffe Institute, Harvard University, Cambridge, MA, *Women 1980* [Newsletter No. 3] Issued by Division for Economic and Social Information/DPI, U.S. State Department.

16 Frieda S. Miller Papers 1909–1973, Schlesinger Library, Radcliffe Institute, Harvard University, Cambridge, MA (hereafter FSM), Mrs A. H. Johnstone, League of Women Voters, to Anna Lord Strauss, 21 June 1945, re: 'United Nations conference and the status of women', box 7.

17 Virginia Gildersleeve quoted in Devaki Jain, *Women, Development and the UN: A Sixty-Year Quest for Equality and Justice* (Bloomington, IN: Indiana University Press, 2005), p. 17.

18 Kenyon, 'Victories on the international front', p. 20.

19 Laura Reanda, 'The Commission on the Status of Women', in Philip Alston (ed.), *The United Nations and Human Rights: A Critical Appraisal* (Oxford, UK: Oxford University Press, 1992), p. 267.

20 Stienstra, *Women's Movements and International Organizations*, pp.79–81; FSM, Rachel C. Nason, Secretary Pro Tem, 'Report of informal conversations on the proposed Commission of Women under the Social and Economic Council of the United Nations Organization', c. June 1945, box 7.

21 MAD, 'An experiment in cooperation', box 1.

22 DK, 'History of the committee on legal status of women appointed by the League of Nations in 1938', 12 September 1945, box 53.

23 Stienstra, *Women's Movements and International Organizations*, pp. 157–8.

24 FSM, Memo from Anna Lord Strauss, President National League of Women Voters, to American Association of University Women, General Federation of Women's Clubs, National Federation of Business and Professional Women, Women's Action Committee, 14 August 1945, box 7.

25 FSM, 'Proposed agenda for conference on the United Nations and the special interests of women', 19 September 1945, box 7.

26 DK, 'Report of the conference on the United Nations and the special interests of women', 19 September 1945, box 53.

27 Jain, *Women, Development and the UN*, p. 14.

28 'Report of the conference on the United Nations and the special interests of women.'

29 DK, Mary Anderson, chair, Washington committee on arrangements, conference on the United Nations and the special interests of women, to all who attended the conference, 27 December 1945, box 53.

30 DK, National League of Women Voters, 'Suggested content for covering letter to Secretary of State when endorsing attached recommendations of the conference on the United Nations and the special interests of women', 27 December 1945, box 53.

31 WYWCA, Liaison Committee meeting minutes, c. January 1946, box 291.

32 FSM, US Department of Labour 'Women delegates and advisers to the general assembly of the United Nations Organization', London, January-February 1946, box 11.

33 WYWCA, Special meeting of the Liaison Committee, 4 February 1946, box 291.

34 Jain, *Women, Development and the UN*, p. 13.

35 'Short history of the Commission on the Status of Women', United Nations, Division for the Advancement of Women (un.org/womenwatch/daw/CSW 60YRS/CSWbriefhistory.pdf); J. R. Mathiason, 'The long march to Beijing: the United Nations and the women's revolution, vol. I, The Vienna Period, 2006 (intlmgt.com/longmarch/Long%20March%202006.pdf).

36 Jain, *Women, Development and the UN*, p. 22.

37 J. R. Mathiason, 'The Long March to Beijing', p. 18; The Human Rights Commission was also charged with drawing up an international bill of rights, international conventions or declarations on civil liberties and the prevention of discrimination on grounds of race, sex, language, religion and with the pro tection of minority rights.

38 DK, 'Commission on Human Rights and Sub-Commission on the Status of Women', Resolution of the Economic and Social Council of 16 February 1946, Document E/20 of 15 February 1946, box 53.

39 Reanda, 'The Commission on the Status of Women', p. 269.

40 'Engendering the Global Agenda', UN Nongovernmental Liaison Service (unsystem.org/ngls/gender%20part%203%20main.pdf).

41 DK, 'Report on conference between representatives of the National [USA] women's organizations and members of the staff of the State Department', Washington, DC, 29 March 1946, box 53.

42 Bodil Begtrup's speech quoted in Jain, *Women, Development and the UN*, p. 17.

43 'Short History of the Commission on the Status of Women', United Nations, Division for the Advancement of Women. The original delegates to the Commission on the Status of Women included: Jessie Mary Grey Street,

Australia; Evdokia Uralova, Belorussian Soviet Socialist Republic; Way Sung New, People's Republic of China; Graciela Morales F. de Echeverria, Costa Rica; Bodil Begtrup, Denmark; Marie Hélène Lefaucheux, France; Sara Basterrechea Ramirez, Guatemala; Shareefah Hamid Ali, India; Amalia Gonzales Caballero de Castillo Ledon, Mexico; Alice Kandalft Cosma, Syria; Mihri Pektas, Turkey; Elizavieta Alekseevna Popova, Union of Soviet Socialist Republics; Mary Sutherland, United Kingdom; Dorothy Kenyon, USA; and Isabel de Urdaneta, Venezuela.

44 DK, Dorothy Kenyon to Alice Shaffer and Mrs. Hendricks, Division of Social and Health Affairs, US State Department, 9 April 1946, box 55; FSM, Frieda S. Miller to Eleanor Roosevelt, 25 April 1946, box 7.

45 DK, Dorothy Kenyon to Katherine Bompas, International Alliance of Women, 4 February 1947, box 56.

46 'Short History of the Commission on the Status of Women', United Nations, Division for the Advancement of Women.

47 Reanda, 'The Commission on the Status of Women', p. 276.

48 Jain, *Women, Development and the UN*, p. 19.

49 DK, Press release no. 138 'Statement by Judge Dorothy Kenyon, US Representative on the Commission on the Status of Women, delivered at the Commission meeting on Tuesday, 11 February 1947', box 54.

50 Leon Gordenker and Thomas G. Weiss, 'Pluralizing global governance: analytical approaches and dimensions', in Thomas G. Weiss and Leon Gordenker (eds), *NGOs, the UN and Global Governance* (Boulder, CO: Lynn Rienner Publishers, 1996), pp. 21–2.

51 FSM, 'Report of Frieda S. Miller, Director, Women's Bureau, before Conference of Women's Organizations, 14 March 1946, on United Nations Sessions in London', box 2.

52 WYWCA, Ruth Woodsmall to Lilace Barnes, 27 July 1946, box 291.

53 DK, 'Non-governmental organizations arrangements for consultation described', *UN Weekly Bulletin*, 7 October 1946, box 53; Peter Willetts, 'Consultative status for NGOs at the United Nations', in Peter Willetts (ed.), *'The Conscience of the World': The Influence of Non-Governmental Organizations in the UN System* (London: Hurst & Company, 1996), pp. 37–40.

54 WYWCA, The enlarged meeting of the World's YWCA executive committee, Geneva, 28 May – 4 June 1946, Executive Committee meeting minutes; Gwendolen Home Peel, Liaison Committee of International Women's Organisations to Ruth Woodsmall, May 1947; UN General Secretary Trygve Lie to World YWCA General Secretary Ruth Woodsmall, 21 May 1947.

55 Berkovitch, *From Motherhood to Citizenship*, p. 108.

56 Willetts, 'Consultative status for NGOs at the United Nations', p. 43.

57 WYWCA, 'CONGO: Conference of Non-Governmental Organizations in Consultative Status with the United Nations Economic and Social Council', c. 1979, Conference of NGOs in Consultative Status with ECOSOC.

58 WYWCA, Anne Guthrie to Helen Roberts, 26 April 1948, World YWCA and United Nations Consultative Status, 1979–1985; Carole Seymour-Jones,

Journey of Faith: The History of the World YWCA 1945–1994 (London: Allison and Busby, 1994), pp. 119–21.

59 WYWCA, Ruth Woodsmall to Gladys Bretherton, 1 November 1946; Ruth Woodsmall to Gwendolyn Home Peel, 10 December 1946, Correspondence and Minutes, Liaison Committee, 1945–46, box 291.

60 WYWCA, Helen Roberts to Gwendolyn Home Peel, 7 March 1950, Liaison Committee, Documents and Correspondence, 1947–50.

61 RW, World's Young Women's Christian Association Leaders Study Course, Schlosshunigen, Switzerland, June 1946, box 45.

7

Allied post-war reconstruction projects

Linking 'women and democracy'

The post-war focus on women's political participation in the World Young Women's Christian Association (YWCA) was a long-running theme that women's organisations had often expressed during the interwar era: they believed that women's equal participation was necessary to establish just, peaceful, democratic societies.[1] Immediately after the war ended a gender discourse linking 'women and democracy' emerged again, inspired in part by the spread of the women's organisations' influence and in part by the new 'human rights' agenda that post-war global governance bodies incorporated. In her book *From Motherhood to Citizenship: Women's Rights and International Organizations*, Nitza Berkovitch has identified a critical moment after the Second World War when the United Nations (UN) was founded and a political shift occurred. At that time 'the emergence of human rights as an international concern . . . changed dramatically the way women have been discussed globally. For the first time women's rights as individual citizens were articulated and promoted by major global actors.'[2] As discussed previously, women's rights language was insinuated throughout the system of the UN – in the Charter, and in the documents of UN commissions, agencies International Labour Organization and the (ILO), as all articulated the goal to promote 'fundamental freedoms for all without distinction as to race, *sex*, language or religion'. In the post-war period 'women's rights' became an issue that demanded modern state intervention. With the notion of women's rights accepted by Western-defined 'world culture' Berkovitch argues that 'women as a group now can make legitimate claims on the state and can demand action on their own behalf'.[3]

Consequently equal participation in democratic nation-states in the post-war era could be claimed as every woman's 'right'. However, continued patriarchal resistance to notions of women's social, political, and economic equality, or to so-called 'women's rights', led some Western feminists who promoted women's full participation in all realms of society to employ other more 'neutral' and less overtly feminist language in order to forge alliances within patriarchal power structures. Liberal Western feminists within women's organisations followed this strategy in the post-war era and created with Western government policy makers a discourse linking 'women and democracy'. According to their formulations, women's political participation in a democratic society was sought as a functional goal; societies must utilise all of their human resources in order for a 'true' democracy to function optimally.

Within the 'women and democracy' framing discourse, women's organisations continued to promote the expansion of women's presence and attention to 'human issues' at the international level of politics through integration of well-qualified and well-connected women into existing patriarchal political bodies within the UN system and within UN member governments. Like other Western women's organisations at the time the World YWCA clearly articulated this goal:

> By no means the least responsibility of the YWCA in all parts of the world is to help make it possible for competent women to make their contribution to international affairs through direct participation in the work of the United Nations. This is no mere feminist ambition; in present day society it is still widely taken for granted that public life is the sphere of men. Women, therefore, must accept the obligation of ensuring that all the resources of the community are used in the achievement of world cooperation that is so essential to the future of civilization.[4]

The discourse linking women and democracy became an effective way to expand alliances with patriarchal power, as became evident during the Allied Occupations of Japan and Germany. These episodes reveal, however, the drawbacks of working within patriarchal governing institutions. This strategy imposes narrow limits on the benefits accrued to women and slows the advance of global feminist goals. Some critics have argued that the strategy of working with patriarchal institutions merely reinforces existing and unequal global power relations. In the post-war period the victorious Western Allies sought to transform the defeated fascist powers into reliable political allies and capitalist trade partners and to 'contain' the global influence of the totalitarian Soviet state and its communist ideology and economy. These political goals encompassed but did not always privilege the women's organisations' 'women and democracy' agendas.

Women's role in the post-war reconstruction of Japan

As the World War in Asia ended with the dropping of atomic bombs on Hiroshima and Nagasaki and the Japanese surrender to the Allied Powers in August 1945, Ruth Woodsmall was already planning her return to China and Japan as well as for the first post-war YWCA World Council meeting scheduled to take place in Hangzhou, China in October 1947.[5] Prior to the World Council Woodsmall brought the YWCA vice presidents from China and Japan to Geneva for an Executive Committee meeting in January 1947. The Chinese vice president, Madame Chu Shiming, was the wife of a high-ranking Nationalist Government General Chu Shiming who had served as Generalissimo Chiang Kai-shek's Military Attaché in Washington, DC during the Second World War and had been appointed as head of the China Mission in Occupied Japan. The Japanese vice president, Tamaki Uemura, had served as president of the Japanese YWCA throughout the Sino-Japanese War.

The Geneva meeting was a triumph for YWCA diplomacy and it demonstrated that the YWCA had built influential relationships with Allied governments during the war. United States General Douglas MacArthur, the Supreme Commander of the Allied Powers (SCAP) Occupation forces based in Tokyo, had granted Tamaki Uemura extraordinary permission to travel to the United States and Canada in summer 1946 as the special guest of the Presbyterian Church and Institute of World Missions. Uemura, an ordained Presbyterian Minister, was the first and for several years afterwards the only Japanese civilian allowed to leave Occupied Japan. Following Uemura's North American tour Ruth Woodsmall requested permission through her State Department contacts for Tamaki Uemura to travel onto Geneva to attend the World YWCA Executive Committee meeting and this extraordinary permission was also granted.

In addition to her YWCA connections there were other reasons that explain why Tamaki Uemura was allowed to travel to the West as a spokeswoman for the 'new' Japan the Allied Occupation force hoped to create. Accounts of Uemura's visits to the United States and Canada have described her appearance as 'diminutive, cultured, charming, dressed in her national costume in a soft blue shade', commented on her flawless English that was the product of a Wellesley College and University of Edinburgh education and years of involvement in the international women's and Christian movements, and denied that Uemura personally gave any direct assistance to the war effort. Uemura was also quoted asking for forgiveness on behalf of the Japanese people and expressing obeisance to the Western Christian Church and bowing to Western leadership.[6]

Uemura's remarks resonated with General Douglas MacArthur,

whom Uemura praised as 'wise and understanding'. [7] A devout Christian himself, General MacArthur believed that Christianity was the spiritual foundation of democracy and that the Christian conversion of Japan should accompany the Occupation force's liberal-democracy-building project.[8] Moreover MacArthur and his Occupation deputies believed that Japanese women were destined to play a key role in Japan's post-war 'democratisation'.[9]

One of General MacArthur's first acts as Supreme Commander of the Occupation force had been to extend suffrage to Japanese women on 11 October 1945 and to pressure the Japanese Diet to confirm women's voting rights through election law revision in December.[10] The draft constitution that Occupation forces presented to the Japanese Diet for confirmation in March 1946 on MacArthur's orders included Article 14, the 'Japanese ERA', outlawing discrimination in all forms based on race, creed, social status, family origin or sex, and Article 24 that extended women's equality into the private sphere with equal rights to choose a spouse, divorce and to own and inherit property.[11]

Even though Japan's male legislators resisted these constitutional provisions that undercut male dominance in Japanese society unyielding pressure from SCAP administrators forced their acquiescence. Susan J. Pharr has explained the linkage of 'democracy and feminism' during the Allied Occupation of Japan as a result of four special circumstances. First, the 'idealistic' Americans serving the Occupation force defined women's suffrage as a human right and not a 'women's right' per se. Second, the Americans did not have to live with the effects of the constitutional provisions that granted Japanese women equality. Third, the Occupation force's extraordinary authority allowed it to impose a wide range of reforms, with or without Japanese officials' support. And fourth, a mutually beneficial and therefore particularly effective alliance was forged among American women, civilian and military, who served in the Occupation force and politically astute Japanese feminists who had waged a women's suffrage campaign since the 1920s. Together, American and Japanese women advocated successfully for Japanese women's political and civil rights.[12]

At the January 1947 Executive Council meeting in Geneva where Woodsmall intended to lay the groundwork for post-war reconciliation among Japanese, Chinese and Western YWCA women Tamaki Uemura's remarks expressed the tone of abasement that she had adopted during her North American travels and that Japanese YWCA women expressed generally during the post-war period.[13] Uemura praised the wisdom of General MacArthur and Allied Occupation policy for preserving the Japanese Emperor as Japan's ceremonial head of state. Echoing the Occupation force's revisionist history she assigned sole responsibility for Japan's war policy to the militarists who 'took advantage' of the Emperor and 'fooled' the misguided Japanese people and she praised the moral superiority of the Chinese Nationalist President Chiang Kai-shek and his wartime leadership of the Chinese people – all in an effort to regain partnership in the global community of Christian womanhood.[14] Tamaki Uemura won over Western YWCA women; Chinese women, however, were not able to forgive or accept Japan's olive branch of friendship before or after the October 1947 Hangzhou World Council meeting.

Reconciling Asian women was only one consideration in the World YWCA's decision to hold the first post-war World Council in China. From the late 1920s onward the YWCA planned to hold a World Council in China but these plans had been postponed repeatedly by international and civil conflicts. As the first post-war World Council was organised, Chinese YWCA leaders pushed for a China location. Ruth Woodsmall was convinced that key government support gained through Madame Chu Shiming's close connections to the Chinese Nationalist government and the World YWCA's relationships with US Military and State Department officials would facilitate World Council arrangements and would guarantee that even her most ambitious plans to bring YWCA women from defeated Germany and Japan into China would succeed.[15] Woodsmall believed that if women from former enemy nations talked face to face their shared concerns would foster international collaborative projects to promote peace and advance women's economic and political status worldwide.[16] Moreover, the World Council would prove to male-led governments that the international women's movement had survived wartime divisions and was ready to move forward to address women's needs at the national and international levels.

Reuniting Asian women and involving them in post-war politics were major goals of the World Council meeting that convened in October. Yet in the very last days before the Council opened Woodsmall's plans to bring Japanese women into China and to inaugurate officially the China-Japan reconciliation process were thwarted. The Japanese delegation's requests for exit visas were denied. China's Nationalist government and two other governments represented on the Allied Powers Far Eastern Commission denied the visa requests because Japan had not yet signed a peace treaty concluding the Second World War.[17] Nevertheless, World YWCA leaders welcomed national delegates to China from thirty nations around the world, from Western Europe including Germany, the United States, Canada, Latin America, India, Korea, Australia, New Zealand, the Philippines and from China, the host nation. China's first lady Madame Chiang Kai-shek was an honoured guest along with representatives from the International Council of Women, the International Missionary Council, the International Federation of University Women, the World Bureau of Girl Guides and Girl Scouts, the World Council of Churches and the ILO. New regions of the world were targeted for YWCA development in the Caribbean, Middle East and West Africa, and new emphasis on programming for women in rural regions of member nations was stressed. And the schedule for the World YWCA leaders' post-Council visitation to Occupied Japan was finalised.[18]

When initial plans were made to visit Japan the US State Department and General MacArthur's Occupation forces at SCAP Headquarters strongly supported the World YWCA request. A State Department memo sent to SCAP headquarters in Tokyo in August 1947 asserted that 'The Y.W.C.A. is basically a democratic and international organization with outstanding women leaders throughout the world who have made significant contributions to their community and national life. It is believed that first-hand relationships with some of these leaders at the present time will have significant influence in furthering the cause of democracy and the participation of women in all phases of national life.'[19]

In the view of World YWCA women and Allied Occupation forces, Japanese women had to overcome their culturally bred tendencies to be 'too self-effacing and docile' and to 'confine themselves' to the domestic sphere, neglecting their obligations to the public sphere.[20] Sex-role traits that Westerners appreciated in Japanese women in some situations were in other circumstances used to criticise them. Whereas Western observers like Harold Wakefield described Japanese women in positive terms as 'graceful, brave, cultivated, and selflessly devoted to duty . . . centered primarily on family and secondarily on the state', these feminized behaviours could also be interpreted negatively, as potential hindrances to Japanese women's emancipation.[21] When that seemed to be the case, Westerners advocated behaviour modification. Addressing a group of Japanese women at Ushiromachi Middle School in Nagano during the November 1947 visitation Ruth Woodsmall clarified the Western liberal feminist agenda for Japanese women's liberation:

Although every citizen should be engaged in this work [reconstruction], women's responsibility is especially significant. A family lacks richness if a woman doesn't make efforts for the household. As well, women's contribution to society, to the nation, is needed. The idea that women's responsibility is for the household alone, and not for the well-being of society, is wrong. It is a mistake for women to separate society from the family and just put their efforts into the household . . . In Japan, the new constitution granted women great responsibility in reconstructing the nation. Things have changed from the time when only political leaders could contribute to society. Today, anyone has the right to contribute and women's organizations have to understand the new role they can play; this includes the YWCA and its role in promoting women's position in society.[22]

According to the Westerners – including YWCA women and the Allied Occupation force alike – Japanese women needed to learn ambition and derive inspiration from Western women, particularly from American women, to lead their society out of its heathen, anti-Western, anti-democratic past and onto the path of Christian, enlightened democracy.[23] Lulu Holmes, SCAP's Adviser on Women's Education, had written to Ruth Woodsmall in October 1946 to alert Woodsmall to the Japanese women's needs, as SCAP defined them:

> Miss Hikaru who is the national [YWCA General Secretary] is a very sensitive, fine Christian woman but she is not the person to develop the strong national group. I am satisfied that most of the Japanese women who are members of the national board are not the aggressive capable type who will help to build such a program. It seems imperative to me that if the national Y.W.C.A. of Japan is to take any part in the reconstruction of this country they will have to have official help from the International Organization in terms of a well-trained and far-seeing official who will come out here and work from the ground up to rebuild the organization.[24]

Education could facilitate this transformation of Japanese women, that is, through a Western curriculum that included social studies courses that would train women and girls to 'participate eagerly' in democratic local, national and international politics and to interject Christian morality into all policy debates.[25] This was the Christian internationalist and liberal feminist agenda for women's liberation that included both an outward-directed focus on global society and an inward-directed focus on character building that World YWCA women brought to Japan. It coincided with the women's agenda that the Allied Occupation force promoted. The Allied Occupation force did not co-opt the Western YWCA women, rather they shared similar goals.

World YWCA women believed that their own experiences as Christian feminists in Western nations offered tested and proven models to raise women's status and to increase women's role in the public sphere. When the UN granted the organisation consultative status with the Economic and Social Council (ECOSOC) the World YWCA's faith in its political efficacy seemed confirmed.[26] In Japan, World YWCA leaders were granted audiences with the Emperor and Empress, as well as meetings with General MacArthur, Prime Minister Tetsu Katayama, Foreign Minister Ashida Hitoshi and Diet member Hiroo Sasa and many other governors, mayors and Japanese diplomats. All these male leaders praised the YWCA leaders of 'Christian womanhood' who would teach Japan's 'long-oppressed womanhood' democratic values and would provide spiritual rejuvenation that would 'save' Japan and promote world peace.[27] When Foreign Minister Ashida hosted a luncheon for the World YWCA delegation and Japanese women leaders, the *Nippon Times* reported:

> 'Out of the ashes of war, a new nation has emerged in our midst,' the Foreign Minister said, 'a nation dedicated to the cause of peace, where its long-oppressed womanhood has been freed from feudal chains and now stands shoulder-to-shoulder with men in building a commonwealth which can take its place in the family of nations.' Stressing that the Japan of former days was no more, he made a plea for guidance and friendship and at the same time pledged to the Y.W.C.A. that Japan would cooperate and exert its utmost efforts in furthering the noble work of the organization.[28]

This male approval reaffirmed the World YWCA's liberal feminist agenda. Women had seemingly succeeded within the male-dominated system in achieving their objective to bring women's issues to the forefront of national and international policy. The public accolades that the World YWCA received in Japan capped Ruth Woodsmall's twelve-year long tenure as World YWCA general secretary and she concluded triumphantly:

> Without any qualification this mission to Japan was the most remarkable single experience in reference to the contact of the World's YWCA with a national movement. This was due to the unusual situation of Japan today. It far exceeded even my most sanguine anticipation. It had meaning not only for the YWCA in Japan but for the general public. It had the full endorsement of the Occupying Authority as was evident from all the official recognition and concentrated front page publicity and editorial comments in the Japanese and English press . . . The World's YWCA was certainly in visible form an instrument of Christian international relations.[29]

Japanese YWCA women embraced the World YWCA's and Allied Occupation force's agenda for women in the reconstructed Japanese democracy and in the post war international world order. Japanese YWCA General Secretary Shizue Hikaru spoke for the organisation during the visitation with World YWCA leaders when she stated that:

> With our newly acquired freedom, we must bear a greater responsibility. We must first arouse social consciousness in the Japanese women . . . This war has taught us that we cannot stand as we did before. Each enforced difficult situation can be turned into a useful experience and from these experiences we can rise, stronger and more useful as a youth organization and an international organization, striving for the uplifting of womanhood and for the brotherhood of mankind.[30]

Japanese YWCA women were among a small segment of the population of educated Japanese women who from the late nineteenth century
onwards looked to the West for models of 'ideal womanhood'. The World
YWCA had historically appealed to these so-called 'internationalist'
Japanese feminists. The anthropologist Karen Kelsky has explained how
Japanese women who adopted a Western-defined 'internationalist identity' historically and in contemporary Japan have displayed *akogare*, that
is, 'longing, desire, or idealization' of the West that has implicated Japanese
women in 'eroticized Western agendas of modernity and universalism
and [in] the emergence of a global cosmopolitan class that contains its
own hierarchies of race, gender, and capital'. During the Occupation era
Japanese women who adopted this internationalist identity participated
in 'a discourse of women's "deliverance" at the hands of the United States,
from what women insisted were the odious and intolerable oppressions of
the patriarchal Japanese family system'. American men in the Occupation
forces began to imagine themselves as Japanese women's saviours, 'not
only . . . generous father figures to young Japanese children, but "loving,
supportive, democratic" husbands to Japanese women whom they had
freed from a medieval patriarchal system'.[31]

Western YWCA women, too, saw themselves as saviours, and 'loving,
supportive, democratic' mothers to Japanese women – or perhaps as sisters
in an idealized and universalized 'global sisterhood'. Japanese YWCA
women certainly participated in this 'discourse of women's deliverance'
at the hands of the Occupation forces and the Western-led international
women's movement. The legacy of Allied Occupation force's and the
World YWCA's coinciding agendas for Japanese women's liberation was
ambiguous. As the historian John Dower has explained SCAP's plan for
Japan's national liberation – to liberate Japanese men and women from
their nation's militarist and fascist past and to reincorporate Japan into the
Western capitalist, anti-Communist orbit – the Occupation forces sought
to instigate a 'genuinely democratic revolution' but they did so through
the machinery of a 'neo-colonial military dictatorship'.[32] Dower has
defined the uniquely confounding neo-colonial relationship the American
occupiers forged with post-war Japan:

> There was no historical precedent for this sort of relationship, nor any-
> thing truly comparable elsewhere in the wake of the war. Responsibility for
> Germany, Japan's former Axis partner, divided as it was among the United
> States, England, France and the Soviet Union lacked the focused intensity
> that came with America's unilateral control over Japan. Germany also
> escaped the messianic fervor of General Douglas MacArthur, the postsur-
> render potentate in Tokyo. For the victors, occupying defeated Germany had
> none of the exoticism of what took place in Japan: the total control over a

pagan, 'Oriental' society by white men who were (unequivocally in General MacArthur's view) engaged in a Christian mission. The occupation of Japan was the last immodest exercise in the colonial conceit known as the 'white man's burden.'[33]

Yet ironically the national constitution that MacArthur and SCAP imposed on Japan in 1946-47 created, on paper, one of the most liberal and democratic governments throughout the world.

Moreover although the post-war constitution guaranteed women's full equality in Japanese society, Japan's patriarchal social order remained fundamentally intact. MacArthur's Occupation forces temporarily emasculated Japanese men to punish them for waging imperialist war but SCAP did not seriously undercut Japanese male power. General MacArthur saved the Japanese Emperor and retained most of his patriarchal authority in Japanese society by denying the Emperor's responsibility for waging imperialist war. SCAP acted to give Japanese women entrance into the political system in 1946 but did not level the playing field to allow women to compete for power as equals beyond the first post-war election cycle. [34]

World YWCA women led by Ruth Woodsmall attempted a feminist intervention to benefit Japanese women. Their visitation to Japan in 1947 and the subsequent elevation of women's issues in Japan's public sphere may have challenged Japanese male privilege but they did not effectively challenge Western patriarchy and its race, class and gender hierarchies, nor did the YWCA leaders reduce their own power as Western women vis-à-vis Japanese women.

Women's role in the post-war reconstruction of Germany

World YWCA general secretary Ruth Woodsmall masterminded the plan to lead the first international delegation of women into Occupied Japan. She arranged for special permissions granted at the highest levels of Allied power because she was well connected to Allied intergovernmental bodies and well known to US government policy makers. After her retirement from the World YWCA in 1947 at the age of 64, Woodsmall began to work directly with the United States government.

Beginning in 1948 and through January 1949 Woodsmall served as informal adviser to Dorothy Kenyon, the US delegate to the UN Commission on the Status of Women (CSW). Woodsmall and Kenyon were long-time friends who had collaborated for years through women's NGOs. When the March 1949 session of the UN CSW was scheduled to take place in Beirut, Lebanon, Kenyon and Rachel Nason who was then working for the State Department asked Woodsmall to draw on her network of friends and former colleagues and on her own first-hand knowledge of the region to advise the US delegation about the Middle Eastern women's movement and about Middle Eastern society and politics, in general. In particular, the State Department wanted Woodsmall to gather information about the regional activities and influence of the Women's International Democratic Federation (WIDF), a new association that was formed in Paris in 1945 by socialist women's organisations that were sympathetic to the Soviet Union.[35] The State Department feared 'that the meeting of the United Nations Commission on the Status of Women to be held in Beirut . . . may be used by the USSR to agitate against the United States in the Middle East'.[36]

During the Cold War era as women's international organisations adjusted to new political alignments, the WIDF, representing 'eight million women from fifty countries', often set itself up as an 'Eastern' counterpoint to the Western-led women's international organisations and, in particular, to American women's organisations. The WIDF challenged the Western women's claims to represent global feminist perspectives. The Soviet Union and socialist women in the WIDF advocated immediate emancipation for women and presented themselves as the champions of peace, human rights, anti-colonialism, and women's and children's welfare campaigns during the Cold War.[37] The longstanding Western women's organisations, in contrast, advocated a more evolutionary liberal democratic approach to achieving women's political rights through educational and legislative initiatives.[38]

The State Department watched WIDF activities carefully and defined the WIDF as a Soviet-front organisation that did not represent women's interests. Rather, the State Department claimed that the WIDF repeated Soviet propaganda when it asserted that women had already achieved equality in socialist societies and advocated socialist strategies for women's liberation within international forums, especially during the annual sessions of the UN Commission on the Status of Women.[39]

The State Department staff that coached the US delegation to the CSW had opposed ECOSOC's decision to award consultative status to the WIDF but the United States was overruled. Thereafter, the US government considered the CSW to be 'a very lively and prize-worthy propaganda vehicle – of first class interest in the East-West contest'.[40] Dorothy Kenyon and her adviser Ruth Woodsmall concurred with the State Department's designation of the WIDF as a tool of the Soviet Union.[41] Kenyon spent a great deal of energy at the March 1949 Beirut CSW sessions discrediting WIDF 'propaganda', debating with the Soviet CSW delegate Elizavieta Popova, and guarding 'against the Communist Fifth Column and all frontal attacks'.[42] Woodsmall planned to accompany Kenyon and the State Department delegation to the CSW meetings in Beirut. In January 1949, however, the US Military Occupation Force in Germany asked Woodsmall to lead its Women's Affairs Division and she eagerly accepted this new post.[43]

When Germany was defeated in May 1945 the Big Four anti-fascist Allies – the United States, Great Britain, France and the Soviet Union – together formed an Allied Council that divided Germany into zones of occupation where each occupying power was responsible for 'denazification and democratisation' as well as for collecting war reparations. Dividing Germany was seen as the practical solution to avoid the difficulties of reaching agreement on reparations policy or on post-war reconstruction policy between the rival Western Powers and the Soviet Union. Within its occupation zone the Soviet Union Military Administration implemented Stalinist policies for social transformation. They created 'anti-fascist' and socialist political parties, enacted land reform policies and created a collective farm system, and transferred the industrial infrastructure and all capital assets to the Soviet Union.[44] The Soviets recognised, as the Western Allies recognised, women's important role in Germany's reconstruction. Demographics alone demanded attention to women's contributions. German women outnumbered men three to two in the 25 to 40-year-old age range in the immediate post-war years. Women's full participation in the productive labour force and their incorporation into public life were policies instituted for practical as well as ideological reasons. Even though the Soviet-sponsored state failed to provide much childcare or other forms of welfare for working mothers through the 1950s women still entered the workforce, schools and governing structures in East Germany in large numbers.[45] Differences among the Western allies prevented them from uniting to oppose Soviet initiatives or from devising a common approach to German reconstruction in the Western zones.

As General Douglas MacArthur directed the post-war government of Japan, within his more limited American occupation zone in Germany US General Lucius Clay headed the Office of the Military Government of the United States (OMGUS) and directed German governing policy. Clay proved to be '"an intense and disciplined Army technocrat" whose imperious personality hid his sensitivity to Washington's criticism and his concern for the welfare of "his" Germans . . . He believed that his first responsibility was to get Germany "on its feet", thus reducing the cost of the occupation to the American taxpayer.' Clay sympathised with German suffering as he viewed destroyed cities and farmlands across Germany and the consequent critical food shortages, widespread hunger and lack of functioning industries. He tried to persuade the Allies to adopt a unified economic policy to promote German recovery but got little support from the Soviet Union or from France and limited support from Britain.[46]

Allied occupation efforts remained stalemated and economic recovery stalled until the US State Department proposed a massive and coordinated European Recovery Programme known as the Marshall Plan, so-named for the US secretary of state, George Marshall, who announced the Plan to include all the German occupation zones in June 1947.[47] The Soviet Union refused to participate in the Marshall Plan as developed by the Americans. The Marshall Plan would have weakened Soviet influence in Eastern Germany by flooding the Soviet sphere with American dollars and it would have increased Eastern European dependence, as providers of raw materials, on the industrialised Western European nations. Eventually in the years following 1949 the Marshall Plan sparked Western European post-war recovery with $12.4 billion invested to rebuild industries and to promote self-sustaining economic growth. As it was initially envisioned and presented to US Congress by the State Department, the Marshall Plan served American global interests but it also served humanitarian purposes. Ultimately, however, it increased tensions between the West and the Soviet Union and intensified the Cold War rivalry. By 1952 Marshall Plan dollars funnelled mostly anti-Soviet military aid to Western European nations.[48]

As part of the Marshall Plan aid package the US government maintained an Occupation force in Germany until a formal peace treaty was signed in 1952. General Clay's Office of the Military Government continued its supervisory operations and initiated programmes to build democratic institutions. According to the political scientist C. R. Hiscocks who had studied democracy building in West Germany between 1945 and 1949, 'the Allies realized that if Germany was to become a democracy, the German people must play a part in the government of their country as soon as possible and while the Allied authorities were still present to supervise the early stages of the new democratic experiment'. The Allies lifted a post-war ban on political parties soon after they established their authority within the Western zones. And the Cultural, Educational and Information Divisions of the Allied governing councils pursued 'less direct but more fundamental' development of democratic institutions.[49] In February 1948, OMGUS established a Women's Affairs Division as part of the American projects to incorporate German women into the denazification and democracy-building project. Lorena Hahn who worked with the OMGUS in its Welfare Division and was a former national president of the Women's Auxiliary of the American Legion was named as the first Chief of Women's Affairs Division. She remained in that post until October 1948. Ruth Woodsmall was hired to lead the Division in January 1949.[50] As Woodsmall wrote to her friends after accepting the leadership position:

The Women's Affairs Section, as I envision it, has a wide responsibility for stimulating and encouraging women's activities in all fields – in education, public health, and welfare, labor unions, government and politics, and religious affairs. To work alongside German women leaders and help them in every way possible in their efforts to promote the full contribution of women to rebuilding the life of Germany will be my special task. There will be much in this day by day work which will never be summed up in official reports.[51]

The historian Helen Laville has written that in their collaborations with Ruth Woodsmall and the Women's Affairs Division, American women's organisations provided 'The Recipe for American Democracy' in Occupied Germany. This was a social feminist recipe as opposed to an egalitarian feminist one that engaged German women in politics through voluntary associations with the message that women's political participation was a 'responsibility' in a democratic state rather than emphasising participation as a 'right' of 'equal citizenship'.[52] Ruth Woodsmall invited World YWCA vice president Cornelia van Asch van Wijck to speak at a Women's Affairs Division international conference in 1950 that she organised around the theme of 'The Individual Responsibility of Women in Meeting Critical Issues of Today'. Van Asch van Wijck expressed the social feminist perspective when she spoke to German women and 'described the "new feminism" which had developed during the conference, a feminism which placed emphasis on women's service and co-responsibility with men in civic affairs rather than on an aggressive but misguided struggle for women's rights'.[53]

According to Helen Laville, 'The Women's Affairs Bureau . . . saw it as their responsibility to educate previously politically innocent German women about their civic responsibilities. This education was a two-stage process. First, Germany women must be awakened from the political apathy with which Americans were convinced they approached life. Once German women were aroused from apathy, they could be "re-educated" in the ways of democracy'.[54] The Women's Affairs Division policies deliberately incorporated the 'good mother tradition' that Americans expected would appeal to German women, who were constructed as politically naive and innocent of war crimes, in order to engage these women in political activities.[55] In fact, Laville asserts, German women were war-weary, 'drained and apathetic to anyone offering political solutions'.[56]

The sociologists Marilyn Rueschemeyer and Hanna Schisler have contrasted the role of women in Germany's post-war reconstruction in the Eastern and Western occupation zones. Their research revealed that West German women did not define their own roles in society. Rather, the reconstituted but still patriarchal state and social institutions determined women's roles. After 1949 the American, British and French

Occupation zones were consolidated into the Federal Republic of Germany and a new Basic Law established women's equality and banned laws that discriminated against women. However, as in other Western nations the German state was reluctant to intervene to promote women's equal status. The equal rights clause of the Basic Law did not match social practices. 'Traditional gender roles and the male/female division of labor were quickly restored in post-war West Germany, and the example of "forced emancipation" [of women] in East Germany deterred further steps toward equality in the crucial years of the late 1940s and early 1950s.'[57]

Nonetheless, between 1949 and 1952 Ruth Woodsmall designed a plethora of programmes linking women and democracy building that 'aimed at training women for more effective citizenship in their own communities, increasing their professional opportunities, improving their position in economic life, and developing international contacts'.[58] Woodsmall sent German women to the United States for training in democratic politics, held international women's conferences in Germany, restored German women's national chapter affiliations to women's international organisations, and initiated new international relationships among German women and UN commissions and specialised agencies.[59]

In her position as Chief of the Women's Affairs Division Woodsmall drew on her network of female friends and associates to implement the programmes that she designed. At the end of 1949 Woodsmall asked Dorothy Kenyon to share her legal expertise and join the Women's Affairs Division for several months in 1950 to 'help the German women rewrite their laws [the Civil Code] relating to women'. Kenyon expressed interest in this project but hesitated to commit until she knew whether she would be reappointed to represent the United States on the CSW.[60] Woodsmall was eager to recruit Kenyon but noted that Kenyon would need to be cleared by the Federal Bureau of Investigation, a seemingly pro forma background check.[61]

Neither Woodsmall nor Kenyon anticipated that Kenyon's past political associations would be considered pro-Communist or that her loyalty to the United States would be questioned. But in the intensely anti-Communist climate in Cold War America Kenyon became a victim of Senator Joseph McCarthy's attack on her character and record of public service. Even before Woodsmall contacted Kenyon, the State Department was already scrutinising Kenyon's record as it determined the next delegate for the upcoming 1950 session of the CSW. Kenyon never knew whether it was her past associations with the American Civil Liberties Union, the Inter-American Commission of Women, or the Women's Trade Union League or her contributions to the League of Nations Inquiry on the Status of Women during Franklin Roosevelt's administration that had raised McCarthy's suspicions.[62] Nonetheless Senator McCarthy accused Kenyon of being a Communist at hearings before the Tydings Committee, the Senate Foreign Relations Subcommittee convened to investigate McCarthy's charges that 250 Communists had infiltrated US State Department operations before and during the war and had betrayed the 'Democratic Christian world'.[63]

During her testimony before the Senate Subcommittee Kenyon answered McCarthy's charges and forced him to back down. As she told Woodsmall 'we had a battle royal and I think I came out on top'.[64] McCarthy's accusations nevertheless ended Kenyon's government service career.[65] In response to Woodsmall's repeated requests that the State Department approve Kenyon's appointment to the Women's Affairs Division because Kenyon was 'the international authority on this subject' of Civil Code revision,[66] Rachel Nason informed Kenyon 'for the moment the Department is not moving on controversial people and may not even until [after] the next elections'.[67]

Increasingly, Cold War anti-Communist dictates transformed the Women's Affairs Division and its programmes more often 'focused on propaganda aimed at refuting the allegations of the Soviet Union and winning the loyalty of the women of Germany and elsewhere to the American cause'.[68] In April 1951 Woodsmall invited a group of fifteen leaders from American women's organisations to tour Germany, meet with German women, and celebrate the role that women's organisations had played in the United States social and political life. Woodsmall involved the leaders of the British and French Women's Divisions so that all West German states were visited and the Americans met with German women in Frankfurt, Wiesbaden, Heidelberg, Stuttgart, Freiberg, Munich, Nuremburg, Berlin, Bremen, Hamburg, Hanover, Kiel, Düsseldorf and Bonn.

The Americans discussed a wide range of political, labour and social issues with women from all realms of German society: those who served in government, education and business, and those who represented the middle and working classes, and rural farm women. During the same visit Woodsmall provided the Americans with a cautionary 'glimpse' of the Soviet-dominated East Germany where, according to the director of Christian World Relations Luella Rockmeyer, 'The prostitution of the terms "peace", "freedom" and "democracy" has to be seen to be truly appreciated. The "iron curtain" is a tragic reality. What is happening to the children and youth beyond that curtain is a repetition of what happened to German youth under National Socialism.'[69]

By the time that the Allied Occupation of Germany ended in 1952 US foreign policy priorities had shifted from 'democratisation and denazification' to anti-Communist containment. The priorities of the Western feminists who led American NGOs and who participated in US global gender policy making were likewise transformed. Helen Laville has concluded, 'The rhetoric of American women's organizations, which had in the immediate aftermath of the Second World War proclaimed them internationalists and women, became increasingly focused on their role as Cold War warriors and Americans.'[70]

Indeed, Ruth Woodsmall had transformed from the internationalist general secretary of the World YWCA into the American director of the Women's Affairs Division in Occupied Germany. These two very different professional positions dictated Woodsmall's shifting loyalties but in many respects she was blind to the contractions between 'internationalism' and the Cold War version of American nationalism. Woodsmall certainly believed that the American democratic system more closely matched her Christian internationalist values than the totalitarian governing system of the Soviet Union. She sought to restore collaborative relationships between German women and Western-led women's international organisations and she believed that the Women's Affairs Division succeeded in achieving this goal. Moreover, she believed that she had instilled a faith among German women in the UN as a new world organisation that could promote peace and other global social policies and programmes that would benefit women worldwide. Woodsmall promoted an American nationalist version of 'internationalism' yet she continued to define her perspective as a universal and 'feminist' vision.[71]

Notes

1 The author thanks the editor of the *Journal of World History* for permission to include excerpts from a previously published article. Karen Garner, 'Global feminism and post war reconstruction: the World YWCA "visitation" to occupied Japan, 1947', *Journal of World History* 15:2 (June 2004), pp. 191–227.

2 Nitza Berkovitch, *From Motherhood to Citizenship: Women's Rights and International Organizations* (Baltimore, MD: Johns Hopkins University Press, 1999), p. 16.

3 Ibid., p. 3.

4 WYWCA, Marion V. Royce, 'World organizations and the World's YWCA', [pamphlet prepared for 1947 World's Council].

5 RW, Ruth Woodsmall to Mrs John D. Rockefeller, 23 August 1945, RW, box 17; Anne Guthrie to Ruth Woodsmall, 12 December 1945, box 42.

6 WYWCA, 'Mrs. Tamaki Uemura, only civilian released from Japan since the war speaks at 10:45', c. summer 1946, unidentified newspaper clipping; 'College honors Tokyo Christian leader' [Wooster, OH] *Daily Record* (6 March 1947), Who's Who Files: Tamaki Uemura. See also: WYWCA,

Mildred Roe to 'Friend of Japan', 30 June 1946, Country Files, Japan 1940–1946.

7 WYWCA, 'Reverend Tamaki Uemura, Japanese woman, visits Canada', *United Church Observer* (Toronto), 1 September 1946, Who's Who Files: Tamaki Uemura.

8 General Douglas MacArthur Memorial Library and Archives, Norfolk, Virginia, 'Christianity seen as chief hope of Japan by Gen. MacArthur', *Washington Post* (11 January 1947), p. 13; press release, Civil Information and Education Section, Occupation Forces, 12 January 1947.

9 Mire Koikari, 'Exporting democracy? American women, "feminist reforms", and the politics of imperialism in the U.S. occupation of Japan, 1945–1952', *Frontiers* 23:1 (2002), pp. 23–45.

10 Beate Sirota Gordon, *The Only Woman in the Room: A Memoir* (New York: Kodansha International, 1997), p. 109.

11 Ibid., pp. 106–8. Beate Sirota Gordon, a 22-year-old assigned to the SCAP Cultural Affairs Section, wrote these provisions, even though, by her own admission, Gordon knew little of constitutional theory or content. She was selected because she was the only woman on the writing team, and therefore her colleagues Colonel Kades and Colonel Roest assumed that it was most appropriate for her to compose the women's rights section.

12 Susan J. Pharr, 'The politics of women's rights', in Robert R. War and Sakamoto Yoshikazu (eds), *Democratizing Japan: The Allied Occupation* (Honolulu: University of Hawaii Press, 1987), pp. 221–52.

13 YWCA of Japan Archives, Tokyo, Report of the General Secretary YWCA of Japan, Shizue Hikaru, 11 November 1947, translated for author by Eiko Isogai Williams.

14 RW, Report on talks given at World YWCA Executive Committee Meeting, 19 January 1947, box 63.

15 WYWCA, Ruth Woodsmall to Mildred Roe, 3 February 1947, Japan Country Documents II; RW, Ruth Woodsmall to World YWCA Executive Committee, 26 June 1947, box 18.

16 WYWCA, Hangchow World's Council meeting minutes, 15 October 1947.

17 WYWCA, Emma Kaufman to Friends in Toronto, Canada YWCA, 3 October 1947, Japan Country Documents II.

18 RW, World's YWCA Council Meeting Hangchow, Chekiang, China, interim release no. 2, 29 October 1947, box 47.

19 YWCA of Japan Archives, Tokyo, Japan, Memo from American Advisory Secretary [US State Department] to Section G 1 General Headquarters SCAP, 19 August 1947.

20 Harold Wakefield, *New Paths for Japan* (New York: Oxford University Press, 1948), p. 76; Frank Kelley and Cornelius Ryan, *Star-Spangled Mikado* (New York: Robert M. McBride & Co., 1947), pp. 160–2; Elizabeth Gray Vining, *Return to Japan* (Philadelphia, PA: J. B. Lippincott Co., 1960), p. 38; Lucy Hendon Crockett, *Popcorn on the Ginza: An Informal Portrait of Postwar Japan* (London: Victor Gollancz, 1949), pp. 152 and 158; RW, Lulu Holmes, Adviser

on Women's Education, SCAP, 1946–48, 'The education of women in the new Japan', March 1949, box 45.

21 Wakefield, *New Paths for Japan*, p. 76.

22 YWCA of Japan Archives, Tokyo, Japan, Ruth Woodsmall, 'Women's role in post-war reconstruction', address at Ushiromachi Middle School in Nagano, 19 November 1947, translated for author by Eiko Isogai Williams.

23 Crockett, *Popcorn on the Ginza*, pp. 163 and 273–4; WYWCA, 'Japan YWCA to mark golden jubilee', *Nippon Times* (21 October 1955); YWCA of Japan Archives, Tokyo, Japan, Tsugi Shirashi, 'Patience, hope, needed for peace, declares new president YWCA', *Nippon Times* (16 November 1947); 'WYWCA Leaders Visit Osaka', *Osaka Times* (18 November 1947), translated for author by Eiko Isogai Williams.

24 RW, Lulu Holmes, SCAP Headquarters, Tokyo, to Ruth Woodsmall, 30 October 1946, box 42.

25 WYWCA, Ruth Woodsmall to Emma Kaufman, 20 August 1947, 'World Council Hangchow'; RW, Lulu Holmes, 'Education in the new Japan', May 1948 and 'The education of women in the new Japan', March 1949, box 45.

26 RW, Ruth Woodsmall, 'The meaning of consultative status with the Economic and Social Council of the United Nations', 1947, box 47.

27 RW, Remarks by Hiroo Sasa, Kyushu University, member House of Councilors, managing editor of *Asahi Shimbum* on 'Japan's current situation and women', box 45; YWCA of Japan Archives, Tokyo, Japan, Tsugi Shirashi, 'Visiting YWCA leaders to attend 4-day convention opening today', *Nippon Times* (11 November 1947).

28 YWCA of Japan Archives, Tokyo, Japan, 'Ashida plays host to YWCA leaders', *Nippon Times* (16 November 1947).

29 RW, Ruth Woodsmall to Marianne Mills, 28 November 1947, box 18.

30 Shizue Hikaru, 'Report of the general secretary', 11 November 1947.

31 Karen Kelsky, *Women on the Verge: Japanese Women, Western Dreams* (Durham, NC: Duke University Press, 2001), pp. 22–80.

32 John Dower, *Embracing Defeat: Japan in the Wake of World War II* (New York: W. W. Norton & Co., 1999), pp. 80–1.

33 Ibid., pp. 23–4.

34 Sally Ann Hastings, 'Women legislators in the postwar Diet', in Anne E. Imamura (ed.), *Re-Imagining Japanese Women* (Berkeley, CA: University of California Press, 1996), pp. 271–300; Sachiiko Keneko, 'The struggle for legal rights and reforms: a historical view', in Kumiko Fujimura-Faneslow and Atsuko Kameda (eds), *Japanese Women: New Feminist Perspectives on Past, Present and Future* (New York: The Feminist Press, 1995), pp. 8–10.

35 RW, Ruth Woodsmall to Dr Martin, American Christian University in Cairo, 21 December 1948, and Ruth Woodsmall to Mrs James (Matilde) Keeley, Jr., Damascus, Syria, 21 December 1948 and Ruth Woodsmall to Mrs Frederick (Bertha) Vester, Boston, MA, 22 December 1948, box 18.

36 Helen Laville, *Cold War Women: The International Activities of American Women's Organizations* (New York: Palgrave, 2002), p. 115.

37 Mire Koikari, *Pedagogy of Democracy: Feminism and the Cold War in the US Occupation of Japan* (Philadelphia, PA: Temple University Press, 2008), pp. 151–2.

38 Laville, *Cold War Women*, pp. 116–17.

39 DK, Incoming Telegram United States [CSW] Delegation, New York Infotel No. 384 from Moscow dated 12 February 9 p.m., from the Secretary of State, box 53; Laville, *Cold War Women*, pp. 113–16.

40 Frieda Miller quoted in Laville, *Cold War Women*, p. 114.

41 DK, Dorothy Kenyon to Miss Mary Sutherland, c/o the Labour Party, London, England, 8 April 1947, box 56; RW, Ruth Woodsmall to Dr Martin, American Christian University in Cairo, 21 December 1948, box 18.

42 DK, Ruth Woodsmall to Dorothy Kenyon, 28 March 1950, DK, box 37; 'Commission on the Status of Women, third session', by Margaret Hickey, Chairman, UN Committee, International Federation of Business and Professional Women, May 1949, box 55; press release: 'Statement for the press by Judge Dorothy Kenyon, representative of the US on third session of the UN CSW meeting in Beirut, March 21–April 4 1949,' 19 May 1949, box 54.

43 RW, Ruth Woodsmall to 'Friends', 25 January 1949, box 18.

44 Thomas Alan Schwartz, *America's Germany: John J. McCloy and the Federal Republic of Germany* (Cambridge, MA: Harvard University Press, 1991), p. 30.

45 Marilyn Rueschemeyer and Hanna Schissler, 'Women in the two Germanys', *German Studies Review* 13 (1990), p. 72.

46 Schwartz, *America's Germany*, p. 30.

47 Ibid., p. 31.

48 Thomas G. Paterson, J. Garry Clifford and Kenneth J. Hagan *American Foreign Relations A History Since 1895*, vol. II, 4th edition (Lexington, MA: D. C. Heath and Company, 1995), pp. 293–4.

49 C. R. Hiscocks, 'The development of democracy in Western Germany since the Second World War', *Canadian Journal of Economics and Political Science* 20:4 (November 1954), pp. 496–7.

50 'Personalities and projects – social welfare in terms of significant people: new hopes and plans for German women', *Survey* (March 1949), pp. 174–5.

51 RW, Ruth Woodsmall to 'Friends', 25 January 1949, box 18.

52 Laville, *Cold War Women*, p. 78.

53 Papers of the High Commission of Occupied Germany, 1949–1985, Sophia Smith Collection, Smith College, Northampton, MA (hereafter HCOG), 'Women's responsibilities' report on the conference 'The individual responsibility of women in meeting critical issues of today' reprinted from the [US State Department] *Information Bulletin*, November 1950, box 1.

54 Laville, *Cold War Women*, p. 72.

55 Ibid., p. 78.

56 Ibid., p. 74.

57 Rueschemeyer and Schissler, 'Women in the two Germanys', pp. 73–4.

58 HCOG, 'Women in West Germany', box 1; Morgan–Howes Papers, Ruth Woodsmall to friends and associates, 20 July 1952, box 5.
59 Morgan–Howes Papers, Ruth Woodsmall to Laura Puffer Morgan, 20 July 1952, box 5.
60 DK, Dorothy Kenyon to Ruth Woodsmall, 13 December 1949, box 37.
61 DK, Ruth Woodsmall to Dorothy Kenyon, 6 January 1950, box 37.
62 Kate Weigand and Daniel Horowitz, 'Dorothy Kenyon, feminist organizing, 1919–1963', *Journal of Women's History* 14 (2002), p. 128.
63 Melvyn P. Leffler, *A Preponderance of Power: National Security, the Truman Administration and the Cold War* (Stanford, CA: Stanford University Press, 1992), p. 343.
64 DK, Dorothy Kenyon to Ruth Woodsmall, 31 March 1950, box 37.
65 Weigand and Horowitz, 'Dorothy Kenyon, feminist organizing', p. 128.
66 HCOG, Memo: To Mr William Johnstone, Chief, Division of Cultural Exchange, Department of State; From Miss Ruth Woodsmall, Chief, Women's Affairs Branch, Educational and Cultural Relations Division; DK, 'Appointment of Judge Dorothy Kenyon for expert legal advisory service in Germany', 29 April 1950, box 37.
67 DK, Rachel Nason to Dorothy Kenyon, 20 April 1950, box 37.
68 Laville, *Cold War Women*, p. 90.
69 HCOG, Luella Rockmeyer, 'Report to the Department of State, American Women's Panel in Germany, April 20, 1951–June 4, 1951,' c. June 1951, box 1.
70 Laville, *Cold War Women*, pp. 90–1.
71 Morgan–Howes Papers, Ruth Woodsmall to Laura Puffer Morgan, 20 July 1952, box 5.

8

The Cold War

Collaborations with the Commission on the Status of Women

In its earliest years of operation the Commission on the Status of Women (CSW) addressed some of the long-standing goals that Western-led women's organisations had articulated during the League of Nations era. For example, CSW delegates supported the drafting of a Universal Declaration of Human Rights by the Human Rights Commission (HRC). The Declaration asserted 'universal respect for the observance of human rights and fundamental freedoms' followed by a listing of 'the political, civil, economic, social and cultural rights to which every human being is entitled'.[1] However, in the Declaration's first draft the first article stated that 'all *men* are created equal'. Consequently, the Commission lobbied for the addition of gender-inclusive language in the Declaration's final form and succeeded in changing 'all *men*' to 'all *human beings*' and persuaded some reluctant HRC members that the language – and implied gender hierarchy – mattered.[2]

During its first sessions the CSW also advocated for women's rights to participate equally in politics and to maintain their own national citizenship and ownership of property after marriage. Eventually the CSW proposed a Convention on the Political Rights of Women that the UN General Assembly adopted in 1952 and a Convention on the Nationality of Married Women adopted in 1957, followed by the Convention and Recommendation on Consent to Marriage, Minimum Age for Marriage, and Registration of Marriages. At the urging of women's organisations, the CSW also addressed women's economic rights. In collaboration with the International Labour Organization the CSW initiated a study of women's wages that led to the 1951 Convention on Equal Remuneration for Men and Women for Work of Equal Value.[3] The CSW's early Cold War era agenda and record of accomplishments certainly revealed the strong and effective influence of the women's international organisations.

Throughout this era women's organisations also continued to push for the appointment of more women to the UN secretariat as well as to government delegations through the forum provided by the CSW's annual sessions. In 1949 the Women's International League for Peace and Freedom (WILPF) conducted a study of employment patterns at the United Nations. Their investigation revealed how superpower politics determined the appointments of government delegates from Eastern and Western countries but their final report asserted that sexism rather than geopolitical considerations prevented women from gaining appointments to secretariat or other United Nations leadership posts. WILPF's report, 'Women in the United Nations' presented to the Commission on the Status of Women concluded:

> The main barrier to a liberal and just policy as regards the use of women in the UNO seems to be prejudice, conscious or unconscious, even in countries we call liberal and where there have long been movements for women's rights. The facts as shown in this compilation speak for themselves. Whether there is a woman more or less on the staff of the Secretariat or in the national delegations does not change the character of their composition. There is discrimination, there is inequality, in spite of all the declarations to the contrary. It is up to the women in each Member State of the UN to call attention to the facts and figures and to take energetic steps to bring about an adequate representation of women in the UN.[4]

To overcome persistent patterns of discrimination at the UN, women's organisations continued to identify and promote the appointments of qualified women to male-led UN agencies.[5] Other organisations including the International Federation for Business and Professional Women and the International Council of Women echoed the WILPF report in subsequent years. They made official statements at CSW meetings, calling attention to the persistently small numbers of women appointed to national delegations or employed in positions of authority within the UN secretariat. These statements were officially entered into the Commission session records. The women's organisations also pressed the CSW to request yearly reports on employment status of women from the UN secretariat.[6]

Over the years, women's organisations recommended many projects to guide the CSW's agenda. For example, at the 1949 CSW session in Beirut women's organisations urged the CSW to use the media 'to promote and further the political, social and economic education of women, to accelerate women's progress toward higher professional positions nationally and internationally'. They suggested that the CSW should publicise the fact that United Nations Educational, Scientific and Cultural Organization (UNESCO) and other international fellowships were available to fund higher education for female students. They called on the CSW to recommend that the Economic and Social Council (ECOSOC) expand research and education initiatives generally and especially in regard to political education that could prepare women for appointments and work in diplomatic and international fields. They prompted the CSW to conduct its own studies regarding the extent and conditions of child labour and the impact of post-war relocations on women and their families and to coordinate these efforts with the United Nations Social Commission.[7]

This wide range of recommendations demonstrated that women's organisations believed in the CSW's potential to serve global women's interests and to raise women's status even as the fifteen-member Commission moved slowly towards those goals, meeting only once a year for a two-week long session (these later increased to three-week sessions).[8] The Commission had limited powers to conduct surveys and studies and then to recommend further actions to ECOSOC but women's organisations urged the CSW to exercise the full extent of its power. The organisations also used their own considerable influence with national governments to promote CSW recommendations to advance the status of women in their home countries.[9]

Nonetheless, Cold War politics unavoidably affected women's activism. As they lobbied CSW delegates regarding the Commission's agenda Western-led women's organisations strove to identify 'universal women's issues' but they often refused to acknowledge their own obviously Western biases and this caused some awkward internal debates. In one instance during the 1955 annual session the CSW discussed the 1952 Convention on Women's Political Rights and whether women's status had risen internationally as a consequence. Socialist delegates from the Soviet Union, Belarus and Poland asserted that the exercise of women's political rights globally was closely linked to the maintenance of peace. Therefore they argued that the CSW should support the Soviet Union's proposal to the UN General Assembly to ban nuclear weapons in order to halt the international arms race and create more favourable conditions for peace.

In this case the Soviet women were taking a stand to promote peace achieved through disarmament similar to the one that Western-led women's international organisations had advocated during the 1930s. During the Cold War era, however, Western women considered this peace proposal to be a form of Soviet 'propaganda'. Western women who spoke at the CSW session not only opposed Soviet-sponsored disarmament plans, they argued that discussion of the Soviet initiative 'was outside the Commission's terms of reference', thus effectively shutting down a discussion of women's role in peacemaking in the CSW forum.[10]

During the Cold War era the Soviet Union presented itself as the champion of world peace in UN meetings, opposed by the 'warmonger-ing' United States. The US government on the other hand characterised Soviet peace initiatives as insincere and duplicitous proposals for 'negative peace', that is, peace defined narrowly as the absence of war or openly violent conflict but without guarantees for personal freedoms, protection of human rights or realisation of social justice. Throughout the 1950s when anti-Communist containment policy dictated foreign as well as domestic politics in the United States the US government's perspective strongly influenced American and Western-led women's organisations. Consequently Western women opposed international peace initiatives that originated in the Women's International Democratic Federation (WIDF) or from other Eastern bloc sources. The Western women generally shared the US government's perspective but they also feared being labelled as pro-Communist agents or dupes of Soviet propagandists and suffering political reprisals in their own countries as a consequence.[11]

Alliances with Western governments

East-West power politics had also determined the UN policy towards Second World War refugees since its inception. From its origins in 1943, the United States had dominated the United Nations Relief and Rehabilitation Administration (UNRRA) by providing the major source of funding and organisational leadership. Although the forty-four nation alliance that fought the fascist powers together joined UNRRA, soon after the war con-cluded the Soviet Union rejected UNRRA's American-inspired policies and refused to allow the UN agency to operate in its European zones of occu-pation. For its part, the United States resisted Soviet policies that forced repatriation of Eastern Europeans into Soviet-controlled countries against the will of the displaced persons who preferred to emigrate to the West. For these reasons, UNRRA was dissolved in 1947. In his study *Refugees in International Politics* the political scientist Leon Gordenker concluded '[in] seeking the dissolution of the UNRRA, the United States reflected the growing Soviet-American animosity. The United States wanted to eliminate the Soviet voice from refugee policy, to prevent the forcible repatriation of displaced persons and refugees to the Soviet Union and to cut off the dribble of economic aid to the USSR that UNRRA provided.' The International Refugee Organization (IRO) replaced UNRRA and operated until 1950. Eighteen Western states joined the IRO that was funded pri-marily by donations from the United States and Britain. The IRO assisted the still-unsettled European war refugees and helped them relocate to 'depopulated Western European countries and "under-populated" Canada and Australia'. The Soviet Union did not join the IRO, and the IRO did not operate in Soviet-sphere countries. Although Soviet delegates criticised the IRO policies in UN forums, 'during the years of the Cold War, the United States and its allies succeeded in excluding the Soviet Union from any significant influence on the international treatment of refugee affairs.'[12]

Under the general supervision of Alice Arnold the World Young Women's Christian Association (YWCA) continued to build its alliance with Western governments and, at the same time, to carry out a humanitarian agenda aiding refugees and women prisoners of war in Germany and Austria. The World YWCA sent Western secretaries from Sweden, Great Britain, Canada and Australia to work with local refugee operations through its Mutual Service Committee, bridging the global agency transition from UNRRA to IRO with no break in YWCA activities. From the very beginning of the European war YWCA secretaries dispatched to refugee camps had distributed emergency material aid and then helped to organise recreation, schools, or other activities for women and children.[13] In 1950 the World YWCA estimated that 150,000 Second World War refugees 'ineligible for emigration due to age, illness, or other disability' remained in West Germany and required continuing services. A steady stream of new populations of refugees also arrived in West Germany in flight from Eastern European Soviet-controlled territories. After the State of Israel was founded in 1948 the YWCA initiated service to Palestinian refugees forced to relocate to Lebanon and Syria, where national YWCAs operated. Funds were scarce but YWCA secretaries provided services to Palestinian women's groups as they had to European women and organised informal educational opportunities, leadership training, employment counselling and operated summer camps for children. The World YWCA estimated that 100,000 Palestinians were in Lebanon and Syria in 1950 and that only 1,700 hundred had found work through UN agencies.[14] When the UN opened Palestinian refugee camps in Jordan, YWCA refugee services expanded into Jordan as well.

In 1951 the YWCA World Council meeting held in Beirut determined that 'work with victims of international conflicts can no longer be considered to be a field of work assumed merely as a temporary basis . . . The responses to such situations must be seen as an integral part of our work and program.' The YWCA Executive Board established a permanent Committee on Refugee and Emergency Work.[15] In 1952 the YWCA earned a commendation for its service to refugees from the IRO's American director general, J. Donald Kingsley, as the IRO dissolved and a new United Nations High Commission for Refugees was created.[16] In 1963 the UN High Commissioner for Refugees awarded the World YWCA and its fellow members of the International Council of Voluntary Agencies the Nansen Medal for outstanding humanitarian services to refugees.

The non governmental organization (NGOs) that had focused on refugee service, international migration issues and international development initiatives, were all recognised for 'their major contribution to the solution of refugee problems throughout the world and to their indispensable role in fostering international solidarity toward this end'.[17] Yet in many ways the critical assessment of World YWCA historian Carole Seymour-Jones captures the essence of the UN and NGO refugee services. They were mere 'palliative measures . . . [that] eased the conscience of the world' rather than furthering political solutions to world conflicts that created refugee populations.[18]

Continuing into the 1950s as Cold War conflicts created new populations of refugees, ECOSOC organised multiple new refugee agencies. The World YWCA collaborated with these new agencies to provide emergency services and longer-term education and recreation services for women and children whenever possible. The refugee populations in Europe were served by United Nations Office of the High Commissioner for Refugees (UNHCR); in Asia refugees were served by the United Nations Korean Reconstruction Agency (UNKRA); and in the Middle East they were served by the United Nations Relief and Works Agency (UNRWA). These agencies all influenced the development of new fields for YWCA refugee service work for the very practical reason that they allocated funds to the voluntary agencies that performed emergency relief and developed educational projects for refugee populations.[19] Through its refugee service work the YWCA increased its organisational and Christian influence among women in refugee camps, refined its women's leadership development and educational programmes, and built stronger relationships with UN agencies and personnel.[20]

The World YWCA drew on these relationships and on UN resources when it planned conferences and training seminars around the globe and included UN secretariat personnel in YWCA programmes on a regular basis.[21] When UN agencies hosted conferences and training sessions they also recruited participants from among YWCA chapters in Western and Third World nations and offered travel grants and other incentives to YWCA women.[22] In a seminar that the World YWCA held in Geneva in 1956 to introduce some of its young leaders to the work of the Commission on the Status of Women Alice Arnold asserted proudly that 'The United Nations count on women's organizations to promote their aim and to influence public opinion. The resolutions of the Economic and Social Council and of its Commissions mention [input from] non-governmental organizations (NGOs) more and more frequently.'[23]

Throughout the 1950s and 1960s the World YWCA participated regularly in numerous UN agency surveys and inquiries and in dedicated UN policy and programme years such as the 'Year of the Refugee' in 1960.

The YWCA was also invited to comment on UN agency special reports. In the case of the YWCA's consultative status with UNESCO that was established in 1948, the YWCA provided feedback in regard to the design of UNESCO educational programs and programme budgets.[24] In 1958 Alice Arnold became the first woman to chair the Conference of NGOs in Consultative Status with UNESCO, a peer-elected leadership position that she maintained for several years. From this position Alice Arnold raised the international profile of the World YWCA even further and positioned YWCA educational programmes for women and girls – including those in ongoing refugee camps – in line for more funding from intergovernmental agencies and international donors.[25]

The symbiotic relationships that developed between the Western-government-dominated UN agencies and women's NGOs through consultative relationships during the Cold War years furthered the agendas of the women's international organisations in many positive ways. Their efforts were responsible for developing with the governmental delegates 'the five great international instruments . . . since the Second World War, enunciating the principles of equality for women': two UN Conventions on Political Rights of Women and Nationality of Married Women, two ILO Conventions on Equal Remuneration for Men and Women for Work of Equal Value and on Discrimination in Employment and Occupation and the UNESCO Convention Against Discrimination in Education.[26]

Beginning in 1962 women's international organisations and the CSW also began developing an all-encompassing statement opposing all aspects of discrimination against women and drafted the Declaration on the Elimination of Discrimination against Women between 1965 and 1967. This Declaration, like the Universal Declaration of Human Rights, confirmed international norms promoting equality between men and women; when governments signed the Declaration it could be used as a lever to exert pressure on the individual states to amend national laws and practices that compromised women's rights.[27]

Clearly, since the founding of the UN global governance system in 1945-46 Western-led women's organisations had created and exploited relationships with powerful Western governments through UN Commissions and agencies in order to promote international acceptance of women's equal rights. Yet there were unacknowledged problems associated with the mutual dependence between the Western governments that dominated UN forums and NGOs that created an exclusive, rather than inclusive, global governance system. For one, there was the systemic problem of awarding 'consultative status' to selected NGOs. In a report issued in 1962 only ten mixed-gender NGOs held Category A Consultative Status with ECOSOC and 124 NGOs, including approximately 20 per cent of women's organisations, held Category B Consultative Status. These were the NGOs that ECOSOC had vetted and that could utilise formal UN channels for information sharing and other influential activities.[28]

Western-led women's organisations with consultative status jealously guarded the insider privileges they had earned through years of collaboration with UN member states. In one instance when delegates to the 1955 CSW session discussed a draft resolution calling for a survey to determine women's political rights in UN trusteeships and other non-self-governing territories this exclusivity was revealed. Eastern bloc delegates suggested that the Commission on the Status of Women survey also include women's organisations in those territories that did not have consultative status with ECOSOC. To Western-led women's NGOs with consultative status and to Western government delegates this proposal seemed radical and fraught with 'legal' difficulties. The UN legal counsel was called in to explain the prohibitions and the suggestion was dropped.[29] Consultative NGOs, Western governments and the UN secretariat had developed a system of global governance with rules of engagement that women's international organisations could and did use to their advantage on occasion – but these rules also prevented them from defining a truly global women's agenda.

Contributions to UN development initiatives

During the Cold War era as superpower conflicts played themselves out in violent but 'limited' regional wars and in national liberation movements they also shaped global economic and social development programs at the UN. By the 1950s ECOSOC agencies had initiated 'technical assistance' programmes for unindustrialised, underdeveloped and conflict-ridden Third World nations – the former colonies of Western nations that gained independence during the early Cold War years – in efforts to rebuild political allegiances between these nations and the US-led Western governments that directed most UN forums. Yet these Western-led development programmes often privileged male participation by funding projects in the technology-driven modern industrial or agricultural export economies while they ignored or minimised women's economic participation in small-scale handicraft production or family farming activities.

From their inception, women who represented a wide range of global locations challenged the gender biases built into UN development programmes. As newly independent Third World nations were incorporated into the UN as member states, many sent women who had participated in the wars for national liberation to the UN forums as their national delegates. These non-Western women were quick to promote the case for women's 'equal participation in nation-building, social and economic development, the strengthening of civic responsibilities, and the overall improvement of the status of women' at the UN.[30]

At the same time, Western-led women's international organisations used their established consultative status with UN agencies to advocate for inclusion of women in new UN development programmes. Pursuing their long-running goals to increase opportunities for women worldwide and to improve women's status and access to resources for women and their families, women's NGOs constructed new arguments that 'would transform women into beings as capable of yielding production as their male counterparts'. Rather than arguing that women *as women* or *as mothers* had a distinctive contribution to make to international development, new arguments constructed women as de-gendered human resources that could be employed to advance the world's economic progress.[31]

At the urging of the YWCA and other women's organisations the CSW discussed women's participation in UN technical assistance programmes at its 1953 session.[32] CSW delegates voted unanimously to request that ECOSOC appeal to member states to appoint women development experts to plan and implement technical assistance programmes and 'to encourage increased participation of women in conferences, seminars, and training courses in regions where the position of women in the community needs to be raised'.[33]

Within its own organisational ranks, too, the YWCA focused on its role in international development programmes and debated its historic Christian mission in the former Western colonies in the Third World. In 1953 the YWCA examined its Western biases and surveyed its national chapters in Asia, Africa and Latin America, and asked the probing questions: 'How can we make the YWCA an instrument of social development? How can we help the YWCA Associations to help themselves? In the whole problem of "give and take" [between Western and non-Western YWCA chapters], how can we make the giving sufficiently effective to develop independence? What is to be done about leadership training, about the exchange of experts, of staff, of scholarships, etc?' This self-examination refocused the attention of women's international organisations on North–South issues, between the industrialised wealthy Western countries of the Northern hemisphere and the unindustrialised and cash-poor Third World nations of the Southern hemisphere, and redirected some of the overemphasis on the East–West Cold War conflict as defined by the US-Soviet superpower rivalry.[34]

During the 1950s and early 1960s women's organisations gradually raised awareness of women's special needs in rural and community development, in agricultural work, in family planning and in technical assistance to developing nations in UN forums.[35] For example, the YWCA

addressed women and development issues through its consultative relationships with United Nations (International) Children's (Emergency)
Fund (UNICEF), UNESCO, the Food Agriculture Organization (FAO) and
the International Labour Organization (ILO), and in its work with UN
refugee agencies, making statements and interventions at various agency
meetings and seminars on topics including 'Concerns of Women and
Girls, in reference to Family, Work, Education', 'Technical Assistance and
Aid to Economic and Social Development', and 'The Human Factor in
Technology and Urbanization'.[36] By the mid-1960s the World YWCA had
established its development expertise drawing on the practical experiences
of its national chapters, now seventy-five in number, and on its many local
chapters that worked directly with women and girls in developing nations.
Through these on-the-ground contacts the World YWCA staff believed
they had accurate first-hand and global knowledge about women's and
girls' access to education, social welfare, vocational training, community
development, human nutrition and labour conditions, and they drew on
this knowledge to assess the efficacy of UN agency development programs
vis-à-vis women.[37]

When the UN launched a decade-long focus on development in 1961
'women' were not specifically mentioned in the UN Development Decade
Plan. Nonetheless the YWCA and other women's NGOs joined the UN
campaign to publicise Development Decade goals and brought their organisational priorities and programming suggestions targeting women into
UN forums. During this decade the number of UN agencies focused on
development and the scope of their work expanded greatly. In 1962 the
UN General Assembly requested that the Commission on the Status of
Women 'prepare a report on the role of women in the social and economic
development plans of member governments'. Although Devaki Jain has
argued that 'the issue of women and development was not a major part of
the CSW's agenda during these very early years of the [first development]
decade',[38] women's NGOs added new dimensions to UN development
programmes to include women-related activities. Women's NGOs argued
that women's integration into the public sphere – especially in regard to
women's participation in waged labour and economic production – was
necessary for economic and social development. Therefore it was critical to
raise women's status in order to promote development.[39]

At its 1965 session the CSW shared the results of its extensive study on
the advancement of women in developing countries that was based on
information gathered from UN agencies, governments and from women's
NGOs. At that time the Commission identified an 'urgent' need to dedicate
a much larger proportion of the UN Development Fund to long-term programmes for the advancement of women and girls within national and

international development plans. The CSW requested that women's NGOs collect more information on the controversial topic of family planning policies and programmes as they were linked to social and economic development goals.[40] An interim report based in part on the data that women's organisations collected was distributed through ECOSOC to UN member states with a resolution in 1968:

> to undertake national surveys or case studies on the status of women and family planning, taking into account such factors as the implication for the status of women of the effects of population growth on economic and social development; factors affecting fertility that relate directly to the status of women; the implications of family size for maternal and child welfare; the scope of existing family planning programs in relation to the status of women; and current trends in population growth and family size, and the protection of human rights, in particular the rights of women, [and] to make their findings available to the Secretary General as the basis for a further report on this question.[41]

With the long-term focus on international development as their model, the CSW and women's organisations gathered data and developed proposals for a sustained intergovernmental effort to promote the global advancement of women.[42] UNESCO, too, began to emphasise the 'advancement of women' at its December 1966 General Conference. UNESCO delegates authorised an agency-wide focus on 'long term action to achieve full equality for women; to hasten their advancement and full participation in the economic and social development of their countries; and to assist member states, at their request, in their efforts to elaborate and apply a general policy directed to this end'. UNESCO planned research projects, social and natural science education and training programmes, and technical assistance projects that were all aimed at involving women and girls in the economic and social development of their nations.[43]

In 1967 ECOSOC also requested that member governments develop long-term national plans for women's advancement. This coincided with the passage of the UN General Assembly resolution to adopt the Declaration for the Elimination of all forms of Discrimination against Women that had been discussed in its various draft stages at the CSW since 1965 and that specifically connected women's status to development goals.[44]

The focus on women's contributions to economic and social development proceeded as a process of step-by-step collaboration between women's international organisations, UN agencies and female government delegates. The idea that 'woman power' represented 'untapped brains and skills' and should not be 'wasted' became an accepted premise and the basis of international development initiatives by the end of the First UN

Development Decade (1961–1970). During the Second UN Development Decade (1971-1980) 'women' became a focus of programming and activities, 'especially,' Nitza Berkovitch notes, 'when [the Second Development Decade] coincided with the UN Decade for Women (1976-85).'[45]

An influential UN survey entitled 'The Role of Women in Development' published in 1970 proposed the long-term international focus on women's advancement that women's organisations had been promoting for years. Drawing on the UN survey and on the research in the Danish economist Ester Boserup's path-breaking book, *Women's Role in Economic Development*, also published in 1970, women delegates to the UN and women's NGOs could document with authority women's historic contributions to national economic productivity in traditional societies and the ways that Western-led UN development programmes had privileged male roles.[46] As Part III of this book will document, during the 1970s and 1980s the long-running efforts of women's international organisations to shape a global women's agenda for development, equality and peace within the post-war system of global governance came to fruition during the UN Decade for Women.

Notes

1 Margaret K. Bruce, 'An account of United Nations action to advance the status of women', *Annals of the American Academy of Political and Social Science* 375 (January 1968), p. 165.

2 Devaki Jain, *Women, Development and the UN: A Sixty-Year Quest for Equality and Justice* (Bloomington, IN: Indiana University Press, 2005), p. 20.

3 'Short History of the Commission on the Status of Women', United Nations, Division for the Advancement of Women; Laura Reanda, 'The Commission on the Status of Women', in Philip Alston (ed.), *The United Nations and Human Rights: A Critical Appraisal* (Oxford, UK: Oxford University Press, 1992), pp. 282–3.

4 DK, 'Women in the United Nations', 1 April 1949, box 53.

5 WYWCA, Liaison Committee meeting minutes, New York, 7 March 1949.

6 DK, 'Twenty-five women who participate in the work of the United Nations', c. 1951, box 53.

7 WYWCA, 'Statement of working party of representatives of Women's International Organisations present at the Third Session of the United Nations Commission on the Status of Women held in Beirut, Lebanon, March 21–April 3, 1949,' 30 March 1949.

8 Yale University Divinity School Library, Alice Arnold, 'Commission on the Status of Women report', *World's YWCA Monthly* (July–August 1950).

9 DK, The National Federation of Business and Professional Women's Clubs, Inc., NYC, 'International Issue of the Month', March–April 1950, 'What the United Nations is Doing to Advance the Position of Women', box 53.

10 JS, 'Report of the Ninth Session of the Commission on the Status of Women, UN Headquarters', 14 March–1 April 1955, box 10.

11 Helen Laville, *Cold War Women: The International Activities of American Women's Organizations* (New York: Palgrave, 2002), pp. 124–39.

12 Leon Gordenker, *Refugees in International Politics* (New York: Columbia University Press, 1987), pp. 27–9.

13 WYWCA, Executive Committee meeting minutes, Geneva, Switzerland, 26 February–4 March 1950; Yale University Divinity School Library, Alice Arnold, 'Emergency and community', *World's YWCA Monthly* (November 1950).

14 WYWCA, Executive Committee Meeting Minutes, St. Cergue, Switzerland, 19–25 June 1949 and Nybourg, Denmark, 4–12 November 1950; Yale University Divinity School Library, 'What the World's YWCA is doing' [in worldwide refugee services], *World's YWCA Monthly*, (March 1952).

15 Carole Seymour-Jones, *Journey of Faith: The History of the World YWCA 1945–1994* (London: Allison and Busby, 1994), p. 267.

16 Yale University Divinity School Library, 'IRO thanks the World's YWCA', *World's YWCA Monthly* (June 1952).

17 Yale University Divinity School Library, 'The Nansen Medal, 1963', *World's YWCA Monthly* (March 1964).

18 Seymour-Jones, *Journey of Faith*, p. 272.

19 WYWCA, Report of the Executive Committee to the World's Council, Social and International Responsibilities, November 1954, WEC [World Ecumenical Council], Social and International Questions, 1947–56.

20 WYWCA, Report to the World's Council on the Work of the Executive Committee, 1951–1955, 'Service to refugees', 1955.

21 WYWCA, International YWCA Seminar, in relation to the 11th Session of the Commission on the Status of Women, New York City, 25–29 March 1957, World YWCA Documents in Relation to the UN Commission on the Status of Women.

22 WYWCA, Pre-Council Consultation on 'Methods of Developing Public Affairs Programs in YWCAs: Methods of Work Used by the World's YWCA in the Field of Social and International Responsibilities', 1956, WEC, Social and International Questions, 1947–56.

23 WYWCA, Alice Arnold, 'Introduction to the program of the seminar', 12–17 March 1956, World YWCA Seminar on the Status of Women.

24 WYWCA, Executive Committee Meeting Minutes, Céligny, Switzerland, 1–13 May 1960.

25 Yale University Divinity School Library, 'NGOs working with UNESCO', *World's YWCA Monthly* (October 1958).

26 Morgan–Howes Papers, Eleanor Hindler, 28 October 1961, box 7; Bruce, 'An account of United Nations', pp. 167–72.

27 Reanda, 'The Commission on the Status of Women', pp. 284–5.

28 Charles S. Ascher [President of CONGO], 'The review of activities of NGOs by the UN Economic and Social Council, an interpretation', *International Associations* (June 1962).

29 JS, 'Report of the Ninth Session of the Commission on the Status of Women' 14 March–1 April 1955, box 10.

30 Jain, *Women, Development and the UN*, pp. 24–5.

31 Nitza Berkovitch, *From Motherhood to Citizenship: Women's Rights and International Organizations* (Baltimore, MD: Johns Hopkins University Press, 1999), p. 146.

32 WYWCA, 'Intervention by Mrs. C. Anderson, World's YWCA Consultant at UN Headquarters, New York, at the 7th Session of the Commission on the Status of Women', 31 March 1953, World YWCA, Statements, 1967–75.

33 Yale University Divinity School Library, 'Consultant at the UN Commission on the Status of Women', *World's YWCA Monthly* (June 1953).

34 Yale University Divinity School Library, Alice Arnold, 'World's YWCA seminars', *World's YWCA Monthly* (October 1953).

35 'Short history of the Commission on the Status of Women', United Nations, Division for the Advancement of Women (un.org/womenwatch/daw/CSW 60YRS/CSWbriefhistory.pdf).

36 WYWCA, 'Guide for World YWCA representatives and observers at United Nations and its Specialized Agencies', World Young Women's Christian Association, Geneva, 1963, Consultative Status Documents.

37 Yale University Divinity School Library, Report on Melbourne World Council, 'The role of the YWCA as a non-governmental organization', *World's YWCA Monthly* (1968).

38 Jain, *Women, Development and the UN*, p. 35.

39 Berkovitch, *From Motherhood to Citizenship*, p. 142.

40 WYWCA, Executive Committee Meeting Minutes, Mont Pèlerin, Switzerland, 12–22 May 1965.

41 WYWCA, Margaret K. Bruce, Chief, Section on the Status of Women, to 'All NGOs concerned' on the subject 'Further study of the relationship of the status of women on family planning', 25 June 1968, World YWCA Status of Women Inquiries, 1951–67.

42 WYWCA, Executive Committee Meeting Minutes, Mont Pelerin, Switzerland, 5–18 June 1966.

43 Bruce, 'An account of United Nations', pp. 172–3.

44 Jain, *Women, Development and the UN*, p. 48.

45 Berkovitch, *From Motherhood to Citizenship*, pp. 141–3.

46 Jain, *Women, Development and the UN*, pp. 45 and 51–3.

Part III

Women's NGOs and the United Nations, 1970–85

During the 1970s and continuing through the UN Decade for Women (1976–85), the global feminist movement changed in qualitative and quantifiable ways.[1] Newly organised non-governmental organizations (NGOs) and women leaders from the global South challenged the long ascendancy of Western-led women's international organisations within the United Nations (UN) system of global governance and transformed women's participation in the international arena. These activists represented less-institutionalised associations and more fluid networks, defined new goals and set new priorities among global women's issues, and were more willing to formulate radical feminist analyses that recognised the interconnectedness of patriarchal and other oppressive power structures based on class or race or heteronormative sexuality.[2] Yet the new global feminist movement did not exclude Western women's international organisations. As their consciousness was raised, Western feminist leaders and their organisations evolved. A number of these longstanding women's associations including the Young Women's Christian Association (YWCA) did not become irrelevant as the new global feminist leadership emerged in the 1970s. Rather, the established groups incorporated new leaders, innovative ideas and fresh energy that emanated from the global South while retaining faith in the creation of a just and humane world community achieved through the efforts of activist women who transformed global governance structures from within.

Several YWCA leaders played influential roles in the evolving global feminist movement during this transformational era. Mildred Persinger who had served for many years as the World YWCA's NGO consultant at the UN headquarters in New York, chaired the NGO tribune that ran parallel to the 1975 International Women's Year conference in Mexico City and then founded and led the International Women's Tribune Centre from 1976 to 1982. Elizabeth Palmer, World YWCA general secretary from 1955 to 1978, chaired the NGO forum 1980 at the Copenhagen mid-decade UN conference. Dame Nita Barrow chaired NGO forum 1985 at the Nairobi end of decade conference. Barrow had been a World YWCA vice president during the 1960s and was president of the World YWCA from 1975 to 1983. Persinger and Palmer were white Western women, both born in the United States. Nita Barrow was an Afro-Caribbean woman whose family ranked among the powerful political elite in Barbados. Because of their birthrights, these three women lived relatively privileged lives compared to most of the world's women. However, they each confronted the limitations of their particular worldviews, created new feminist identities and redefined feminist activism in collaboration with less-privileged women.

Persinger, Palmer, Barrow and the World YWCA organisation found effective ways to bridge class- and race-based divisions as they fostered new international feminist networks among long-established NGOs and new NGO actors within UN world forums. They worked closely with women leaders at the UN, including the women who presided over the three government conferences held during the Decade for Women: Helvi Sipilä from Finland, Lucille Mair from Jamaica and Leticia Shahani from the Philippines. Cultivating relationships to powerful women and men and sharing their extensive knowledge and influence Persinger, Palmer and Barrow introduced a new generation of women activists to global gender politics as practised by UN member states. Their activism allows examination of critical questions about 'power' within the global feminist community. Whether power is conceptualised as a neutral resource that men have more of and women are concerned with gaining an equal measure of, or is defined negatively as a tool of domination used by a stronger group to wield coercive influence over a weaker group, or is understood in its positive manifestation as 'empowerment' to achieve radical transformation from patriarchal to more humanistic value systems,[3] these three women and their NGO and UN cohorts used power in all these ways. At times Persinger, Palmer and Barrow were accused of undermining feminist goals. Nonetheless their record of accomplishments as they redefined a global women's agenda during the UN Decade for Women was significant even though it was limited.

Women's activism during the 1970s and 1980s encompassing old and new NGOs transformed the global feminist movement; it also transformed the institutional agenda at the UN. 'Women's issues' – especially those broadly related to global development – were seriously considered by governments and UN agencies. Women activists influenced the framing of some women's concerns as 'problems' that demanded collective state actions and they offered 'solutions' in terms of policies and programmes in ways that demonstrated their understanding of international political contexts as well as their ability to work effectively within institutional structures. Building on their historic gains, women's organisations also continued to improve their access to UN agencies and offices and to increase NGO participation at intergovernmental meetings. They cultivated influential allies among governments, funding foundations and the UN secretariat. They learned to better utilise the media to promote their causes and they adopted new communication technologies to expand and improve the efficacy of their activist networks.[4]

UN world conferences held during these decades provided NGOs with multiple opportunities to interact with government leaders and the UN secretariat. NGOs with consultative status were particularly well situated to influence government policy making at conference preparatory meetings. When they were invited to conference sessions as official observers, consultative NGOs aggressively lobbied government delegates and UN officials behind the scenes and utilised rare opportunities to address delegate assemblies publicly. Women's international organisations in the Conference of NGOs in consultative status with the UN Economic and Social Council (CONGO) steadily expanded their influence within the system of the UN through their participation in world conferences; in particular, this occurred at the World Population Conference held in Bucharest in 1974, at the International Women's Year Conference in Mexico City in 1975, and at the mid-decade and end of decades conferences held during the UN Decade for Women in Copenhagen and Nairobi in 1980 and 1985. At these conferences and at the parallel NGO meetings, the long-established women's international organisations effectively advocated for global recognition of women's oppression and elevation of women's status and improved access to material resources worldwide.

The accounts of women's organising at these conferences related here reveal how the NGO activists' feminist principles were forged in practice. They provide evidence of the 'circular and reinforcing' links between feminist theory and praxis that women's studies scholar Ime Kerlee explained in 2006:

> When women come together they inevitably discuss their lived experiences rendering the hegemonic presence of systematic male privilege visible regardless of location. In confirming a shared disparity based on gender, and multiplied by race, class, sexuality, ability language, and location, women around the world articulate a theory of gendered oppression based in specificity and capable of solidarity across differences. Rather than reifying, in its best sense, experience as a basis for theory and action allows us to move past the tendency to universalize a single woman's experience or to claim that gender eclipses other metalanguages by acknowledging the specific embodied locality of theory. The coming together of women (practice) and

the articulation of gendered oppression (theory) move the movement/s forward co-equally.[5]

Like the previous generations of Western feminists who had led the international organisations, these women were pragmatic and persistent in promoting a women's agenda within global governance settings. During the UN Decade for Women some of that pragmatism and persistence found its rewards.

Notes

1 The author thanks the editor of the online *Journal of International Women's Studies* for permission to include excerpts from a previously published article in Part III of this book. Karen Garner, 'World YWCA Leaders and the UN Decade for Women', *Journal of International Women's Studies* 9:1 (November 2007) (bridgew.edu/SoAS/jiws/Nov07/YWCA.pdf).

2 Nitza Berkovitch, *From Motherhood to Citizenship: Women's Rights and International Organizations* (Baltimore, MD: Johns Hopkins University Press, 1999), 156–9; Martha Alter Chen, 'Engendering world conferences: the International women's movement and the UN', in Thomas G. Weiss and Leon Gordenker (eds), *NGOs, the UN and Global Governance* (Boulder, CO: Lynne Rienner Publishers, 1996), p. 141.

3 Amy Allen, *The Power of Feminist Theory: Domination, Resistance, Solidarity* (Boulder, CO: Westview Press, 1999), pp. 1–3.

4 Jutta M. Joachim, *Agenda Setting, the UN, and NGOs* (Washington, DC: Georgetown University Press, 2007), pp. 16–29.

5 Ime A. S. Kerlee, 'Theory and Praxis: An Introduction,' Special Issue *FemTAP: A Journal of Feminist Theory and Practice* (summer 2006) (femtap.com/id11. html).

8 Mildred Persinger, convenor of the 1975 International Women's Year NGO Tribune. The World Young Women's Christian Association.

9 Elizabeth Palmer, convenor of the 1980 UN Decade for Women mid-decade NGO Forum. The World Young Women's Christian Association.

10 Eddah Gachukia (centre, front row), head of UN Decade for Women NGO Forum 1985 local arrangements committee and Dame Nita Barrow (second from right, front row), convenor of NGO Forum 1985, Nairobi, Kenya, with Kenneth Matiba, Kenya Minister for Culture and Social Services and John Michuki, Kenya Assistant Minister for Commerce and Industry.

11 At the closing session of the UN Decade for Women NGO Forum 1985.

9

Transforming the global development
agenda

Linking 'women and development'

Perceptions of women within the global governance system had begun
to change as the First UN Development Decade progressed through the
1960s; after the inauguration of the Second Development Decade in
1971 these changes accelerated. During these decades United Nations
(UN) agencies and member nations slowly incorporated consideration of
women's reproductive and productive roles into global development policies and programmes and reshaped the formerly gender-blind UN development agenda. Women were primarily responsible for raising gender
consciousness in UN forums and for creating what became known globally
as a 'women and development' movement. As the movement gained
strength, women's organisations diagnosed significant obstacles to social
and economic development globally that related to a lack of women's participation and then positioned themselves within the UN system as legitimate and necessary 'experts' who proposed likely solutions to overcome
those obstacles.

Women's activism took place within the context of a general expansion
of the non-governmental organizations (NGOs) within the UN governance system. Beginning with the World Conference on the Environment
held in Stockholm in 1972 and continuing through the 1970s, some
of the most effective NGO activism was organised in conjunction with
UN-hosted government conferences and the NGO meetings that accompanied them. International NGOs identified problems that were included
on conference agendas and then proposed solutions that included legal
instruments such as treaties and declarations. They also called for new
research, redistribution of government resources and new educational
and other programming initiatives. And very importantly, NGOs mobilised
support worldwide among governments and within 'civil society' to carry
out the proposed actions.[1] In particular, women's organisations took the
lead in performing these functions at the World Population Conference in

Bucharest in 1974 and during the three world conferences held during the UN Decade for Women.

In order to implement their agenda-changing proposals within UN bodies NGOs have relied on the influence of dynamic leaders who have acted as 'organisational entrepreneurs' and who possessed in-depth subject area expertise and were able to rally broad-based international constituencies.[2] These influential components were all evident as NGOs mobilised support for the 'women and development' movement at UN meetings beginning in the 1960s. Among the recognised organisational entrepreneurs who concurrently demonstrated significant subject area expertise regarding 'women and development' issues and who also represented broad international constituencies of women as well as their national governments were Aida Ginty from Egypt, who served a term as chief of the UN Social Affairs Section and who had worked on the Economic Commission for Africa; Aziza Hussein, also from Egypt, who served as Egypt's delegate to the Commission on the Status of Women and was president of International Planned Parenthood Federation from 1977 to 1983; Justice Annie Jiagge from Ghana who was active in the YWCA of Ghana, on the Executive Board of the World YWCA, and was Ghana's delegate to the Commission on the Status of Women (CSW); along with Vida Tomsic from Yugoslavia, Leticia Shahani from the Philippines and Inga Thorsen from Sweden.[3]

Additionally, many of the new women's NGOs that formed during the UN Development Decades were based in the developing world and their members brought specific situational knowledge to 'women and development' policy debates when they participated in UN-funded programmes. Finally, during these years many of the established women's international organisations reset organisational priorities and designed seminars and training courses that incorporated women from developing nations as they focused on 'women and development' issues. They did so in order to acquire up-to-date subject area expertise and to better address the needs of their international constituencies even as they were responding in practical ways to the UN agencies' changing funding priorities. The activities of all these international players were mutually reinforcing, adding, Nitza Berkovitch has argued, 'more layers of coherence to the overall global effort for the sake of women, rights, and development'.[4]

Women activists opened discussions regarding women's reproductive roles as governments and UN agencies debated causal relationships that linked global population growth to economic development. By the 1960s and 1970s improvements in food production and rising nutritional standards had led to larger populations especially in the world's developing nations although poverty-linked hunger continued to pose global challenges.[5] While there was near-universal acknowledgement among governments that population growth and economic development were linked, there were distinct differences in the ways that the nations and financial institutions of the industrialised North identified cause and effect relationships compared to developing nations located in the unindustrialised South. Northern nations of the so-called First World controlled a disproportionately large share of the world's wealth and provided development aid and programme funding. In general they advocated for state-sponsored population controls such as state-distributed contraceptives to limit population growth. Northern nations argued that slower population growth in developing nations would reduce 'drains' on national resources and that, in turn, would allow for greater economic development.[6] Southern nations of the so-called Third World that received aid generally pushed for further economic development before population controls were introduced. They argued that economic development would lead to reduced fertility rates as soon as families realised that they could limit their numbers of working children and still survive as the basic economic unit of production.[7]

At the instigation of women activists in the 1960s, UN commissions and agencies slowly and tentatively opened discussions of 'family planning' – the code words for distribution of contraceptives and other birth control methods – as these discussions related to population growth and development debates. Family planning discussions were highly controversial within UN forums because they seemed to threaten certain traditional religious authorities and patriarchal 'sovereign' state autonomy. Even within the CSW when Egyptian delegate Aziza Hussein suggested that the CSW discuss family planning at their 1963 session she provoked an alarmed reaction. She later recalled: 'The effect of my words thundered like an explosion. "You have, in your mild manner, exploded a bomb," the French delegate told me in the corridors. "No one has ever dared to approach this subject, which is so crucial for the status of women. Some of us would go to jail over it."'[8] In 1965 Hussein co-sponsored a CSW resolution directing the UN secretariat to report on the relationship between the status of women and women's fertility rates and to focus on developing countries. At that time, half of the CSW members abstained from voting on the resolution. By 1968, however, the CSW grew bolder and Finland's CSW delegate, Helvi Sipilä, headed a new CSW project to study the Status of Women and Family Planning.

Much less controversially within intergovernmental UN bodies, economic development was also linked to women's participation in national production. Following this line of argument, women's NGOs effectively mobilised support to change the UN development agenda through the combined pressures of their well-known and respected organisational entrepreneurs, their vocal international constituencies and their recognised expertise. The Danish economist Ester Boserup was particularly influential as she provided subject area expertise through her seminal study *Women's Role in Economic Development* published in 1970. As discussed previously, Boserup documented women's necessary contributions to national productivity, redefined women as human and economic development resources, and mapped women's inequality and lack of access to national and international development resources in a comprehensive global survey. The evidence that Boserup compiled provided women who worked for the UN secretariat or who served as national delegates to the Commission on the Status of Women and their allies in women's international organisations with new ammunition to define women's limited role and unequal status within global development initiatives as a 'problem' that must be addressed.[9] They were able to focus male attention on the problem and redirect government funding to programmes where women as well as men participated and benefited. In 1972 the CSW and UN Commission on Social Development co-sponsored an Interregional Meeting of Experts on the Integration of Women in Development and invited Ester Boserup to share her research with other women who occupied leadership positions within the UN system.

In these UN forums women's abilities to contribute to national production in positive, significant and sustainable ways were connected to women's roles and status in society. Activists made the case that in societies where women's status was more equal to that of men's and where women were educated and had 'rights' to make decisions about their own lives women were better able to contribute to national development. These arguments had global policy and programming implications attached to them and activists worked hard to interject an awareness of gender into the North-South debates that dominated the preparatory meetings leading up to the 1974 World Population Conference. While male-led governments and demographers – the so-called 'population experts' – most often conceptualised women as 'targets' of population control policies, women activists redefined women as 'active participants' in setting national development strategies and in making decisions about their own lives, particularly decisions regarding their fertility.

After a July 1973 meeting was held at the US State Department to confer with NGOs that planned to attend the 1974 World Population Conference, Young Women's Christian Association (YWCA) UN consultant Mildred Persinger reported:

> I had been waiting all afternoon to hear some reference to the relationship of women to population growth – or even some recognition that there were two

sexes, one of which bears children. Typically there was no such recognition. In the UN papers, the chairman said he had found nothing about the participation of women. Finally I pointed out the obvious, that development raises opportunities for women as well as men, that the status of women appears to be key to the level of birthrate, that a strong drive for the advancement of women at the Bucharest Conference, pressure for access of girls and women to education, training, and employment, if accepted by governments, could have a profound influence on future growth patterns. Recognizing that poor countries cannot provide these opportunities for everyone, I argued that the US should press for policies of equal access to what there is.[10]

With the interest in women's fertility as it related to economic development growing, in April 1974 the CSW co-sponsored a global forum on Women, Population and Development that was held in the United States to prepare reports for the World Population Conference to be held in August. Helvi Sipilä who was then serving as UN assistant secretary general for Social Development and Humanitarian Affairs was also named as secretary general at the CSW global forum. Sipilä brought her concerns about the lack of attention to women's role in population planning to the forum that was attended by 116 prominent women activists and academics who shared strategies to educate the gender-blind male population experts and government representatives as they prepared Population Conference documents. The forum wrote policy recommendations, which the CSW endorsed and forwarded to the world conference preparatory commission.[11]

Aziza Hussein has recorded her experiences regarding the collaborative and mutually reinforcing relationships that developed between NGOs, UN officials and government delegates as they related to population policy and programming during the UN Development Decades. Her testimonial explains how NGOs expanded their influence and gender perspectives among governments at the UN:

> [T]he UN picked up the family planning angle from the IPPF [International Planned Parenthood Federation] then pioneered a new strategy linking family planning to the status of women and launching it throughout the world. This initiative in turn influenced the NGO family planning movement world wide, and IPPF itself began to center itself on the role of women as a focal entry point in its programs and for the first time established its own women's department. I believe that the pioneering and advocacy role played by the population and women's NGOs, in which I played a modest role, climaxed in the official mobilization of governments and the UN, spurring them on to launch global conferences. Conversely, the outcome of UN decisions in these conferences had an important effect on the thinking and direction taken by NGOs in Egypt and worldwide, by virtue of the moral weight and authority that they carry with governments and NGOs alike.[12]

Hussein and the IPPF played important entrepreneurial leadership roles that led to the incorporation of family planning into global population policy at the UN. Helvi Sipilä and Mildred Persinger and their well-established networks of women's international organisations were also influential in the agenda-changing process.

Helvi Sipilä and Mildred Persinger

Helvi Sipilä and Mildred Persinger were well-known leaders within established Western-led women's organisations who played the role of 'activist brokers' and who 'bridg[ed] the gap between the beliefs and goals of NGO members and policy makers'.[13] This type of interlinking leadership was necessary in transforming both the UN governance system and the global feminist movement during the 1970s and 1980s. Sipilä and Persinger shared long-running and passionate commitments to advancing women's status globally as their personal histories reveal. Sipilä and Persinger also shared a Western liberal feminist political orientation and were committed to working within the UN global governance system. Throughout their careers as feminist activists they cultivated influential relationships with governments and the UN secretariat, they developed deep knowledge about how the UN system worked, and they shared that knowledge with broad networks of women activists. As builders of bridges between governments in power, liberal feminist women's organisations that sought power within the intergovernmental system, and more radical feminist women's organisations that sought to revolutionise the global system, it is not surprising that Sipilä and Persinger became targets for criticism as well as for praise. They tended to seek common ground and to make compromises and these were not always popular actions among the various groups negotiating for power within the global governance system. Yet during their activist careers they drew on the foundational Christian internationalist and liberal feminist values of their historic home organisations – the Girl Scouts and the YWCA – and they broke new ground to expand the global feminist movement during the 1970s and 1980s. Their efforts raised women's status in the realm of international politics.

Helvi Sipilä was the first woman appointed at the elevated rank of assistant secretary general at the UN. Her appointment was the result of various concessions that the secretary general Kurt Waldheim had made to appease women in the secretariat who had documented women's generally low-ranked appointments within the UN system.[14] Trained as a lawyer, Sipilä had led the Girl Scouts organisation in Finland and had served as Finland's delegate to the CSW since the 1960s. In 1971 she was named as chair of the UN General Assembly's Third Committee, the Social

Committee – or, as it was referred to somewhat derisively in the 1970s, the 'Ladies' Committee'.[15] In these posts Helvi Sipilä made it clear that she was not willing to play the oblique games of traditional diplomacy. John R. Mathiason, former Deputy Director of the Division for the Advancement of Women in the UN secretariat from 1987 to 1996, worked with Sipilä and knew her well. He explained Sipilä's unorthodox style:

> Not having come from a government bureaucracy, Mrs. Sipilä, a small woman with a high forehead and white hair, was never daunted by arguments about why something could not be done. Her response was always, 'we can find a way'. . . Her management style was also 'un-UN.' She would bring her staff together and, occasionally, ask them to join in singing, as befitted someone who lead [*sic*] her country's girl scouts. Many of the staff, particularly the men, were considerably discomfited by the experience, which was rather standard at women's organization gatherings but not at all usual at the United Nations.[16]

Sipilä's appointment as assistant secretary general led to a reorganisation of offices within the UN secretariat. The Status of Women section was removed from the Division for Human Rights and a new bureaucratic office, the Centre for Social Development and Humanitarian Affairs, was created under Sipilä's oversight at the Department of Economic and Social Affairs. The Status of Women section was upgraded to a branch and renamed the Branch for the Promotion of Equality between Men and Women and it also fell under Helvi Sipilä's purview.

Mildred Persinger was a self-defined 'housewife' and unpaid volunteer; she was active in local, national and international organisations throughout her adult life after she moved to Dobbs Ferry, New York as a young bride in 1944.[17] In addition to serving in her hometown League of Women Voters and on the Tarrytown, New York Junior League Persinger also worked with the National Board of the YWCA of the USA in New York City. In the early 1960s she was appointed to the US President's CSW, the New York Governor's Consumer Advisory Committee, the New York State Committee Against Discrimination in Housing and the Race Relations Committee of the American Civil Liberties Union. She developed a broad and deep expertise in regard to the organisation and work of the UN governance system as a member of the National Committee of the American Association for the United Nations (AAUN). From 1969 to 1972 she chaired the Conference of UN Observers that brought together a council of 150 NGOs associated with the AAUN. In 1970 she was appointed to the US Presidential Commission on the Twenty-fifth Anniversary of the UN. From that time, beginning in 1970 and continuing through the 1980s, Persinger also served as the World YWCA NGO consultant at the UN along with her colleague Mildred Jones.[18] As a staunch liberal, Persinger's activist strategy was to identify social and political injustices and to advocate for reform of unfair systems working from inside democratic governments and intergovernmental organisations.[19]

The 1974 World Population Conference in Bucharest, Romania

Until the 1970s UN member states as well as the UN secretariat rarely recognised that 'gender mattered' or that women's needs and interests were distinct from men's as they determined global political or social policy. As John R. Mathiason recalled, 'while it may be considered bizarre today, population issues in the 1970s were not considered from a gender perspective'. He explained that 'this was because demographers were the intellectuals behind the issue and population was considered a technical [i.e. 'gender-neutral'] subject'. But Mathiason also noted at that time men headed the UN Population Division, men directed the UN Fund for Population Activities (UNFPA), and conservative male forces led by the Roman Catholic Church tried to limit any discussion of family planning and especially any discussion of abortion in UN forums.[20] With men in charge of these key agencies and institutions women's participation was limited and feminist perspectives were nearly excluded as World Population Conference preparations began.

Women's coalitions working inside and outside the UN system, however, challenged UN members to include women participants at the upcoming conference and to consider women's concerns during population policy debates. Helvi Sipilä played a 'pivotal' role mobilising these coalitions according to many accounts. She co-organized the April 1974 global forum on Women, Population and Development as well as a series of regional seminars to prepare for the World Population Conference to be held in August. Indian development economist and feminist activist Devaki Jain has noted the importance of Sipilä's interventions that:

> set in motion the inclusion of women's participation in this subject and helped in the evolution of ideas about women's rights, empowerment, power relations, and structures in succeeding world conferences. They also acted as a stimulus to research, including gendered data collection, in this key topic . . . Pivotal figures such as Sipilä were sometimes able to merge the male dominated areas of the UN with the research skills and expertise of the CSW for specific projects, and such temporary unions sometimes led to lasting influences. For example, the leading body in the promotion of population programs, which had been established as a trust fund for work on population by the Secretary General in 1967, has emerged as a forerunner in the engagement of the UN in women's rights, albeit slowly.[21]

Mildred Persinger and her NGO colleagues also contributed in critical ways to the World Population Conference preparatory discussions. They argued that women's 'real world' situations must be considered in all family planning initiatives. The following statement drafted by an NGO committee on which Persinger served was submitted to the conference preparatory commission. It revealed how women's NGOs struggled with male conference delegates for some recognition of women's global inequality as it related to population policy making.

> Another human rights area . . . essential to any consideration of birth rates is the situation of women, far from the equality proclaimed in the UN Charter and numerous statements of the principle [of equality] adopted by world bodies. Third World women tend to be the 'most unequal.'
>
> The right of women and girls of all races 'to decide the number and spacing of their children' which presupposes access to family planning resources is the key which could unlock the population puzzle. But in order to exercise their right they must be able to throw off their colonial status within the society, the economy and the family. They must be able to decide on roles other than as tillers of the soil, purveyors of food and subjects of maximum human fertility. Equal rights to education, employment and a share in community decision-making, even if they are not exercised, can contribute to changing women's self-image, the first step toward full personhood. [22]

Persinger recalled the important role that women's international NGOs played to counterbalance patriarchal resistance that inhibited consideration of women's needs at the World Population Conference. As her remarks illustrate, Persinger learned the necessity of working through organised coalitions including women who held formal positions of power in the UN and women who worked informally through NGOs in order to advance women's interests.

> My Eureka! moment occurred in 1973 as I was representing the World YWCA at the UN Population [Conference Preparatory] Commission. The delegates, mostly men except for a couple of female demographers, were debating the draft of the World Population Plan of Action to be adopted (they assumed) the following year at the Bucharest World Population Conference. They did not seem to know that women had anything to do with fertility rates. I remember the draft's twenty-two pages had initially contained *one sentence* specifically related to women. It invited governments to '*give particular consideration to fertility at the extremes of female reproductive ages.*' That turned me on. Later, after much lobbying by women's organizations and Assistant Secretary Helvi Sipilä, we managed to achieve *another sentence with several sub clauses in the final document.* That huge effort with so little result made me realize that the men just did not get it.

> Women delegates HAD to attend the conference. We worked through the NGOs to urge governments to send women. We worked with the organizers of the parallel NGO Population Tribune to assure women's participation, including a woman editor of the Tribune newspaper, a daily distributed also to the government conference . . . We helped women delegates, most of whom had never been in such a gathering, with their interventions; we wrote a statement offered to NGOs for endorsement and tried to help the government men to see our point.[23]

Although the results of women's efforts to amend the final World Population Plan of Action were meagre, their activism led to greater NGO influence at subsequent UN conferences. Following the Population Conference women's NGOs produced a Statement for the Commission on the Status of Women: Study of the Interrelationship of the Status of Women and Family Planning that was used by the CSW as it developed proposals for programmes and a conference to commemorate International Women's Year in 1975.[24] Irene Tinker who attended the Population Conference in 1974 recalled: 'At both UN world conferences held in 1974, one on population and one on food, women formed ad hoc groups to draft and lobby for additional paragraphs about women in the respective Plans of Action. At every subsequent world conference women with increasing sophistication inserted language concerning women's work and responsibilities into the appropriate sections.'[25] Moreover, Persinger noted that even though their influence on conference documents was limited, women participants were present in record numbers at the Population Conference attended by 153 nations and at the concurrent NGO tribune.[26]

The World Population Conference created another important legacy in regard to global women's activism: it institutionalised the NGO forum. In Bucharest in 1974 Rosalind Harris, a leader of the International Social Services NGO who was serving a term as president of the NGOs in Consultative Status with UN ECOSOC (CONGO), took on the organisation of this new 'citizen conference' named the NGO Population Tribune. NGOs had already gathered spontaneously and informally at the 1972 World Conference on the Environment that had been held in Stockholm. At that time, NGOs focused on environmental research and activism had camped out in Stockholm, lobbied government delegates and pressed for their concerns to be part of the UN conference agenda and debates. NGOs had organised panels of experts and published a newspaper that reported on the conference and tribune events. This ad hoc gathering set a precedent that Harris would revive, expand upon and begin to formalise when she organised the Population Tribune in Bucharest. The Romanian government and the UN secretariat welcomed CONGO's organisational assistance, acknowledging that interested NGOs would attend the World Population Conference with or without government or UN recognition.[27] Harris formed a nine-member NGO organising committee headed by the IPPF.[28]

Mildred Persinger worked closely with Rosalind Harris on the NGO tribune committee and she attributed much of the success of the meetings to Harris's visionary leadership:

> Rosalind Harris ... believed that CONGO was in a position to broaden the discussion more effectively by actually organizing a parallel forum rather than just letting it happen. The resulting NGO 'Population Tribune,' or forum, initiated a major NGO effort that for the next twenty years vastly enlarged constituencies for other world conferences on public concerns such as racism, human rights, women's status and urban development.
>
> Luckily for us, the design of the Population Tribune provided a template for the hastily organized [International Women's Year] Tribune the following year. When [Harris], the CONGO president, persuaded me to take on the IWY Tribune, her design of the previous Tribune, her advice and guidance, were invaluable. She also did much of the management and fund raising from the contacts she had made for the population forum.[29]

Harris formed a guiding vision for the NGO Population Tribune: a cooperative model that she articulated in a publication announcing the tribune and explaining its purpose.

> Meeting together in Bucharest both in scheduled meetings and meetings arranged on the spot, persons from many backgrounds will be able to discuss a wide range of topics. Common interests can be identified and collective programs may be found. The Conference of Nongovernmental Organizations in Consultative Status with UN ECOSOC, which undertook to organize a Planning and Management Committee for the Population Tribune, believes the success of this venture lies in the cooperation found among the nongovernmental groups, the United Nations bodies, and the member governments. The Tribune is more than a clearinghouse of information; it is also the springboard to future understanding and action.[30]

In many respects, the tribune proceeded according to Harris's vision. In Bucharest, demographers, anthropologists and population planners met social workers, medical doctors and theologians in a programme of lectures, panels and films, and held discussions with fellow NGO activists, the UN secretariat and government representatives. Many population issues were raised in tribune sessions that focused on demographic trends, population policies, new contraceptive methods, internal and international migration, children, traditional and new family patterns, population education and abortion. As anticipated, North-South perspectives on population policy clashed at the World Conference and at the tribune.

The Northern developed countries generally promoted programmes aimed at zero population growth; the Southern developing countries generally asserted that 'development was the best contraceptive' and promoted a more equitable distribution of global resources and a new international economic order to inspire development in the Third World.[31]

Yet as Harris also planned it, the tribune was supposed to accommodate different perspectives; it was not designed to produce a formal statement or adopt any singular political positions: 'The Tribune does not have a point of view on the issues involved, other than that they are important for all of us to consider. No formal statement of a Tribune position on any or all of the issues will be forthcoming at the end of the two weeks in Bucharest. Individuals and groups may make whatever statements they wish, but not in the name of the Tribune.'[32]

Nonetheless, some 500 tribune participants agreed on a statement of principles that they submitted to the Economic and Social Council (ECOSOC) for consideration in the aftermath of the conference with the introduction: 'Signatories believe the following principles should guide UN and governments' population policies.' These principles recognised the need for global coordination to deal with the dramatic world population growth projected for the next several decades. The principles linked population policies to social and economic development policies and rejected nationalistic solutions regarding consumption of global resources. Moreover, they asserted the primacy of human rights and stated:

> the success of population policies depends on the full participation of women. Women should have the opportunities to obtain full human dignity for them to exercise responsible choice as persons. Governments should take particular steps to achieve integration of women into every stage of the development process of the Second Development decade. The economic contribution of women as mothers and providers of food both in rural and urban areas should be fully recognised.[33]

NGO meetings became more formalised beginning with the Population Tribune and continuing through the UN Decade for Women because they followed Rosalind Harris's tribune template. Even so, NGO forums remained far more freewheeling than the UN-hosted government conferences that followed established protocols. Prior to the 1970s UN member governments had invited selected NGOs with consultative status to attend UN conferences as official 'observers', but this was a prescribed role. Invited consultative NGO observers could attend conference sessions and could lobby government delegates in the conference halls; they were rarely given the opportunity to present formal statements before conference delegates. During the formal conference sessions governments typically hashed out the fine points of the conference document language that had already been substantially determined by preparatory commissions. Government delegates presented their official positions on conference topics and they also seized the opportunity to comment on pressing global political issues.

In relation to these established UN conventions international relations scholar Peter Willetts has explained that:

> Diplomats like to see NGOs as useful advisers having 'consultative status' but definitely not as equal participants in diplomacy. Thus NGOs are usually very careful not to step beyond the bounds of accepted procedure. They have much less ability to take part in formal public UN meetings than in informal private meetings. Most of their influence in invisible except to the immediate participants and it is therefore easy to underestimate the impact of NGOs on UN proceedings.[34]

Consultative NGOs, however, continued to expand their influence with governments throughout the 1970s and 1980s in both hidden and observable ways. One visible marker of NGOs' impact was demonstrated by the fact that consultative NGOs were increasingly invited to participate in UN world conference preparatory meetings where government decisions were made regarding global policy and programming. Consultative NGOs used these opportunities to influence conference documents as they were drafted rather than lobbying after the fact at the official conference sessions.

Whether or not NGOs had formal consultative status with ECOSOC, however, was not a consideration for participation at the NGO forums that were established in the 1970s and that have continued since that time. All individuals and organisations with interests in the conference topics were welcome to attend these gatherings. The growing numbers of participants in the forums held in conjunction with the UN Decade for Women conferences demonstrate that women activists found the NGO meetings to be vital and useful. At Mexico City, 114 NGOs registered as organisations and 6,000 activists attended the NGO Tribune. These numbers rose to 134 NGOs registered and 7,200 activists at the Copenhagen NGO Forum, and 163 NGOs and 13,500 participants at the Nairobi Forum.[35]

Following the model that Rosalind Harris set at the Population Tribune in 1974, NGO forum-organising committees during the UN Decade for Women established minimal formal programming and provided time and space for spontaneous meetings and networking. Although individuals and NGOs that did not take part in the formal forum planning often criticised the forum structures, they vented their criticisms freely. Moreover, new NGOs that emerged during the 1970s and 1980s learned valuable information about the UN system through forum participation. Many of these new NGOs originated in the global South. As these NGOs applied the knowledge they acquired through participation in NGO forums their advocacy became more effective. They assumed leadership roles within the global feminist movement and in the international political arena.

And as the numbers of UN member states expanded from fifty in 1946 to over 180 during the 1980s the UN governance system expanded to include many Southern leaders and new NGOs in its operations. The numbers of NGOs awarded consultative status rose dramatically over the years from forty in 1947 to over 800 by the mid-1980s to nearly 1,500 by the mid-1990s.[36] These rising numbers of consultative NGOs also indicate increasing NGO influence within the UN system, or, at the very least, they indicate increasing NGO interest in participating in the UN system.

Notes

1 Jutta M. Joachim, *Agenda Setting, the UN, and NGOs: Gender Violence and Reproductive Rights* (Washington, DC: Georgetown University Press, 2007), pp. 20–1.

2 Ibid., pp. 32–3.

3 Devaki Jain, *Women, Development and the UN: A Sixty Year Quest for Equality and Justice* (Bloomington, IN: Indiana University Press, 2005), pp. 51–3.

4 Nitza Berkovitch, *From Motherhood to Citizenship: Women's Rights and International Organizations* (Baltimore, MD: Johns Hopkins University Press, 1999), p. 161.

5 Jain, *Women, Development and the UN*, p. 58.

6 Jane S. Jaquette, 'Crossing the line: from academia to the WID office at USAID', in Arvonne S. Fraser and Irene Tinker (eds), *Developing Power: How Women Transformed International Development* (New York: Feminist Press, 2004), p. 192.

7 Irene Tinker, 'Introduction' in Fraser and Tinker (eds), *Developing Power*, p. xxi.

8 Aziza Hussein, 'Crossroads for women at the UN', in Fraser and Tinker (eds), *Developing Power*, p. 6.

9 Berkovitch, *From Motherhood to Citizenship*, p. 152.

10 WYWCA, Mildred Persinger to Alice Paquier, Re: Preparations for the World Population Conference, 31 July 1973, World YWCA World Consultants at UN and Specialized Agencies, 1973–76.

11 Hussein, 'Crossroads for women', p. 7; Jain, *Women, Development and the UN*, p. 60.

12 Hussein, 'Crossroads for women', p. 12.

13 Joachim, *Agenda Setting*, pp. 33–4.

14 Jain, *Women, Development and the UN*, pp. 59–60.

15 Ibid., p. 173, note 67. 'Margaret Bruce noted that the Third Committee was disparagingly called "the ladies' committee" in the 1970s. She wrote "It is as

if men would have no concern with women's issues, and women nothing to contribute to world issues."'

16 John R. Mathiason, *The Long March to Beijing: the United Nations and the Women's Revolution*, vol. I. The Vienna Period. (2006), pp. 33–4 (intlmgt.com/longmarch/Long%20March%202006.pdf).

17 'Persinger speaks on women's conference', *Hollins [College] Columns*, 48:4 (14 October 1977).

18 Mildred Persinger, 'Not all wine and roses', *YWCA [of the USA] Magazine* (October 1971); J. Stern, 'Dobbs resident is a long-time advocate for women', [Dobbs Ferry, NY] *Enterprise* (29 September 1995).

19 Mildred Persinger, 'The poor, the black, the young, all of us have a stake in the United Nations', *YWCA Magazine* (October 1969), pp. 14–15, 31.

20 Mathiason, *The Long March to Beijing*, p. 36.

21 Jain, *Women, Development and the UN*, pp. 60–1.

22 Mildred Persinger, 'Some comments on draft Plan of Action for World Population Conference', 31 January 1974. [Copy of this document on National Board of the YWCA of the USA letterhead was sent by Mildred Persinger to the author in April 2002.]

23 Mildred Persinger in email to the author, 7 April 2002; author's emphasis.

24 IWTC, Esther Hymer, Chairman Protem to Members of the NGO Committee on International Women's Year, 14 December 1973, box 1; WYWCA, Mildred Persinger to Alice Paquier, 11 January 1974, World Consultants at UN and Specialized Agencies.

25 Irene Tinker, 'Challenging wisdom, changing policies: the women in development movement', in Fraser and Tinker (eds.), *Developing Power*, p. 72.

26 WYWCA, 'The YWCA was there: World Population Conference – Bucharest 1974', YWCA *Interchange* (November 1974).

27 IWTC, Meeting of WINGOs, Sub-Committee on Status of Women, Geneva, Switzerland, 21 May 1973, box 1.

28 Arvonne S. Fraser, *The UN Decade for Women: Documents and Dialogue* (Boulder, CO: Westview Press, 1987), pp. 55–6.

29 'Personal narrative, Mildred Emory Persinger', Hollins University (www1.hollins.edu/classes/anth220s06/lynskeyk/persinger_lynskey_narrative2.htm; accessed 21 October 2007).

30 WYWCA, 'Population tribune planning and management committee', (Apimondia Publishing House, Bucharest, Romania, c. August 1974), Youth Population Conference.

31 WYWCA, Alice Paquier, 'International Population Year', World YWCA *Perspective* (November–December 1974).

32 WYWCA, 'Population tribune planning and management committee'.

33 WYWCA, 'Bucharest-NGO statement', *Common Concern* Newsletter (November 1974).

34 Peter Willetts (ed.), *'The Conscience of the World': The Influence of Non-Governmental Organizations in the UN System* (London: Hurst & Company, 1996), p. 54.

35 Judith P. Zinsser, 'From Mexico to Copenhagen to Nairobi: the United Nations Decade for Women, 1975–1985' *Journal of World History* 13:1 (spring 2002), footnote 5, p. 141; Jane Connors, 'NGOs and the human rights of women at the United Nations' in Willetts (ed.), *'The Conscience of the World'*, pp. 158–60.
36 WYWCA, 'Report of the 19th General Assembly of the Conference of Nongovernmental Organizations in Consultative Status with the Economic and Social Council of the United Nations (CONGO), the future of the NGO–UN partnership', (Geneva, Switzerland: International Labour Office, 1994).

10

International Women's Year

Planning for International Women's Year

When the Commission on the Status of Women (CSW) proposed to the UN General Assembly that 1975 be designated International Women's Year the CSW was inspired by the long-established Western-led women's international organisations and by the Women's International Democratic Federation of socialist women's organisations. The Commission also relied on the established East-West women's non-governmental organizations (NGOs) to marshal international support for the Year's activities.[1] According to Arvonne Fraser who attended all three Women's Decade conferences and served as adviser and later as US delegate to the CSW 'the [very] idea for an international women's year and a decade for women did not come from the United Nations. Rather it was proposed by a group of traditional women's organizations who had consultative status with the UN Commission on the Status of Women.'[2] Historian Arnold Whittick confirms this: 'A group of non-governmental organizations having consultative status with the United Nations Economic and Social Council conceived of the idea of an International Women's Year. As non-governmental organizations cannot introduce resolutions to a UN Commission, Florica Andrei, a government delegate of Romania, did so on the group's behalf at the 24th session of the Status of Women Commission in early 1972.'[3]

In 1972, on the occasion of its twenty-fifth anniversary session, the CSW decided that because 1975 was the midpoint of the Second UN Development Decade and because governments and United Nations (UN) agencies were beginning to recognise that women were vital participants in global economic development, and the time was right to propose a year of research and programming focusing on the status and needs of women. Prompted by women's international NGOs, the Commission proposed a resolution to the UN General Assembly. United Nations General Assembly Resolution 3010 approved on 18 December 1972 proclaimed 1975 as International Women's Year (IWY). Margaret K. Bruce, deputy director of the UN Branch for the Promotion of Equality of Men and Women from Great Britain and Assistant Secretary General Helvi Sipilä were directed to plan and oversee IWY programmes.[4] A separate proposal to hold an intergovernmental IWY conference was formally approved by the UN General Assembly in May 1974.[5] Originally set to take place in Bogotá, Columbia, in October 1974 the world conference venue was changed to Mexico City.[6] Sipilä was also named secretary general for the IWY conference.

Margaret Bruce, Sipilä's assistant in IWY programmes and conference preparations at the UN secretariat, had served in the British military during the Second World War and was among the first group of civil servants hired to work in the new United Nations Organization (UNO) in 1945. Bruce knew the bureaucratic ins and outs of the UN system and had built strong relationships with the women's international organisations that supported IWY. She had worked in the Division of Human Rights when the Section on the Status of Women was located in that Division and she led the Section from 1966 onwards. When the UN Centre for Social Development and Humanitarian Affairs was created in 1972 and the Branch for the Promotion of Equality between Men and Women was established Bruce moved to the new Centre to take charge of the Branch.[7]

After a working group made up of members of the UN secretariat, the CSW and women's organisations held discussions to determine the IWY objectives,[8] the CSW named the Year's themes: 'equality, development, and peace', at its 14 January–1 February 1974 session.[9] The original purpose of IWY as Western-led women's organisations conceived it was to continue their long-running emphasis on the advancement of women and to highlight their campaign for women's equality. These women's organisations lobbied unsuccessfully to have the name of the UN year entitled more to the point as the 'International Year for Equality between Men and Women'.[10] The second emphasis of IWY grew out of the UN's emphasis on integrating women into development initiatives that had been spearheaded and promoted most strongly by women leaders and organisations from the global South. The third emphasis of IWY – recognising and expanding women's necessary contributions to peace building – was most strongly promoted by the Soviet Union and the socialist countries of Eastern Europe that continued to be locked in a Cold War nuclear arms race and an ideological and political struggle for the allegiance of Third World nations with the United States and Western Europe, and by the Women's International Democratic Federation (WIDF).[11]

Soon after IWY themes were determined in early 1974 two NGO sub-committees formed to plan NGO activities: the Sub-committee on International Women's Year chaired by Esther Hymer of the International

Federation of Business and Professional Women (IFBPW) that met in New York and the Sub-committee on the Status of Women chaired by Shahnaz Alami of the WIDF that met in Geneva. Both sub-committees were attended by representatives of women's international organisations that were members of the NGOs in Consultative Status with UN ECOSOC (CONGO) but liberal Western-led organisations strongly influenced the New York Committee and the ideas of the Eastern European socialist and working women's organisations more strongly influenced the Geneva committee. Already in February, 1974, Mary McGeachy Schuller, long-retired from the UN secretariat but still active in the International Council of Women, was urging the CONGO president Rosalind Harris to establish the primacy of the New York sub-committee and award it the official CONGO sanction or, as she put it, 'to give the New York sub-committee its proper place and authority' to organise NGO participation during IWY.[12]

Since the inception of the UN governance system and continuing with its expansion during the Cold War era UN activities had been dispersed among several world capitals. International NGOs with consultative status tried to maintain consultants wherever UN bureaucratic offices were headquartered but especially in New York and Geneva, the cities that were most prominent in the UN system. In the 1970s the Young Women's Christian Association (YWCA) maintained its World headquarters in Geneva and general secretary Elizabeth Palmer and World staff member Alice Paquier attended UN agency and CONGO meetings in Geneva on a regular basis. Mildred Persinger and Mildred Jones were designated YWCA NGO Consultants who attended UN sessions and CONGO Committee meetings at UN headquarters in New York City. Frequent communications flowed between New York and Geneva within the World YWCA organisation but reports and letters that passed between the two UN locations were summaries of activities and YWCA women expected and exercised some latitude to act independently.

The rival NGO sub-committees operating in the two United Nations capitals did not handle these logistical challenges as smoothly. Tensions between NGO committees in New York and Geneva surfaced at the earliest stage of organising IWY activities and continued throughout the UN Decade for Women. These tensions reflected both bureaucratic and geopolitical rivalries within the UN system. One of the earliest conflicts focused on the IWY conference location. The New York sub-committee supported the Columbian government's offer to host the world conference in Bogotá but the Geneva-based sub-committee expressed reservations about holding a conference so far from European organisational headquarters on such short notice. On behalf of the WIDF Shahnaz Alami proposed that an IWY Conference on the Elimination of Discrimination against Women be held in East Berlin in October 1975, since 1975 would mark WIDF's thirty-year anniversary as well.[13]

In April 1974 CONGO president Rosalind Harris stepped in to establish the chain of command regarding NGO participation in IWY. She wrote to Niall MacDermot who chaired the Geneva-based CONGO Committee on Human Rights and who oversaw the Sub-committee on the Status of Women that was chaired by Alami. Harris asserted the authority of the New York-based Committee to develop NGO IWY activities, thus ensuring that Western-led NGOs would dominate the planning process:

> I have discussed this with the Chairman of the NGO Committee for International Women's Year [Esther Hymer], which was established here [in New York City] last fall. The members of this Committee represent 43 of the consultative NGOs and all but 3 of the member organizations of the Geneva Sub-Committee on the Status of Women.
>
> The purpose of this Committee is to work with the Secretariat and the CSW on plans and programs for the IWY, and it is the successor to the Working Group we had last year on the integration of women into development. The minutes of its meetings are forwarded to Geneva regularly. I may add that this has been an exceptionally active committee, meeting twice a month and following the sessions of the CSW closely. I am enclosing a statement of the work of the Committee recently circulated to New York NGO representatives.[14]

After the UN General Assembly finalised the decision to hold a UN world conference for International Women's Year CONGO resolved to sponsor an NGO forum to be held in conjunction with the world conference. At that time CONGO determined officially that the New York NGO Sub-committee on International Women's Year would organise the NGO forum.[15]

By the time that the decision to hold an IWY world conference in June and July 1975 had been made and the conference venue had been changed to Mexico City it was October 1974 and there was not much time or money available for conference preparations. By October 1974 the UN budget for the 1974-75 fiscal year had already been approved and it did not include provisions for the IWY conference. Moreover, the CSW would not be involved in conference preparations. During the 1970s the CSW no longer held annual sessions; it convened every other year and was not scheduled to meet again until 1976. Therefore the UN secretariat – primarily represented by Helvi Sipilä and Margaret Bruce – had to invite governments, organise the Mexico City meetings and draft the conference document – the World Plan of Action – that governments would consider and approve at the conference. They also had to develop a conference budget and apply for funds through voluntary contributions.[16] These daunting tasks had to be accomplished in an 'abysmally short' amount of time. As Arvonne

Fraser and Irene Tinker recalled, 'Neither the UN bureaucracy nor most member countries were enthusiastic about the conference [although] they were pressured by women's organizations and supportive NGOs.'[17] With 'six months and less than $350,000' to plan the IWY conference, Sipilä and Bruce had one-tenth of the funding that had been made available to the World Population conference, which had taken over two years to organise.[18]

In order to draft the conference document Sipilä and Bruce mined the statements that women activists had prepared for the World Population conference and reports that had been prepared for previous CSW sessions on women's equal rights. They also formed a consultative committee with interested government representatives to review the draft conference document in March 1975.[19]

In her evaluation of the Mexico City conference World Plan of Action, Arvonne Fraser emphasised Helvi Sipilä's influential role in its drafting its provisions. The Plan, Fraser asserted, reflected:

> Sipilä's views that having equal legal capacity, education, economic means, access to family planning, and having women in decision making positions were all necessary to improve the status of women. These views were reflected in her own experience as a lawyer, her experience on the Commission on the Status of Women and those of the women's organizations she headed. As secretary general for the conference, she had a strong hand in the draft plan.[20]

Women's organisations in CONGO also sought to shape the UN conference document. Although their direct input into the document drafting process was limited, the long-established women's organisations had laid the groundwork for IWY during many years of activism at the CSW and in other UN agencies and commissions. Their ideas infused the draft World Plan of Action and they monitored UN conference preparations at every opportunity.

In early February 1975 World YWCA staff member Katherine Strong reported on a briefing that Helvi Sipilä had held for the Geneva-based NGO Sub-committee on the Status of Women. Sipilä had reported on the IWY conference-planning process as NGO representatives quizzed her about the draft World Plan of Action and asked whether NGOs could review the draft before Sipilä presented it to her consultative committee of government representatives in March. According to Strong, Helvi Sipilä 'obviously hasn't considered the question before and at first was quite negative. However, Mrs. Bruce was with her and whispered some suggestions, so she finally agreed that the draft which is now being worked on here in Geneva will be given to Mme. Giuriati, who will let some of us [NGO representatives] at least have it and can then send our reactions to Mrs. Sipilä before the meeting of the [government] Consultative Committee, which will be meeting in New York on March 3–14.[21]

At the end of February, just prior to meeting with the government committee, Margaret Bruce briefed the New York NGO IWY sub-committee chaired by Esther Hymer on the draft World Plan of Action. Bruce characterised the draft as 'a working paper, which needed to be strengthened and made more precise'. She invited comments from the NGOs before she met with the government consultative committee that included Princess Ashraf Pahlavi of Iran, the Attorney General Pedro Ojeda Paullada of Mexico, Elizabeth Reid of Australia and Leticia Shahani of the Philippines, among its twenty-three members.[22] Rosalind Harris sent a copy of the draft World Plan of Action to the Geneva NGO sub-committee for its review and comments as well.[23]

According to Marianne Huggard, an invited NGO observer at the consultative committee sessions, government delegates voiced competing perspectives and the draft World Plan of Action incorporated all their views. Huggard was a British woman who revealed her Western biases when she described the four major 'world' views: 'the African view with the major thrust on development, the Mexican emphasis on the Charter of Economic Rights and Duties of States, the Communist bloc concerned with Peace and the moderate view of the U.S. and Western Europeans'.[24]

In her report back to the NGOs after the consultative committee sessions Margaret Bruce assured the NGOs that their input was evident throughout the draft plan and she was certain that the women's organisations would continue to play critical roles, along with the CSW and the UN secretariat, in tracking and appraising the implementation of the World Plan of Action after its approval by governments at the IWY conference.[25]

Organising the IWY NGO tribune

Just as Helvi Sipilä and Margaret Bruce led the UN secretariat that organised the IWY World conference, Mildred Persinger led the NGO committee that organised the NGO tribune. In early October 1974 Persinger wrote to Elizabeth Palmer to report that she had been asked to take charge of NGO tribune planning. At that time she voiced reservations:

> The Women's Year Committee here has decided to go ahead with plans to put on an NGO Conference which would begin about two days ahead of the official [UN government] conference in Bogotá. Mildred Jones takes a very dim view of the amount of organization which has taken place, but if money comes from somewhere they may be able to employ someone to work on it. Offers were made to me to take on the job of coordinating these efforts – the 'Ros

Harris' of Bogotá. But I know what Ros went through for Bucharest and even 20 percent as many headaches are too many. Besides it would cut into my work here which seems to occupy every waking hour, whether or not the results are noticeable.[26]

Not only was time short but in October 1974 no funding had yet been collected for the NGO tribune. Moreover, the Geneva Sub-committee on the Status of Women were already objecting that they were being left out of IWY tribune planning process even though it had barely begun.[27]

In early November 1974 Rosalind Harris visited Geneva and met with the Sub-committee on the Status of Women to assure them that their input would be incorporated into future tribune planning, but she also learned that the WIDF was moving forward with its plans for a 'World Congress for the International Women's Year' to be held in East Berlin in October 1975.[28] This rival NGO meeting was being organised by the WIDF along with a number of international women's groups including the Women's International League for Peace and Freedom, International Federation of Women in Legal Careers, the Pan African Women's Organisations and some twenty others. The Congress planning committee had met with Helvi Sipilä in Geneva and Budapest in July and November 1974 and they believed they had the assistant secretary general's full support for their IWY NGO Congress.[29]

Although women's organisations were reluctant to host two global NGO forums during IWY, Sipilä did not recognise the undercurrents of the NGO conflict. Following her trip to Geneva, Helvi Sipilä travelled to Mexico City to confer with the Mexican government in early December. There she learned that Mexico would sponsor the UN World conference and a concurrent NGO tribune, although the two meetings would not be held on the same site; the conference would be held at the Foreign Ministry in the Mexico City centre and the tribune would take place at the National Medical Centre in an outlying district of Mexico City. When Sipilä returned to New York, she urged the New York-based women's organisations to move forward with plans for the Mexico City NGO tribune and she promised funding from the Mexican government. With Sipilä's support and promise of funding the New York NGO IWY sub-committee continued tribune planning and Rosalind Harris persuaded Mildred Persinger to take charge of the organising committee.[30]

World YWCA general secretary Elizabeth Palmer would later assert that 'The Mexico Meeting was Mildred Persinger's creation.'[31] As leader of the tribune organising committee, Mildred Persinger's overriding goal was to provide a space for the free and open exchange of ideas among women's international organisations from developed and developing nations, government delegates and UN secretariat representatives. Between January and June 1975 Persinger and the eleven NGO representatives who made up the organising committee created a space for 6,000 activists who represented 114 international NGOs to meet with each other and to discuss the conference themes of equality, development and peace. Twenty-five tribune panel sessions focused on the basic issues that were raised at the government conference. The panels featured representative women who presented case studies describing specific 'women and development', peace and leadership projects that were operating in various parts of the world. In addition to the planned panels, women who attended the tribune organised nearly 200 additional meetings on the spot in Mexico.[32] All were reported on in the tribune newspaper *Xilenon. Xilenon*, named after an Aztec goddess, included daily briefings of UN conference sessions as well as highlights of the tribune activities and up-to-date schedules of tribune meetings and announcements.[33]

From the first, Persinger's committee was concerned with including activists from the developing world and they 'strongly encouraged' participating NGOs 'to make possible the attendance of members in Asia, Africa and Latin America' to balance the large numbers of women they expected from the United States and Canada.[34] Also from the beginning, Persinger focused on fundraising, which ultimately raised $191,000 to cover the salaries of a few paid staff members, office rental and supplies, travel expenses for Committee and staff members, publishing costs for the tribune newspaper and travel grants for Third World participants. Over one-half of the budget, approximately $100,000, was dedicated to funding travel for participants from developing countries. The Mexican government provided crucial support for the tribune by donating the use of the National Medical Centre conference facilities. The Mexican government also paid for local interpreters, secretarial staff and translation services in English, French and Spanish.[35]

While striving for the broadest, most diverse participation at the tribune, the organising committee comprised only a few individuals; all were Westerners and the majority were Americans. They represented the long-established consultative NGOs that had insider connections with the UN secretariat and with their governments' UN delegations. Led by Mildred Persinger of the World YWCA, the NGO tribune committee included Robert W. C. Brown of the International Association for Religious Freedom, Richard C. Fagley of the Committee of the Churches on International Affairs, Kay Fraleigh of the International Alliance of Women, Rosalind Harris of International Social Services and the president of CONGO, Harriet Hollister of the Friend's World Committee, Esther Hymer of the IFBPW, Mary McGeachy Schuller of the International Council of Women,

Fanny Simon of the International Council of Social Democratic Women, Annabelle Wiener of the World Federation of UN Associations and Page Wilson of the Population Crisis Committee.[36]

Of these eleven committee members, Persinger and Harris travelled to Mexico to meet with government officials and settle logistical details and conducted most of the fundraising for the tribune. In February 1975 the committee hired Marcia Ximena Bravo who had worked on Harris's Population Tribune staff as director of the IWY tribune programme. Thereafter Bravo took charge of many of the day-to-day details and sent out 'literally thousands' of letters of invitation to activists worldwide.[37] The committee also enlisted the aid of Frances Dennis, the information director for International Planned Parenthood Federation (IPPF) who had organised the publication of the 1974 Population tribune newspaper, *Planet.* [38] Dennis hired the IWY tribune newspaper editor, Marjorie Paxson, who had been an assistant metropolitan editor at the Philadelphia *Bulletin.*[39]

It was rare for newly organised NGOs to have developed contacts that would have enabled them to join the 'inner circle' that led international NGO activism at the UN. Nonetheless, Persinger's committee cooperated with one newly formed NGO, the Women's International Network (WIN) founded in Boston, Massachusetts in February 1975.[40] Franziska (Fran) Hosken, an architect, photographer, journalist and activist who had been born in Vienna and emigrated to the United States in the 1930s established WIN and defined its purpose: to create 'a worldwide multi-media communication system' connecting women activists to each other and publicising their work among governments and the general public. Fran Hosken compiled an International Directory of Women's Organisations and published a newsletter, *WIN News*, to promote networking and collaborations among the many women's NGOs that were forming as a consequence of IWY and due to a generalised increase in global feminist activism during the 1970s.[41]

Fran Hosken, like Persinger and her tribune organising committee, strongly believed in sharing knowledge about the UN governance system and developing effective lobbying skills among feminists and NGO activists who were newcomers to international politics.[42] By sharing information with young activists Hosken hoped to avoid conflicts among women in Mexico that she believed were already brewing:

> I believe it is essential to make young women welcome and to give them essential information in the clearest form (charts and graphs and other visual aids) and to instil a sense of purpose and participation from the start.
>
> I know the women's movement pretty well and I am saying this from experience: the young women who will come I believe in large numbers to

the Conference and from the USA are not impressed by rules and authority. I have constant contact with students here at Harvard, MIT, BU, etc. They do not know the UN. They will get very angry if they are told they 'are not allowed' to attend meetings and to feel that they are not wanted – after they have scraped together the money to come to Mexico. The spectacle of young American women and feminists denouncing traditional women and women's organizations in front of an international audience in the international press must be avoided.

The international press, Hosken asserted, were 'extremely chauvinistic and will pounce on any problems. I saw male journalists time and again deliberately creating dissent among women in order to get a good story.' Hosken also shared her strategies for diversifying the participants who would come from the United States with the tribune organising committee:

> WIN is planning orientation meetings in the Boston area with the purpose to raise funds to bring third world women to the Conference. This includes third world women from the U.S. What, if anything, has been done to get black women, Chicano, and Puerto Ricans (in the U.S.) involved? It seems to me that this is the sort of thing that should be proposed to feminist organizations all over the country. [43]

The tribune organising committee shared these goals to promote diversity among participants and broad participation among women's NGOs. However, in setting up the programme, determining panel topics and selecting the panellists, programme director Marcia Bravo surveyed the consultative women's organisations that were affiliated with CONGO. The programme suggestions that she heard most often focused on 'women and development' issues as these issues had been discussed in UN commission and agency meetings since the 1960s. Consequently, a number of the tribune panels focused on women living in rural areas in developing countries and emphasised practical considerations regarding the expansion of education and vocational training programmes to promote women's contributions to their national economies. Other suggestions for panel topics included promoting inclusion of women in government policy making and leadership positions and women's role in peacemaking[44] (see the Appendix to this book). After the week of planned panel sessions, several days were reserved for NGOs to meet in ad hoc sessions.

Following Rosalind Harris's guidelines Persinger informed all participants serving on panels and attending the sessions that the tribune would not adopt any formal political statements. If NGO activists produced such statements they could present them to the assembled participants and request signatures but no single statement would speak for 'the Tribune'.[45]

In spite of many complaints, tribune sessions generally followed these broad guidelines formulated by Persinger's committee.

The IWY conference and tribune

When the UN secretary general Kurt Waldheim called to order the opening session of the World Conference for IWY he welcomed a historic crowd of 5,000 government representatives and activists; for the first time at a UN world conference women made up the majority of the government delegates and attendees.[46] The conference president and Mexican host attorney general Pedro Ojeda Paullada followed Kurt Waldheim to address the IWY conference delegates. He prefaced his remarks with a political appeal for the adoption of the New International Economic Order (NIEO) and called on the governments attending the IWY conference to make its provisions a reality.

After the men had spoken IWY conference secretary general Helvi Sipilä, whose zealous advocacy and hard work had made the conference a reality, addressed the assembled government delegations. Arvonne Fraser summarised Sipilä's remarks that directed the government delegates' attention back to the subject and the purpose of the conference – raising the status and addressing the needs of the world's women: 'Social and economic ills were rooted, she said, in the denial of women's rights and opportunities, a situation profoundly dangerous to world order. Sipilä urged the conference to forge a new approach to development and to work for partnership between women and men in implementing the World Plan of Action.'[47]

During the conference sessions, from 20 June opening to 2 July adjournment, government delegates debated and amended the World Plan of Action and devised some concrete measures to evaluate progress toward achieving IWY goals. The conference delegates identified specific areas for government action in regard to increasing women's political participation, expanding education, training and employment of women, improving levels of health and nutrition for women, implementing programmes to benefit families, developing gender-conscious population policies, improving housing and addressing other social issues affecting women. Delegates agreed to expand research and data collection specifically in regard to women and to improve media coverage and communications about women.

The government representatives also discussed the World Plan of Action's provisions for international and regional action and the proposed UN review and appraisal instruments to measure progress for women at these supranational levels. Nearly universally, conference delegates supported the drafting of the Convention on the Elimination of all Forms of Discrimination against Women, which had been under development in the CSW. Delegates also recommended the establishment of two new UN offices: the International Research and Training Institute for the Advancement of Women (INSTRAW), and a UN Voluntary Fund specifically targeting women and development projects.

Although the conference had reached broad agreement on objectives to promote women's global advancement as specified in the World Plan of Action, government delegates were divided along East–West and North–South lines on several geopolitical issues of the day including the proposed NIEO. The NIEO was formulated in 1973 by a coalition of developing countries among the UN member states. It called for substantial revisions of the post-Second World War global economic order as defined by the United States and Britain in the 1944 Bretton Woods Agreements that favoured the First World nations; the NIEO outlined more equitable international trade policies regarding pricing, national controls over the sale of raw materials and commodities produced in developing nations, more liberal financing for economic development and increased technology transfer from the developed Northern nations to the global South.[48] Third World nations that promoted the adoption of the NIEO asserted that the UN must address worldwide economic inequities in the distribution of wealth globally before inequalities between men and women could be addressed effectively within nations.

Third World nations also condemned South Africa's policy of racial apartheid; they defined Israel's Palestinian policy as 'oppressive' and they denounced Zionism and defined it as racism. More often than not public debates among government delegates and demonstrations at the conference site – including a dramatic walkout staged by Asian and African nations when Lea Rabin, wife of the Israeli prime minister, rose to speak at the conference – focused on these political issues rather than on 'women' specifically.

A second IWY conference document – the Declaration of Mexico on the Equality of Women and Their Contribution to Development and Peace – addressed these divisive geopolitical issues. The Declaration stated among its thirty principles that: 'Women and men together should eliminate colonialism, neo-colonialism, imperialism, foreign domination and occupation, Zionism, *apartheid*, racial discrimination, the acquisition of land by force and the recognition of such acquisition, since such practices inflict incalculable suffering on women, men and children.' The Declaration also asserted that 'Peace requires that women as well as men should reject any type of intervention in the domestic affairs of States, whether it be openly or covertly carried on by other States or by transnational corporations.

Peace also requires that women as well as men should also promote respect for the sovereign right of a State to establish its own economic, social and political system without undergoing political and economic pressures or coercion of any type.'[49] Although the conference general assembly approved the Declaration by a vote of 89 nations in favour, the United States, Israel and Denmark rejected it and eighteen nations, most of them US allies in Western Europe, abstained from voting. These political issues dominated the media coverage of the conference, a fact which disappointed many Western feminists.[50]

The Declaration of Mexico clearly exposed global fault lines among world governments. On the other hand, the World Plan of Action that had won general government approval conversely drew criticisms from feminists. Judith Zinsser who has analysed the language of the UN Decade for Women official conference documents asserted that neither the Mexico City World Plan of Action nor the Declaration of Mexico could be defined as feminist documents. Instead she has argued that:

> The language of the various documents from Mexico City defined women according to traditional patriarchal images and within the patriarchal ideologies and structures of national and international relations. Women were either victims of forces beyond their understanding and control, or so marginal to the implicit model of the world that the Declaration and the Plan of Action asked only that women be given 'access' to training, be 'integrated' into development programs, and allowed to 'participate' in the political life of their country. Explicit distinctions between women, even simple acknowledgements of class, race, and ethnicity were lost in the collective, essentializing images of 'mother, worker, citizen.'[51]

Moreover, Zinsser has concluded that the Mexico Plan of Action was inherently flawed because it, like other UN documents, left implementation to the discretion of national governments. As in the past, the UN secretariat had the power to advise governments but the member governments retained ultimate sovereignty and could follow or reject UN advice.

> Women remain subject to the same inherent contradictions that govern all legalistic societies in which the state has both the authorization to give rights in principle through legislation, and to curtail them in practice through lack of enforcement. In the Mexico City Plan of Action, as in other UN documents, national governments remain the final arbiters. The Plan explains 'Since there are wide divergences in the situation of women in various societies, cultures and regions . . . each country should decide upon its own national strategy, and identify its own targets and priorities.' This paramount role assigned to the state in Mexico leaves women in a passive role.[52]

Despite these significant weaknesses the IWY conference documents were landmarks in articulating global goals for the advancement of women. They inspired further NGO activism that led to new UN programmes and redistribution of government resources directed at improving women's status. As weak as the language of the Mexico City World Plan of Action appeared to be, it ultimately led to government actions that benefited women.

The NGO tribune also fell short of the goals set by many feminist activists and organisations even though it, too, contributed to the expansion and transformation of the global feminist movement in ways that increased women's influence in the UN governance system.

Having attended numerous UN meetings throughout her tenure as YWCA NGO consultant and having had very recent experience lobbying governments and UN secretariat officials at the World Population conference, Mildred Persinger who led the tribune organising committee was well versed in the rules of UN politics. She knew the limits of NGO influence in setting global policy but she also knew how and when and where to push those limits in the long policy-making process. In her communications with NGO activists from January to June 1975 she had tried to convey some of this knowledge to prepare NGO participants with realistic expectations regarding what they could achieve in Mexico City. Nonetheless, Persinger's insider information and liberal feminist orientation had shaped the organisation and content of the tribune programme and for many of the uninitiated and more radical feminist activists who came to Mexico City, the tribune structure and programme agenda were the source of numerous and deep frustrations.

Feminist activists who were new to the UN governance system objected to their seeming lack of power to shape government gender policies during and after the two-week-long Mexico City events. Many criticised the great divide between the government delegates who attended the UN-hosted conference at the Mexican Foreign Ministry offices in Tlatelolco, in the centre of Mexico City, and the NGOs and activists who gathered for the tribune at the National Medical Centre in an outlying sector of the city, five miles away. The physical distance between the two meetings was a real challenge to the NGOs as they sought government and media attention for their concerns. The NGOs invited the government delegates to cross the city to attend any and all tribune sessions and some, such as special adviser to Australia's prime minister and head of the Australian delegation Elizabeth Reid, joined the NGO meetings. Others, including the conference president Pedro Ojeda Paullada, dismissed the tribune as irrelevant and told the news media: 'There is nothing really new in what they are saying [at the tribune]. Everything has been said before.'[53]

The political distance between the government conference and NGO tribune, however, was even more difficult to travel than the few miles to cross the city. To their great annoyance, many of the new NGO activists discovered that UN conference sessions were only open to consultative NGOs with UN-designated 'observer' status. On 26 June some 2,000 NGO activists who expected to revise the draft World Plan of Action in Mexico City organised a delegation, named themselves the Voice of the United Women of the tribune, and intended to present their 'demands' to the government delegates at the UN conference.

The vocal NGO delegation leaders denounced the government delegates for focusing their public debates on criticisms of Western imperialism, Zionism and apartheid, and seeming to ignore 'women'.[54] The NGO delegation called for revisions of the World Plan of Action to include statements about women's 'rights' to control their own bodies, to healthcare, and to participate in global development policy making and programming. They demanded funding to combat discriminations against women and the creation of a new UN Office for Women's Concerns headed by an official at the elevated under-secretary general rank that would monitor implementation of the World Plan of Action, investigate violations of women's rights, and analyse the gender impact of UN-sponsored development programmes. Finally, they met with Helvi Sipilä and appealed for time to speak before the conference general assembly.[55]

Helvi Sipilä answered these activists who were frustrated that the conference was not responding to their demands with the message: 'Take your fight home.' Sipilä advised the NGO delegation: 'The UN is nothing when it comes to implementation. We cannot change your [country's] laws, your education, your economic plans. You are the ones who can elect people to the parliaments and municipal councils where all the decisions are made – the UN cannot. You should be involved in national planning and you should be heard.'[56]

The well-known American feminist Betty Friedan, leader of the National Organization for Women (NOW), became a Western media-appointed spokeswoman for many of the feminist critics who attended the Mexico City tribune. Friedan brought attention to herself and to the shortcomings of the IWY conference and the NGO tribune as she used provocative rhetoric that the world press quoted widely. Leading the NGO delegation to the conference site she announced that the IWY meeting was merely 'a callous manipulation of women by their governments'. She pledged to present the NGO tribune's statement on women's rights to the UN General Assembly.

Many Southern feminists, however, who attended the tribune denounced Friedan and denied her the right to speak about their concerns:

Latin American delegates to the tribune accused the United States of preparing official statements without consulting them after Ms. Friedan announced she and other tribune delegates planned to prepare a women's rights paper to present to the United Nations.

One Latin American delegate said her group would not support the Friedan statement because 'their interests are not relevant to ours. And besides, we were never involved in the statement.'

Another tribune delegate called Ms. Friedan's statement 'typically American. First they do it, then they ask us to go along.'[57]

The Mexico City world conference and tribune were not the only global gatherings for women during IWY. The World Congress for IWY, organised by a coalition of the world's socialist women's organisations within the WIDF convened for five days, from 20 to 24 October, in East Berlin, the German Democratic Republic. Nearly 2,000 delegates from 140 countries gathered for several plenary sessions and three days of planned discussions. The World Congress emphasised political issues of the day and asserted that 'women's problems' could not be discussed separately from the context of world conflicts and the widespread oppression, exploitation, and discrimination that the conflicts created and exposed. Emphasising their non-Western perspectives, Eastern bloc women and Third World women held Congress sessions that focused on critiques of Zionism and the Arab–Israeli conflict in the Middle East and that supported peace initiatives and revolutionary movements in other zones of conflict around the world including those in Vietnam, Cuba and Chile.

The Congress reacted to the World Plan of Action and the Declaration of Mexico that came out of Mexico City and Helvi Sipilä spoke at the opening session, but the UN did not direct the Congress agenda nor was the UN the centre of attention at the World Congress. Moreover, the long-established Western-led women's organisations did not take charge of defining global women's issues at the Berlin Congress. Although the Western women's international organisations were represented among the participants, Alice Paquier reported for the International Federation of University Women that the World Congress 'offered the picture of a world other than the one we [usually] meet in our own international meetings. Not only were there participants from countries where we have no affiliates (North Korea, Cuba, Eastern European countries, etc.), but also the participants from countries where we have . . . associations were usually very different [ideologically and politically] from our members.'[58]

The Congress also set its own women's agenda reflecting its collective definition of global women's issues that prioritised 'peace, disarmament, and ending the arms race, elimination of illiteracy, UN International Children's Year, [and] the problems of working women'. In February

1977 the 'Continuing Committee of the World Congress for International Women's Year' met again in East Berlin to evaluate the progress that had been made towards meeting its IWY goals.[59]

The significance of the IWY tribune

Post-conference analyses also revealed conflicting opinions within the global women's movement. The criticisms directed at Betty Friedan were only one manifestation of a fundamental North-South division among global feminists who met in Mexico City. Women who represented vastly different global locations struggled to determine who had the power to define 'women's issues' at the IWY meetings and they continued to debate with one another throughout the UN Decade for Women.

According to non-Western women, white Western women monopolised power and used it coercively in the international political arena. A group of Native American women published one such critique denouncing white Western women's misuse of power at the IWY conference and tribune. These Native American women argued that they had been denied access to the official conference site because the US government delegation did not represent their interests, [60] but they also argued that they had been denied a voice at the NGO tribune. This, they argued, was due to the way that Mildred Persinger organised the tribune programme as a series of planned panel sessions that did not allow for open discussion of the issues that they determined were most important to non-white, non-Western women:

> The Tribune consisted of two seminars held at the same time in the two largest rooms of the Centro Medico convention facilities, one half in the morning, and the other half in the afternoon of each meeting day. *According to its organizers, this plan would best fulfil the purposes of the Tribune – to let women tell each other about their problems.* There were no session at which all participants could attend at once, no conclusions, no resolutions or recommendations, and no statements could be made in the name of the whole Tribune – and no communication with the national delegations across town was encouraged.
>
> Native American women who attended the Tribune were denied any voice at the official UN conference. Unrepresented by the official U.S. delegation, they could only use the Tribune as a means of informing many women from other parts of the world of the general Native American situation . . .
>
> But the Tribune was organized so that participation was very limited excepting for those officially on the program. After each of the four sessions everyday, anyone could ask questions about the subject, but since listeners were frustrated by the lack of opportunity to make speeches on their own issues, many women took these opportunities to speak out, whether their remarks fitted with the topic or not.
>
> The three major topics of the whole year – Equality, Development, and

Peace – were general enough, but the viewpoint from which they were approached was extremely narrow. *No discussion of such important subjects such as racism, imperialism, and colonialism were scheduled anywhere . . .*

[At the Seminar on Agriculture and Rural Development] we realized that others besides ourselves wanted to talk about different topics, not to have 'show and tell' about their situations. Women wanted to talk about the political facts that make those situations the way they are. But the chairwoman – who like other U.S. experts wanted to keep the topic as narrow and specific as possible – became impatient and soon time ran out.[61]

Moreover, well-known and media savvy Western feminists like Betty Friedan and her sisters in NOW had claimed the power to define 'global women's issues'. Yet according to the Native American women, these organisations represented primarily white Western women who narrowly defined feminist issues to include only those that focused on women's lack of power in relation to men. White Western women seemed to exclude discussions of global economic, social and political inequalities that were the legacies of Western colonialism. Criticisms of entrenched racist hierarchies, for example, were categorised as 'political' questions that went beyond the scope of 'feminist' concerns by Western organisations like NOW. Native American women voiced their strong objections to the Western feminists' limited ways of thinking and the control they had exercised over tribune discussions.

Many of the U.S. women such as the National Organization of Women members were concerned only with so-called 'women's problems': abortion, rape, women's right to vote, job equality and so on. Their position was that talk of politics gets in the way of women's communication. *The reply from many of the Third World women was that 'they were compelled to talk about the realities of the lives of their people before any discussion of special women's problems could take place.'*[62]

Considering the IWY conference and tribune from their relatively privileged perspective, predominantly white Western women's organisations in the United States and Canada that had lobbied for years within the UN system to organise an international women's conference emphasised many positive outcomes from Mexico City, in addition to the shortcomings. The political 'factionalism' that was evident at the government conference, as one Canadian observer defined it, had focused on 'socio-economic inequalities' and the global political power structure and did not address 'women's interests' as she defined them, namely the 'strategies for achievement of equality between the sexes, integrating women in the development process as equal partners with men, and the involvement of women nationally and internationally in the real quest for peace'. Yet she asserted that the IWY conference was hardly a 'total failure' as *Time Magazine* quoted French delegate Françoise Giroud's post-conference appraisal. Instead, she interpreted the criticisms expressed about the conference and the World Plan of Action as a clarion call to mobilise NGOs and to inspire them to exert even more pressure on governments to overcome discriminations against women in law and practice.[63]

The United States ambassador to the UN Barbara M. White also emphasised the positive significance of the IWY NGO tribune at a press conference held in mid-July:

> The Tribune had an essential role in the interaction with governments, not just at the conference but more importantly afterwards. If changes in women's role depended upon governments alone, we probably wouldn't see much happen that fast. But the women at the Tribune are the women who are going to go home and see that their governments do something to follow up on the Plan of Action and on the resolutions. I have been here as one of the U.S. representatives at the UN for not quite two years now, and I was struck with the fact that at the conference I heard more discussion – both by governmental representatives and by non-governmental – of what people intended to do after they got home than at any other UN meeting I have participated in.[64]

According to the report of one post-conference meeting hosted by the US State Department for CONGO representatives that was attended by Mildred Persinger and other tribune organisers:

> The Tribune was referred to as 'frustrating' for its narrow substantive focus and its inability to have any input to the [World Conference], but it was also called 'essential' and 'positive'; many of the people at the meeting seemed indignant when they heard that [Pedro Ojeda Paullada] said that no communication with the Tribune was necessary because nothing was being done there, and they were pleased to hear that Helvi Sipilä said that the Tribune was valuable. Many positive comments about the Tribune were made by several NGOs who were in Mexico City. One said that it was a 'consciousness raising session of world-wide proportion.'[65]

From Mildred Persinger's perspective, the IWY conference and tribune represented the realisation of a long-running goal of women's international NGOs and it marked a rare moment when women had shared governing power with the world's male leaders. 'It was the year that worked', she declared in an interview published by her alma mater in the *Hollins College Newsletter*. Women delegates were in the majority at the Mexico City IWY events, even if these women did not represent the 'inner circle of power in their governments'. The conference delegates certainly represented their national political agendas but Persinger asserted that the women delegates also represented a 'human agenda' at the conference. North-South global politics were incorporated into the conference documents but so was the basic feminist notion that 'equality between men and women means equality in their dignity and worth as human beings'. Although male delegates resisted acknowledging 'women's rights to control their own bodies', women compromised and inserted alternate language into the conference documents recognising the 'inviolability of the human body'. According to Persinger, women delegates 'used their limited power for limited objectives' but the more significant outcome was that these women utilised opportunities to connect with the grass-roots organising that took place at the NGO tribune.

The tribune was the main source of energy that animated the UN commemoration of International Women's Year according to Persinger and other observers. Arvonne Fraser would later write that 'International Women's Year was not an end in itself, but a beginning. The chaos and uproar created at Mexico City along with the more sedate analysis and information exchange, stimulated numerous activities, energized and motivated thousands, if not millions of women and accelerated the momentum of the resurgent women's movement. It began to become truly international at the grass-roots level as well as at the highest government levels.'[66] Persinger's post-tribune report concluded that it was significant because it brought together a wide range of viewpoints that raised the consciousness of all who attended, most particularly American women. At the tribune American women, including Persinger:

> heard the women of the world say that injustice is indivisible; that . . . gaps between rich and poor, lettered and illiterate, over-fed and starving, do not discriminate on the basis of sex. When some said, 'We demand access to professional education,' others said, 'we have no schools.' When some said 'we demand equal participation in the political process,' others said 'our brothers and sisters are in prison because they tried it' . . .
>
> They said to each other: 'Women must work for justice within their countries as well as justice among countries.' And they said to each other 'The brains, the energy, the creativity and the $300 billion the world devotes to weapons of war and military establishments is too mass a problem for men only.'[67]

These were the lessons of the IWY conference and the NGO tribune, as Mildred Persinger defined them.

Notes

1 Jane Connors, 'NGOs and the human rights of women at the United Nations', in Peter Willetts (ed.), *'The Conscience of the World': The Influence of Non-Governmental Organizations in the UN System* (London: Hurst & Co., 1996), pp. 158–60.

2 Arvonne S. Fraser, *The UN Decade for Women: Documents and Dialogue* (Boulder, CO: Westview Press, 1987), p. 1; Arvonne S. Fraser, 'Seizing opportunities: USAID, WID, CEDAW', in Arvonne S. Fraser and Irene Tinker (eds.), *Developing Power: How Women Transformed International Development* (New York: Feminist Press, 2004), p. 164.

3 Arnold Whittick, *Woman into Citizen: The World Movement Towards the Emancipation of Women in the Twentieth Century with Accounts of the Contributions of the International Alliance of Women, the League of Nations and the Relevant Organizations of the United Nations* (London: Athenaeum, 1979), p. 267; Martha Alter Chen, 'Engendering world conferences: the international women's movement and the UN', in Thomas G. Weiss and Leon Gordenker (eds), *NGOs, the UN and Global Governance* (Boulder, CO: Lynne Rienner Publishers, 1996), p. 140.

4 IWTC, United Nations, 'What is International Women's Year?' c. January 1974, box 1.

5 IWTC, NGO Committee on International Women's Year Meeting Minutes, 15 May 1974, box 1.

6 IWTC, NGO Committee on International Women's Year Meeting Minutes, 30 October 1974, box 1.

7 John R. Mathiason, *The Long March to Beijing: The United Nations and the Women's Revolution*, vol. I, The Vienna Period (2006), p. 23 (intlmgt.com/longmarch/Long%20March%202006.pdf).

8 IWTC, NGO Committee on Integration of Women in Development, c. March, 1973; Notes on WINGOs' meeting with Helvi Sipilä, Geneva, Switzerland, 7 July 1973, box 1.

9 Whittick, *Woman into Citizen*, p. 268.

10 Mildred Persinger, 'YWCA Participation in World Population Year', *YWCA Magazine* (December 1973), pp. 24–6.

11 Mathiason, *The Long March to Beijing*, pp. 35–6; Judith P. Zinsser, 'From Mexico to Copenhagen to Nairobi: the United Nations Decade for Women, 1975–1985', *Journal of World History* 13:1 (spring 2002), p. 146.

12 IWTC, Mary Craig Schuller-McGeachy, President, International Council of Women, to Rosalind Harris, International Social Service, New York, 19 February 1974, box 1.

13 IWTC, NGO Committee on Status of Women (Geneva), Minutes of the Meeting, 22 February 1974; NGO Sub-committee on International Women's Year (New York), 6 March 1974, box 1; WYWCA, Alice Paquier to Mildred Jones, 2 April 1974, WYWCA World Consultants at UN and Specialized Agencies, 1973–76.

14 IWTC, Rosalind Harris to Niall MacDermot, Chair NGO Committee on Human Rights (Geneva), 4 April 1974, box 1.

15 IWTC, NGO Committee on International Women's Year, Minutes of Meeting, 29 May 1974, box 1.

16 Mathiason, *The Long March to Beijing*, p. 37.

17 Fraser and Tinker (eds), *Developing Power*, p. xxii; Fraser, *The UN Decade for Women*, p. 22.

18 Zinsser, 'From Mexico to Copenhagen to Nairobi', p. 146.
19 Fraser, *The UN Decade for Women*, p. 32.
20 Ibid., p. 22.
21 WYWCA, Katherine Strong to Mildred Persinger and Mildred Jones, 5 February 1975, World Consultants at UN and Specialized Agencies, 1973–76.
22 IWTC, NGO Committee on International Women's Year, Minutes of Meeting, 26 February 1975, box 1.
23 IWTC, Rosalind Harris to Shahnaz Alami, 3 March 1975, box 1.
24 IWTC, NGO Committee on International Women's Year, Minutes of Meeting, 19 March 1975, box 1.
25 IWTC, NGO Committee on International Women's Year, Minutes of Meeting, 2 April 1975, box 1.
26 WYWCA, Mildred Persinger to Elizabeth Palmer, 3 October 1974, World Consultants at UN and Specialized Agencies, 1973–76.
27 WYWCA, Alice Paquier to Mildred Jones, 14 October 1974, World Consultants at UN and Specialized Agencies, 1973–76.
28 WYWCA, Alice Paquier to Mildred Jones, 8 November 1974, World Consultants at UN and Specialized Agencies, 1973–76.
29 IWTC, Dorothy R. Steffens, Executive Director, Women's International League for Peace and Freedom to Margaret K. Bruce, Deputy Director, Centre for Social Development and Humanitarian Affairs, IWY Secretariat, 11 November 1974, box 2.
30 WYWCA, Mildred Jones to Elizabeth Palmer, 19 December 1974, World Consultants at UN and Specialized Agencies, 1973–76.
31 Carole Seymour-Jones, *Journey of Faith: The History of the World YWCA, 1945–1994* (London: Allison & Busby, 1994), p. 320.
32 Virginia R. Allan, Margaret E. Galey and Mildred E. Persinger, 'World conference of International Women's Year', in Anne Winslow (ed.), *Women, Politics and the United Nations* (Westport, CT: Greenwood Press, 1995), p. 40.
33 WYWCA, Mildred Persinger, 'Summary report [to the funders] on the IWY tribune', November 1975, World Consultants at UN and Specialized Agencies, 1973–76.
34 IWTC, IWY tribune organizing committee meeting, c. January, 1975, box 2.
35 IWTC, IWY tribune 1975 budget, 1 January–15 August 1975, box 2.
36 IWTC, IWY tribune organizing committee, 29 January 1975, box 2.
37 Fraser, *The UN Decade for Women*, p. 40.
38 IWTC, Memorandum from Mildred Persinger and Rosalind Harris, IWY tribune organizing committee, 11 March 1975, box 2.
39 IWTC, 'Status report – IWY tribune daily newspaper', c. March, 1975, box 2.
40 IWTC, Mildred Persinger to Fran Hosken (WIN News), 11 February 1975, box 2.
41 IWTC, Women's International Network organised February 1975, box 2.
42 IWTC, Fran Hosken, Women's International Network, IWY WIN Orientation Session, IWY Tribune, 6 February 1975, box 2.
43 IWTC, Fran Hosken to Mildred Persinger, 1 March 1975, box 2.

44 IWTC, IWY tribune organizing committee, 13 March 1975, box 2.

45 IWTC, 'Guidelines for the conduct of IWY tribune sessions', 27 May1975, box 2.

46 Allan, Galey, and Persinger, 'World conference of International Women's Year', p. 33.

47 Fraser, *The UN Decade for Women*, p. 22.

48 Robert Looney, 'The New International Economic Order', in R. J. B. Jones (ed.), *Routledge Encyclopedia of International Political Economy* (London: Routledge, 1999) (online: web.nps.navy.mil/~relooney/routledge_15b.htm).

49 'The Declaration of Mexico on the Equality of Women and their Contribution to Development and Peace', United Nations Document E/conf.66/34 (online: un-documents.net/mex-dec.htm).

50 Allan, Galey and Persinger, 'World conference of International Women's Year', pp. 35–9.

51 Zinsser, 'From Mexico to Copenhagen to Nairobi', p. 143.

52 Ibid., pp. 148–9.

53 Barbara M. White Papers, Schlesinger Library, Radcliffe Institute, Harvard University, Cambridge, MA (hereafter BMW), 'Private women ask voice at UN parley', *Los Angeles Times*, 27 June 1975, box 1; IWTC, '"I've heard it" Says Ojeda', *Xilonen* Mexico City, 24 June 1975, on microfilm.

54 IWTC, 'Daniel in the lioness's den', *Xilonen* Mexico City, 23 June 1975, on microfilm; 'Report on the World Conference on International Women's Year', Congressional Record, 94th Congress, 1st Session, 121:133 (11 September 1975), pp. S15823–S15829.

55 IWTC, press release, 25 June 1975, box 1; 'Tribune's voice to be heard in Tlatelolco?', *Xilonen* Mexico City, 26 June 1975, on microfilm; BMW, UPI press release, 'Women,' 26 June 1975, box 1.

56 IWTC, 'Take your fight home, says Sipilä', *Xilonen* Mexico City, 30 June 1975, on microfilm.

57 BMW, UPI press release, 'Women', 26 June 1975, box 1.

58 WYWCA, Alice Paquier, 'World Congress for International Women's Year, Berlin, GDR, 20–24 October 1975', International Women's Year.

59 WYWCA, Freda Brown Women's International Democratic Federation to the World YWCA, 29 October 1976, International Women's Year.

60 BMW, box 1. The US Delegation to the International Women's Year Conference included: Patricia Hutar, US Rep on the Commission on Status of Women; Jewel LaFontant, Deputy Solicitor General, Department of Justice; Daniel Parker, Administrator, Agency for International Development; and Jill E. Ruckelhaus, Presiding Officer, National Commission on Observance of IWY. Alternate Representatives who accompanied the Delegation included: Virginia Allan, Deputy Assistant Secretary for Public Affairs, State Department; Anne Armstrong, Member National Commission for Observance of IWY; Ruth Clusen, President, League of Women Voters; Arvonne S. Fraser, Former President, Women's Equity Action League; Joan Goodin. Assistant Director, Brotherhood of Railway, Airline and Steamship Clerks; Rita Hauser, Member US Advisory Commission on International Educational and Cultural Affairs;

Rita Johnston, US Delegate Inter-American Commission of Women; Joseph Jova, US Ambassador to Mexico; Patricia Lind, Special Assistant to the President for Women, White House; Carmen Maymi, Director, Women's Bureau, Department of Labour; Virginia Trotter, Assistant Secretary for Education, Department of Health, Education and Welfare; and Barbara M. White, Ambassador, Alternate Assistant for Special Political Affairs, US Mission to the UN.

61 IWTC, 'Native American women denied a voice at International Women's Year conference', *AKWESASNE Notes* (early autumn, 1975), p. 33, box 3; author's emphasis.

62 Ibid.; author's emphasis.

63 WYWCA, Freda L. Paltiel, 'International Women's Year: its significance for the future', Remarks at World YWCA World Council in Vancouver, 12–26 July 1975.

64 BMW, press release USUN 79 (75), 'Transcript of a press briefing by ambassador Barbara M. White, United States alternate representative for special political affairs at the United Nations headquarters on the results of the International Women's Year conference in Mexico City', 14 July1975, box 1.

65 BMW, 'Eyewitness report from Mexico City', Jacki Ratner to ambassador Barbara White, 23 July 1975, box 1.

66 Fraser, *The UN Decade for Women*, pp. 64–5.

67 Mildred Emory Persinger, 'On stage at last', *Hollins College Newsletter* (May 1976).

11

Taking the world's 'women' seriously

Inaugurating the UN Decade for Women

According to Leticia Shahani who would later be named as secretary general for the third United Nations (UN) World Conference on Women at Nairobi in 1985, after the International Women's Year (IWY) 'governments accepted the issue of women, the status of women, as a governmental concern. It wasn't just a social welfare [issue] handled only by NGOs. Now governments took a serious look at how half the population in their societies lives.'[1] The General Assembly designated 1976-85 as the UN Decade for Women and resolved to convene another world conference in 1980 at mid-decade to evaluate the progress in implementing the Mexico City World Plan of Action. And the UN secretariat and 127 member states established new bureaucratic offices or ministries to focus specifically on women's concerns.

Governments at the UN began to take the needs of women throughout the world seriously because women researchers and activists from developed and developing nations became 'a communicating club' after they met in Mexico City. Women had learned to use their collective power and expertise to gain leverage in UN forums. Women shared information with one another and increased their influence at UN agency meetings including those held by the International Labour Organization (ILO), UN Educational, Scientific and Cultural Organization (UNESCO) and the Food and Agriculture Organization (FAO), and at regional UN social and economic commission meetings held in Asia, Africa and Latin America.

As Devaki Jain had described the transformation of the UN and of the global women's movement after Mexico City:

The entire system came alive through the knowledge base that was being provided by the combinations of activists, writers, researchers, and the UN family of organizations. Such gatherings added to the understanding of gender, showing both the differences in values arising out of location and political systems and the universality of the nettles in gender relations. It also enabled those who were designing policies in the South to examine critically the policy approaches and programs of the Eastern and Western blocs.[2]

After IWY, UN agencies addressed women's inequality through expanded and improved methods of data collection that mapped women's lives in societies throughout the world. To conduct and oversee this new research on women, the UN General Assembly established the Institute for Training and Research for the Advancement of Women (INSTRAW), which was inaugurated in 1980. In reference to 'women and development' the General Assembly resolved to integrate women fully into the development process, acknowledging both women's rights as human beings and women's productive role as social and economic resources.

In 1976, the UN General Assembly also created a new Voluntary Fund to pay for the UN Decade for Women programming. In 1985 the fund became permanent and was renamed the UN Development Fund for Women (UNIFEM). Since that time UNIFEM has continued to fund programmes to eradicate illiteracy among women and girls, to promote equal pay for women, to provide healthcare and maternity care for women, to provide women with access to family planning methods and to increase women's participation in national and public life.

The American sociologist Margaret Snyder who had worked with the UN Economic Commission for Africa from 1971 until 1978 when she was invited to manage the UN Voluntary Fund for Women also recalled the fruitful collaborations among what she called the 'tripartite coalition of UN civil servants, government delegates from both industrial and developing countries, and NGO representatives'.[3] This was the coalition whose joint activism provided the world's needy women with 'a fund of their own'. With the UN resources dedicated to funding women's projects, the women's fund managers also gained the power to define those projects and to actually direct resources to poor women in developing societies at the village level.

These funding decisions both defied and redefined the conventional bureaucratic wisdom that had prevailed in UN agencies, in global funding agencies, and in private commercial banks. The UN Voluntary Fund for Women and its successor the UN Development Fund for Women radically changed UN funding practices; the women's fund bypassed the governments and channelled resources directly to village women through local savings societies. Fund manager Margaret Snyder recounted a few of the successes that were a result of this strategy. She has explained the revolutionary impact of UNIFEM on women's access to development resources and its role in developing new world leaders:

UNIFEM invested in women who would become world leaders such as Ela Bhatt, the gentle but steel-strong founder of India's Self-Employed Women's Association (SEWA), a remarkable instrument for poor women ... Wangari Maathai, Africa's foremost environmentalist and founder of the Green Belt Movement, which received its first major financial grant from UNIFEM in 1981 ...

UNIFEM also assisted women in strengthening their influence on multi-country economic groups, such as the Southern African Development Community (SADC), starting with their own priority, food security, and supporting technical seminars and policy-oriented women staff within its secretariat. Those actions were the first of what became women's strong political and economic influence in that sub-region ...

We developed 'the UNIFEM system' to generate economic growth while improving people's lives through investing in the women who create wealth rather than simply demanding its redistribution. We implemented strategies to systematize the inclusion of women and their concerns in the allocation of national resources. We faced the futile and distracting debate over women-specific issues versus integrated (mainstream) activities and institutions by recognizing that both types of investment are needed and that situations must dictate the choice.[4]

Under Snyder's management UNIFEM steadily increased the number of projects it funded and administered from fifty in 1978 to over 400 in 1984.[5]

Ongoing UN Decade for Women activism

Following the IWY conference and tribune, Mildred Persinger fielded criticisms directed at her organisational leadership. Nonetheless, Persinger had been energised by the intensity and passion of the non-governmental organization (NGO) activists that she encountered in Mexico City. She was determined to respond to the many thousands of appeals that her tribune committee had received for more information, more communication, and for financing and other technical assistance from activists who had met and interacted with one another in Mexico.

A thoroughgoing pragmatist, Persinger immediately focused on the future and on what she could do to sustain the enthusiasm for advancing women's status and improving women's lives. She sought to translate that enthusiasm into some concrete and beneficial programmes for women.[6] With a start-up grant of $50,000 from the Canadian International Development Agency (CIDA), Persinger's plans came to fruition in 1976 with the creation of the International Women's Tribune Centre.[7]

In establishing the International Women's Tribune Centre in New York City, Persinger collaborated again with Rosalind Harris and with Gail

Gowanlock, who had worked on a special IWY project with CIDA and who managed the CIDA grant money. She also recruited a young woman who had been trained in the Young Women's Christian Association (YWCA) organisation, Anne Walker, to direct the Centre. While Persinger, Harris, and others volunteered their time, Walker and a few paid staff members ran the Tribune Centre for many years.

Anne Walker was born in Melbourne, Australia and had worked with the Australian national YWCA and with the YWCA of Fiji during the 1960s. She was enrolled in graduate studies at Indiana University when Persinger asked her to join a group of women from Fiji who were participating in one of the tribune panel sessions that described women's participation in the anti-nuclear movement in the Pacific. After the Mexico City meetings Persinger asked Walker to help her respond to the deluge of requests for aid from women activists. In the spring and summer of 1976 Walker, Persinger and Harris formulated a plan to provide resources for women involved in development initiatives and to facilitate women's networking and exchange of news and information on a global scale through the organisation they named the International Women's Tribune Centre.[8]

By 1977, Walker hired two more paid staff members, Vicki Semler and Marina Midence. Together they established the resource centre and produced a newsletter, the *Tribune*, which circulated among a global mailing list of women's NGOs and activists. Walker also compiled a computerised resource database to track women and development projects worldwide.

In its early days, the Tribune Centre collaborated with Peggy Antrobus who directed the Women's Bureau in Jamaica and who had established contacts with women and development projects throughout the Caribbean. The Tribune staff and Antrobus devised training programmes and resource kits that included manuals to share organisational skills, along with workbooks, posters and postcards that publicised women's local organising efforts throughout the region. These kits provided the model for similar resources that the Tribune Centre later produced in collaboration with women in Asia and the Pacific, Africa and Latin America.

The small Tribune Centre staff travelled frequently to developing nations to host training sessions and to promote women's networking and share fundraising skills. They also brought women from developing nations to New York to participate in trainings at the UN headquarters. These activities strained the Tribune Centre's own limited financial resources and demanded continual fundraising efforts. Yet from its modest inception in 1976, the International Women's Tribune Centre expanded its networks and influence for over twenty six years and claimed a 'constituency' of 26,000 women and NGOs in over 160 countries by 2004.[9]

In an oral history interview conducted in 2006 Persinger recalled her experiences founding the Tribune Centre and she defined the Centre's significance within the global women's movement. The Centre had provided training and funding for Third World activists. Moreover, it had compiled data and facilitated communications among feminist activists around the world at a critical moment in the history of the global women's movement:

> That was a very exciting time because we had to do something, we were getting so many communications. After the Mexican meeting these women desperately needed something to hang on to. We had thousands of people on our mailing list . . .
> And I just think we were the thing that kept the [global women's] movement going at a time when it might have foundered, had it not a communication medium. Because the UN, as I said yesterday, they didn't get out a newsletter about this conference and about what was happening, to follow it up and implement the decisions that were made, for two years! And we had ours out within a couple months . . . and that kept the momentum going. Kept the people involved. Kept us in touch with the leaders in these various countries. The thing that, I think, we contributed to the [UN Decade for Women] conferences was having really good attendance and enthusiasm about the next conferences.[10]

Persinger ended her direct involvement with the Tribune Centre in 1982 when its governing board determined that the Centre's operations should be formalised and a CEO should be hired to oversee those operations. At that point the Centre's activities were transformed in ways that reduced some of the personal contacts between the Centre staff and global women's organisations while other electronic communications among women expanded. From the 1980s onward the Tribune Centre continued to cultivate women's global networking through an electronic newsletter that reported on women's projects and research to NGOs throughout the world.

Persinger's and Walker's accounts of the Tribune Centre's growth in the decades following IWY are a testament to the Centre's positive impact on women in First and Third World nations. The Centre connected women with public and private resources in order to promote social and economic development. It trained and equipped women leaders with political skills that enabled them to enter governments at the local, national and international levels.

Women who were left out of the process of establishing and determining the programme of the International Women's Tribune Centre criticised Persinger's actions as they had criticised the exclusive organisation of the Mexico City NGO tribune. From Geneva in May 1976 Shahnaz Alami wrote to Persinger as Persinger shared her post-Mexico City IWY report and announced plans to establish the Tribune Centre with CIDA grant money. Alami criticised Persinger for writing her IWY report without taking into account all the activities that had taken place during the Year. Persinger had privileged some events and left out other national and international events – such as the World Congress for International Women's Year that took place in East Berlin – that had also inspired and animated the IWY and the UN Decade for Women. Alami suggested the inclusion of several additional international organisations in the planning of the post-tribune project. Alami noted 'Since the work has not yet begun, we felt we could still submit suggestions to you on how the project should be carried out.'[11]

Persinger responded to Shahnaz Alami's letter but she did not change plans that had already been made in New York. As she explained to Alami:

> Many thanks for your letter of 24 May . . . As the Canadian funds to *follow-up on the IWY Tribune* were given for that purpose rather than for a general evaluation of IWY, NGOs here have proposed the continuation of the original IWY organizing committee.[12]

Based in Geneva, the World YWCA general secretary Elizabeth Palmer attended the meetings of the NGO Sub-committee on the Status of Women. At these meetings Shahnaz Alami and other NGO representatives continued to question Palmer about Persinger's actions throughout 1976. Palmer relayed these questions to Persinger, asking for clarifications regarding the terms of the CIDA grant, and whether the NGOs in consultative status with UN ECOSOC (CONGO) or the NGO tribune committee that Persinger headed was 'legally and technically responsible' for the dispersal of the Canadian grant money. Palmer pressed Persinger: 'There seems to be considerable confusion about who the Committee is that is responsible for the program which is being carried on with this money.' Palmer asked 'could you, or have someone else, put on paper exactly what is being done and what the plan is? I think I know but I keep hearing different things and I hesitate to be authoritative without being sure that I have checked with you.'[13]

Persinger immediately sent a detailed financial account and provided again the names of the eleven NGO representatives who had served on the NGO IWY tribune organising committee and who then consequently became the founding members of the International Women's Tribune Centre Board, but she did not back down in response to Geneva's challenges.[14] In Persinger's view consultations for the Tribune Centre's structure and activities were being carried out through the communications she maintained with NGOs worldwide. These NGOs had requested resources and had shared information about their activities. She considered these consultations to be evidence that her methods were inclusive and that her work style was collaborative. Yet from the perspective of some of the Geneva-based NGOs, Persinger operated in an elitist manner that limited participation at the level where decision making took place and where power resided.

The IWY conference and its World Plan of Action had generated an outpouring of women's activism in nations worldwide. Mildred Persinger was not only involved in international women's organising through the newly established Tribune Centre in New York City, she also became involved in organising a National Women's Conference to identify national priorities for American women in reference to the global goals and targets set by the World Plan of Action. Following the IWY conference in Mexico City several US congresswomen, including Bella Abzug, Patsy Mink and Margaret Heckler, took the lead in sponsoring a bill and in persuading Congress to fund a National Women's Conference. The conference eventually took place in Houston, Texas in November 1977 and was attended by 2,000 official state delegates and 20,000 observers.

President Gerald Ford appointed Jill Ruckelshaus who had served on the US delegation to the IWY conference in Mexico City as the chair of the National Commission on the Observance of International Women's Year (NCOIWY) to organise the National Women's Conference. Mildred Persinger and thirty-five other women and men were appointed as commissioners. After the election of President Jimmy Carter in 1976, Carter appointed Bella Abzug to replace Ruckelshaus as chair of the commission and appointed several additional NCOIWY commissioners.[15] In the original congressional bill authorising the national conference, states were directed to host state-wide conferences prior to the national event.

With the assistance of NCOIWY commissioners the state conferences collectively identified a core agenda addressing American women's needs that were included in the conference document 'To Form a More Perfect Union'. The agenda outlined twenty-six broad issue areas directing national attention to the inequalities experienced generally by women in US society and that specifically identified the needs of battered women and the need to strengthen rape laws, the need for affordable child care, the need to expand women's healthcare, the need for bank credit that was accessible women, the need for equal employment opportunities for women, the need to address inequalities in education for women and girls, the need for women's equal participation in electoral politics and appointive office, the need for an equal rights amendment to the US Constitution, the need for women's participation in international relations, the need to address negative images of women in the media, the needs of women in the criminal justice system, the needs of older women and the need to protect women's reproductive rights.[16]

During the state conferences and at the national conference in Houston conservative American men and women attacked the 'feminist' orientation of the National Plan of Action. They accused the NCOIWY and its chair, Congresswoman Abzug, of misusing federal funds to lobby for the equal rights amendment. New Right neo-conservatives denounced the state-wide meetings for promoting lesbian sexuality and abortion rights and tried to eliminate public support for the National Conference. The Ku Klux Klan, the John Birch Society, the Mormon Church and Phyllis Schlafly's ultra-nationalist and anti-feminist Eagle Forum, all opposed the National Plan of Action and staged protests at state gatherings. Nonetheless the National Conference generated widespread grass-roots activism among 'pro change' women's groups across the country and rallied support for the core agenda as outlined in the National Plan.[17]

While the media labelled the controversies surrounding the National Women's Conference as the 'War between Women' and predicted the implosion of the feminist movement, activists like Persinger were not daunted by the heated debates about – or among – women. 'Why should women agree?' Persinger asked. 'Men have been meeting for years and they aren't expected to agree . . . I'm not sure what a women's movement or feminism are, per se . . . [but I know that] the end of women seeking equality in the institutions of society can't really happen, a whole change of attitude, can't appear overnight . . . The goal of the conference . . . is to establish a firm women's plan of action, a plan that will carry us into the 21st century.'[18]

Persinger headed a sub-committee of the NCOIWY that planned the international component of the National Conference programme. Although American women were focused on defining a national agenda Persinger reminded them that Americans should be involved in setting an international agenda for women's advancement as well. Drawing on her connections at the US State Department Persinger persuaded the US government to provide travel funds that brought seventy women from various nations to Houston. These international women observed the American conference, honed their networking skills, and shared news about their own national responses to the IWY World Plan of Action. Persinger believed that it was important for women from other nations to observe the United States conference; it was also beneficial for American women to connect with women living in other parts of the world. Through these contacts American women became more aware of the global needs of women and were better able to interject feminist values into US foreign policy. 'How should [American] women relate to the vast influence of the United States in an interdependent world?' Persinger asked, and she responded:

> Women must be where their foreign policy is made. They are already forming support communities to promote women's appointments and candidates [for political office in the United States]. They need to seek out women who understand what the sisters of the developing world are saying and women who will make an adequate response. They need women who honor cultural differences and who will work for greater inclusiveness of both men and women of diverse economic, ethnic, social, and racial backgrounds in the foreign policy establishment.
> It is essential to [formulating] valid U.S. decisions in the world community that decision makers reflect the diversity which has infused such vitality into 200 years of U.S. history ... Involving oneself in foreign policy is all very hard work, but if women are indeed the only new force for change, their multiple roles will have to include the assertion of their right and their competence to be part of the great global decisions. These decisions must recognize humanity's interdependence and accept earth's finite resources – to ensure human survival.[19]

As chair of the international program committee in Houston, Persinger persuaded anthropologist Margaret Mead, whom she had met during the World Population conference in 1974, to join a National Conference panel. Mead shared her knowledge of women and development projects in Africa. To Persinger's satisfaction, Mead highlighted the role that the YWCA had played in initiating some of these projects. This amused a few audience members who thought of the YWCA as 'white-haired women in tennis shoes', well-meaning but ineffectual. According to Persinger Mead stared them down and asserted, 'Don't laugh, the YWCA has done more for the women of Africa than any other organization!'[20]

Transforming Western women's organisations: the case of the YWCA

Although many activists within the established international NGO community were aware of the wide-ranging and progressive political, social and economic development programmes that the World YWCA had sponsored throughout the world, among the newly formed and more radical feminist organisations the YWCA was defined by its white, Western, middle-class and colonialist roots. Historically the YWCA's most elite leadership had been drawn from its privileged Western membership. Although the World YWCA governing Executive Board had incorporated a few non-Western women into its ranks beginning in the 1920s, beginning in the 1960s, non-Western

women challenged the Association to diversify its leadership and to transform its programming to meet the needs of the majority of its worldwide
membership. Real changes in the organisation occurred as a result of these
disputes and non-Western women joined the YWCA's decision-making
elite.

The YWCA's general secretary from 1955 to 1978, Elizabeth Palmer,
promoted these changes. Born into an Episcopalian family in Connecticut,
Palmer came of age during the Great Depression of the 1930s. After
working at YWCA summer camps in her youth she joined the YWCA of
the USA staff in New York City during the Second World War. Following
her graduation from Columbia University, Palmer was sent to work with
the British YWCA in Manchester for the duration of the war. When the
war ended in 1945, she joined the World YWCA staff and served as youth
programming secretary from 1946 to 1948 and then as a foreign secretary
in East Asia and the Pacific from 1948 to 1951. Palmer returned to Geneva
headquarters in 1951 and began working as the World YWCA finance
secretary 'where her genius for figures and fundraising first became apparent'.[21] After she demonstrated her leadership skills in all these positions
the World YWCA Executive Board selected Elizabeth Palmer to head
the organisation in 1955 when her predecessor, Helen Roberts, retired.
Palmer, then in her early thirties, became the youngest general secretary
that the World YWCA had ever employed; she became one of the longest
serving general secretaries and retired from the position after twenty-two
years in 1978.

In conjunction with elected Executive Board members Palmer presided
over the post-Second World War growth of the YWCA as the Association
expanded to over eighty national chapters by the 1970s. Palmer oversaw
a paid staff at the international headquarters in Geneva and designed
and implemented programmes to carry out global policy that she and the
Executive Board determined. She facilitated communications between the
international, national and local levels of the organisation and travelled
widely to attend international conferences and national chapter meetings and to visit many women and development projects sponsored by
the World Association and its Third World affiliates. During her tenure as
general secretary Palmer also served on numerous CONGO committees
in Geneva and collaborated with various Christian, women's, youth, and
peace advocacy NGOs, whose headquarters were also based in the UN
European capital.

Like Ruth Woodsmall before her, Elizabeth Palmer expanded the World
YWCA's distinctive leadership role among the international NGO community. YWCA colleagues praised Palmer for her 'openness, her quick
understanding, unerring political sense, and genius for finance'. She was

described as 'a natural leader with a passion for justice' who displayed a 'strong, vital, matriarchal personality'. She had 'invested her life' in the YWCA and she served the association with 'missionary dedication'. According to the YWCA historian Carole Seymour-Jones, 'during her twenty-two year reign an era of [post-war] reconciliation gave way to one of expansion during which the name of the World YWCA became increasingly respected in the international and NGO communities for its pioneering work with women and youth, with refugees, and at the UN.'[22]

During the 1960s and 1970s Palmer worked with YWCA President Athena Athanassiou to integrate the YWCA leadership and staff at the world headquarters. Athanassiou pushed the white, Western, Protestant Christian women who dominated the Executive Board to share power and brought in new leaders drawn from non-Western nations. Born into an elite Greek family and raised within the Greek Orthodox Church Athena Athanassiou gained international experience at a young age; her father was Prime Minister during King Constantine's reign and her family fled to Europe with the royal family when Italian and German forces occupied Greece during the Second World War.

After she became a leader within the YWCA organisation, Athanassiou often bridged the gap between some of her more conservative colleagues who led the established European YWCA national chapters and the rising leaders who hailed from national associations in Africa and the Middle East. She denounced the thinly veiled racism expressed by her more timid European colleagues who served on the World YWCA Executive Board and later asserted that 'working with other women with power pushed us forward'. Athanassiou worked well with Elizabeth Palmer who had also embraced the global changes in the organisation and who had involved the World YWCA in the UN's technical assistance, development, and family planning initiatives within Third World nations since the earliest years of their emergence in the 1950s and 1960s when these initiatives seemed most radical.[23]

The 1975 World Council Meeting in Vancouver marked a turning point for the YWCA organisation and culminated a decade of transformations led by Palmer and Athanassiou at World headquarters. At Vancouver, the World Council documents that defined the Association's global policy were infused with language that recognised the interconnectedness of the unequal distribution of wealth and power in the world, the declining state of the global environment, the world food, population, energy crises and the global status of women.

Lucille Mair was among many invited speakers at the World Council. Mair represented the YWCA of Jamaica and she also served as Jamaica's delegate to the United Nations. She called upon the YWCA to return to its 'radical traditions' in order to address world problems. According to Council reports:

> Mair outlined the situation of voluntary organizations today, both at the international and national level. Many of them, she said, tend to reflect the traditional pattern of resources at one end of the scale and recipients at the other, but this is now being challenged, and the voluntary organizations themselves more and more are questioning their position and their task . . .
>
> History is now turned on its head, said Dr. Mair, and these groups, which were pioneers in the past, are today considered part of the establishment. Yesterday's heresies are today's orthodoxy. 'I would like us to recall our radical past . . . There may be friction, but friction too can be creative, and voluntary organizations are freer than many governments to experiment with new ways, while at the same time to keeping their inherent concern for the human person, a concern which is apt to get lost in bureaucracy.'[24]

The Vancouver World Council meeting focused its wide-ranging discussions on examining and questioning the YWCA's foundations. YWCA women asked whether the predominantly white, Euro-American, middle-class leadership could in fact diversify its racial composition and consequently transform its conservative politics because there had been stubborn resistance to such changes in the past. By electing Dame Nita Barrow from Barbados as their new YWCA president, World Council members chose the path of change.

Following Nita Barrow's leadership after 1975 the YWCA continued in the progressive direction initiated by Athena Athanassiou and Elizabeth Palmer; the Association recruited non-Western leaders who were often drawn from their nations' first generation of professionally trained women and incorporated these women into a truly multiracial World Executive Board. Among these Board members were pioneering Southern leaders including Madie Hall Xuma from South Africa, Lettie Stuart from Sierra Leone, Irene Ighodaro from Nigeria, Annie Jiagge and Delphina Bartlett-Vanderpuye from Ghana, Leonor Stok de Lovlovet from Argentina, Iris Haberli from Uruguay, Marly de Barros from Brazil, Phoebe Shukri from Egypt, Aurea del Carmen from the Philippines and Carmen Lusan from Jamaica. These women 'gradually tilt[ed] the balance away from an overwhelmingly WASP leadership, despite sometimes feeling like poor relations' on the World Executive Board.[25] When Elizabeth Palmer retired as general secretary of the World YWCA in June 1978 the transformation of the World YWCA leadership was well under way although it was far from complete.

The mid-decade women's conference at Copenhagen

In 1978 the UN General Assembly initiated the planning process for the mid-decade UN world women's conference called to 'readjust programs for the second half of the Decade in light of new data and research', although the process was in considerable flux.[26] Responding to pressures from Third World nations the general assembly decided to name three mid-decade conference sub-themes – education, health and employment – all related to the Decade for Women theme of development. The Princess Ashraf Pahlavi of Iran, the sister of Shah Reza Pahlavi, had offered to host the mid-decade conference. However, the Islamist revolution threatened and ultimately overthrew the Shah's regime in 1979 and Iran withdrew its offer – but not before Western feminist groups denounced the prospective host country for claiming to support women's rights while violating fundamental human rights. American feminist historian Joan Kelly had asserted that 'If the conference meets in Iran it will be used to disguise a reality of gross human abuse in that country behind a veil of pseudo-feminist reform'.[27] After Iran's withdrawal, Denmark stepped in to host the mid-decade conference and corresponding NGO forum in Copenhagen and UN plans went forward.

Power shifts within the UN secretariat also affected planning for the mid-decade conference. UN secretariat officials assumed that the Branch for the Promotion of Equality between Men and Women led by Margaret Bruce, operating within the Division for Social Development and Humanitarian Affairs led by assistant secretary general Helvi Sipilä, would again take charge of conference preparations as they had at Mexico City. Sipilä, however, had prompted a mutiny within her own Division when she agreed to UN secretary general Kurt Waldheim's plan to move the Division and its Branch for the Promotion of Equality between Men and Women from the UN headquarters in New York City – 'the center of the United Nations political universe' – to Vienna, Austria – 'the equivalent of exile to a desert island' – for secretariat officials. Margaret Bruce refused to move from the hub of UN activities in New York to Vienna and took early retirement. The UN General Assembly had also passed a resolution stipulating that the 1980 women's conference secretary general must come from a developing nation; Helvi Sipilä no longer qualified and Lucille Mair was appointed conference secretary general at the institutional rank of under secretary for the duration of the conference preparations.[28]

Lucille Mair walked into a political minefield when she agreed to serve as secretary general for the Copenhagen conference yet she did so knowingly and willingly. Her strongly held political convictions were drawn from her life experiences growing up in Jamaica, a Third World nation. Trained as a historian, she began her professional career teaching at the University of the West Indies and then entered government service during Michael Manley's tenure as Jamaica's Prime Minister. Mair had been active in NGOs before her first government appointment as Jamaica's first adviser on women's affairs. This experience led to her appointment as head of the nation's Agency for Public Information in 1974 and then onto a series of diplomatic posts at the UN.[29]

Lucille Mair had also served as Jamaica's delegate to the Mexico City IWY conference and had been a vocal member within the UN member-state coalition of developing nations, the Group of 77, or G77. According to Devaki Jain, Mair 'was in many ways as committed to Third World concerns as she was to those of women. She was able to link quite explicitly macro issues of imperialism and the "violence of development" with the violence women face within more intimate spaces.'[30]

Following the Mexico City conference Mair served as Jamaica's deputy permanent representative at the UN from 1975 to 1978; she was elected chair of the UN's Third Committee on Social Issues, a post that Helvi Sipilä had held in the early 1970s. When she was interviewed by the *New York Times* after she was named secretary general for the mid-decade conference Mair openly acknowledged that she had been selected because she was a black woman from a developing nation. She accepted the post because she had a political agenda that she hoped to further. Mair told the *Times* reporter 'Third World women are acutely conscious of their condition. There comes a time when we need to put the problem in a global context. This is it.'[31]

The UN mid-decade conference preparatory committee headed by Lucille Mair was far more inclusive than the IWY conference preparatory committee led by Helvi Sipilä had been. Mair relied on women's NGOs to mobilise support for the conference through their established communication networks and publications but she also included representatives of twenty-eight consultative NGOs as official members of the UN conference committee. These NGOs joined government delegates from Australia, Brazil, Cuba, Egypt, German Democratic Republic, India, Iran, Japan, Mexico, Netherlands, Niger, Nigeria, Pakistan, Philippines, Senegal, the Soviet Union, Uganda, United Kingdom, the United States, Venezuela, Yugoslavia and representatives from seventeen UN agencies.[32] Mair also included representatives from the African National Congress, the Palestinian Liberation Organization (PLO), the Pan-African Congress, and patriotic front groups from Zimbabwe on the conference preparatory committee.

It was clear from the start of preparations for the mid-decade conference that the outstanding political issues of the day – the continuing

Israeli-Palestinian conflict and the policy of apartheid in South Africa – would command the government delegates' attention at the conference. Additionally Western feminists at conference preparatory meetings were condemning the practice of female circumcision in African countries, claiming that the practice was in fact 'female genital mutilation', and this controversy also became a major political issue in Copenhagen. Debates addressing these divisive conflicts dominated many of the pre-conference meetings as well as the Copenhagen conference sessions.[33]

The conference preparatory committee drafted the Copenhagen conference document – the Programme of Action for the Second Half of the United Nations Decade for Women. This document like the IWY conference documents reflected the geopolitical priorities that divided the Western bloc, Eastern bloc and Southern bloc powers. Nonetheless, according to Judith Zinsser's analysis, the Copenhagen Programme of Action 'did advance women's interests'. Differences among women were acknowledged and the essentialist categories of the Mexico City documents were abandoned; more specific women's needs were identified and more active and participatory roles for women in setting national and international development goals were defined. Assessments were made to measure women's access to education, healthcare and employment – the sub-themes of the mid-decade conference. This data helped to build a 'world profile of women' that revealed continuing and deep inequalities between women and men, and between urban women who were generally more privileged and rural women who were among the world's most disadvantaged groups. Although the Copenhagen conference document did not criticise patriarchy in overt ways 'men's and women's attitudes toward their roles and responsibilities in society' and 'biases and prejudices' were named as limiting progress toward women's equality. The Programme of Action identified the negative impacts that the global capitalist economy and world trade structures had on women's employment and wages and raised awareness that women's unpaid work in the home and in the agricultural sector prevented women from attaining economic equality.[34]

Arvonne Fraser and Irene Tinker have further argued that 'despite the political static, the Copenhagen conference produced the best researched documents of the decade'. This was due to Lucille Mair's leadership during conference preparations. Mair recruited women scholars and development specialists from Southern nations to draft sections of the Programme of Action. The UN conference secretariat also organised regional meetings prior to the conference to gather input from women around the world in order to define global women's concerns. The practice of holding regional preparatory meetings would be repeated at the end of decade conference in Nairobi.[35]

The Copenhagen NGO forum

Once again, CONGO – a coalition that included 130 consultative NGOs in 1980 – planned a parallel NGO forum to coincide with the mid-decade UN women's conference. Edith Ballantyne, the president of the Women's International League for Peace and Freedom that located its organisational headquartered in Geneva, had been elected as the president of CONGO to replace Rosalind Harris. In consultation with leaders of several women's NGOs Ballantyne selected Elizabeth Palmer as the convenor for the 1980 NGO forum.[36]

Edith Ballantyne, born Edith Mueller in the Bohemian region of Czechoslovakia, had experienced the dislocated life of the twentieth-century European refugee first-hand. Her parents were socialists and anti-fascists. When German armies invaded the Sudetenland in 1938 the Muellers were forced to flee their home. Edith Mueller, then a young girl, escaped with her mother and an aunt to Plzeň and then emigrated to London and eventually to the Canadian West. When she was a young woman Edith moved to Toronto where she joined the local chapter of the Women's International League for Peace and Freedom (WILPF) and developed a strong sense of social justice as she engaged in campaigns for workers' rights. Later Edith moved to Montreal where she met and married Cam Ballantyne. The Ballantynes moved to Geneva in 1948. Edith Ballantyne initially worked for the World Health Organization (WHO) but she soon rejoined the WILPF organisation at its international headquarters and worked on international peace and justice campaigns for the next several decades. In 1969 Ballantyne was hired as WILPF's secretary general and was elected president of the WILPF organisation in the 1970s.[37]

When Edith Ballantyne and her CONGO colleagues unanimously agreed to invite Elizabeth Palmer to convene the Copenhagen NGO forum 1980 the location of the forum planning committee meetings became an issue. The tension between the New York- and the Geneva-based NGOs surfaced again. There were several logical reasons for the forum 1980 planning committee to meet in New York City. For one, after her retirement from the YWCA, Elizabeth Palmer had returned to live in New York. For another, the mid-decade conference preparatory committee headed by Lucille Mair was also based at the UN headquarters in New York. It seemed most efficient for Palmer's NGO forum-planning committee to be located in New York, too. Ballantyne, however, pushed for forum committee meetings to be held in Geneva in addition to New York.

The NGO representatives hoped to avoid a repeat of the New York-Geneva power struggle but these hopes were thwarted and the rivalry was revived. Although Elizabeth Palmer and Edith Ballantyne conferred frequently on forum matters from their bases of operations in New York and Geneva questions about the coercive use of decision-making power were raised again, even among the relatively tight-knit cohort of leaders of women's international organisations in CONGO.

At the outset Palmer tried to define the NGO forum 1980 planning committee, which was composed of representatives of thirty four NGOs, as a special event committee, distinct from the two ongoing CONGO committees concerned with the UN Decade for Women: the Committee for NGO Activities during the UN Decade for Women based in New York, and the CONGO Sub-committee on the Status of Women based in Geneva.[38] The forum 1980 planning committee represented thirty-four women's international NGOs and therefore, Palmer asserted, by inference it represented 'global women's interests'. It was organised for the duration of the mid-decade conference only, after which the forum 1980 planning committee would dissolve.[39]

Although Palmer travelled to Geneva numerous times to meet in person with Ballantyne and the NGO Sub-committee on the Status of Women, she coordinated the forum from office space that was rented from the YWCA of the USA in New York City. As the following dispute revealed, Edith Ballantyne's believed that Palmer and the New York-based planning committee often acted too independently and made decisions that should have been made in joint consultation with the NGOs in Geneva.

Ballantyne wrote a long letter of complaint to Palmer after Palmer planned to hire Marcia Ximena Bravo to serve as the forum 1980 programme director. Ballantyne's concerns illuminated the difficulties in reconciling organisational efficiency with truly democratic and feminist participatory decision making that takes time and focuses on process rather than on result. Ballantyne wrote to Palmer in November 1979:

> I assumed the post [of program director] would be advertised, with a job description, at least among the member organizations of the two most concerned NGO committees in New York and Geneva . . . I am aware of the problems of time and the other difficulties of 'communication,' but it is for these reasons that I feel every effort needs to be made to avoid having decisions of such import made by a small group of individuals. The Planning Committee was set up early this time to avoid the problems of (and accusations against) the Mexico planning group and more recently that of the Vienna Forum. I gather nothing can be done concerning the post of director. But there are other problems . . .[40]

Ultimately Palmer's forum 1980 planning committee hired two program co-coordinators – a British woman, Marianne Huggard, and a Ugandan woman, Hilda Paqui – who both had experience working for the UN secretariat and with NGOs.[41] Although it exposes tensions among women, this dispute demonstrated that the leaders of these NGO forums were continually learning and adjusting to new circumstances and that they were developing leadership styles that were less autocratic and more collaborative throughout the UN Decade for Women.

In her letter to Palmer, Ballantyne, although a white, Western European woman herself, also urged Palmer to include a large contingent of women from the Third World at the Copenhagen forum. This was Palmer's concern as well. Throughout the forum 1980 planning process, Palmer worked hard to ensure representation of the 'world's women' by dedicating travel subsidies and other funding to bringing women from Asia, Africa, and Latin America to Copenhagen. Over $200,000 of the nearly $490,000 forum 1980 budget-funded travel costs for Third World women.[42]

However, the non-Western women who received travel subsidies were nominated by the consultative NGOs associated with CONGO. Insider connections played an important role in bringing the names of specific non-Western women who needed financial assistance to the attention of the forum-planning committee.[43] The forum committee's resources were finite and personal connections were an important factor determining the distribution of those resources. [44] For example, Palmer's committee paid travel expenses for six women nominated by the World YWCA who participated on forum panel sessions; all were from developing nations who either worked in Geneva on the YWCA staff or who were leaders of Third World YWCA national chapters. The US Agency for International Development (USAID) also funded four additional Third World women nominated by the World YWCA and Elizabeth Palmer helped the YWCA apply for US government funds.[45]

Beyond her concern to include broad-based non-Western participation in Copenhagen, Edith Ballantyne was also interested in the content of the forum programme. She wanted to ensure that the New York-based committee played a coordinating role only and incorporated the substantive ideas proposed by forum participants rather than determining the contents of forum sessions themselves.[46] Palmer took these concerns seriously, and consultations among women's international NGOs in New York and Geneva and Lucille Mair's UN conference preparatory committee took place on a regular basis.

Palmer played the key role in facilitating the NGO forum 1980, but she did not shape the forum program with the same measure of controlling influence that Mildred Persinger had exercised at the 1975 tribune and this was by her conscious design. Palmer turned over the responsibility for organising workshops and panel sessions that were focused on the UN Decade for Women themes and sub-themes to specific NGOs, and so, for example, WILPF selected and coordinated sessions related to the theme of peace.[47] Other NGOs took charge of coordinating sessions focused on development, equality, education, employment, migrants and refugees, family, health, racism and sexism.[48]

To deflect other criticisms related to the forum programming, Palmer utilised the records of the Mexico City IWY tribune planning commit-tee that were collected at the International Women's Tribune Centre. Consequently, the forum 1980 structure became more fluid and allowed for more spontaneity than the 1975 tribune. Arvonne Fraser reported that:

> Palmer and the planning committee could see the handwriting on the wall. They had the experience of Mexico City behind them and they understood the dialogue and the activities going on among women's groups around the globe. On the basis of this, Palmer had simply decided to take care of the logis-tics and the funding, put together a minimal program, and 'let it all happen,' according to one of her co-coordinators. The Tribune Centre and others facilitated the happening.[49]

At the Copenhagen forum, nearly 175 meetings, panels, workshops, demonstrations, exhibits and films took place daily for ten days running from 14 to 24 July. An open meeting place was established at the Copenhagen University Amager campus, the site of forum 1980, for infor-mal activities, discussions and workshops, with an open microphone set up for performers and display space provided for visual artists. The organ-isers named this flexible-use open space 'Vivencia!', to express its vibrant nature.[50]

Palmer also made it clear that the purpose of the forum was 'to enable women and men from all geographic areas and diverse backgrounds to exchange information and perspectives on the situation of women at the Mid-Decade and devise strategies for change . . . The Forum will take no position on issues discussed and will not adopt formal resolutions in its own name.'[51] To make this open forum a reality, Palmer took the lead in the mammoth task of raising the $490,000 needed to run the programme from governments, international development agencies, charitable foun-dations, NGOs, businesses, and individual donors.[52] At the same time, Palmer and CONGO also pressed the UN secretariat to arrange greater opportunities for NGOs to express their views to the government delegates at the conference, which would amend the Copenhagen conference rules adopted by Mair's preparatory committee.[53] And in July 1979 Palmer also began working with the Danish Council of Women to coordinate local arrangements for accommodation, food, transportation and other needs of the NGO forum.

Although Elizabeth Palmer led the NGO planning committee that organised forum 1980, for the most part she operated behind the scenes. In one exception to her usually hidden work Palmer joined the UN conference secretary general Lucille Mair and the conference president Lise Ostergaard in the spotlight at the forum 1980 opening ceremony. Together, Palmer, Mair and Ostergaard welcomed 8,000 forum participants who converged on Copenhagen on 14 July. Interviewed by the *Forum 80* newsletter about her role as forum convenor Palmer asserted, 'What women wanted most from such a gathering was an opportunity to exchange ideas on the things they'd been doing and to find out how to do them better.' Palmer emphasised practical action as she had at the YWCA for many years as its general secretary. She explained that her forum-planning committee had not scheduled any plenary sessions for the full contingent of NGO activists to meet as a group, to discuss the concurrent UN conference sessions, or to formulate joint political statements.[54] Instead NGO participants could choose to attend any of the 175 workshops, panel sessions and informal meetings that took place each day at the forum site.[55]

Some NGO participants believed that the absence of any forum-wide meetings was a serious flaw in the forum 1980 organisation and they tried to correct this when they met in Copenhagen.[56] Sixty activists organised an impromptu plenary session to address the need for more communication between the forum and the UN conference sites and for more opportunities for non-consultative NGOs to address conference delegates on substantive women's issues.[57]

As a result of the spontaneous plenary meeting, several thousand NGO activists marched to the Bella Convention Centre to address government delegates who attended the UN mid-decade conference. Responding to a pressing conflict of the day, the activists declared their support for Bolivian miners who were on strike and were being suppressed by government troops, an issue raised dramatically and persuasively by mine worker Domitila Barrios de Chungara. They also made additional demands directing global attention to women's human rights and nuclear disarmament campaigns. Anne Walker described the women's march from the forum site to the UN conference centre and assessed its significance in terms of NGO contributions to the government-led debates:

> The organizing for what became known as Domitila's March from the Forum to the official conference also took place in Vivencia! Domitila, the tireless activist who fought for miners' rights in Bolivia held the floor for days surrounded by crowds of women painting banners, T-shirts, posters, and whatever else was needed for the march across Copenhagen to the Convention Center where the UN Conference was being held.
>
> The day of the march was unforgettable. Tiny Domitila led the way in full

Bolivian attire, holding high a banner demanding human rights for miners in Bolivia. Thousands of women streamed behind her, singing chanting, waving banners. Demands had been expanded to include women's human rights, labor rights, calls for nuclear disarmament, and more in the document being forged at the Conference. At the Convention Center we were met by heavily armed police and militia attempted to stop the marchers from reaching the doors of the Convention Center. Then Lucille Mair appeared before the crowd and finally agreed that Domitila and two or three others could go to the plenary meeting and place our demands before the delegates.

It was a major step in forging a greater role for civil society in global decision making. It followed in the tradition established in 1975 when women NGOs, led by feminist writer Betty Friedan, marched across Mexico City to the IWY Conference to demand more participation by NGOs in the conference.[58]

The NGOs created a spectacle that gained media attention and that resulted in a unique opportunity to address the government delegates in a highly publicised conference session. In general, however, forum 1980 participants focused their attention on sharing practical strategies for women's empowerment and on networking with one another on the Amager campus. NGOs forged new connections and held ground-breaking conversations with one another and these developments also defined the significance of forum 1980 for the global feminist movement. For the first time in such an international and public setting, activists discussed many previously taboo topics, including domestic violence, sexual abuse, female circumcision, contraception and abortion. These issues raised at the NGO forum also penetrated discussions at the government conference site. One specific and immediate impact of these discussions was registered when the United Nations (International) Children's (Emergency) Fund (UNICEF) pledged to work with governments to eradicate female circumcision.[59]

Polling forum participants one week after the meetings began the *Forum 80* newsletter reported that activists found the gathering to be 'stimulating', 'frustrating' and 'confusing'.[60] Reflecting on these mixed evaluations from a few months' distance, the American scholar Irene Tinker who was then working at the Equity Policy Center in Washington, DC, echoed these on-the-spot mixed reviews. She published her 'Feminist View of Copenhagen' in *Signs* journal in 1981:

> The NGO Forum abounded with dynamic women of every creed and country whose interaction created stimulating new ideas and a proliferation of new networks. But at what cost, not only in money but in world opinion! I think women must look for new methods of influencing the United Nations and world opinion, and I seriously ask, What purpose would a repetition of a women's conference such as this one or that in Mexico City serve? . . . The

challenge, success, and inefficiency of the NGO Forum was the plethora of
women's groups; there were so many tunes and tempos that the too-frequent
result was simply noise. The problem that presents itself is simple: How do
you take one tune and encourage variation while at the same time eliciting
orchestral support?[61]

Tinker recounted criticisms that she heard at the forum site. Again,
as in Mexico City, some forum participants asserted that 'political issues'
rather than women's gender-specific oppression dominated UN conference
discussions. For example, when Jehan Sadat of Egypt addressed the conference general assembly many delegates from Arab nations, the Soviet
Union, several Eastern bloc nations and the anti-apartheid South African
National Congress, all walked out in support of the PLO. The PLO had
denounced Egypt for recognising the state of Israel and this demonstration
of support for the PLO captured international press attention. Moreover,
when the Copenhagen Programme of Action officially recognised the
legitimacy of PLO opposition to Israel and explicitly named Zionism as a
form of racism, the United States, Australia, Canada and Israel rejected the
Conference document, and twenty-two US-allied nations abstained from
voting on the document.[62] This, according to Tinker, was a tragedy. As she
explained, 'The confrontation over the Palestine issue spilled over into . . .
the NGO Forum, sending out waves of anti-Semitism that raised tempers,
divided delegations, and again diverted energy from the real point of the
conference: women's status and welfare.'

Women's issues, Tinker and others asserted, were 'controlled by male
debate' at the mid-decade events in Copenhagen. Women had been 'set up
by the UN and ridiculed by the world press'.[63] The mainstream news media
focused on political controversies at the conference and forum and was
especially captivated by Leila Khaled. Khaled, an attractive and politically
savvy Palestinian revolutionary who had taken part in an airline hijacking in 1969, had gained international notoriety when she was captured
after a second attempt at hijacking failed in 1970. Television cameras
and news reporters followed Khaled during the Copenhagen meetings
and documented her condemnations of the state of Israel.[64] The mainstream media's focus on sensationalised news coverage of conference and
forum events was, in Tinker's view, evidence that the media failed to take
women's issues seriously.[65]

Tinker's criticisms of the Copenhagen meetings did not go unchallenged. Nilüfer Çağatay and Ursula Funk argued in response to Tinker
that elite and middle-class women *should* acknowledge 'political issues'
and must openly oppose their governments' policies when those policies
oppressed Third World women. They asserted that 'women who tacitly

give support to countries with repressive political systems by claiming to be apolitical help perpetuate these systems. That is why it is so important to discuss the situation of women under *apartheid* and to try to understand the particular oppressions that Palestinian women and other refugee women's experience.'[66]

Lourdes Arizpe also called on feminists to recognise connections that linked oppressive forces and to oppose oppression in all its forms. She argued that *all political issues* were *all women's issues* whether women were located in the First or Third Worlds, and that the UN women's conference was justified in debating world politics:

> [I]t seems that feminism is sometimes ascribed a certain 'purity' which then leads to judgments that feminist issues become 'contaminated' when mixed up with other political issues. Is not feminism also political in the sense that it is fighting for certain principles of social organization in the public arena? If it is not a political or ideological movement, what is it? . . . Only when we are able to prove that sexual, psychological, and emotional relations of women and men in a patriarchal society are inextricably linked to women's economic deprivation, their political exclusion, and their religious or cultural oppression in all systems – both developed and underdeveloped – will women in different countries be able to agree on immediate strategies and tactics for change. For the time being, we have to have different strategies in different countries, but this does not mean that we do not share the beginnings of a common goal.[67]

After the conference dispersed, the UN secretariat published the newsletter that assessed the world conference and NGO forum. Despite the fact that the United States, Israel and several other allied governments would not sign the Programme of Action because of its political content, the UN secretariat did not agree with mainstream media reports that the conference had been diverted from its main focus on women's issues. The newsletter argued:

> [T]he women of the world were not 'sidetracked' onto political matters. The debates that raged at the Bella Center showed that the majority of women there felt that discussion of the so-called political issues was an integral part of the Conference debate, that political issues, along with economic and social issues and the international situation, were of as much concern to women as to men because women are as much affected by them as men are . . .

In assessing the NGO forum the UN secretariat also emphasised its practical orientation. Whereas the Mexico City tribune had been a 'consciousness-raising' session, the secretariat asserted that by 1980 the world was well aware of the issues and objectives of the UN Decade for Women, and NGOs were consequently focused on taking practical action to achieve those objectives. The UN newsletter quoted one of the forum organisers who said 'At the Forum [women] discussed how to move the world in the way they wanted it moved and this showed the success of the Decade and how far women have come since 1975.'[68]

From the vantage point of 1995, a decade after the UN Decade for Women officially concluded, international relations scholar Jane Jaquette re-evaluated the mid-decade conference in an essay entitled 'Losing the battle/winning the war'. Jaquette acknowledged the controversies that divided the government delegates at the Copenhagen conference and forum and the entrenched Western, Eastern and Southern 'bloc perspective on women's issues' that dominated the more polite conference debates and less-restrained forum 'shouting matches'. Nonetheless, Jaquette argued that:

> [T]he case can be made that the Mid-Decade Conference has been dismissed too readily and that its long term impact is more positive than the conventional wisdom allows. The Program of Action is an important bridge between Mexico City and Nairobi, giving strong legitimacy to the international norm of legal equality for women and elaborating a more effective and detailed women in development agenda. The Program of Action breaks new ground on a number of issues, including recognition of violence against women, an emphasis on the importance of women-headed households, encouragement of women's empowerment through grassroots organizations and attention to racism and refugees . . .
>
> Finally the 'politicization' of the conference served the international women's movement in two important ways. The debates over structuralist and feminist perspectives changed views on both sides and helped contribute to the consensus that was later formed at Nairobi – the 'coming of age' of the women's movement. The vote in Copenhagen, though difficult for the U.S. and Israel, helped legitimize women as an issue not just for the West but for the world.[69]

Following the Copenhagen conference in December 1980 the UN General Assembly passed several resolutions that endorsed the Programme of Action for the Second Half of the UN Decade for Women and urged UN member governments to implement the programme and to sign and ratify the Convention on the Elimination of All Forms of Discrimination Against Women (CEDAW). Prior to the mid-decade conference in December 1979 the General Assembly had adopted CEDAW, as it had been drafted by the Commission on the Status of Women (CSW) based on the 1967 Declaration on the Elimination of All Forms of Discrimination Against Women. At the mid-decade conference opening ceremony CEDAW was presented to government delegates for signatures. Demonstrating widespread support for the CEDAW, fifty nations signed it during the mid-decade conference sessions.[70]

CEDAW was conceived as an 'international bill of rights for women'. The Convention affirmed women's equal access to political and civil rights, and to education, health, employment, reproductive and nationality rights. It included a preamble and thirty articles defining discrimination against women and it prescribed how nations should act to eliminate gender-based discrimination. Nations that signed and ratified CEDAW agreed to include in their national laws the principle of women's equality. Even more significantly, national signatories agreed to adopt laws to enforce prohibitions on discrimination against women, to prosecute trafficking and all other forms of exploitation of women, and to report back to UN agencies on implementation of CEDAW every four years.[71]

Although political controversies surrounding the Copenhagen Programme of Action at the mid-decade conference overshadowed the great accomplishment of CEDAW, its importance has continued to be manifested. Laura Reanda who wrote about the CSW's role in drafting the Convention has asserted: 'The Convention is the first international treaty dealing with the rights of women in a global manner and including provisions for a reporting system and review machinery. It is considered the crowning achievement of the Commission in the field of standard-setting.'[72] In 2004 Aziza Hussein of Egypt also identified CEDAW's long-term significance: 'It is still engaging the world as a watchdog for the status of women worldwide and as a morale booster for feminist activities.'[73]

Notes

1 Devaki Jain, *Women, Development and the UN: A Sixty-Year Quest for Equality and Justice* (Bloomington, IN: Indiana University Press, 2005), p. 72.

2 Ibid., p. 79.

3 Margaret Snyder, 'Walking my own road: how a sabbatical year led to a United Nations career', in Arvonne S. Fraser and Irene Tinker (eds), *Developing Power: How Women Transformed International Development* (New York: Feminist Press, 2004), p. 44.

4 Ibid., pp. 46 and 48.

5 Jain, *Women, Development and the UN*, p. 94.

6 WYWCA, Mildred Persinger, 'Following up on the IWY tribune', c. December 1975, World Consultants at UN and Specialized Agencies, 1973–76.

7 'Personal narrative; Mildred Emory Persinger', Hollins University (www1. hollins.edu/classes/anth220s06/lynskeyk/persinger_lynskey_narrative2. htm).

8 IWTC, 'Progress report of IWY tribune activities August 1976', box 1.

9 Anne S. Walker, 'The International Women's Tribune Centre: expanding the struggle for women's rights at the UN', in Fraser and Tinker (eds), *Developing Power*, pp. 90–3.
10 'Personal narrative Mildred Emory Persinger'.
11 WYWCA, Shahnaz Alami to Mildred Persinger, 24 May 1976, World Consultants at UN and Specialized Agencies, 1973–76.
12 WYWCA, Mildred Persinger to Shahnaz Alami, 14 June 1976, World Consultants at UN and Specialized Agencies, 1973–76; emphasis in original.
13 WYWCA, Elizabeth Palmer to Mildred Persinger, 25 August 1976, World Consultants at UN and Specialized Agencies, 1973–76.
14 WYWCA, IWY Follow-up project, financial report, c. August 1976, World Consultants at UN and Specialized Agencies, 1973–76.
15 Kathryn Kish Sklar, 'Introduction', in 'Women and social movements in the United States, 1600–2000' document project 'How did the National Women's Conference in Houston in 1977 Shape an Agenda for the Future?' (alexanderstreet6.com.library.esc.edu/wasm/wasmrestricted/DP59/intro.htm).
16 Caroline Bird, 'State meetings: every woman has her say', ibid., pp. 99–113.
17 Sklar, 'How did the National Women's Conference in Houston in 1977 Shape an Agenda for the Future?', ibid.
18 'Persinger speaks on women's conference', *Hollins [College] Columns*, 48:4 (14 October 1977).
19 Mildred Emory Persinger, 'On stage at last', *Hollins College Newsletter*, (May 1976).
20 'Personal narrative Mildred Emory Persinger'.
21 Carole Seymour-Jones, *Journey of Faith: The History of the World YWCA, 1945–1994* (London: Allison and Busby, 1994), p. 86.
22 Ibid., p. 114.
23 Ibid., pp. 322–3.
24 WYWCA, 'Council highlights . . . our radical traditions', World Council in Vancouver, 12–26 July 1975.
25 Seymour-Jones, *Journey of Faith*, pp. 325–9.
26 Arvonne S. Fraser, *The UN Decade for Women: Documents and Dialogue* (Boulder, CO: Westview Press, 1987), p. 69.
27 Joan Kelly, 'Comment on the 1980 international women's decade conference in Iran', *Signs* 4:2 (winter 1978), p. 388.
28 John R. Mathiason, *The Long March to Beijing: The United Nations and the Women's Revolution*, vol. I, The Vienna Period. (2006), pp. 46–8 (intlmgt.com/longmarch/Long%20March%202006.pdf).
29 Peggy Antrobus, 'A Caribbean journey: defending feminist politics', in Fraser and Tinker (eds), *Developing Power*, p. 139.
30 Jain, *Women, Development and the UN*, p. 89.
31 Fraser, *The UN Decade for Women*, p. 71.
32 WYWCA, Planning committee for the world conference of the UN Decade for Women, minutes of the meeting, 4 July 1979, NGO Forum, Copenhagen July 1980.

33 Fraser, *The UN Decade for Women*, pp. 75–8; IWTC, UN press release, 'Preparatory committee for world conference of Decade for Women discusses effects of apartheid on women in Southern Africa', 14 April 1980, box 1; UN press release, 'Preparatory committee for world conference of Decade for Women discusses effects of Israeli occupation on Palestinian women', 14 April 1980, box 1.

34 Judith P. Zinsser, 'From Mexico to Copenhagen to Nairobi: the United Nations Decade for Women, 1975–1985', *Journal of World History* 13 (spring 2002), pp. 154–7.

35 Fraser and Tinker (eds), *Developing Power*, p. xxiv.

36 IWTC, Board of the CONGO, minutes of meeting, 7–8 November 1978; Planning committee for NGO activities at the 1980 world conference of the UN Decade for Women, 12–13 March 1979; Edith Ballantyne to Elizabeth Palmer, 19 March 1979, box 4.

37 'Too bad I didn't take notes: the autobiography of Edith Ballantyne', Women's International League for Peace and Freedom (wilpf.int.ch/events/2006IEC/other_reports/Edith_ballantyne_message.htm); Edith Ballantyne, UNESCO round table, 'Culture of peace and the foundations of reconciliation', 8 September 2003 (wilpf.int.ch/statements/2003UNESCO-reconciliation.htm).

38 WYWCA, NGO Activities at the world conference of the UN Decade for Women, memorandum, 7 April 1980, NGO Forum, Copenhagen July 1980.

39 WYWCA, Planning committee for the world conference of the UN Decade for Women, minutes of the meetings, 7 May 1979 and 4 July 1979 NGO Forum, Copenhagen July 1980.

40 IWTC, Edith Ballantyne to Elizabeth Palmer, 3 November 1979, box 4.

41 IWTC, Elizabeth Palmer to Edith Ballantyne, 12 December 1979, box 4.

42 WYWCA, Elizabeth Palmer to Arvonne Fraser, Coordinator, Office of Women in Development, USAID, 7 April 1980, NGO Forum, Copenhagen July 1980.

43 WYWCA, 'Criteria for granting financial aid', NGO activities at the world conference of the UN Decade for Women, minutes of the meeting, 31 January 1980; Elizabeth Palmer to Erica Brodie, general secretary World YWCA, 11 March 1980, NGO Forum, Copenhagen July 1980.

44 IWTC, Elizabeth Palmer to executive officers of CONGO organisations, February 1980, box 4.

45 WYWCA, 'Funding – mid decade conference at Copenhagen', c. August 1980, NGO Forum, Copenhagen July 1980.

46 IWTC, Edith Ballantyne to Elizabeth Palmer, 3 November 1979, box 4.

47 WYWCA, 'Preparation of women's NGO forum in Copenhagen: workshop on peace', 17 April 1980, NGO Forum, Copenhagen July 1980.

48 IWTC, 'Planning committee assignments at NGO forum', 14–24 July 1980, box 4.

49 Fraser, *The UN Decade for Women*, pp. 145–6.

50 IWTC, Anne Walker, 'Vivencia! At the NGO Forum', 9 April 1980, box 5; Anne S. Walker, 'The International Women's Tribune Centre: expanding the struggle

for women's rights at the UN', in Fraser and Tinker (eds.), *Developing Power*, p. 93.

51　WYWCA, Pre-registration brochure, c. 1980; Minutes of meeting, 31 January 1980, NGO Forum, Copenhagen July 1980.

52　IWTC, 'Grants and Contributions', 1980 Forum, Accession 97s–53, box 1.

53　WYWCA, Planning committee for the world conference of the UN Decade for Women, minutes of the meeting, 7 May 1979, NGO Forum, Copenhagen July 1980; IWTC, Memorandum on NGO participation in the 1980 world conference of the UN Decade for Women, box 4.

54　IWTC, 'It's ideas that matter says Elizabeth Palmer', Forum 80 *Newsletter*, 17 July 1980, on microfilm.

55　Jane Connors, 'NGOs and the human rights of women at the United Nations', in Peter Willetts (ed.), *'The Conscience of the World': The Influence of Non-Governmental Organizations in the UN System* (London: Hurst & Company, 1996), pp. 159–60; Fraser, *The UN Decade for Women*, pp. 147–8.

56　WYWCA, J. Patricia Morrison, International Section Program Department, '[Evaluation] mid-decade forum for women, Copenhagen, 14–24 July 1980', NGO Forum, Copenhagen July 1980.

57　IWTC, 'Call for NGO plenary', Forum 80 *Newsletter*, 17 July 1980 and 'NGO "plenary" makes an action plan', Forum 80 *Newsletter*, 18 July 1980, on microfilm.

58　Walker, 'The International Women's Tribune Centre', p. 94.

59　Fraser, *The UN Decade for Women*, p. 151.

60　IWTC, 'So what do you think of it so far?' Forum 80 *Newsletter*, 21 July 1980, on microfilm.

61　Irene Tinker, 'International notes', *Signs* 6 (spring 1981), p. 532.

62　Ninety-four nations voted to approve the Copenhagen Programme of Action document. United Nations Division for Economic and Social Information/ Department of Public Information Newsletter No. 6, *Women 1980*, Schlesinger Library, Radcliffe Institute, Harvard University, Cambridge, MA.

63　Irene Tinker, 'A feminist view of Copenhagen', *Signs* 6 (spring 1981), pp. 531 and 534.

64　Fraser, *The UN Decade for Women*, p. 152.

65　Tinker, 'A feminist view of Copenhagen', p. 534.

66　Nilüfer Çağatay and Ursula Funk, 'Comment's on Tinker's "A feminist view of Copenhagen"', *Signs* 7 (spring 1982), p. 778.

67　Lourdes Arizpe, 'Comments on Tinker's "A feminist view of Copenhagen"', *Signs* 7 (Spring 1982), pp. 714–715.

68　UN DPI Newsletter No. 6, *Women 1980*.

69　Jane S. Jaquette, 'Losing the battle/winning the war: international politics, women's issues and the 1980 mid-decade conference', in Anne Winslow (ed.), *Women, Politics and the United Nations* (Westport, CT: Greenwood Press, 1995), p. 57.

70　Arvonne S. Fraser, 'Seizing opportunities: USAID, WID, CEDAW', in Fraser and Tinker (eds.), *Developing Power*, p. 171.

71 United Nations A/CONF.94/35, 'Report of the world conference of the United Nations Decade for Women: equality, development and peace', 14–30 July 1980, Copenhagen, Denmark.

72 Laura Reanda, 'The Commission on the Status of Women', in Philip Alston (ed.), *The United Nations and Human Rights: A Critical Appraisal* (Oxford, UK: Oxford University Press, 1992), p. 286.

73 Aziza Hussein, 'Crossroads for women at the UN', in Fraser and Tinker (eds.), *Developing Power*, p. 11.

12

Concluding the UN Decade for Women

'Old' and 'new' women's NGOs at the end of the decade

After working with the Commission on the Status of Women (CSW) to promote the Convention on the Elimination of all forms of Discrimination Against Women for years (CEDAW), the World Young Women's Christian Association (YWCA) and other historic women's international organisations strongly supported CEDAW and urged their national chapters to monitor local implementation. In addition to widely publicising the provisions of CEDAW, the YWCA also advised its global membership to know and understand the international agreements that had come out of the Mexico City International Women's Year conference and the mid-decade UN women's conference:

> Women have a special obligation to be informed and articulate about the existing conditions which deny people their rights to freedom and dignity. Woman power is necessary to provide the education, training, and support needed for women who are seeking out new roles in a changing society and to give a new sense of global interdependence. The broad issues of common concern to women include food and hunger, racism and sexism, education, employment, changing family and cultural values, environment and energy, health, peace and development, justice and equality, oppression and empowerment . . . The YWCA needs to become more effective in mobilizing women to improve their condition and status and help raise the consciousness of women to the issues which affect their lives.[1]

To maintain its currency in the widest range of international women's issues, so that it could continue to influence global gender policy and respond to the changing needs of its membership, World YWCA staff and volunteers attended well over 100 meetings each year at international agencies in United Nations (UN) capitals around the world; the YWCA also maintained an active and leading presence in the NGOs in consultative status with UN ECOSOC (CONGO) and other non-governmental organizations (NGO) networks based in New York and Geneva.[2]

From the late 1970s through the 1980s the YWCA sponsored women's leadership development programmes that recruited young women, many from developing nations, for international training seminars and study tours. It funded these training sessions primarily through grants from the UN and government development agencies, private philanthropic foundations and numerous Christian church ministries.

The YWCA also sponsored projects that established small-scale industries run by women in developing countries. These projects had the potential to provide livelihoods for many women even though they operated in only a few locations. The YWCA consultant who monitored these projects in the early 1980s, Tapati Das, pushed the Executive Board to expand these programmes:

> I am totally convinced that through these kinds of projects women can benefit. I have seen from my own experience that when an underprivileged woman starts to earn money, her status goes up as a result. She asks for her rights, she wants to be treated properly, she voices her feelings; in short, she has regained her dignity . . . All of these projects need people who really know about business and personnel management . . . It is very clear from my [international] visits and from management workshops that the [national chapters] need help in management to run these income-generating projects economically and successfully. It should be noted that through this kind of project the YWCA will be able to reach the grass-root level.[3]

This orientation towards practical development projects determined the World YWCA's participation at the end of decade conference in Nairobi, Kenya when Tapati Das and other World YWCA staff worked with Anne Walker at the International Tribune Centre to sponsor a Tech and Tools workshop that focused on defining and demonstrating 'appropriate technologies' that would not exploit or exclude Third World women from participating in and benefiting from development projects.

The World YWCA's emphasis on developing sustainable technologies and redefining the goals of development projects to better meet poor women's needs was shared by many of the newly formed NGOs during the 1980s. In particular, the NGO Development Alternatives with Women for a New Era (DAWN) that formed in 1984 operated from a similar impulse to redefine and redirect international development goals and strategies.

From the 1950s onwards state-sponsored development programmes had focused on national wealth-generating development that was driven by export production for the international market. This type of economic development usually benefited the national elite and business classes and rarely redistributed resources to the working classes or to the poor. DAWN advocated a redefinition of the central goal of development projects to focus on meeting the needs of the nation's poorest members. According to

DAWN researchers and activists, the disproportionately large segment of poor women in the Third World would then become essential participants in development programmes.

DAWN also criticised excessive state spending on weapons and military equipment as well as the lack of global business and trade regulations to standardise and humanise the operations of multinational corporations. DAWN condemned national and international governmental bodies for failing to address these key factors that perpetuated underdevelopment and exacerbated mal-distribution of the world's resources. Founded by Southern feminists, DAWN advocated political coalition building among women's and other NGOs that represented radical social movements in order to link political and economic analyses and activist organisations throughout the global South. Like the World YWCA, DAWN advocated this new development philosophy through the workshops it designed for the 1985 NGO forum programme and through its proposals for the end of decade UN women's conference documents. These proposals were included in a report entitled 'Development, Crises, and Alternative Visions: Third World Women's Perspectives'.[4]

Both the long-established and the newly formed NGOs expanded their influence in planning for the Nairobi end-of-decade women's conference when the CSW was designated as the official conference-planning body within the UN system. Unlike the first two world women conferences when the CSW played a limited role in preparations, the CSW, now chaired by the Nigerian delegate Olajumoke Oladayo Obafemi, called a special session to meet in Vienna in February 1983 to take charge of the planning process with assistance from the UN secretariat. Leticia Ramos Shahani, the new assistant secretary general in charge of the Vienna-based Centre for Social Development and Humanitarian Affairs, had replaced Helvi Sipilä after she left the secretariat in 1981. Shahani, from the Philippines, had long associations with the CSW and she worked closely with it over the next two years to plan the Nairobi conference.

The end-of-decade conference at Nairobi

Assistant secretary general Shahani was also named secretary general for the Nairobi conference.[5] During her public service career Shahani had filled several diplomatic posts at the UN; she had represented the Philippines on the CSW and she had chaired the Third Committee of the Economic and Social Council (ECOSOC) after Sipilä left that post in 1974. Although Shahani's family ranked among the Philippines governing elite and her brother led the Philippines Army, according to John Mathaison, Shahani met the UN General Assembly's political criteria to lead the women's conference. She came 'from a developing country and could blunt any criticism that the [conference] secretariat was dominated by Western feminists'. Moreover, both the CSW and Shahani welcomed the input of women's international NGOs into the conference planning process.

In 1983, as UN conference plans were getting under way, the General Assembly accepted Kenya's offer to host the end-of-decade conference and also accepted ECOSOC's resolution to formally invite NGOs to participate in UN conference preparatory meetings.[6] This invitation, John Mathiason asserted, represented the UN's recognition of the integral role of NGOs in the Decade for Women and 'set the stage, as well, for the NGO Forum that became famous at Nairobi'.[7] Virginia Sauerwein of the UN secretariat acted as liaison between CONGO committees and Shahani's conference secretariat, advocating for office space and other accommodation for NGO observers at the 1985 conference, as she had during the Copenhagen conference preparations in 1980.[8]

The new CONGO president elected at the end of Edith Ballantyne's term of office was a well-known leader within the international NGO community. Alba Zizzamia, born into an Italian-American Catholic family in Hartford, Connecticut in 1910, spent her adult life as a scholar and activist who focused on Catholic social theology. In her scholarly life Zizzamia had translated the works of Italian Catholic social thinkers, and in her professional life of service to the church she had worked for the US Catholic Conference Office for the United Nations and directed the New York Catholic Archdiocese Office for Justice and Peace. From the founding of the UN in 1946 Zizzamia also dedicated service to the International Union of Catholic Women's Leagues that had consultative status with ECOSOC and that was renamed the World Union of Catholic Women's Organizations (WUCWO) in 1952. Zizzamia had focused her NGO activism on status of women issues and especially on women's needs in underdeveloped African nations and UN trusteeship territories. She was also an active member of the coalition of NGOs in consultative status with United Nations (International) Children's (Emergency) Fund, UNICEF.[9]

Beginning in August 1983 Zizzamia organised CONGO participation at the UN end-of-decade conference preparatory meetings that were held in five regional capitals of the world: Tokyo, Arusha, Havana, Baghdad and Vienna. Over the next two years the preparatory sessions for the end-of-decade conference gathered input from a broad representative sample of the world's women to draft the conference document: the Forward Looking Strategies for the Advancement of Women to the Year 2000.[10] In order to collect the widest possible input from women around the world, the International Women's Tribune Centre, the UN secretariat, and the programme committees circulated multiple surveys; in addition NGOs attended the five regional conference preparatory sessions as well as an additional meeting called for NGOs held in Vienna in October 1984. NGOs contributed their ideas regarding the conference documents and forum programme in those arenas.[11]

In September 1983 Alba Zizzamia formed a planning committee to organise the NGO forum in Nairobi. At the time CONGO represented a membership of 200 NGOs out of a group of over 800 NGOs with designated consultative status to ECOSOC.[12] There were fifty-three CONGO member organisations who volunteered to serve on the forum 1985 planning body. Although the forum-planning committee later grew to sixty-four NGO members, a steering committee comprised of twenty-two women formed its coordinating and decision-making body. Altogether, the final forum 1985 report recorded, 'The Planning Network involved some 378 persons, although even that large number included few Third World women.'[13]

At the September 1983 CONGO meeting World YWCA president Nita Barrow was named as convenor of the NGO forum 1985 committee; Virginia Hazzard was named as the forum programme coordinator. Three additional programme leaders were designated to develop forum sessions addressing the three themes of the UN Decade for Women at the forum: Kay Fraleigh of the International Alliance for Women for the theme of 'equality', Bettina Corke of the Society for International Development for 'development', and Edith Ballantyne for 'peace'. At a later date, programme committees were formed to address the Decade's sub-themes and focal points, as well. These included the areas of education, employment, health, young women, girls and older women.

Forum 1985 convenor Nita Barrow was a member of a prominent family of public servants in Barbados; she was the daughter of Reverend Reginald Barrow and sister of Prime Minister Errol Barrow. Because of her background and her training she was viewed as a strong role model for women in both the First and Third Worlds. Barrow was described as a 'strong leader with a mild manner'[14] and as someone who possessed finely honed 'political skills, supreme patience, and tact and low-keyed but absolutely magnetic personal charisma'.[15]

Barrow had trained as a nurse in Barbados, at the School of Nursing at Toronto University, at the Royal College of Nursing at Edinburgh University and at Columbia University in New York. As her professional career developed she earned many distinctions. Barrow became the principal Nursing Officer advising the Minister of Health in Jamaica, West Indies, and she served eight years as a consultant to the World Health Organization (WHO). In 1980, British Queen Elizabeth named Nita Barrow a Dame of St. Andrew in recognition of her public health service to the Caribbean and to the Commonwealth.

Barrow was also was an active leader in several ecumenical Christian organisations. She directed the international Christian Medical Commission from 1975 to 1981 and served as president of the World Council of Churches and on the International Council for Adult Education during the 1970s and 1980s. She was a vice president on the World YWCA Executive Board during the 1960s and 1970s and was president of the World YWCA from 1975 to 1983. Barrow entered government service soon after the Nairobi conference ended when she was appointed as Barbados ambassador to the UN; in 1990, she became Governor-General of Barbados.[16]

The programme coordinator for forum 1985, Virginia Hazzard, was based in New York City in office space at UN headquarters that was provided by the UN secretariat. Virginia Hazzard was an American woman who had built a long record of service in NGOs and in UN agencies. After graduating from Columbia University, Hazzard had gone on to work for the Red Cross and the American Friends Service Committee and with the UN Food and Agriculture Organization (FAO) in Algeria. After completing projects with the FAO, Hazzard went to work for UNICEF. She evaluated women's education programmes in Senegal and Sierra Leone, prepared guidelines regarding programming for women and girls, and was an adviser to Ethiopian women's organisations for three years. She then returned to New York and worked in UNICEF agency offices at the UN headquarters until her retirement in 1982. After retirement, she rejoined the NGO community and began working with the New York-based CONGO planning committee for NGO activities during the UN Decade for Women.[17]

It was clear from the beginning of the forum 1985 planning process that NGO participation would exceed that of the two previous NGO meetings and that one of Nita Barrow's major concerns would be fundraising for the July 1985 gathering, which had a budget of $772,000.[18] Overall, including funds for the preparatory meetings as well as funds for the Kenyan local arrangements committee, the NGO forum 1985 planning committee raised $1,247,548. These funds were provided through governments, private foundations and individual donations; intergovernmental agencies also provided grants, NGOs contributed funding and forum participants paid a $10 registration fee.[19]

Forum 1980 convenor Elizabeth Palmer had excelled in the role of fundraiser and she had left the forum 1985 planning committee with start-up funds of $6,000, which allowed the committee to pay for some immediate and necessary travel and office expenses. Yet Palmer had devoted great amounts of time and energy to fundraising and she recommended that the task should be shared by the convenor and all forum 1985 planning committee members, who should commit to raising money as well as to programme planning.[20] As was the case with Persinger and Palmer, Nita

Barrow volunteered her services and was reimbursed only for the travel and expenses she incurred in organising the forum. She took no salary for the two-year long post as forum convenor.[21] Despite these arrangements and Palmer's recommendations, forum fundraising remained a constant challenge; it nearly defeated Barrow who threatened to resign her leadership post in October 1984 when she felt that planning committee members were not supporting her decision to hire additional staff.[22]

In addition to the challenge of raising money to cover forum expenses and travel expenses for women from developing countries the forum planning committee faced many logistical difficulties associated with the location of the end-of-decade conference in Nairobi, Kenya. The UN decision to accept Kenya's offer to host the conference was based on political rather than practical considerations. African women and Southern feminists had attached great symbolic importance to hosting a world woman's conference and NGO forum in an African nation. The Kenyan women's planning committee asserted that the end-of-decade events would mark 'the first time that women in the African region have undertaken to organise an international conference of major proportions. It is obvious that the success of the work of the Kenya NGO organizing committee in hosting the 1985 forum will boost the morale and the status of women throughout the developing world.'[23]

Yet the Kenyan government and some of the more conservative African women's NGOs were anxious about 'excited or extremist participants' – their code words for radical Western feminists, particularly those who were outspoken lesbians – who challenged African social norms and cultural practices.[24] Kenya's President Daniel Toroitich Arap Moi nearly cancelled the NGO forum in spring 1985 rather than allow lesbian and other radical women to speak out freely at the forum sessions; Nita Barrow had to persuade him to allow the forum to go forward without censorship of its participants.[25]

Moreover, the infrastructure needed to host over 17,000 delegates and participants who would attend the UN conference and forum seemed inadequate. Questions were raised about the wisdom of holding the conference and forum simultaneously when it appeared that the airport and existing hotels could not accommodate such a large influx of global visitors. Nairobi's Kenyatta International Conference Centre was equipped to provide simultaneous translations required at international meetings, but the University of Nairobi campus where the NGO forum would be held did not have these capacities.[26] To address these logistical concerns the forum began one week ahead of the conference opening and the overlap of the two meetings was reduced from two weeks to one week.

During the forum 1985 planning process the Kenyan women's

committee played a larger role in forum programme planning than pre-vious local arrangements committees had played in Copenhagen or in Mexico City.[27] In addition to offering logistical support, the Kenyan com-mittee organised trips to rural villages for the international visitors and established the 'Karibu Centre', an interfaith church available for worship services that also housed a café and provided rooms for meditation.[28] Nita Barrow worked closely with Dr Eddah Wacheke Gachukia who chaired the Kenyan committee.[29]

Born and raised in rural Kenya, Eddah Gachukia was educated at Makerere University in Uganda, at Leeds University in Britain and at the University of Nairobi where she taught literature courses until 1974 when she was elected to Kenya's national Parliament. Gachukia had focused on women's issues as a scholar, teacher and politician. She chaired the Kenyan National Council of Women and had worked with international agencies as a consultant for WHO and UNICEF. She was active in the Kenyan chapter of the Associated Countrywomen of the World, an international NGO that focused on the needs of women in agricultural communities. And she had been Kenya's delegate to the International Women's Year confer-ence in Mexico City and to the mid-decade conference in Copenhagen.[30]

Although Eddah Gachukia's Kenyan forum-planning committee played a significant part in shaping the end-of-decade forum activities, the Kenyan women nonetheless raised questions about the coercive use of power by the NGO forum committee located in New York. Gachukia believed that Nita Barrow's 'international' NGO forum-planning commit-tee operated from a privileged position of power as they determined the 1985 programme. She was determined that less-privileged African women who provided alternative perspectives regarding women's interests and needs would be heard by the New York-based forum planners.

In her many communications with Nita Barrow, Eddah Gachukia repeatedly stressed the 'Kenyan women's perspective' and the 'African women's perspective' that defined economic development as the key to women's liberation. In June 1984 Gachukia met with Barrow and the NGO committee in New York. She voiced the 'concerns of the women of Kenya: . . . That the Forum should reach out to the "ordinary woman;" that the needs of rural women should be carefully considered; [that] each country had its priorities, in Kenya it was water before education; that women can be the instruments of peace, carrying the message right into the rural areas . . . that women should prove to the world watching the Forum that women had come a long way since 1975.'[31] In her report at the pre-conference Consultation for NGOs hosted by the UN secretariat held in Vienna in October 1984 Gachukia asserted: 'Given [the] urgent situation, Kenya hoped that famine and drought in Africa would take precedence over controversy, that there would be much constructive dialogue, and that Nairobi would be the venue where Third World Women would be taken seriously.'[32]

The 'controversy' that Gachukia referred to included the global political conflicts that had raged throughout the UN Decade for Women and that had overshadowed the government discussions at the previous world women's conferences as well as the contentious differences among feminists who spoke from the standpoint of white privilege in the West and feminist women of colour who expressed the standpoint of the underprivileged global South.

Gachukia's appeals recognised real divisions among the world's women but her goal to head off controversy was not realistic. In 1984 a radical feminist NGO – the Women for Racial and Economic Equality (WREE) that was founded in the United States in 1975 and was affiliated with the Women's International Democratic Federation – published its critiques of 'Western feminism' in a 'Dialogue' written by South Korean feminist Soon Young Yoon. Soon wrote that, in 1984, as the world's women prepared for the conference and forum in Nairobi, 'An international feminist movement – united, embracing all races, raising a single voice of protest against world hunger and political oppression – is still a dream.' She argued that Western feminists were promoting a version of 'global sisterhood' that did not represent a global constituency of women. It was in fact a 'Western feminist agenda' that included campaigns that opposed female circumcision in Africa, the veiling of women and the practice of Purdah in Islamic countries, and all practices that 'sensationalize[d] patriarchal violence among Asians and Africans and ignore[d] the greater violence of infant deaths due to hunger and wars', for which Western imperialist nations bore some responsibility.

Soon Young Yoon criticised the 'high-handed missionary zeal' demonstrated by 'imperialist' Western feminists. She argued that Third World women did not need to be schooled in internationalism; rather, Western women needed re-education regarding the principle of equality. She wrote that:

> The truth is that Third World feminists are often isolated but this has little to do with states of consciousness; it has to do with survival. In Egypt, Nawal el Saadawi was imprisoned for her writings advocating feminism. In India, girls may be impoverished or disinherited for open protests against dowry and arranged marriages. The consequences of confrontation must be borne by those who struggle, and these are the realities that so often escape outsiders. The histories of women's struggles and their sociopolitical contexts are different, and when Third World women say they do not want to carry on their movement like 'western feminists' they are expressing this simple truth.

As Soon explained, Southern feminists understood that 'political' issues like apartheid in South Africa, human rights in South Korea and under-development in many African nations 'have priority over others such as lesbian rights'.[33]

The UN Decade for Women conferences and forums exposed funda-mental differences within the global women's movement but did not resolve them. Yet Nita Barrow's goal for forum 1985 was not to silence controversial political discussions or to reach an artificial agreement but to provide space for political and feminist debates. In a press conference held in New York in the spring of 1985 as various partisan groups began their pre-conference lobbying Nita Barrow announced to the press: 'The Forum is a place for all women.'[34] Political issues would be discussed at the UN conference and forum because, as Barrow explained, 'Almost everything is political. The air we breathe is political. Equality, development, and health are all political. But our major plan is to put the concerns of women in the middle.'[35] Barrow organised the forum to allow those with opposing viewpoints their opportunity to speak, but not to allow the 'loudest', most media-savvy groups to dominate the forum proceedings.[36] Arvonne Fraser later recalled 'Like Palmer before in Copenhagen, Barrow understood that Nairobi would be a "happening." She also understood that the best forums require a structure open to all and an acceptance of responsibility by many.' Running from 10 to 19 July the forum hosted over 1,200 pre-arranged workshops and panel sessions as well as many meetings organ-ised on site.[37] Nearly 14,000 activists – 'professional and grass roots, poor, rich, and middle class women' – attended forum 1985 and over 3,000 of those activists were from Kenya and nearly half were from Africa.[38]

Nita Barrow supported several new initiatives at forum 1985 that were aimed at sharing practical knowledge to improve women's lives and pro-viding space for uncensored feminist debates. Many participants identified these initiatives as the key components of the forum's success.[39] Barrow supported the Tech and Tools appropriate technology workshop organised by the World YWCA and International Women's Tribune Centre that impressed rural African women and the Kenyan president Daniel Moi, who visited the forum site with television cameras in tow. Moi praised the practical projects that were being demonstrated including 'smokeless stoves, water pumps, drum ovens, beehives, hand washing machines, solar ovens and cookers, and more'.[40]

Barrow also supported Edith Ballantyne's brainchild – the Peace Tent – a space set aside on the University of Nairobi campus where women could talk out their conflicts with one another in a neutral setting and avoid the escalation of emotions and rhetoric that occurred in more public and political arenas, where the media sought out sensational confrontations.[41]

Barrow brought women with opposing viewpoints to the Peace Tent and urged them to explain their positions to one another.[42] Referred to by Barrow as the forum's 'safety valve', the Peace Tent became a 'visible symbol that even women with diametrically opposed views on some issues could openly discuss their differences with respect and tolerance'.[43]

As African women in traditional dress danced and sang in Swahili to welcome the international guests at the forum 1985 opening ceremony Nita Barrow explained her inclusive philosophy and her focus on open debate.[44] Barrow asserted that '"Woman-Time" is here . . . There can be no one [feminist] strategy because although we have common roots of women's oppression and inequality, one woman's liberation is another's destruction. That is why consensus is not possible, but understanding can be.'[45] Barrow was adamant on this point. Following the practice set at Mexico City and Copenhagen, no political statements were made in the name of the whole forum, even though activists tried to define common causes.

Yet from its earliest meetings, the forum-planning committee had insisted that 'a forum is not designed to take formal positions; it has no fixed "agenda" and does not adopt resolutions as a body, instead it should be viewed as a "mass meeting" or "happening" where women from different backgrounds and perspectives may meet to share their experiences and stimulate ideas for the future.'[46] According to Arvonne Fraser, 'Barrow was not to be pressured . . . firmly declaring that anyone could say anything at the workshops but nobody spoke in the name of the Forum.' Ultimately, 'What happened at Nairobi was that a critical mass of women had decided that they could be feminists and still disagree on certain issues.'[47]

In their post-forum assessment the feminist scholars Nilufer Cagatay, Caren Gowan and Aida Santiago commented on the Nairobi forum, which they defined as the starting point rather than the culmination of the UN Decade of feminist activism:

> Nairobi marks a new stage in our understandings about the struggle for social transformation. The Forum discussions could not generate the blueprints for such global or regional strategies, nor should we have expected them to. What can be achieved in a ten-day conference, especially one that 'officially' prohibits final resolutions, platforms or statements, is limited. Women have only recently begun to identify and discuss ways to tackle problems that are the product of complex historical processes. It would be naïve to expect that women alone will or can devise the solutions to world scale questions. As feminists we are striving for a fundamental restructuring of the economic and social order, one that does not reproduce the hierarchies under which we presently live. To accomplish this, we need to develop more concrete and powerful strategies at the local, regional and global levels;

to strengthen our links and networks; to be supportive and aware of each others' struggles; and to be in positions to ensure that the implementation of our visions have a longer-lasting impact.[48]

Assessing the achievements of forum 1985 Nita Barrow concluded that:

> Nairobi was a coming of age for women. After Copenhagen networks which had been in the formative stage grew in numbers and in international linkages between Copenhagen and Nairobi . . . Unlike government representatives who, of necessity, had to reflect the views of their governments, participants at the Forum were free to speak from their own perspectives. A very wide cross section of women willing and ready to share opinions, ideas and leanings were included in the group. The experience was a very rich one. The progress made by women in articulating their own views was evident . . . There was more willingness to listen to others by a growing number of women . . . Women talked to each other on many different levels.[49]

At a later date, Barrow further articulated the philosophy that guided her feminist leadership at the Nairobi forum, 'I will never define for other women their needs. I can suggest some principles: one person should not choose priorities for others. We can find groups of women with common priorities. Others may go along with them. But other people have to know where their objectives lie. Every woman has to know her own priorities. The mistake is to place the responsibility on other people.'[50]

Arvonne Fraser praised the accomplishments of the Nairobi forum that she argued were a 'new model' for NGO meetings:

> The forum at Nairobi was also a new model, reflecting women's sense of solidarity and interdependence through a highly democratic structure and method of operation. Led by two strong women from developing countries, it was organized by an independent, diverse, and collaborative group of volunteers and staff and it attracted worldwide attendance and attention. The NGO Forum was much more structured than previous forums, but it allowed participants to make up their own program and follow-up agenda. A fee was charged, a tacit acknowledgement of women's growing economic self-reliance. Reams of documentation were produced, making a record for future historians and future organizers of women's meetings. The forum and its participants recognized the differences among women.[51]

In part due to Nita Barrow's guiding influence, forum 1985 incorporated many conflicts between women yet it was still perceived as a productive gathering. There was 'talk, talk, talk' but no organised demonstrations or march to the conference site as had occurred in Mexico and Copenhagen. These marches had, according to some critics, 'little impact on the UN conference and only divisive repercussions for the forum'.[52]

At the UN conference site political controversies that had played out

over the UN Decade for Women were evident again but the final conference document – the 'Forward Looking Strategies for the Advancement
of Women to the Year 2000' – was adopted by consensus. In Nairobi
government delegates agreed to compromises in the language that did not
prohibit them from signing the final much-debated conference document;
this outcome was also considered a major advance towards addressing the
needs of the world's women. The influence of the 'emergent global feminism' expressed by NGO activists throughout the Decade and especially at
the Nairobi preparatory conferences helped move the government delegations beyond 'specific national issues' and to the point where they could
develop 'an international working agenda for women'.[53]

As had occurred at Mexico City and Copenhagen, the Israeli–Palestinian
conflict, South African apartheid policy and global inequities defined by
Third World nations in the New International Economic Order (NIEO),
all caused heated debates among the government delegates. Yet many
East–West and North–South political and ideological differences regarding the conference document language as well as definitions of obstacles
and proposed strategies to achieve women's equality were worked out
at the regional preparatory conferences, before the Nairobi meetings
took place.[54] The final conference document adopted in Nairobi excised a
controversial condemnation of 'Zionism' and substituted the more widely
acceptable language condemning 'all forms of racism and racial discrimination'. The final document also 'emphasized action over intention' and
defined specific actions that governments should take to achieve women's
equality and to recognise women's central roles in realising national development and international peace. National ideologies and institutions that
discriminated against women were specifically criticised within the final
conference document that was ratified by government delegations.[55]

Assessing the Nairobi conference, forum 1985, and the UN Decade for Women

John Mathiason has identified what he has termed the 'passive' language
of the Forward Looking Strategies that specified government actions as a
fundamental weakness of the Nairobi conference document. 'Since most
governments were run by men', he explained, 'in effect the Strategies asked
men to do the right thing by their women, a kind of Victorian approach that
essentially left no one really responsible for implementing the Strategies
and made monitoring extremely difficult, it was soon learned.'[56]

Yet Mathiason's criticisms were not shared by women who evaluated
the conference outcomes and who recognised the significant and progressive changes that the Nairobi conference and the Decade for Women

represented for the women globally. According to Arvonne Fraser's analysis, the Nairobi conference document articulated 'aggressive strategies, asserting that a women's perspective on all issues is critical, beginning with the issues of development and peace . . . What is implied rather than stated is that women must accept much of the burden for advancing their own status. They must act like equals in order to become equal.'[57] The implication that women had to play an active role in realising the goals of the Forward Looking Strategies was also Leticia Shahani's message when she discussed the Forward Looking Strategies that were adopted by the government delegates: 'While these strategies will be mainly directed towards governments, they will also be your [women's] blueprint for action during that period. We in the UN Secretariat rely on your efforts in the implementation of these strategies. We recognize the hard work and the dedication of those women's NGOs which have worked closely with the UN since it was established 40 years ago.'[58]

Significantly, the Forward Looking Strategies emphasised the mainstreaming of gender considerations into all programmes and areas of the UN system, rather than promoting separate women-focused programmes or bureaucratic offices as previous world women's conferences and UN Decade for Women activities had advised. Mainstreaming of women and gender considerations into male-dominated governing bodies has been considered a more progressive strategy to achieve women's social and political equality by some feminist scholars. According to Laura Reanda, as evaluations of established 'women and development' programmes were shared in Nairobi, government delegates recognised that:

> projects designed only for women had performed a useful function in apprising policy makers of women's needs, but had not succeeded in improving their overall position and that such activities had tended to remain marginal compared to development planning at the national level. It was also increasingly recognized that strategies for the advancement of women would remain ineffective unless they were accompanied by empowerment of women through participation in decision making in all areas.[59]

The feminist peace educator Betty Reardon has written that the Forward Looking Strategies recognised the value of a 'feminine mode of thinking' that feminist researchers such as Carol Gilligan and Robin Burns have explored in their scholarship. According to their essentialist feminist theories, women have perceived reality through interconnected relationships and have considered the human consequences of their actions as the first priority in determining their actions. Women have resolved conflicts through 'open communication, free access to information, and honest discussion of differences and dialogue among all concerned', which explained why, in Reardon's view, women have been adept peacemakers. According to Reardon, 'Women can do, and are doing, much to bring about a nonviolent world. But perhaps the most effective thing women can do is to become significant voices in policy making, to bring feminist perspectives, values, and modes in confronting the major questions of peace and security.' This recognition of women's strengths in building relationships and in resolving conflicts peacefully was incorporated into the Forward Looking Strategies, which also set targets with specific goals for mainstreaming women into all UN policy-making bodies.[60]

Women activists gained valuable knowledge and learned strategic lessons through participation in the world conferences and forums during the UN Decade for Women. Women learned that deliberate and concerted activism captured the attention of the world's governments and UN officials and they were able to focus male attention on the goals of the UN Decade: women's equality, sustainable development and peace. The political scientist Amrita Basu has noted that:

> The UN Decade for Women at the least forced governments to pay lip service to women's issues – and sometimes encouraged them to do more. Ninety percent of the world's governments have created official bodies that are devoted to the advancement of women; half of these were created during the decade. Sixty governments have ratified the UN Convention for the Elimination of all forms of Discrimination against Women, sixty-two have special programs for women in their national development plans, and forty-five provide women with free legal aid to fight for their rights.

Moreover, 'The Decade also witnessed the creation of a Voluntary Fund and a Development bank, as well as an international research and training institute for women.'[61] As the economist and development specialist Martha Alter Chen has noted, women activists learned how the UN system worked and were able to act effectively within the system. This was evident in the input women had in crafting the Forward Looking Strategies. Finally, in order to create a truly global women's movement, women activists learned that they must address global inequalities and material differences among the world's women, as well as the ideological differences that were based on material differences.[62]

The evaluations of the UN Decade for Women that were formed in the late 1980s and 1990s identified the beginnings of positive changes in women's global status as the Decade concluded, yet they also recognised that the world's women still faced 'dramatic' inequalities. Amrita Basu reported in 1986 that 'Women still perform two-thirds of the world's work, earn one-tenth of its income, and own one-hundredth of its property.' Moreover, patriarchal backlash in the form of anti-feminist religious fundamentalism was on the rise in nearly all regions of the world by the 1980s and traditional patriarchal attitudes continued to challenge women's rights to 'property, constitutional equality and reproductive choice'.[63]

In other words, the Decade inspired progressive developments for women throughout the world – albeit in a very uneven distribution. The feminist achievements of the UN Decade for Women were tentative and were hotly contested by patriarchal structures and authorities. Whether the progressive ideas and programmes that emerged during the Decade would continue to impact women's lives in positive ways was far from guaranteed.

The women's international organisations that were in large part responsible for raising the consciousness of the world's male-dominated governments and intergovernmental bodies throughout the twentieth century saw many of their long-term feminist goals to raise the status of the world's women come to fruition during the UN Decade for Women. Yet as new NGOs representing the interests of the global South moved to the forefront of the international feminist movement the dilemmas that the long-established women's international organisations had faced historically remained: how to define a truly global women's agenda that encompassed egalitarian, inclusive, just, humane and peaceful values, and how to incorporate feminist women into positions of power where they could carry out that agenda. By the end of the UN Decade for Women the global women's movement was well on the way to transforming itself but was only beginning to transform the world.

Notes

1 WYWCA, Minutes of the meeting of the World YWCA Executive Committee, Annecy, France, 28 June–10 July 1982.
2 WYWCA, 'United Nations and other NGOs' 21 October 1982 and 'Four year report, 1979–83,' Consultative Relations with UN and UN System Agencies.
3 WYWCA, Minutes of the meeting of the World YWCA Executive Committee, Annecy, France, 28 June–10 July 1982.
4 Devaki Jain, *Women, Development and the UN: A Sixty Year Quest for Equality and Justice* (Bloomington, IN: Indiana University Press, 2005), pp. 96–97. 'DAWN: Development Alternations with Women for a New Era' (dawnnet. org/about.html).
5 Arvonne S. Fraser, *The UN Decade for Women: Documents and Dialogue* (Boulder, CO: Westview Press, 1987), p. 159.
6 IWTC, UN Division for Economic and Social Information, Info sheet, January 1984 'General Assembly decides to hold 1985 women's conference in Kenya and approves draft agenda', box 7.

 7 John R. Mathiason, *The Long March to Beijing: The United Nations and the Women's Revolution*, vol. 1, The Vienna Period (2006), pp. 51 and 53 (intlmgt. com/longmarch/Long%March%202006.pdf).
 8 IWTC, Virginia Sauerwein, Chief NGO Unit, DIESA to Mr. C. Constantinou, Office of the Under-Secretary General DIESA, 21 September 1984, box 7.
 9 John S. Rossi, '"The status of women": two American Catholic women at the UN', *Catholic Historical Review* 93 (April 2007), pp. 304–5; 'Women Active in NGOs Honored', *Off Our Backs* (April 1997).
10 IWTC, 'Planning Committee for NGO activities in relation to the world conference to review and appraise the achievements of the UN Decade for Women', 15 August 1983, box 11.
11 IWTC, NGO Planning Committee meeting minutes, Vienna, 8–9 March 1984, box 11; 'Pre-Conference Consultation on the 1985 World Conference on the UN Decade for Women, Vienna International Centre', 22–25 October 1984, box 8; 'Progress report, NGO Forum Planning Committee,' 12 February 1985, box 7.
12 WYWCA, Mildred Jones and Mildred Persinger, 'Thoughts about the United Nations at forty and the YWCA connection', 22 January 1985; Roshan R. Billimoria, 'YWCA of the USA at the United Nations', *YWCA Interchange* (summer 1986), United Nations Consultative Status, 1979–85.
13 IWTC, Summary of the meeting of the Planning Committee for NGO activities in relation to the 1985 conference on the Decade for Women', 19 September 1983, box 11; 'Update on activities of the NGO Planning Committee', July 1984 , box 7; 'Forum '85 NGO Planning Committee final report: Nairobi, Kenya', box 15.
14 IWTC, 'Strong leader, mild touch' (profile of Nita Barrow), *Forum 85* newspaper, 10 July 1985, box 9.
15 WYWCA, Michelle Landsberg, 'Nita Barrow', *Toronto Star* (23 December 1995), Who's Who File: Nita Barrow.
16 Fraser, The UN Decade for Women, p. 206; 'Ruth Nita Barrow 1916–1995, Women Leaders and Transformation in Developing Countries' (people.brandeis.edu/~dwilliam/profiles/barrow.htm).
17 IWTC, 'Planning Committee: NGO activities for the 1985 World Conference of the UN Decade for Women, resume of Virginia Hazzard', c. January 1984, box 7.
18 IWTC, Summary of steering committee meeting, 2–3 July 1984, box 7.
19 IWTC, Forum '85 NGO Planning Committee final report: Nairobi, Kenya, c. December 1985, box 15.
20 IWTC, 'Second meeting of the Planning Committee, New York', 8 December 1983, box 10.
21 IWTC, Alba Zizzamia to Nita Barrow, 3 October 1983, box 11.
22 IWTC, 'Notes on informal meeting held on October 29, 1984, at IFUW Headquarters, Geneva', box 11; 'Memorandum to steering committee members from Dame Nita Barrow convenor', 12 November 1984, box 7.
23 IWTC, 'The Kenya organizing committee for the activities of the 1985 World Conference of the UN Decade for Women: project proposal for the funding of the committee's activities in organizing and hosting the NGO Forum 1985', box 11.

24 IWTC, Alice Paquier, International Federation of University Women in Geneva, to Nita Barrow, Virginia Hazzard, Alba Zizzamia and cc to Edith Ballantyne, 18 October 1983, box 7.

25 Carole Seymour Jones, *Journey of Faith: The History of the World YWCA, 1945–1994* (London: Allison and Busby, 1994), pp. 320–1.

26 IWTC, Alice Paquier, International Federation of University Women in Geneva, to Nita Barrow, Virginia Hazzard, Alba Zizzamia and cc to Edith Ballantyne, 18 October 1983, box 7.

27 IWTC, Mid Decade Forum 1980 in Copenhagen, report prepared by the Danish National Council of Women chair Karen Ytting, May 1984, box 7.

28 IWTC, Forum '85 NGO Planning Committee final report: Nairobi, Kenya, c. December 1985, box 15.

29 IWTC, Nita Barrow, 'Visit to Kenya', 29 August–8 September 1984, box 7.

30 IWTC, 'Dr. Eddah Wacheke Gachukia', c. April 1984, box 7; Eddah W. Gachukia, 'Education, women and politics in Kenya', in Arvonne S. Fraser and Irene Tinker (eds), *Developing Power: How Women Transformed International Development* (New York: Feminist Press, 2004), p. 324.

31 IWTC, Minutes of the fourth meeting of the NGO Planning Committee, 11 June 1984, box 11.

32 IWTC, NGO Forum, Nairobi, pre-conference consultation, Vienna, 22–24 October 1984, box 8.

33 IWTC, Soon Young Yoon, 'Dialogue, Third World women and Western feminism', *WREE View: Bulletin of Women for Racial and Economic Equality* (October 1984), Accession # 97s–53, box 2.

34 IWTC, *Backgrounder* (published by the Heritage Foundation) 410 (25 February 1985), box 8.

35 Judy Klemesrud, 'Forum '85: "place for all women"', *New York Times* (February 27, 1985).

36 IWTC, Nita Barrow, 'Woman time is here', *Forum 85*, 11 July 1985, on microfilm.

37 Fraser, *The UN Decade for Women*, pp. 199 and 202; IWTC, 'Forum '85 NGO Planning Committee final report: Nairobi, Kenya', box 15. The final Forum 1985 report recorded that 1,500 workshops had taken place at the Nairobi forum.

38 Nilufer Cagatay, Caren Gowan and Aida Santiago, 'The Nairobi women's conference: toward a global feminism?', *Feminist Studies* 12 (summer 1986), p. 402; Tami Hultman, 'Reflections on forum 85 in Nairobi, Kenya: voices form the international women's studies community', *Signs* 11 (spring 1986), p. 591.

39 Fraser, *The UN Decade for Women*, p. 211; IWTC, communiqué (published by the International Federation of University Women, Geneva, Switzerland, November 1985), box 16.

40 IWTC, 'Appropriate technology trade fair end of decade conference Nairobi', 23 April 1984, box 7

41 Fraser, *The UN Decade for Women*, p. 210.

42 Anne S. Walker, 'The International Women's Tribune Centre: expanding the

struggle for women's rights at the UN', in Fraser and Tinker (eds), *Developing Power*, p. 95.

43 Fraser, *The UN Decade for Women*, pp. 199 and 210; Cagatay, Gowan and Santiago, 'The Nairobi women's conference', p. 409.

44 IWTC, communiqué (published by the International Federation of University Women, Geneva, Switzerland, November 1985), box 16.

45 IWTC, Nita Barrow, 'Woman time is here', *Forum 85* (11 July 1985), on microfilm.

46 IWTC, Marianne Huggard Hasslegrave, 'Dateline Nairobi, 1985: how to organize your own NGO forum', c. January 1984, box 7.

47 Fraser, *The UN Decade for Women*, pp. 206 and 210.

48 Cagatay, Gowan and Santiago, 'The Nairobi women's conference', pp. 409–10.

49 IWTC, Nita Barrow, 'Reflections on the women's decade, 1976–85', c. mid July 1985, box 7.

50 WYWCA, *Convergence* 29:1 (1996), Who's Who File: Nita Barrow.

51 Fraser, *The UN Decade for Women*, p. 216.

52 Irene Tinker, 'Reflections on forum 85 in Nairobi, Kenya: voices from the international women's studies community', *Signs* 11 (spring 1986), p. 587.

53 Jean F. O'Barr, 'Reflections on forum 85 in Nairobi, Kenya: voices from the international women's studies community', *Signs* 11 (spring 1986), p. 585.

54 Leticia Shahani, 'UN celebrates 30 years promoting gender equality', Commission on the Status of Women, Forty-ninth Session, 9th Meeting (AM), 4 March 2005 (online, International Federation of Settlements and Neighbourhood Centres website: ifsnetwork.org/news/item.asp?offset=108).

55 Judith P. Zinsser, 'From Mexico to Copenhagen to Nairobi: the United Nations Decade for Women, 1975–1985', *Journal of World History* 13 (spring 2002), pp. 158–64; Leticia Ramos Shahani, 'The UN, women and development: the world conferences on women', in Fraser and Tinker (eds), *Developing Power*, p. 34.

56 Mathiason, *The Long March to Beijing*, p. 59.

57 Fraser, *The UN Decade for Women*, p. 169.

58 IWTC, Statement of Ms. Leticia Shahani, secretary-general of the world conference to review and appraise the achievements of the UN decade for Women to forum 85, Nairobi, 10 July 1985, box 8.

59 Laura Reanda, 'The Commission on the Status of Women', in Philip Alston (ed.), *The United Nations and Human Rights: A Critical Appraisal* (Oxford, UK: Oxford University Press, 1992), p. 298.

60 Betty A. Reardon, *Women and Peace: Feminist Visions of Global Security* (Albany: State University of New York Press, 1993), pp. 141–7.

61 Amrita Basu, 'Reflections on forum 85 in Nairobi, Kenya: voices from the international women's studies community', *Signs* 11 (spring 1986), pp. 604–5.

62 Martha Alter Chen, 'Engendering world conferences: the international women's movement and the UN', in Thomas G. Weiss and Leon Gordenker (eds), *NGOs, the UN and Global Governance* (Boulder, CO: Lynne Rienner Publishers, 1996), pp. 141–3.

63 Basu, 'Reflections on forum 85', p. 605.

Conclusion

During the course of the twentieth century, non-governmental organisations (NGOs) have made significant impact on intergovernmental bodies and have transformed the global system of governance. If the generous praise that UN Secretary General Boutros Boutros-Ghali heaped on NGO representatives in 1994, to the effect that 'Non-governmental organisations are now considered full participants in international life' is not the reality, it is nonetheless true that NGOs have made far-reaching and critical contributions to the work of the United Nations (UN) and to the League of Nations which preceded it in all realms of social, economic, and political operations.[1] NGOs have not only mobilised public opinion in support of the idealistic and internationalist goals and values articulated in the charters of the League of Nations and the UN, they also helped to shape those goals and to craft the charter language. NGOs have also participated in the practical policy and programme development that has benefited needy populations and alleviated global social and political crises. Their hands-on assistance in implementing these policies and programmes on the ground has been invaluable to the global governance system. In 1997, UN Secretary General Kofi Annan recognised the 'crucial' role NGOs have played in providing UN agencies and governments with 'information, guidance and inspiration' most particularly in the realms of 'preventative diplomacy, in humanitarian work, in development and human rights'.[2]

The long-established women's international organisations founded in the West at the turn of the twentieth century have been in the vanguard of NGO efforts to expand the role of 'civil society' in global governance. They have pushed for humanising changes in international relations in order to transform patriarchal power structures and realist international relations models that have oppressed and excluded over one-half of humanity. As this book documents, women's international organisations succeeded through deliberate and sustained activism in interjecting women's and human needs and interests into the agendas of male-led global governance bodies. Though not the sole instigators behind these initiatives in many cases the women's international NGOs provided crucial leadership for their male and female allies.

Because of the activism of Western-led women's international organisations language recognising women's equality and human rights was included in the League of Nations and UN charters. During the League era the Liaison Committee of Women's International Organisations was recognised in League of Nations forums as the 'voice of women' on global social and political issues. Most particularly the Liaison Committee articulated women's perspectives in its call for an international disarmament conference during the 1920s, at the League of Nations Conference for the Reduction and Limitation of Armaments when it was finally convened in 1932, and in peace and disarmament debates responding to international conflicts throughout the 1930s. Women's international organisations also initiated the campaign for recognition of married women's rights to retain their nationality and citizenship status and they led the subsequent campaign to open a League of Nations Inquiry into the Status of Women.

Women's organisations provided humanitarian service to refugees during and after the Second World War. These same women's organisations were at the forefront of non-governmental coalitions that defined the scope and meaning of NGO consultative status to the United Nations Economic and Social Council (ECOSOC) and United Nations Special Agencies after the UN was founded in 1945. The women's international organisations were responsible for the establishment of the UN Commission on the Status of Women (CSW) in 1947. They also lobbied for and influenced the language of the 1948 Universal Declaration of Human Rights.

Women's international organisations were among the pioneering voices involving women in population policy and national development strategies during the 1960s and 1970s. They were further responsible for the designation of the United Nations International Women's Year in 1975, for defining its goals of equality, development and peace, and for the policy statements and programmes that came out of the subsequent UN Decade for Women including the landmark Convention on the Elimination of all forms of Discrimination Against Women in 1979. During the UN Decade for Women the male-led global governance system acknowledged women's value, abilities and necessary contributions to the world community. While it was preceded by a long feminist pre-history, the UN Decade for Women represented a fundamental shift in global governance norms and recognition among many male holders of power that women's rights are human rights and that a true democracy must include women leaders.

During the UN Decade the women's international organisations also acknowledged and addressed the vast material and ideological differences between First and Third World women.

These recognitions on the part of men and feminist women in the international political arena are a legacy of the UN Decade for Women and of the women's international organisations whose long-running activism made the Decade possible. Patriarchal power structures that undergird global governance bodies have not, however, been dismantled, and equality between men and women everywhere and among different groups of women in various locations around the globe has not been achieved. These inequalities present an ongoing challenge and illuminate the need to assess the feminist strategies that have achieved these past and partial accomplishments.

The women who led the historic organisations analysed here were activists and not theorists. Few individual women within these organisations sought fame or personal power for themselves yet they were proud of the liberal feminist and humanist agenda they collectively defined to fight for equality and social justice for all and for recognition of women's intrinsic value and personhood.[3] In the name of their organisations and the millions of women they claimed to represent worldwide they applied moral and political pressures on male power holders to adopt their agenda. They practised 'feminist politics' – albeit imperfectly – as Peggy Antrobus has defined the term. 'Feminist politics', Antrobus has written:

> starts with the understanding of the way injustice is embedded in the social relations of gender and grounded in a politics informed by that analysis. It ends with a passionate commitment to work for gender justice as a way of addressing all other issues . . . There is a need for leadership informed by a politics grounded in a consciousness of the ways in which women's subordinate position in society serves as the basis of an economic system that is fundamentally exploitative of people. We need a politics that understands the links between women's oppression and the oppression of other marginalized groups and sectors. We need a politics committed, on the basis of this consciousness, to challenging these structures of oppression and the institutions that promote them. We need a politics that seeks to work through the mobilization of women to demand policies that would put the interests of people first.[4]

Women's international organisations devised practical and progressive programmes of action to further their feminist and humanist goals. They adopted liberal feminist strategies to enter the patriarchal institutions, learned well how those institutions operated, and tried to reform them from within. They relied on the intuitive assumption that the unified voice of the relatively powerless peoples of the world as they demanded their just rights had both a moral and political power that male leaders could not deny, although this had been proven to be a false assumption in many historic instances. Men in power have ignored the 'voice of women' and the 'voice of the people' even when the 'voice' spoke for vast numerical majorities on many occasions. Nonetheless, when coalitions of women or like-minded individuals have united behind a proposal the chances for its success have increased and the successes of the women's international organisations catalogued here have been achieved.

Yet in order to define a global feminism that could begin to address the needs of the many diverse women of the world whose political voices were raised to audible levels once decolonisation got under way after the end of the Second World War, the women's international organisations needed to make stronger connections with non-Western feminist theorists and activists – the women who held even less power in the international system than did Western women. The encounters, consultations, data collection and dialogues that took place during the UN Decade for Women had to continue and expand during the global women's activism of the 1990s, and they did expand as NGOs participated in the 1992 World Conference on the Environment and Development, the 1993 World Conference on Human Rights, the 1994 International Conference on Population and Development and the 1995 United Nations Fourth World Conference on Women held in Beijing. During these years broader and better-educated global women's networks participated in planning committees for these intergovernmental conferences; beginning with the World Conference on the UN Environment and Development (UNCED) membership on planning committees was opened to interested NGOs that did not have consultative status with UN agencies. The parallel NGO forums for these world conferences also incorporated NGOs without consultative status on forum-planning committees and consequently the numbers of participating NGOs mushroomed.

In regard to the participation of NGOs at the Beijing Fourth World Conference on Women, Hilkka Pietilä and Jeanne Vickers have reported that, 'A record 4,035 NGO representatives attended the official conference, almost as many as the 4,995 government delegates. Many had followed the intergovernmental negotiations throughout the preparatory process and came to influence the Draft Platform for Action . . . The importance of the role played by NGOs in preparing for the conference was emphasized by UN Secretary-General Boutros Boutros-Ghali in his speech to the conference.'[5]

The participation of the NGOs at Forum 1995 was also impressive. The facilitating committee for the Beijing Women's Forum 1995 convened by Khunying Supatra Masdit of the YWCA of Thailand was joined by 250

NGOs.[6] According to a research report prepared after the Beijing Women's Conference:

> The pattern that prevailed at UNCED – of admitting NGOs to a participatory role without going through the formal process of acquiring consultative status – continued for the major conferences thereafter . . . But if the overall forum sometimes has appeared to be a disjointed ten-ring circus, many of the special interest groups within it – women's organisations are a striking example – have organised themselves for many months prior to the conference and have come prepared with a platform for which they are committed to lobby intensely.[7]

Nearly 31,000 activists attended Forum 1995; they chose from among 400 scheduled events and workshops held daily, including among the highlights 'The second World Women's Congress for a healthy planet', 'Breathing fire into feminism: a tribunal on accountability for women's human rights', an 'International symposium on women with disabilities' and an 'International day of action for women's equality'.[8]

The mainstream historic women's international organisations with their long-developed connections and insider knowledge of the patriarchal global governance system were an integral part of the new global women's networks during the 1990s, but they were too intimately connected to the goodwill of the power holders to apply the sharp critiques and more militant pressures that non-Western activists would apply without hesitation. Non-Western women exerted the pressures of outsiders; they applied the 'strategies of disengagement', which proved to be necessary to continually and effectively challenge entrenched patriarchal power in the global governance system.[9] Mildred Persinger, who recognised these dilemmas very early as she looked back on what had been accomplished during the International Women's Year, wrote in 1976 'Possibly only the powerless can bring about real change. Men and the few women in power have too much to lose. It seems that those who work successfully for shared power have only a short period of freedom in which to act. To use power to sustain change, women must be where the decisions are being made. However, soon they become entrenched in the institutions whose very nature is to resist change.'[10]

The very proliferation of new NGOs since the 1960s and 1970s is a consequence of numerous globalising developments inspiring the growth of social movements in general and the international feminist movement in particular.[11] However, the 29,000 NGOs counted in a UN report released in 1995 reveals that many of these new NGOs were not founded by independent, altruistic or independent bodies as much of the general public – the so-called civil society – has assumed. Many, as the *Economist* exposed in a report on international agencies published in 2000, are tied to government and big business interests, that is, to the interests of the traditional male power holders. Governments for example, fund CIDA, the Canadian International Development Agency and USAID, the US Agency for International Development. These agencies in turn fund NGOs so that 'the principal reason for the recent boom in NGOs is that western governments finance them. This is not a matter of charity, but of privatization; many "nongovernmental" groups are becoming contractors for governments.'[12]

NGOs supply governments with information that is used to further governments' political goals. There is a careerist 'revolving door' that exists for many individuals who become global civil servants in UN agencies and subsequently serve terms in governments or join NGOs. Business-funded NGOs, or BINGOs as the *Economist* termed them, employ the large salaries and operating structures of large capitalist corporations. All these newly formed NGOs, as was true for the long-established NGOs that were founded at the turn of the twentieth century, propagate the values of their founders; many of these values are far from altruistic, and most are far from 'feminist' even in the broadest meanings of that contested term.

Many of the new transnational NGOs that transverse the boundaries between the global North and South represent the extreme anti-feminist and fundamentalist religious right. Some of these groups have appropriated the international language of human rights that liberal feminists have historically promoted but they have rejected the liberalising intent of the drafters of human rights charters. For example, newly formed anti-feminist and fundamentalist NGOs advocate for the 'rights' of the unborn child and 'defend the rights' of the Muslim or Christian family in order to impose strict limits on women's choices regarding their lives and their bodies.[13]

Among the many new non-Western women's organisations that have been founded to promote human rights and to address issues of race and class in their national contexts and in the global arena, however, there are a significant number that fall under the broad feminist mantle, even though they may understand 'feminisms' (as Francesca Miller defined this new politically strategic term that emerged in the late 1980s) in very different ways from the white Western middle-class women who defined 'feminism' in the nineteenth and early twentieth centuries.[14] Yet within their own non-Western nations most often it is educated and relatively affluent women who have led the NGOs that participate in global forums with their Western feminist counterparts and they do not always faithfully represent the everyday problems of the diverse underclass and racially oppressed women in their own societies. Nonetheless many non-Western feminist activists and scholars are critically and viscerally attuned to these shortcomings and address them in ways that reveal new directions for 'feminisms' as a transformational and humanising force in international relations in the twenty-first century – the very goal that was set forth by historic Western women's international organisations for 'feminism' in the early twentieth century. Asunción Lavrin has written about Latin American 'feminisms' that have emerged since the 1970s in this way:

> Under historical analysis, the possibilities of revealing the multifaceted nature of Latin American feminisms will allow us not only to stretch the boundaries of our own understanding, but to welcome the experience of women elsewhere, as well as let them see that the mirror of womanhood reflects an imperfect but challenging view that comprises multi-ethnic and multi-racial components. Latin American feminisms have given some key concepts and experiences to the debate of feminisms in the international arena: the extension of the concept of the struggle for political democracy to the home as the initial step in eroding the patriarchal grip of husbands and fathers; the need to engender the concept of human rights to formulate a global concept of female as human and therefore respectable; the debate over the validity of empowering women by casting maternal images (*marianismo*) in critical national as well as in daily political circumstances; the validation of women's economic role in society by academic analyses, whose ultimate symbolism lies in contesting the intellectual hegemony of national and international male economic planners; the reflection on how behavioural stereotypes remain in the allocation of power to women even in 'revolutionary' regimes.[15]

Patriarchal power within various cultural contexts must be challenged at all levels. The historic women's international organisations concentrated on challenging that entrenched male power within the realm of global governance and within national political structures. They based their activism on the basic principle of democracy according to which all adult citizens, from whatever stratum of society and whatever cultural and ethnic group, should have equal access to participation in decision making and leadership, and on the feminist knowledge that men and women, no matter what socio-economic class or cultural context, play different roles in society and therefore have different needs, interests and priorities that men could not adequately represent in decision-making bodies.

Women's activism was necessary and has been partially successful in achieving a measure of recognition of the fact that women are valuable human beings and that women's rights are human rights. Yet it is clear from the historic experience of women activists throughout the twentieth century that women will not enter political institutions in equal numbers to men and equality for women will not be achieved unless patriarchal power is challenged in the realm of personal relations within the family as well. The key to alleviating women's oppression globally is not solely through global campaigns, although such campaigns do provide necessary and powerful material and moral supports, but also through local and particularised expressions of 'feminisms' that can transform patriarchal consciousness within families and cultural communities. Therein lays the real and formidable twenty-first century feminist challenge.

Notes

1 WYWCA, Boutros Boutros-Ghali quoted in Andrew E. Rice and Cyril Ritchie, 'Relationships between international non-governmental organizations and the United Nations, a research and policy paper', Union of International Associations (Secretariat General, Brussels, July 1995).

2 WYWCA, United Nations Sg/SM/97/188, 'United Nations press release: Secretary General cites "profound change" in role of non-governmental organizations, in opening address to fiftieth DPI/NGO conference' (text of speech Sec.-Gen. Kofi Annan presented on 10 September 1997, NYC), 15 September 1997.

3 Mildred Persinger, 'A few notes on events in Nairobi, July 10–24, 1985', prepared by Mildred Persinger for John Mack Carter, editor of *Good Housekeeping* magazine, 1985, sent to author by Mildred Persinger.

4 Peggy Antrobus, 'A Caribbean journey: defending feminist politics', in Arvonne S. Fraser and Irene Tinker (eds), *Developing Power: How Women Transformed International Development* (New York: Feminist Press, 2004), p. 148.

5 Hilkka Pietilä and Jeanne Vickers, *Making Women Matter: The Role of the United Nations* (London: Zed Books, Ltd, 1996), pp. xiv–xvi.

6 WYWCA, United Nations (CONGO), 'The future of the NGO–UN partnership', Geneva: International Labour Office, 1994; Martha Alter Chen, 'Engendering world conferences: the international women's movement and the UN', in Thomas G. Weiss and Leon Gordenker (eds), *NGOs, the UN and Global Governance* (Boulder, CO: Lynn Rienner Publishers, 1996), pp. 144–8.

7 Rice and Ritchie, 'Relationships between international non-governmental organizations and the United Nations'.

8 Pietilä and Vickers, *Making Women Matter*, pp. xiv–xvi.

9 Mary K. Meyer and Elisabeth Prügl (eds), *Gender Politics and Global Governance* (Lanham, MD: Rowman & Littlefield Publishers, Inc., 1999), pp. 10–11.

10 Mildred Persinger, 'On stage at last', *Hollins College Newsletter* (May 1976).

11 Late-twentieth-century globalisation has been defined as global integration of formerly nationally based institutions to rationalise and link the world economy, world polity, civil society and business operations.

12 'Sins of the secular missionaries', *Economist* 354 (29 January 2000), pp. 25–7.

13 Amrita Basu, 'Globalization of the local/localization of the global: mapping transnational women's movements', in Carole Ruth McCann and Seung-Kyung Kim (eds), *Feminist Theory Reader: Local and Global Perspectives* (New York: Routledge, 2002), pp. 71 and 73.

14 Francesca Miller, 'Feminisms and transnationalism', in Mrinhalini Sinha, Donna Guy and Angela Woollacott (eds), *Feminisms and Internationalism* (Oxford, UK: Blackwell Publishers, 1999), p. 225. '"Feminisms" . . . is intended to deny the claiming of feminism by any one group of feminists and to signify the multiplicity of ways in which those who share a feminist critique may come together to address issues. "Feminisms" acknowledged that specific historical and cultural experiences will differently construct understandings of gender at different times and places. "Feminisms" is meant to create a discursive space in a fraught arena. It is quintessentially historical, resisting homogenization, generalization, nostalgia.'

15 Asunción Lavrin, 'International feminisms: Latin American alternatives', in Sinha, Guy and Woollacott (eds), *Feminisms and Internationalism*, pp. 188–9.

Appendix: International Women's Year tribune schedule of events

Source: IWY Tribune, Organising Committee, Tribune Schedule, 19 June–2 July 1975
International Women's Tribune Centre Papers, Sophia Smith Collection, Smith College, Northampton, MA, box 2.

Thursday June 19
Opening Session of the IWY Tribune
Friday June 20
BUILDING A HUMAN COMMUNITY
A discussion of the main themes of IWY: equality, development and peace
THIRD WORLD CRAFTSWOMEN AND DEVELOPMENT
Panel discussion on the role of third world craftswomen in economic development
WOMEN ACROSS CULTURES
Panel discussion of the situation of women in various regions of the world: current activities, major areas of interest, prospects
Monday June 23
ATTITUDE FORMATION AND SOCIALIZATION PROCESSES
A panel will discuss barriers of communication between men and women, the role of childhood experiences in attitude formation, and the role of society and the media as influences on development of a self-image
LAW AND THE STATUS OF WOMEN
A discussion of the ways in which women have been active in legal processes to further their position in society
ATTITUDE FORMATION AND SOCIALIZATION PROCESSES cont.
Examples of consciousness raising in Asia, institutional approaches to the attainment of equality, analysis of the image of women presented in the media
LAW AND THE STATUS OF WOMEN cont.
A panel will discuss how the law affects the status of women and is in turn

affected by it with a view to focusing on the need for legal reform in line with human rights

Thursday June 24

AGRICULTURE AND RURAL DEVELOPMENT

A panel discussion on the situation of rural women, the role of cooperatives, credit systems, self-help projects and intermediate technology, food production

HEALTH AND NUTRITION

Examples will be presented of nutrition projects emphasizing protein consumption, training paramedical personnel and integrated projects designed to serve the community as a whole

AGRICULTURE AND RURAL DEVELOPMENT cont.

Examples will be presented of self-help projects in rural areas and organization of migrant workers

HEALTH AND NUTRITION cont.

A panel will discuss the special health needs of women, new trends in the delivery of health care and training needs for auxiliary personnel to ensure improvement of delivery systems

Wednesday June 25

EDUCATION

Examples will be shown of non-formal education projects involving the community in the design and revision of materials and the image of women presented in texts

WOMEN AT WORK

A panel will discuss the situation of women working in marginal occupations, the role of trade unions in bettering the working and training opportunities for women and the problems arising in the implementation of equal pay for equal work legislation

EDUCATION cont.

A panel will discuss the need to plan curricula to reflect national development goals, equal access to educational opportunities for women, and the role of functional, non-formal literacy programs

WOMEN AT WORK cont.

Examples of self-management and trade union organization will be presented. The role of women in management will be discussed.

Thursday June 26

POPULATION

A panel discussion of population trends as they affect the role and status of women; the status of women in relation to the family and social system

WOMEN AND ENVIRONMENT: URBANIZATION

A panel discussion of urbanization processes as they affect women; the migration process, education and job opportunities in urban areas.

POPULATION cont.

Examples of family planning in an agricultural community, and problems of women who migrate to urban areas

WOMEN IN PUBLIC LIFE

A panel discussion of the ways in which women can be integrated into the political processes, including the need to educate and motivate women to enter public life

Friday June 27

THE FAMILY

A panel discussion on differing concepts of family, the role of single person and the childless couple as family unit, the economic role of the family unit and the family as a model of social organization

PEACE AND DISARMAMENT

A discussion of women in the peace movement – the impact of socialization and educational processes, women's activities to bring about peace

THE FAMILY cont.

Examples of different family patterns around the world will be presented, including aspects of joint decision making, women as heads of households and mobilization of family resources for community development

PEACE AND DISARMAMENT cont.

A discussion of the social, environmental and economic implications of disarmament, and the kind of institutional and systems changes that need to be considered in the next 25 years

Select bibliography

Archives

League of Nations Archives, League of Nations Library, Geneva, Switzerland
League of Nations Conference for the Reduction and Limitation of Armaments
League of Nations Inquiry on the Status of Women

Mount Holyoke College Archives, Mount Holyoke College, Holyoke, Massachusetts
Mary Emma Woolley Papers

Peace Collection, Swarthmore College, Swarthmore, Pennsylvania
Papers of the Peace and Disarmament Committee of Women's International
    Organisations, 1931–1940
Laura Puffer Morgan Collection, 1926–1962

Sophia Smith Collection, Smith College, Northampton, Massachusetts
Dorothy Kenyon Papers
International Women's Tribune Centre Records, 1970–2000
Josephine Schain Papers
Papers of the High Commission of Occupied Germany, 1949–1985
Ruth Frances Woodsmall Papers
YWCA of the USA Papers

Schlesinger Library, Radcliffe Institute, Harvard University, Cambridge,
    Massachusetts
Mary Agnes Dingman Papers
Committee on the Cause and Cure of War Papers
Frieda S. Miller Papers
Papers of Laura Puffer Morgan and Ethel Puffer Howes, 1892–1962
Rachel Conrad Nason Papers
Barbara McClure White Papers

The Women's Library, London, England
Kathleen d'Olier Courtney Papers, 1878–1974

World Young Women's Christian Association, Geneva, Switzerland
World Young Women's Christian Association Papers

Yale University Divinity School Library
The World's YWCA *Monthly*

Young Women's Christian Association of Japan Archives
Newspapers and documents in reference to the 1947 World YWCA Visitation

Books and journal articles

Allen, Amy. *The Power of Feminist Theory: Domination, Resistance, Solidarity.* Boulder, CO: Westview Press, 1999.
Alonso, Harriet Hyman. *Peace as a Women's Issue: A History of the US Movement for World Peace and Women's Rights.* Syracuse, NY: Syracuse University Press, 1993.
—— *The Women's Peace Union and the Outlawry of War, 1921–1942.* Knoxville, TN: University of Tennessee Press, 1989.
Alston, Philip (ed.). *The United Nations and Human Rights: A Critical Appraisal.* Oxford, UK: Oxford University Press, 1992.
Arizpe, Lourdes. 'International notes: comments on Tinker's "A feminist view of Copenhagen"'. *Signs* 7 (spring 1982), pp. 714–16.
Baldwin, Hanson W. 'The naval tangle, the need of a new approach is now indicated', *New York Times* (18 December 1932).
Ballantyne, Edith, UNESCO round table. 'Culture of peace and the foundations of reconciliation'. 8 September 2003 (wilpf.int.ch/statements/2003UNESCO-reconciliation.htm).
—— 'Too bad I didn't take notes: the autobiography of Edith Ballantyne', Women's International League for Peace and Freedom (wilpf.int.ch/events/2006IEC/other_reports/Edith_ballantyne_message.htm).
Basu, Amrita. 'Reflections on forum '85 in Nairobi, Kenya: voices from the international women's studies community'. *Signs* 11 (spring 1986), pp. 602–5.
Bendinger, Elmer. *No Time for Angels: The Tragicomic History of the League of Nations.* New York: Alfred A. Knopf, 1975.
Berdahl, Clarence A. 'American foreign policy'. *American Journal of Sociology* 38: 6 (May 1933), pp. 845–6.
Berkin, Carol R. and Clara M. Lovett (eds). *Women, War and Revolution.* New York: Holmes & Meier Publishing, 1980.
Berkovitch, Nitza. *From Motherhood to Citizenship: Women's Rights and International Organizations.* Baltimore, MD: Johns Hopkins University Press, 1999.
Birn, Donald S. *The League of Nations Union, 1918–1945.* Oxford: Clarendon Press, 1981.
Black, Naomi. *Social Feminism.* Ithaca, NY: Cornell University Press, 1989.
Boli, John and George M. Thomas. 'World culture in the world polity: a century of international nongovernmental organization'. *American Sociological Review* 62 (April 1997), pp. 171–91.

Boyd, Nancy. *Emissaries: The Overseas Work of the American YWCA, 1895–1970.* New York: Woman's Press, 1986.

Boxer, Marilyn J. and Jean H. Quataert. *Connecting Spheres: European Women in a Globalizing World, 1500 to the Present,* 2nd edition. New York: Oxford University Press, 2000.

Brandes, Stuart D. *Warhogs: A History of War Profits in America.* Lexington, KY: University of Kentucky Press, 1997.

Bruce, Margaret K. 'An account of United Nations action to advance the status of women'. *Annals of the American Academy of Political and Social Science* 375 (January 1968), pp. 163–75.

Bussey, Gertrude and Margaret Tims. *Women's International League for Peace and Freedom, 1915–1965: A Record of Fifty Years' Work.* London: George Allen & Unwin, Ltd, 1965.

Carroll, John M. and George C. Herring (eds). *Modern American Diplomacy.* Wilmington, DE: Scholarly Resources, Inc., 1996.

Çağatay, Nilüfer, Caren Gowan and Aida Santiago, 'The Nairobi women's conference: toward a global feminism?'. *Feminist Studies* 12 (summer 1986), pp. 401–12.

Çağatay, Nilüfer and Ursula Funk. 'Comments on Tinker's "A feminist view of Copenhagen"'. *Signs* 6: 4 (summer 1981), pp. 771–90.

Crockett, Lucy Hendon. *Popcorn on the Ginza: An Informal Portrait of Postwar Japan.* William Sloane Associates, Inc., 1949.

Davis, Harriet Eager (ed.). *Pioneers in World Order: An American Appraisal of the League of Nations.* New York: Columbia University Press, 1944.

DeBenedetti, Charles. *The Peace Reform in American History.* Bloomington, IN: Indiana University Press, 1984.

—— 'James T. Shotwell and the science of international politics'. *Political Science Quarterly* 89: 2 (June 1974), pp. 379–95.

De Haan, Francesca. 'A "truly international" archive for the women's movement (IAV, now IIAV): from its foundation in Amsterdam in 1935 to the return of its looted archives in 2003'. *The Journal of Women's History,* 16:4 (winter 2004): pp. 148–73.

Dombrowski, Nicole Ann (ed.). *Women and War in the Twentieth Century: Enlisted Without Consent.* New York: Garland Publishing Inc., 1999.

Dower, John. *Embracing Defeat: Japan in the Wake of World War II.* New York: W. W. Norton & Co., 1999.

Duerst-Lahti, Georgia and Rita Mae Kelly (eds). *Gender Power, Leadership and Governance.* Ann Arbor: University of Michigan Press, 1995.

'Eagle, lion, bear'. *Time Magazine* 19:10 (7 March 1932).

Enloe, Cynthia. *The Curious Feminist: Searching for Women in an Age of Empire.* Berkeley, CA: University of California Press, 2004.

Fraser, Arvonne S. *The UN Decade for Women: Documents and Dialogue.* Boulder, CO: Westview Press, 1987.

Fraser, Arvonne S. and Irene Tinker (eds). *Developing Power: How Women Transformed International Development.* New York: Feminist Press, 2004.

Fujimura-Fanselow, Kumiko and Atsuko Kameda (eds). *Japanese Women: New Feminist Perspectives on the Past, Present and Future.* New York: Feminist Press, 1995.

Garner, Karen. *Precious Fire: Maud Russell and the Chinese Revolution.* Amherst, MA: University of Massachusetts Press, 2003.

—— 'Global feminism and post war reconstruction: the World YWCA "visitation" to occupied Japan, 1947'. *Journal of World History*, 15:2 (June 2004), pp. 191–227.

—— 'World YWCA leaders and the UN Decade for Women', *Journal of International Women's Studies*, 9:1 (November 2007): (bridgew.edu/SoAS/jiws/Nov07/YWCA.pdf).

Goldstein, Joshua S. *War and Gender: How Gender Shapes the War System and Vice Versa.* New York: Cambridge University Press, 2001.

Gordenker, Leon. *Refugees in International Politics.* New York: Columbia University Press, 1987.

Grimshaw, Patricia, Katie Holms and Marilyn Lake (eds). *Women's Rights and Human Rights.* New York: Palgrave, 2001.

Haslam, Beryl. *From Suffrage to Internationalism: The Political Evolution of Three British Feminists, 1908–1939.* New York: Peter Lang, 1999.

Hiscocks, C. R. 'The development of democracy in Western Germany since the second World War', *Canadian Journal of Economics and Political Science* 20:4 (November 1954), pp. 493–503.

Hooper, Charlotte. *Manly States: Masculinities, International Relations and Gender Politics.* New York: Columbia University Press, 2001.

Hultman, Tami. 'Reflections on forum '85 in Nairobi, Kenya: voices from the international women's studies community'. *Signs* 11 (spring 1986), pp. 589–93.

Imamura, Anne E. (ed.) *Re-Imagining Japanese Women.* Berkeley, CA: University of California Press, 1996.

Jain, Devaki. *Women, Development and the UN: A Sixty-Year Quest for Equality and Justice.* Bloomington, IN: Indiana University Press, 2005.

Joachim, Jutta M. *Agenda Setting, the UN and NGOs: Gender Violence and Reproductive Rights.* Washington, DC: Georgetown University Press, 2007.

Kelley, Frank and Cornelius Ryan. *Star-Spangled Mikado.* New York: Robert M. McBride & Co., 1947.

Kelly, Joan. 'Comment on the 1980 international women's decade conference in Iran'. *Signs*, 4:2 (winter 1978), pp. 388–91.

Kelsky, Karen. *Women on the Verge: Japanese Women, Western Dreams.* Durham, NC: Duke University Press, 2001.

Kenyon, Dorothy. 'Victories on the international front'. *Annals of the American Academy of Political and Social Science*, 251 (May 1947), pp. 17–23.

Kerlee, Ime A.S. 'Theory and praxis: an introduction'. Special Issue *FemTAP: A Journal of Feminist Theory and Practice* (summer 2006: femtap.com/id11.html).

Kinnear, Mary. *Woman of the World: Mary McGeachy and International Cooperation.* Toronto: University of Toronto Press, 2004.

Koikari, Mire. *Pedagogy of Democracy: Feminism and the Cold War in the U.S. Occupation of Japan.* Philadelphia, PA: Temple University Press, 2008.

—— 'Exporting democracy? American women, "feminist reforms", and the politics of imperialism in the US occupation of Japan, 1945–1952'. *Frontiers* 23:1 (2002), pp. 23–45.

Kuehl, Warren F. and Lynne K. Dunne. *Keeping the Covenant: American Internationalists and the League of Nations, 1920–1939.* Kent, OH: Kent State University Press, 1997.

Laville, Helen. *Cold War Women: The International Activities of American Women's Organizations.* New York: Palgrave, 2002.

Leffler, Melvyn P. *A Preponderance of Power: National Security, the Truman Administration and the Cold War.* Stanford, CA: Stanford University Press, 1992.

Looney, Robert. 'The new international economic order'. In R. J. B. Jones (ed.), *Routledge Encyclopedia of International Political Economy.* London: Routledge, 1999 (web.nps.navy.mil/~relooney/routledge_15b.htm).

Lubin, Carol Riegelman and Anne Winslow. *Social Justice for Women: The International Labor Organization and Women.* Durham, NC: Duke University Press, 1990.

Lynch, Cecelia. *Beyond Appeasement: Interpreting Interwar Peace Movements in World Politics.* Ithaca, NY: Cornell University Press, 1999.

Earl of Lytton. 'The twelfth assembly of the League of Nations'. *International Affairs*, 10 (November 1931): pp. 740–59.

McCann, Carole Ruth and Seung-Kyung Kim (eds). *Feminist Theory Reader: Local and Global Perspectives.* New York: Routledge, 2002.

McLaughlin, Audrey. 'The empowerment of women: searching for genuine democracy among the ashes of patriarchal rhetoric'. Speech delivered at the European Forum for Democracy and Solidarity Conference: Women in Central and Eastern Europe at the Threshold of the XXI Century, Prague, Czech Republic. 18–20 April 1997 (gos.sbc.edu/m/mclaughlin.html).

Mathiason, J. R. 'The long march to Beijing: the United Nations and the women's revolution'. Volume I. The Vienna Period. 2006 (intlmgt.com/longmarch/Long%20March%202006.pdf).

Meyer, Mary K. and Elisabeth Prügl (eds). *Gender Politics and Global Governance.* Lanham, MD: Rowman & Littlefield Publishers, Inc., 1999.

Miller, Carol. '"Geneva – the key to equality": inter-war feminists and the League of Nations'. *Women's History Review.* 3:2 (1994), pp. 219–45.

Mowinckel, Johan Ludwig. Nobel Peace Prize 1934, presentation speech. 10 December 1934 (nobelprize.org/nobel_prizes/peace/laureates/1934/press.html).

Noel-Baker, Philip. *The First World Disarmament Conference 1932–33, and Why it Failed.* Oxford, UK: Pergamon Press, 1979.

Northcroft, D. M. *Women at Work in the League of Nations.* London: Page and Pratt, Ltd, 1923.

Northedge, F. S. *The League of Nations, Its Life and Times, 1920–1946.* Leicester: Leicester University Press, 1986.

O'Barr, Jean F. 'Reflections on forum '85 in Nairobi, Kenya: voices from the international women's studies community'. *Signs*, 11 (spring 1986), pp. 584–6.

Offen, Karen. *European Feminisms 1700–1950: A Political History*. Stanford, CA: Stanford University Press, 2000.

Paterson, Thomas G, J. Garry Clifford and Kenneth J. Hagan. *American Foreign Relations A History Since 1895*, 4th edition. Volume II. Lexington, MA: D.C. Heath and Company, 1995.

Persinger, Mildred Emory. 'On stage at last'. *Hollins College Newsletter* (May 1976).

'Persinger speaks on women's conference'. *Hollins [College] Columns* 48:4 (14 October 1977).

'Personal narrative Mildred Emory Persinger', Hollins University (1.hollins.edu/classes/anth220s06/lynskeyk/persinger_lynskey_narrative2.htm).

Pietilä, Hilkka and Jeanne Vickers. *Making Women Matter: The Role of the United Nations*. London: Zed Books, Ltd., 1996.

Rassekh, Shapour. Biographical Materials Hippolyte Dreyfus-Barney and Laura Dreyfus-Barney. *Encyclopedia Iranica* (iranica.com/articles/v7/v7f5/v7f571.html).

Reardon, Betty A. *Women and Peace: Feminist Visions of Global Security*. Albany: State University of New York Press, 1993.

'Report on the World Conference on International Women's Year'. Congressional Record, 94th Congress, 1st Session. 121:133, 11 September 1975.

Rice, Anna V. *A History of the World's Young Women's Christian Association*. New York: Woman's Press, 1947.

Richardson, Laurel, Verta Taylor and Nancy Whittier. *Feminist Frontiers* 5th edition. Boston, MA: McGraw Hill Higher Education, 2001.

Rossi, John S. 'The status of women: two American Catholic women at the UN'. *Catholic Historical Review* 93 (April 2007), pp. 300–24.

Rueschemeyer, Marilyn and Hanna Schissler. 'Women in the Two Germanys'. *German Studies Review*, 13 DAAD special issue (1990), pp. 71–85.

Rupp, Leila J. *Worlds of Women: The Making of an International Women's Movement*. Princeton, NJ: Princeton University Press, 1997.

Schulzinger, Robert D. *US Diplomacy Since 1900*, 4th edition. New York: Oxford University Press, 1998.

Schwartz, Thomas Alan. *America's Germany: John J. McCloy and the Federal Republic of Germany*. Cambridge, MA: Harvard University Press, 1991.

Scott, George. *The Rise and Fall of the League of Nations*. London: Hutchinson & Co. Publishers, Ltd, 1973.

Seymour-Jones, Carole. *Journey of Faith: The History of the World YWCA 1945–1994*. London: Allison and Busby, 1994.

Shahani, Leticia. 'UN celebrates 30 years promoting gender equality'. Commission on the Status of Women, Forty-ninth Session, 9th Meeting (AM), 4 March 2005. International Federation of Settlements and Neighborhood Centres website (ifs-network.org/news/item.asp?offset=108).

Sims, Mary S. and Rhoda E. McCullough (eds). *Women and Leadership*. New York: Woman's Press, 1938.

Simpson, Smith. 'The commission to study the organization of peace'. *American Political Science Review*, 35:2 (April 1941), pp. 317–24.

Sinha, Mrinhalini, Donna Guy, and Angela Woollacott (eds). *Feminisms and Internationalism*. Oxford, UK: Blackwell Publishers, 1999.

'Sins of the Secular Missionaries'. *Economist* 354 (27 January 2000), pp. 25–7.

Sirota Gordon, Beate. *The Only Woman in the Room: A Memoir*. New York: Kodansha International, 1997.

Sklar, Kathryn Kish. 'Women and social movements in the United States, 1600–2000' document project 'How did the National Women's Conference in Houston in 1977 shape an agenda for the future?' (alexanderstreet6.com.library.esc.edu/wasm/wasmrestricted/DP59/intro.htm).

Snyder, Christy Jo. 'The influence of transnational peace groups on U.S. foreign policy decision-makers during the 1930s: incorporating NGOs into the UN'. *Diplomatic History* 27 (June 2003): pp. 377–404.

Spencer, John H. 'The Italian–Ethiopian dispute and the League of Nations'. *American Journal of International Law*, 31 (October 1937), pp. 614–30.

Steiner, H. Arthur. 'The Geneva disarmament conference of 1932'. *Annals of the Academy of Political and Social Science*, 168 (July 1933): pp. 212–19.

Stienstra, Deborah. *Women's Movements and International Organizations*. London: St. Martin's Press, 1994.

Thompson, J. A. 'Lord Cecil and the pacifists in the League of Nations Union'. *Historical Journal*, 20:3 (September 1977), pp. 949–59.

Thorne, Christopher. 'Viscount Cecil, the government and the Far Eastern crisis of 1931'. *The Historical Journal*, 14:3 (September 1971), pp. 805–26.

Tinker, Irene. 'International notes: a feminist view of Copenhagen'. *Signs* 6 (spring 1981), pp. 531–7.

—— 'Reflections on forum '85 in Nairobi, Kenya: voices from the international women's studies community'. *Signs* 11 (spring 1986), pp. 586–9.

Tong, Rosemary. *Feminist Thought: A Comprehensive Introduction*. Boulder, CO: Westview Press, 1989.

Tuttle, Florence Guertin. *Women and World Federation*. New York: Robert M. McBride and Co., 1919.

United Nations A/CONF.94/35, 'Report of the world conference of the United Nations Decade for Women: equality, development and peace', 14–30 July 1980. Copenhagen, Denmark.

Van Vorhis, Jacqueline. *Carrie Chapman Catt: A Public Life*. New York: Feminist Press, 1987.

Vining, Elizabeth Gray. *Return to Japan*. Philadelphia: J. B. Lippincott Co., 1960.

Wakefield, Harold. *New Paths for Japan*. New York: Oxford University Press, 1948.

Walters, F. P. *A History of the League of Nations*. New York: Oxford University Press, 1952.

War, Robert R. and Sakamoto Yoshikazu (eds). *Democratizing Japan: The Allied Occupation*. Honolulu: University of Hawaii Press, 1987.

Weigand, Kate and Daniel Horowitz. 'Dorothy Kenyon, feminist organizing 1919–1963'. *Journal of Women's History*, 14:2 (summer 2002), pp. 126–34.

Weiss, Thomas G. and Leon Gordenker (eds). *NGOs, the UN and Global Governance*. Boulder, CO: Lynn Rienner Publishers, 1996.

White, Lyman C. 'Peace by pieces: the role of nongovernmental organizations'. *Annals of the American Academy of Political and Social Science*, 264 (July 1949), pp. 87–97.

Whittick, Arnold. *Woman into Citizen: The World Movement Towards the Emancipation of Women in the Twentieth Century with Accounts of the Contributions of the International Alliance of Women, the League of Nations and the Relevant Organizations of the United Nations*. London: Athenaeum, 1979.

Willetts, Peter (ed.). *'The Conscience of the World': The Influence of Non-Governmental Organizations in the UN System*. London: Hurst & Company, 1996.

—— 'What is an NGO?' UNESCO Encyclopedia, Article 1.44.3.7 Nongovernmental Organizations (staff.city.ac.uk/p.willetts/CS-NTWKS/NGO-ART.HTM#Start).

Winslow, Anne (ed.). *Women, Politics and the United Nations*. Westport, CT: Greenwood Press, 1995.

'Women Active in NGOs honored'. *Off Our Backs* (April 1997).

Zinsser, Judith P. 'From Mexico to Copenhagen to Nairobi: the United Nations Decade for Women, 1975–1985'. *Journal of World History*, 13:1 (spring 2002), pp. 139–68.

Internet sources

'DAWN: Development Alternations with Women for a New Era'. dawnnet.org/about.html

'The Declaration of Mexico on the Equality of Women and their Contribution to Development and Peace', United Nations Document E/conf.66/34. un-documents.net/mex-dec.htm

'Engendering the global agenda'. UN Nongovernmental Liaison Service. unsystem.org/ngls/gender%20part%203%20main.pdf

'Ruth Nita Barrow 1916–1995, women leaders and transformation in developing countries.' people.brandeis.edu/~dwilliam/profiles/barrow.htm

'Short history of the Commission on the Status of Women', United Nations Division for the Advancement of Women. un.org/womenwatch/daw/CSW60YRS/CSWbriefhistory.pdf

Index

EU authorised representative for GPSR:
Easy Access System Europe, Mustamäe tee 50,
10621 Tallinn, Estonia
gpsr.requests@easproject.com